THREE PATHS TO GLORY

To Roland
with very much love
from Dad
and Mama

Christmas 1993

THREE PATHS TO GLORY

A Season on the Hardwood with Duke,
N.C. State, and North Carolina

BARRY JACOBS

MACMILLAN PUBLISHING COMPANY   *New York*

MAXWELL MACMILLAN CANADA   *Toronto*

MAXWELL MACMILLAN INTERNATIONAL
New York   Oxford   Singapore   Sydney

Macmillan Publishing Company   Maxwell Macmillan Canada, Inc.
866 Third Avenue   1200 Eglinton Avenue East
New York, NY 10022   Suite 200
Don Mills, Ontario M3C 3N1

Macmillan Publishing Company is part of the Maxwell Communication Group of Companies.

Library of Congress Cataloging in Publication Data
Jacobs, Barry.
    Three paths to glory: a season on the hardwood with Duke, N.C. State, and North Carolina/Barry Jacobs.
        p.   cm.
    ISBN 0-02-558400-6
    1. Duke Blue Devils (Basketball team)   2. North Carolina State Wolfpack (Basketball team)   3. North Carolina Tar Heels (Basketball team)   4. Atlantic Coast Conference.   I. Title.   II. Title: 3 paths to glory.
GV7885.43.D85J33   1993
796.323'63'09756—dc20   93-27218
CIP

Macmillan Books are available at special discounts for bulk purchases for sales promotions, premiums, fund-raising, or educational use. For details, contact:

Special Sales Director
Macmillan Publishing Company
866 Third Avenue
New York, NY 10022

10   9   8   7   6   5   4   3   2   1

Printed in the United States of America

To Jan, for being Jan

ACKNOWLEDGMENTS

AUTHORS routinely credit the completion of a book to the assistance of a great many people, and in this case the practice is most amply warranted.

Everything from appointments to practice schedules to insights was provided by the sports information staffs, basketball secretaries, and student-managers at Duke, North Carolina, and North Carolina State. Coaches at the other six ACC schools willingly facilitated my work, as did their sports information offices.

Media colleagues Al Featherston, Dane Huffman, David Teel, Mick Mixon, and Jay Bilas generously shared materials and observations that deepened my understanding of individuals and events. Eddy Landreth was an invaluable sounding board. Photographers Robert Crawford, Gene Furr, and most especially Bob Donnan went out of their way to share their work, too.

I'm grateful to Rick Wolff at Macmillan for the confidence he had in my abilities, and for the prescience to have it prior to a season that proved so rich in drama. Rob McMahon and Dan Pelletier then did much of the grunt work that undergirded my effort.

Any project of this magnitude also exacts its toll on the author, whose friends in turn help bear the burden. Foremost in providing that support were Tony Britt, Cathy Fletcher, Bernice Jacobs, Gary Rosenthal, and, most resolutely, Jan Weaver.

Finally, I wish to thank the coaches and players at N.C. State, North Carolina, and Duke for their patience and openness. A fundamental tenet of good reporting is to maintain a personal distance from those one covers; despite that standard, I find myself counting among my friends many of those about whom I wrote.

BARRY JACOBS

INTRODUCTION

'LL stipulate at the outset that I attended Duke University. Not that it matters to you or, really, all that much to me. But here in north central North Carolina, alma mater matters dearly. Or, more precisely, what matters is a person's allegiance to a particular college basketball program, primarily one of three located along what natives prefer you not call "Tobacco Road."

These days the area's preferred appellative is "Research Triangle," after an impressive array of university, government, and private research facilities that long ago supplanted the rural economy in this three-county area with a population of about seven hundred thousand. No more than twenty-eight miles, a half-hour's drive, separate the points of the triangle: Raleigh, the state capital and site of technically-oriented North Carolina State University; Durham, the nation's former tobacco capital and home of private, Ivy-like Duke University; and Chapel Hill, a suburbanizing college town that grew around the nation's oldest public university, the University of North Carolina.

Around here most people choose sides and proudly wear their allegiance on their sleeves. Literally.

"When I first got here I thought it was unusual, let's put it that way, that colors could evoke such unbridled joy or the wrath of people," said New Yorker Jim Valvano, who coached at N.C. State from 1980 to 1990. "I understand it now. I don't think I'll ever cease to be amazed by it."

North Carolina is not a place of great ethnic diversity, despite a recent influx of people that makes it the nation's tenth most populous state. Differences revolve around growing urbanization, social inequality, and whether you like your barbecued pork chopped or sliced. Jesse Helms has made a career of capitalizing on underlying racial distrust, but for the most part residents choose a leave-alone, get-along way of life. Except where Atlantic Coast Conference (ACC) basketball is concerned. Then it seems everyone's part of one big family.

"In California, I'm just a tall kid," says Duke's Cherokee Parks. "Here when I go to the mall, it's, 'He plays for Duke!'" Nor is the notice entirely benign, Parks adds. "Every time I go to the mall around here, somebody says something like 'Montross is going to take you.'" For North Carolina players like Eric Montross and George Lynch, there's no escaping Duke's shadow either. "By Duke being next door, you ride down the road, you see signs saying two straight national championships," Lynch says. "You see T-shirts. You see those guys all the time." No thanks, he says. "It gets under my skin a little. I'll be a liar if I tell you it didn't."

That traditional level of interest, envy, and downright animosity keeps the social fabric humming, especially in fall and winter. Fans derive pleasure not only from victories by their favorites but from watching particularly hated rivals go down to defeat, then rubbing rival fans' noses in the result.

"You live with the rivalries every day," explains Woody Durham, a North Carolina native whose voice since 1971 has been synonymous with the Chapel Hill brand of ball, broadcast on a fifty-six station radio network. "A guy comes into this state; he went to school in the Ivy League. He went to Dartmouth. He works in the Research Triangle Park. Becomes a basketball fan. Doesn't care who wins. He can't do that. We force him to choose sides. That's just the way we do it, and that's why we've got the tremendous interest we do." Rooting interest is heightened these days by a little-recognized but stunning truth: While most everyone in the sports community jabbers about parity in Division I men's basketball, the focus of national power has settled in the Triangle.

The seeds were sown nearly half a century ago, when Hall of Fame coach Everett Case brought an uptempo "Indiana-style" of basketball to N.C. State. Case's success sparked envious North Carolina to hire Frank McGuire, a winner at St. John's in New York. Duke was in the mix when State and Carolina joined a Southern Conference splinter group that formed the ACC, which began play during the 1953–54 season.

From its start the ACC has remained among the nation's dominant leagues while all except the Big Ten rose and fell. And leading the way, forming the beating heart of the conference, have been Duke, State, and Carolina.

Entering the 1992–93 season, the ACC had produced six national champions, every one from the Triangle — UNC in 1957 and 1982, N.C. State in 1974 and 1983, and Duke in 1991 and 1992. The league also had sent twenty-five teams to the Final Four, with all but four coming from Duke (10), North Carolina (9), and N.C. State (2).

Small wonder the Triangle trio are the only ACC schools that disdain placing a league logo on their playing floors.

Lately the concentration of power has actually intensified, even as parity pap gains currency. From 1981 through 1992, a period of twelve years, the Triangle sent ten teams to the Final Four. They captured four titles among them, lifting their programs into the all-time top ten in NCAA Tournament winning percentage. No other league can match that performance, let alone any threesome of schools.

Nor can you go elsewhere and find a pair of Hall of Fame–caliber coaches shepherding programs in arenas only eleven miles apart, rubbing elbows as they vie for supremacy within the same sport, same league, same state, same media market, even the same watershed.

It's enough to put Mike Krzyzewski (pronounced shush-EF-ski) and Dean Smith, as well as N.C. State's Les Robinson, among the most recognizable public figures in the state.

Few visitors to the Triangle fail to be amazed by the intensity of it all: Local governments reordering schedules so there's no conflict with basketball games; the shrieked support from crowds at Duke's Cameron Indoor Stadium and State's Reynolds Coliseum, and occasionally at Carolina's Dean Dome, their very passion vibrating the fluids in your chest and making conversation almost impossible even at a distance of two feet; the banners, league and national, bristling from rafters like scalps; the great players, young athletic artists discovering and refining their craft, including five national players of the year from the three Triangle schools; the sense of separate, warring city-states, of competing universes of faith; the realization that it never ceases, not even at midsummer, the farthest remove from the basketball season.

"There's no other area like this," says Duke's Mike Krzyzewski, a Chicago native who arrived in Durham in 1980. "It produces things, situations, feelings that you can't talk to other people about. Because they have no understanding of it. They say they understand it, but they don't. You have to be around here all the time." It's as if pro football's Dallas Cowboys and Washington Redskins played in cities separated by eight miles, not half a continent, with the New York Giants just a bit farther down the road.

"This is definitely a different atmosphere," says North Carolina's Derrick Phelps, another New Yorker. "There's definitely more basketball here; it means something more to fans, students, the population around here. I think everybody's into it just as much as the students, that's the thing about it."

College basketball makes the hypotenuse of this Triangle, largely because of Dean Smith, a Kansan who succeeded McGuire as UNC head coach prior to the 1961–62 season. Smith's program first reached the Final Four in 1967, a year before Richard Nixon was elected president, and for decades stood as a standard of measure, a model of the so-called "right way" to compete in big-time athletics.

Smith's players graduate, adhere to rules of academic and social conduct, play team ball and win better than three quarters of their games. They apparently receive no improper inducements to attend. Among their number have been Michael Jordan, James Worthy, Brad Daugherty, Phil Ford, Walter Davis, Bobby Jones, Bob McAdoo, and Billy Cunningham, undisputed stars of the modern game. Along the way Smith's Tar Heels won the '82 title, visited eight Final Fours in four different decades and became a model of consistent excellence—winners of twenty or more games every year since 1971, an NCAA record; invited to the NCAA Tournament every year since 1975, an NCAA record; Sweet Sixteen participants every year since 1981, best current streak and second all-time. Smith also coached a U.S. team to an Olympic gold medal in 1976.

And, in its ACC backyard, UNC for a quarter-century finished no lower than third place.

Not surprisingly, many Carolina fans came to regard success as a sort of birthright. That superior attitude in turn made their darlings the most despised team in the ACC, the haughty giant everyone ached to slay.

The Heels stumbled mightily in 1990, dropping thirteen games, most at the school since 1952. They did manage to win twenty-one times, including both meetings with Duke and an upset of number-one-seed Oklahoma in the Sweet Sixteen. But they played without the discipline, cohesion, and precision characteristic of Smith squads.

Coincidentally, even as Carolina faltered Jim Valvano was ousted at N.C. State. The head coach's acrimonious departure culminated years of controversy that saw his program stutter after winning the '83 title and finally succumb to NCAA probation, the fourth in school history. "He was hired by (athletic director) Willis Casey to win basketball games and he did that pretty well," Dean Smith said in one of his more famous damnings by faint praise. "They never said to graduate players."

The same year that Carolina stumbled and Valvano fell, Duke reached the NCAA title game. The next season, after a nine-year absence Smith took a team to the Final Four, only to see Duke reach the summit by defeating supposedly unbeatable Nevada-Las Vegas and then Kansas.

Led by Christian Laettner and Brian Davis, the Dukies again won the championship in 1992, earning a place on the roster of great ACC squads along with McGuire's 32–0 Tar Heels of 1957, the 57–1 Wolfpack of 1973 and 1974 that featured David Thompson and Tom Burleson, and the 32–2 Tar Heels of 1982 with Jordan, Worthy, and Sam Perkins.

Duke's second consecutive crown was toasted by a *Sports Illustrated* cover that declared "Dynasty," echoing a common theme. Krzyzewski was likened to UCLA's John Wooden, who won ten championships from 1962 through 1975. Called "the perfect program" by *USA Today*, Duke stood as the modern paradigm with its five consecutive trips to the Final Four, its near-spotless graduation rate, and its open, articulate coach and players.

As might be expected, such gushing over Duke was difficult to swallow for Carolina players and coaches, not to mention their legion of loyalists, including nearly three thousand contributors who funded construction of the Dean E. Smith Student Activities Center, at $33.8 million, America's most expensive public monument to a living private citizen.

Smith's twenty-win seasons, NCAA berths and Sweet Sixteens had never been enough to satisfy critics who demanded championships to validate his excellence. Since 1991 and Duke's first title, Smith's achievements hadn't been enough for many of his friends either.

Duke didn't just raise the ante in 1992. It doubled the stakes, returning to the summit while UNC again suffered double-digit defeats.

Thus the '93 season dawned dark for those of the sky-blue persuasion. Duke beat the Heels two of three times in 1992, as it had in 1991, and routed UNC in the '92 ACC Tournament final. A 1990 recruiting class hailed as the best-rounded of all time had made little impact at Chapel Hill. Duke, not Carolina, was everyone's target and measuring stick. Victory over Duke, not Carolina, was cause for the greatest celebration.

Where once talk of Smith's retirement produced anxiety, on the eve of

'93 increasing numbers of Carolina fans quietly wondered when the blessed event would take place.

Duke entered the same season confident and proud of its position at the top of the heap. Wiseguys called the Final Four the Duke Invitational. In fifty-five years of competition for NCAA men's titles, only UCLA had managed three straight; Duke's Devils were intent upon duplicating the feat.

True, without the graduated Laettner, the 1992 national player of the year, Duke wasn't as strong as it had been. But an excellent perimeter corps remained in Bobby Hurley, Thomas Hill, and Grant Hill. And the Blue Devils were in the guiding hands of Krzyzewski, a sensitive, intense guy in his mid-forties now hailed as a basketball grandmaster.

"This team has so much potential it really is scary," Grant Hill said on the eve of the '93 season. "I think we can only get better. Last year's team, there wasn't that much improvement; we were pretty much the same team. If we can stay injury-free this year, I think we can improve and get a lot better and be a great team."

Goals were far more modest at North Carolina State as the '93 season loomed. As recently as 1989, the Wolfpack completed its fifth consecutive twenty-win season under Valvano. Then came a wave of revelations and allegations, and, by 1991, a new coach.

Les Robinson, who played for Case during the early sixties, had brought success to programs in lesser leagues. But as he turned fifty he was steering a State program with a tarnished reputation and a roster decimated by recruiting and scholarship restrictions.

Robinson's timing was lousy too. His first year at Raleigh, though he took the Pack to the NCAAs, both neighborhood rivals reached the Final Four. His second year, State experienced its first losing season in two decades while Duke won the NCAA title. As he faced the 1992–93 season, Robinson dreamt not of championships, but of respectability, of lifting the curtain of turmoil and failure.

Robinson could take solace in the experiences of his illustrious Triangle colleagues—his situation in 1993 virtually matched those encountered by Smith and Krzyzewski in their early years at their respective schools.

North Carolina was recovering from NCAA probation during Smith's first season, 1962, even as nearby Wake Forest went to the Final Four. Then Duke, coached by former Case player and assistant Vic Bubas, reached the Final Four in 1963 and 1964, Smith's second and third years.

Not until Smith's sixth season, long after he'd been hanged in effigy twice by disgruntled Carolina fans, did he take a team to the Final Four.

Krzyzewski's first season at Duke, North Carolina went to the Final Four. Then, while the Blue Devils suffered consecutive seventeen-loss seasons, the Heels captured the NCAA crown on Michael Jordan's shot to beat Georgetown, followed by N.C. State's title triumph on Lorenzo Charles' dunk to beat Houston.

Not until Krzyzewski's sixth season, long after he overcame doubts that he could cut it, did he take a team to the Final Four.

Robinson knew the parallels, knew how far his program had to progress to rejoin the nation's elite. He knew, too, that continued failure would raise the ire of fans tired of recalling past glories instead of experiencing new ones.

All he could do was preach patience and hope for the best as he and the Wolfpack embarked on their season.

"North Carolina has got a personality; Duke's got a personality," Robinson said. "Now that personality changes a little, you know. Cherokee Parks comes in; it does change. It's molded a little more over at those two places right now than here. We're still Bambi out there finding our way and that kind of thing.

"But all teams take on, to a degree, a new personality. It's a new season. Who knows what spring has in store? It's like a ride, a journey, and it doesn't end, but it does. But it will not end until the final gong in April; then it's over. It's over. You never have it back again."

THREE PATHS TO GLORY

PROLOGUE

DEAN Smith immediately states objections.

The last time someone wrote a book about his program he didn't cooperate, not even a little. He had his assistants read the book. He never did. "I don't want to co-author any books," he protests.

Told he's not being asked to do that, he begins enumerating restrictions.

"Of course you can't attend team meetings," he says. This is hardly news; Smith once told me team meetings are so private, he wouldn't even allow the university chancellor to attend. Nor is he interested in revealing much about himself. This is no surprise either. Smith asks friends to decline interview requests for stories about him and once confided he'd have to be "either crazy or retired" to open himself to close scrutiny.

Uttering words of understanding, I follow Smith through a door beside the coaches' locker room and up a largely unnoticed stairwell that leads to the corridor beside the basketball office. As we walk, I ask to attend his closed practices, something writers rarely do, and to speak privately with him and his players on a regular basis.

"What if there's a fight at practice?" Smith wants to know. "Yeah, what if there is?"

"What if there's a fight between Eric Montross and Matt Wenstrom?" he persists. "I wouldn't want you to write about that."

"Well, I'll speak with you first before I do." I remind him I won't be focused exclusively on the Tar Heels, anyway. I'll be writing about Duke and North Carolina State too.

"I'm sure Les Robinson will like that," Smith says of the struggling N.C. State coach, whether cattily or cannily it's difficult to tell.

Again I solicit agreement to speak with Smith more frequently than is his custom; usually interview requests are honored for a specific topic only, and not often.

Smith consents, sort of, then finds another flaw. "What if ten writers wanted an hour with me every week? I don't budget my time very well."

I ignore the Alice in Wonderland quality of his statement, as it comes from a man renowned for his precision, and reply only to his question. "Ten writers aren't going to call you. That's not going to happen. What if there were ten coaches around that were as good as you? There aren't. It's not going to happen." We dicker a while more, setting a tentative timetable for getting together over the course of the season.

And that's how we leave it.

Les Robinson proves quite open and accommodating, in keeping with both his personality and low status on the Triangle's basketball totem pole. Seated in State's fifteen-hundred-square-foot offices, half the size of North Carolina's, Robinson leans back, legs splayed upon the arms of a padded chair, and welcomes requests. Come to practice? Anytime. Come to team meetings? Sure. Get together and talk? Just let me know.

In fact, the only thing that bothers Robinson is Smith's supposition the N.C. State coach will be eager to cooperate. That makes him bristle.

Then there's Mike Krzyzewski, who reacts explosively when I broach the subject of this book prior to a Duke practice.

The high country of success is in many ways less hospitable than people realize, as Dean Smith learned long ago. Smith set his baffles and went on; Krzyzewski is only now discovering the intensity of the maelstrom.

The coach of the defending champs complains he's tired of meeting offcourt demands for his time. He's just completed a wave of preseason interviews and rightly anticipates another when top-ranked Michigan comes to Durham for the second game of the year. The thought of involvement in a book project is too much.

"Our program doesn't need this," he protests while his players stretch in quiet Cameron Indoor Stadium. "We've had eight writers approach us to do a book about this season." And "I told Dave Kindred 'No' last year." And "I just want to coach my team." And "That's why I wrote my book, so we wouldn't have to do this." Krzyzewski's book, *A Season Is a Lifetime*, co-authored by Bill Brill, was an ex post facto look at the 1992 season. The coach's wife, Mickie Krzyzewski, wielded an uncredited editor's pen.

But even as Krzyzewski simmers and protests "distractions," he listens and backpedals. "You're catching me at a bad time," he repeats at intervals, half in explanation, half in apology.

Gradually he calms as I explain the focus is on three teams, not one, that I'm not proposing shadowing a specific player, that I bear witness, not malice. I make sure to mention that Dean Smith is similarly resistant to close scrutiny and that the Carolina coach and I came to terms. More or less.

Ultimately Krzyzewski refers me to Duke's sports information director, Mike Cragg. I tell Cragg more details and answer his questions. He explains Krzyzewski's belief he might not have won the '92 title had a writer gained access to his program, adding an unbalancing element to a delicate equation. Cragg and the coach will discuss the book later in the week.

Krzyzewski tells me he'll extend limited cooperation, or rather will impose no extraordinary limitations. So begins a season rich in illumination by contrast.

SUNDAY, NOVEMBER 1

THE clowns, ghouls, and hobgoblins are scattered throughout the Dean Dome. Usually they're congregated courtside, across from the benches in the fatcat seating. Tonight they're in costume: It's Halloween, the new NCAA-mandated starting time for the 1992–93 college basketball season, and trick-or-treaters are scattered among the five thousand celebrants in the Dean E. Smith Student Activities Center.

Celebrants is probably too strong a word. There isn't much excitement, celebratory or otherwise, in the mammoth, white-domed spaceship nestled in a hollow off Manning Drive. Perhaps the late-night gathering lacks electricity because nearby Duke has stolen so much of the thunder. Perhaps it's because a certain level of success seems almost preordained for Smith's Tar Heels, and where's the excitement in that? Besides, even if they are excited, five thousand people tend to get lost in the vastness of the 21,572-seat arena.

Truth be told, Smith would just as soon skip the crowd, keep the building closed to outsiders and get on with the business of inculcating habits in his players. But Smith is not inflexible, as many outsiders think. "I hope I've changed, let me say that," Smith offers. "The worst compliment you can give somebody at a high school reunion is, 'Oh, you haven't changed a bit!' You hope there has been some growth in a person's life. I'm sure I've changed." After all, he claims he was against funding this building. But here it is. "In fact, as I pointed out on many occasions, there were a lot more important things to spend the money on. You can see my influence." And he was against having the building named after him. But it is. "They said I'm the common denominator of all the players. The way they said it—'You're representing all the players'—I couldn't say no."

So Smith has proven movable under certain circumstances and tonight's show apparently qualifies. "The main reason [I cooperated] was because I wouldn't want the student body or our players to miss class the next morning. But weekend I suppose we could." Actually "Tar Heel Tipoff" is the latest thrust in a quiet campaign being waged to enliven Dean Dome doings. The prodigious arena has been the ACC's least imposing home court since it opened in January 1986. Dome denizens are so subdued Florida State guard Sam Cassell derided them as "a cheese and wine crowd." Cassell's comment gained wide currency because it so aptly captured the somnolent atmosphere in an arena where fans often wait for the team to inspire them, rather than vice versa. The problem traces to the manner in which money was raised for construction. Folks who gave sums five figures or larger—tax-deductible, of course—bought privileges transferable to their heirs that included parking and blocks of courtside seats. That created a favorite venue for the state's political, educational, and business elite to rub elbows, as well as a pocket of emotional dead air.

To help overcome that handicap, Smith has agreed to tonight's "Tar Heel Tipoff," an event whose origins he ascribes to a request from students. Named after a teacher at Pittsburg State in Kansas, where his mother attended college, the sixty-one-year-old son of high school teachers Vesta and Alfred Smith is ever eager to align his program with the university's educational mission. (That's why the Tar Heel basketball media guide proudly lists by academic degree and current occupation the one hundred and ninety-two lettermen, managers included, during Smith's tenure.)

Given the evening's supposed spookiness, Henrik Rodl, who married a woman he met as an exchange student at Chapel Hill High five years ago, has the most memorable line. "We're going to be so good this year," he vows, "it's scaaaaary."

A moment later Smith, wearing a suit, his normal costume, merges that theme with a defensive jab, noting to loud cheers, "If we're as scary as Henrik says we'll be, we won't have a wine and cheese crowd this year."

Smith concludes brief remarks, then leads his team to the locker room. The players reappear for warmups at eight minutes to twelve, their return rousing the crowd to rhythmic clapping. That peters out in about two minutes, well before Tar Heel radio voice Woody Durham, the master of ceremonies, begins an animated countdown to midnight. Durham's gotten a bum steer; he and the crowd reach zero thirty seconds short of their target.

No matter. Smith and three assistant coaches emerge to see their 1992–93 team in action, broken into squads of Blue and White. The head coach parks behind the scorer's table while assistants Randy Wiel and Phil Ford direct the competition.

Ultimately Blue wins by ten points.

"I thought it would be a little more individual than it was, so that's a plus," Smith says. "I thought the defense was way ahead of the offense, and we hadn't even practiced. So at real practice tomorrow, start to build offensively."

Other than that, and the fact that his players worked hard, there's not much to be gleaned from the competition. "I'd probably rather just have regular practice," Smith says. "I control practice. . . . It's still a benevolent dictatorship here."

The coach does notice changes in individuals' games, "more pluses than minuses," but hastens to add, "I'm not going to go into them." By this time it's nearly 1:00 A.M. If he were home, confides Smith, he'd probably still be watching tape of his team in preparation for the season.

Later today, behind closed doors, Smith puts the team through a workout more to his liking. Each player also receives a photo of North Carolina playing in the Superdome in New Orleans, site of the 1993 Final Four. "1993 NATIONAL CHAMPIONS NORTH CAROLINA" is printed across the top. Carolina players are told to keep this exercise in visualization to themselves.

About three in the afternoon, what Krzyzewski calls "seventy-three potential engineers and doctors" gather at Card Gymnasium, used for intramurals since Cameron opened for the 1940–41 season, to audition for a walk-on spot on the Duke men's basketball team. The players come in all shapes and sizes and wear a wide variety of colors. Their skin is mostly white.

Pete Gaudet, Krzyzewski's senior assistant and once his successor as Army's head coach, instructs the students to separate into groups of point guards, "bangers," second guards, and forwards. "Be thinking of where you play best," Gaudet says, voice booming. Few apparently see themselves as bangers, guys who perform dirty work inside.

Among the taller players is Doug Lito, who, like a surprising number of

Duke undergraduates, "came to Duke because I love basketball." The Air Force ROTC member from Oregon played on an intramural squad with Duke's 1992 walk-on, Ron Burt, and says "it's my dream to play with the team."

Sang Chin, a slight electrical-engineering and computer-science major, has no delusions about making the team. He's trying out "just for the experience."

Kenney Brown feels "really, really confident." When the prospects move to Cameron, he sprawls relaxedly near a corner of the basketball court and watches his competitors with little apparent emotion.

Krzyzewski, the 1992 national coach of the year, watches from the scorer's table.

For two months Kenney Brown has prepared for this moment—running, lifting weights, playing pickup games three times a week. Raised in Raleigh, N.C., he played for his high school team and dreamed about earning an ACC scholarship. No offers were forthcoming, so the guard, who defines his height down to the quarter inch (six-one-and-a-quarter), came to Duke.

Brown spent his freshman year fulfilling his work-study obligations as manager for the women's team. He missed playing, though, his appetite whetted by watching Burt share in the men's practices, travels and triumphs. Walk-on Burt had appeared in nineteen games, including the dying seconds of the title contest against Michigan.

Then Brown read in the Duke student newspaper that Krzyzewski intended to add at least one walk-on to the '92–93 roster. With nine scholarship players, the team needs another body to form two five-man units at practice.

Brown figures a year in the women's program has equipped him to understand how coaches think. With his knowledge of the game, athleticism, and willingness to subordinate his ego, he's convinced he'll catch Krzyzewski's eye.

Among those encouraging the twenty-year-old is North Carolina State head coach Les Robinson, whose summer basketball camp used Brown as a counselor. Brown's father works at N.C. State, where for years he coordinated academic support for athletics. He's in attendance this afternoon at Cameron, as are eight members of the Duke women's squad, who perch in the upper reaches of Cameron and cheer loudly for their friend. Brown does well enough, reaching the final group of ten that's taken behind closed doors to speak with the coaches.

The players are told they'll receive a phone call sometime tonight telling them if they made the team.

"I feel like I did great the first game, medium the second game," Lito says. "I got tired. I got really tired. It's a bigger court than we're used to playing. It got pretty frantic. It was hard. I just hope I get a call tonight. It's going to be tough to study." Krzyzewski announces he'll take one to three walk-ons, the taller the better. Or maybe he won't take any. There's nothing sentimental about the decision; he has no interest in contemplating the romance of walking on with the defending national champs. "It's a hammer and nails decision, not a flowery, artistic thing," says a man who's made his fondest professional dreams come true. "That doesn't mean it's not happening for somebody."

TUESDAY, NOVEMBER 3

A YOUNG woman enters the North Carolina basketball office. She's just been released from North Carolina Memorial Hospital, a university facility up the road from the Smith Center, after undergoing a liver transplant. Her visit to Chapel Hill won't be complete without collecting Dean Smith's autograph though. So she waits in the basketball reception area until the great man exits his office en route to practice, then hands him something to sign.

"You're shorter than you look on TV!" she blurts. Smith laughs. "Most people say I look taller." Paunchy and five-foot-ten, Smith hardly cuts an imposing figure. Other than the bushy eyebrows that turn up like Mercury's wings, and the large, fleshy nose that dominates his face, Smith would not stand out in a crowd. (Not that he'd choose to be in a crowd if he could help it.)

But get Dean Edwards Smith near a basketball court and a transformation occurs. There he's in his element, his stature burnished by a record that makes him a giant, investing his actions and demands with the authority of achievement.

Smith enters this season with 740 career victories, more than any active coach. He should move into second place, all-time among major college coaches before the year expires. His rate of success is among the best ever—Smith's teams have won 77.4 percent of their games since John Kennedy's first year as president. Thirteen of Smith's former players are currently in the NBA. He's produced twenty first-round draft choices, nine of them since 1984.

That rich tradition lends a weight to Smith's words and teachings that cannot be overestimated. "Every year for Carolina is part of a tradition because we're out there playing; Coach Smith is out there coaching," Eric Montross says. "Even after Coach Smith retires—some people wonder if Coach Smith will ever retire—there'll be a Carolina tradition."

And that tradition is rooted in Smith's practices, time-tested and exacting, the complex calculations of a former college mathematics major whose chief assistant for a quarter-century, Bill Guthridge, was also a mathematics major.

"We build our whole program really early, and so much of that based defensively," Smith says. "We don't have a system. How many times have I said that? But we do have a philosophy." Call it what you will, Smith's Way requires endless repetition, constant attention to the game's fundamentals, preparation for every eventuality, predictable execution and instantaneous command of an array of offensive and defensive schemes.

"We just repeat, repeat to build habits. You have to get that done, not wait until their junior year," Smith explains.

"There's always something," junior Brian Reese says. "There's never a time that you just run to the side; you're just going to get your man. Or you just want to run on the foul line extended. There's never a time. That's why every single time you look at us we're always huddling up on any deadball situation."

"I still can't believe how many plays we have for everything," says Henrik Rodl, a senior and a member of Germany's 1992 Olympic team. "They all work though."

Smith's Way also requires a peculiar, internalized balance embodied in what's perhaps his more characteristic belief: "The only free person in society is a disciplined person." And for a Tar Heel that discipline starts when North Carolina's professor of basketball draws the curtains around the Smith Center court.

North Carolina practices are closed to the public, facilitating that classroom atmosphere. In order to attend, an outsider must get written permission from Smith on a special blue index card. The card is to be presented to whatever team manager inevitably sprints off the court and upstairs to collect it when you sit down. "Excuse me, sir," the manager will ask, "can I get your pass?" Coach or writer, TV celeb or lowly grad student, visitors watch practice from the upper deck, from which players' voices are heard as indecipherable murmurs. And you can't just sit anywhere—visitors must perch on the north side, opposite the benches.

That way Smith usually has his back to you when he speaks, making it more difficult to hear him distinctly. "I don't care if you can hear me," he explains, "but I don't want the players to know."

Few outsiders are privy to North Carolina's daily practice plan, typed in capital letters on a standardized sheet of white paper and carried by the coaches. The day and date, year included, and a practice number appear at the upper right. Today's is the fourth practice of the season. Toward the upper left there's an offensive and a defensive emphasis of the day and below them a "Thought For The Day." Smith is quick to point out that he includes all religious traditions in the sources for his "thoughts," though as a Baptist he's inclined toward Christianity.

Players memorize the basketball reminders (today's are "SET LEGAL SCREEN" and "MOVE WHEN BALL MOVES") and the thought, which are posted in the locker room. Today's thought is unattributed: "What you believe yourself to be, you are!"

At prepractice "Assembly" the entire squad gathers in a semicircle around Smith, at midcourt, and he randomly calls upon players to repeat the day's nuggets of wisdom. Should the chosen fail to recall the words correctly—paraphrase is acceptable for two-line quotes—the entire squad runs a lengthwise lap of the court as punishment.

Every aspect of Smith's practices is governed by similar ritual, to such an extent he carries clichés about basketball-as-religion to new levels of meaning. (Come to think of it, other than spiritual leaders, who else in our society commands this sort of instant obedience and eager subservience from followers?) When Carolina players pause to drink at practice, they do so from cups lined up just so on a folding table, three-quarters full with Gatorade. When practice ends, players sit quietly in a perfect line, a pair of drink cups placed by the front left leg of each folding chair.

An extra set of practice jerseys is laid out, spread fully, near the bleachers.

Everyone, from managers to coaches to players, wears matched clothing, all variations in light blue and white. There are no words visible on shirts except "North Carolina" and "basketball." Smith proudly notes that no commercial logos are visible in the Dean Dome playing area either, where every imaginable surface from seats to heating ducts is colored sky blue.

When a UNC player falls at practice, a manager sprints onto the court towel in hand to wipe away any perspiration that's caused a slick spot. When two players fall, two managers sprint onto the court towels in hand, rubbing the floor furiously as if fighting the tide.

The six student-managers also record shots, passes, rebounds, turnovers, assists, deflections, charges taken, and most any other quantifiable act by each player. Smith uses these numbers to various ends. "I think when Coach talks to the players," explains Smith's assistant since 1967, Bill Guthridge, "he's got something concrete to show when he says, 'Donald Williams is a better three-point shooter than you are.'" Smith uses the stats to help refine his own thinking too. Consider use of the three-pointer. Despite Smith's reputation for slowdown tactics prior to the advent of the shot clock and three-pointer in 1987, he was among the first to incorporate the new shot into his attack. Then he charted where the rebounds went and adapted accordingly.

Smith's practice plans are defined to the minute, with players hustling from station to station to receive instruction or to execute plays before the coaches' critical eyes. Today "FULL-COURT DEFENSE—AFTER SHOT!—DEFENSIVE BALANCE" is scheduled for 5:12. "WATER BREAK" comes eight minutes later. Smith carries a copy of the practice plan folded lengthwise in his right back pocket, referring to it at intervals throughout the workout. Managers operate the shot and game clocks, and otherwise make sure Smith is aware of the time.

Drills on fundamentals are everyday occurrences, something Smith picked up from Hall of Famer Phog Allen, his coach at Kansas. "My gosh, we pivoted!" Smith recalls. "You know, we'd spend hours just pivoting. Talking about fundamentals. Passing from here to there on the outside." (Frank McGuire recalls rooming with Smith on the road and waking to find his sleepwalking assistant executing Kansas defensive drills, complete with shouts.)

Smith too wants drills executed to perfection, and often interrupts for instructional purposes simply by raising his voice. He never curses, not even in private. He can get his points across quite well without profanity; his nasal twang can crack like a whip or cut the air with the high-pitched intensity of a power saw.

This afternoon "FAST BREAK DRILL #1" has barely begun before Smith stops play to correct the passing. If a drill isn't run to his satisfaction, he'll keep interrupting, pointing out flaws after every exchange. "Try it again!" he shouts, voice resonant in the cavernous arena that bears his name.

Drills aren't just run either. They're won or lost, the subject of eternal competition, with losers running laps. Winners drink first at water breaks; then sips are taken in class order, with newcomers last. This is in keeping with military custom—Smith served in the Air Force and then, in the mid-fifties, was golf coach and assistant basketball coach under Bob Spears at the newly founded Air Force Academy.

So it is that today the current freshman foursome—Dante Calabria, Larry Davis, Ed Geth, and Serge Zwikker—hover, hands on knees, while their elders drink. "I know as a freshman I needed that water more than anybody else did," recalls Montross, laughing at the memory. "And I said, 'Come on, Coach, I don't want to wait a minute to get a drink.'"

Players also respond smartly to the sound of the whistle that dangles from a lanyard around Smith's neck. Certain blasts cause them to stop what they're doing. Others require them to run to Smith's side with the alacrity of iron filings flowing to a magnet or water to an open drain.

In fact, learning how to react to that sound and to Smith's demands for attention and obedience is another part of the indoctrination every Carolina player endures.

No matter how heralded upon entering college, freshmen are shown from the first day their lowly place in the program's pecking order, the gap in expertise between them and the veterans, and the importance of heeding "Coach Smith." Thus they are the ones who run, don't walk, after every loose ball that escapes the borders of the court. They are the ones who drink last at practice despite the fact they least understand how to pace themselves to minimize fatigue.

Freshmen are the ones who carry equipment on the road and must share seats on the team bus, even when there's room for each person to have his own. The Smith System—pardon, Philosophy—creates an equality in subservience that bonds classes, teaches humility, and builds a sense of camaraderie among team members.

"It's hard to be a freshman," Rodl concedes cheerily. The son of a basketball coach ("I think my dad put the basketball next to me when I was born"), Rodl says most players come to understand the freshman experience after the fact.

"That's part of the learning experience—how to deal with obstacles, how to get through things," he says of the ordeal. "I think at the time you really wish you had a drink right now. But by having to be patient and having to overcome certain things, then you learn to deal with those things on and off the court.

"Things on the court just come easier. Because there's always things that come up, new things, new obstacles. Somebody will be in foul trouble. Calls may go against you. You just have to deal with it. If you learn that in some way in practice, then you're going to be able to deal with that in a game."

So it was that, when the freshman class of 1990–91 came to Chapel Hill acclaimed as the best balanced group of prep talents in modern college history, their older teammates looked on with a certain amused anticipation. "Now that I've seen them, I believe what's been written about them," senior Rick Fox said of Montross, Derrick Phelps, Brian Reese, Cliff Rozier, and Pat Sullivan. "Now what I want to know is how they react to Coach Smith."

Fox, now a member of the Boston Celtics, said at the time: "I wasn't used to the yelling or the pointing out of mistakes. When it actually happens you go into a little shock and you go into a shell. You get defensive."

Rozier, a gifted power forward, went a step beyond that. Unable to adjust to Smith's demands, he transferred to Louisville after a year. Many practices during that '91 season were punctuated by Smith yelling at "Clifford" for moving too slowly and failing to exert sufficient effort. Following a practice incident in which Rozier was sent back to the sideline because he didn't hustle onto the court, Smith shouted, "If you want to play here, you run!" Rozier ran, but out of town.

Then there are those who listen too well, like Doug Moe, who played at UNC from 1959 to 1961, when Smith was a McGuire assistant. "I said, 'Box out; you've got to box out,' and he went over and bopped somebody," Smith recalls. "He boxed him out, all right. Knocked him down, so I threw him out."

There are glum faces today around the Duke basketball program. No one's been injured. No games have been lost. But the news is almost as bad—Bill Clinton has been elected president of the United States.

Tommy Amaker, the coaching staff's sole African-American and one of the few Democrats in either the basketball or adjacent sports information offices, tries to stifle his pleasure in deference to his colleagues' feelings. Writer John Feinstein, who's so close to the basketball program he's almost an auxiliary coach, phones to tease Donna Keane, Mike Krzyzewski's administrative assistant. The two have bet five dollars on the election, and Feinstein informs Keane he's donated his winnings to the Democratic party in her name.

When Duke won its first title in 1991, its players, coaches and staff were invited to the White House to meet President George Bush. The visit was repeated in 1992, and Krzyzewski informed the soon-to-be candidate he hoped they would both be back in '93.

Few would guess Krzyzewski's political leanings from his personal style. The forty-five-year-old is an advocate of openness and diversity. He's not big on rules for his players, whom he encourages to speak their minds in dealing with the media. Krzyzewski disdains pretense and isn't afraid to display his emotions in public, including tears of sadness. He says if he weren't in coaching, he'd like to work to improve race relations. And while his teams stress teamwork, they also cultivate individual expression.

In contrast, Dean Smith is happy today.

Smith is known for the translucent veil of secrecy behind which he operates. He sometimes has assistant coaches follow players to class to assure they're in attendance, and records on videotape his players' every move on court or sidelines. His program is predicated upon a high degree of conformity.

Yet Smith's favorite politician is New Jersey's liberal Senator Bill Bradley. The UNC coach has demonstrated in the past for integration and a nuclear freeze and against the Vietnam War. Smith's name has arisen from time to time as a possible candidate for public office in North Carolina, but he laughs off the notion, saying he dislikes hobnobbing and is much too liberal for the state's electorate.

FRIDAY, NOVEMBER 6

N.C. STATE associate head coach Al Daniel takes the stiff upper lip approach. "If you had asked us what's the worst thing that could happen, we would have said Kevin getting hurt." Daniel shrugs, smiles. "As the bumper sticker says, 'Shit happens.'" Last season disaster struck N.C. State on the first day of practice when forward Bryant Feggins blew out his knee and was lost for the year. This time it's taken four days for something to go wrong.

Freshman center Todd Fuller falls across Thompson's leg during a drill and the team's only experienced big man falls to the floor.

"At first I thought I could just get up and walk it off," says Thompson, who worked hard during the offseason to get in the best shape of his career. He even took up running, an activity many big men disdain. "I thought maybe I had a hyperextended knee or something like that. But I sat down to the side with the trainer and it really burned when I started moving it and I realized it was more complex than what I first thought."

"I guess it really made me look at the situation and think about things a little more," Thompson says of his knee injury. "I think I learned about not taking anything for granted. It can go just like that. So, really, I just tried to weigh things and look at the bright side."

Seeing a bright side becomes easier when the diagnosis is nothing more than a slight tear in the medial collateral ligament. Thompson may be out four to six weeks, but won't need surgery. The pain isn't bad either. "Hopefully, I'll be back real quick," says the communications major. "A lot of people in this situation might be a little depressed, but I'm not depressed at all because it could have been a lot worse. I'm just optimistic about getting back."

In fact, two days after getting hurt Thompson is engaged in rehabilitation and walking without crutches or much of a limp. He even shows up at practice in Carmichael Gym, the university's intramural building where the team has moved because its usual haunt, Reynolds Coliseum, is being set up for a concert.

State's practice plan is simple. It consists of drills—full court layups, defensive slides, zigzag, shell breakdown, 2-on-2 interchange drive—listed by the number of minutes they'll take rather than by the time of day they'll occur. No thought for the day. No reminders of what to tell individual players. No division of players into predetermined units. Just a list of drills with "20" here and "10" there to mark their duration.

Fourteen players remain in Wolfpack red and white without Thompson. But four are essentially invisible big men whose limited athleticism makes them dubious contributors—senior Jamie Knox, a longshot prospect permanently hampered by a freshman-year knee injury, juniors Tony Robinson and Marc Lewis, and sophomore Victor Newman.

Four others are freshmen, including walk-on Bill Kretzer, whose father played at N.C. State during the sixties. They'll take awhile to get into the swing of things, a dangerous fact given the team's tough early schedule with games against Connecticut, Princeton and Kansas.

"You're going to be sitting there, and they're going to screw up in December, and you're going to say, 'Man, that's those guys Les was raving about. They don't look so hot,'" Robinson prophesies. "And that will happen in December. But by mid-January I look for some of them to be not only playing important minutes but quality minutes, and make a major impact."

Impressive, though more for his attitude than anything else, is Marcus Antonio Wilson, the freshman from Monroe in the western part of the state.

Away from basketball, the quiet, slender Wilson resembles a musician with his modest goatee and small, squarish eyeglasses. But Wilson is as aggressive on the court as he is unassuming off it. Already he's playing with a plastic mask, the result of having broken his nose on the second day of practice.

Today Wilson and junior guard Curtis Marshall dive to the floor after a loose ball and fight for possession as if a game is on the line. Marshall arises and gives the supine freshman a shove, irritated by his impudence. Wilson jumps to his feet and shoves back. "Easy! Easy!" shouts Robinson.

But the coach loves the show of fire. The State staff also likes Wilson's confidence, however misplaced at this point in his development. Shooting by himself, the eighteen-year-old has been heard to mutter, as if doing radio commentary, "That Wilson boy, he's going to be a star someday."

More likely to be a star in the immediate future is senior Donnie Seale, whose presence at N.C. State marks the culmination of a long, painful climb.

Seale, a muscular, six-foot-five point guard, grew up near Winston-Salem and played for four summers on the same AAU team with Thompson and Bryan Feggins. The trio vowed to attend college together. But while all three made the commitment, Seale couldn't attend because of low SAT scores. Consequently he was ineligible for an athletic scholarship under the strictures of the NCAA's Proposition 48, which requires completion of a minimal core curriculum in high school and a score of at least seven hundred on the SAT. And ACC athletic programs will not accept Prop 48 players.

Most members of Seale's immediate family went to college. His mother is a teacher, his father a high school coach who has known Les Robinson for twenty years. Seale's parents split before he reached teenhood and Seale lived with his mother, who he says "really stressed academics." Nevertheless, as Seale recalls, "I was playing basketball, and just, it really didn't hit me, because that's really what was on my mind, basketball, at that age. Nothing's more important than basketball, bouncing this ball."

Everyone told the 1989 North Carolina high school co-player of the year (with Feggins) that he had a bright future in basketball, the game he'd learned by watching his father's teams and talking about the game with his dad. "That's all I've been around all my life, since he's been coaching for a long time, and I used to go to a lot of games and be at a lot of practices, around a lot of basketball. And he kind of inserted a lot of basketball into my mind. I would like to be a coach after I finish college."

Unfortunately, Seale became a casualty of his own single-mindedness.

"I went to a lot of summer camps and sat there, and people told me it's not easy; you're going to have to hit your books no matter how good you are," he says sheepishly. "They sat right there and told me, but I was thinking about, after they got through we were going to play a game. I was just there to play basketball." So Seale developed his game to the point where he was ready to play at the Division I level, only to find he had to take a two-year detour through junior college.

He chose Anderson College in Anderson, S.C. He played point guard the first year, then after a preseason exhibition quit the team his sophomore year to concentrate on academics.

"It's very tough to give up something you've been doing all your life and not knowing really if you were going to get here, and no telling what could happen in between," Seale says. "But I just kept the faith and things worked out." But not without further difficulty. Seale's junior college credits weren't all transferable to N.C. State, so he had to retake courses and pay his own way during the fall semester in 1991. He couldn't play with the team, either, until he became a full-time student.

Finally, what Seale called his "dream come true" took place in late December. He not only joined the Wolfpack for the second semester, but became an immediate contributor on a squad bereft of experienced back-court players.

"When I got here it was a big relief," Seale recalls. "I couldn't believe the first game when I was here, I was playing. When I put on that uniform. When you finally accomplish something like that, you go through all that and you get here, it's worth it.

"Then, you know, I never let anything jeopardize my playing. Never let anything like missing class or missing this or that. When you get here it all comes in perspective. You want to go to class; you want to do the right thing. You made it on that long a road, and just to come here and mess up, that's ridiculous." Thrown into the breach, Seale struggled to adjust. For about the first month, Robinson found the guard looking to the bench for guidance on almost every play. Seale also had trouble with his shooting and confidence throughout the season. But he played tough, physical defense, led the team in assists and was among the ACC's best in his ratio of assists to turnovers.

"I hope I'm never in a position again to have to play a guy at midterm who hasn't practiced with us," Robinson said when it was all over. "We were in bad shape. That's why we played him." Seale enters preseason practice as the odds-on favorite to start at point guard for N.C. State. He's familiar with Robinson's motion offensive system. He's worked to strengthen his body and to improve his shooting. He knows what it takes to play in the big time.

But already Seale is dashing his coaches' hopes with performances like the one at today's practice. While Seale is creative with the ball, penetrating defenses with dogged determination, he forgets he's supposed to look for his teammates. Robinson's system thrives on quick passes from the inside to three-point shooters poised on the perimeter. Yet no matter how many times this is mentioned to him, Seale persists in attacking the basket with little apparent regard for anything but scoring himself.

Robinson figures it's a correctable problem. Besides, Marshall also can play the position. "I'm seeing that we are going to be able to do some different things, make a substitution here and there," says the coach. "I know it's not going to be a great team, but I think it can be a good team. I think it can be a good team that on a given night is going to play with anybody. On given nights we can upset some people here, and we can do some things on the road.

"After a week of practice I'm still thinking fifteen, sixteen, seventeen wins, something like that. If we really, really caught fire eighteen, nineteen, something like that. If I'm overestimating a little, thirteen, fourteen, fifteen. But we're going to be better. That I say unequivocally unless the bottom falls out."

SATURDAY, NOVEMBER 7

TODAY's main event: The Blue-White game, the first public viewing of the men's mighty Blue Devils.

There's been a football game earlier this afternoon, but this is the team that matters, the time that matters. Thomas Hill, who hails from Texas, where football is king, says of basketball at Duke: "It's big time. That's the only thing that people want to hear about. For instance, there's a kid on the Duke football team who went to my high school, who in high school he loved it because he was a good football player. He thought he might go to Texas A&M or somewhere. But here he tells me every day he's sick of it, because that's all people talk about is basketball, basketball."

Most attention today focuses on freshmen Chris Collins and Tony Moore, and six-eleven Cherokee Parks, Duke's top recruit of two years ago when he was rated on a par with talents like Michigan's so-called "Fab Five." Parks's freshman season began auspiciously, but an ankle injury sidelined him through December. When he returned, a veteran team had hit full stride.

"That train was moving well, and he wasn't on it for a while," says Krzyzewski, who's fond of rail analogies. "In January that team was great; it wasn't good, it was great. The team was steamrolling. We had to hold it back. We got up thirty on everybody in the second half and would end up winning by fifteen or eighteen. We haven't had a team to do that. When Cherokee came back, incorporating him in that, or anybody in that, was very difficult."

Adding to the difficulty, a discouraged Parks "packed it in" for a while, according to a Duke coach. He recovered to play a significant role in

Duke's run to a repeat title, and now is virtually guaranteed the starting job at center as a sophomore, due to the departure of six-foot-eleven Christian Laettner, the third player chosen in the 1992 NBA draft.

Parks, who wears a self-designed tattoo of a Mayan face on the inside of his right ankle, explains his attitude on and off the court as, "I'm just real laid-back."

"He's a free spirit—discipline is just a word in the dictionary," says a coach at another ACC school who nevertheless admires the way Parks plays.

Parks's parents were divorced and Cherokee grew up with his mother in Boulder, Colorado. He played flag football, soccer, softball, whatever. "I was always interested in sports," he says. "In fact, my mother told me the other day, when I was in second or third grade I told her I was going to get an athletic scholarship to UCLA." Then genetic chance and a prodding parent intervened. Parks was already six-eight by the eighth grade, and an obvious future beckoned. But there was a problem about playing basketball. "I didn't like it at all," Parks recalls. "I didn't know any of the rules. I didn't shoot a jump shot until the end of my eighth grade year. I did set shots over everybody's heads. I just didn't enjoy the game." Mother and son moved to Huntington Beach, near Los Angeles. Soon afterward, Parks wound up attending Marina High School, with a proud tradition of producing college players and a respected coach in Steve Popovich. "I got with the right people early," says Parks, a three-year high school starter.

But Parks, who arrived at Duke with hair dyed burgundy, wasn't prepared for the lessons offered.

As Duke assistant Mike Brey puts it: "He really had no idea what intensity was, ever. I mean, no idea about focus and intensity and dedication. I know to him it was just like, 'Hey, man, get out of bed, get a bran muffin and dunk on some guy.'"

For his part, Parks was dismayed at how much of the day was occupied by his tuition-paying extracurricular activity. "It consumed all my time," he protests.

Even now Parks—a jeans and no-socks kind of guy who likes to sleep late, listen to heavy-duty rock and roll, and hang out with non-basketball friends—is convinced the time demands of basketball are "too much." Thus, he's thrilled practice has started two weeks later in 1992–93. "I know all the coaches weren't happy about it," he says easily, "but I don't hear any players complaining about it."

Nor are Duke's players complaining about the increased opportunity a small squad affords. The coaches, though, worry about depth. After the starting five, the team needs contributions from the career substitutes: Marty Clark, a junior forward; third-year guard Kenny Blakeney; sophomore Erik Meek, recovering still from a post–high school run-in with a drunk driver. All have good size for their positions, athletic ability, and experience, and quickly show they're ready to compete for playing time. "Erik Meek is playing great; Kenny Blakeney is playing like I haven't seen him play," enthuses Bobby Hurley. "I think this year's team will be able to play a lot more guys. I think we'll be a more dangerous team."

There'll also be a different look, thanks to Parks, called "Chief" by coaches, teammates, and fans.

Krzyzewski is almost giddy at the prospect of replacing Christian Laettner with Duke's first true center of any consequence since Mike Gminski, whose collegiate career ended the season prior to Krzyzewski's 1980–81 arrival. Parks gives Duke a genuine shotblocking presence, a potential force on the offensive boards and a new dimension in its motion offense.

In a way, Parks is fortunate to be playing at all after suffering a near-disastrous injury during a late-summer pickup game at Cameron.

Former Blue Devil guard Johnny Dawkins, a member of the Philadelphia 76ers, swiped at a ball and inadvertently poked Parks in the left eye. The inner wall at the back of the eye was cut and immediately started bleeding. "It was real nasty looking. It wasn't pretty," says Parks. The pain was severe and the Duke doctor who treated the athlete "said I was just lucky I still have sight in my left eye."

Parks was not allowed to run or jog for six weeks lest he damage the retina. The eye was kept dilated for five weeks to assist healing and, in all, he missed nearly two months of physical activity. So, for that matter, did his backup, Erik Meek, who had an operation on his calf to remove scar tissue left from his '91 accident.

By the time this evening's Blue-White game rolls around, both big men have regained their athletic tone. Parks, however, is adjusting to the plastic goggles he wears during games on doctor's orders.

Judging by his performance, the adjustment is progressing just fine. Along with his new insect-like appearance, Parks unveils a more assertive oncourt persona that produces sixteen points, eleven rebounds, and words of appreciation from his coach. "He's not Christian," Krzyzewski says, referring to the player, not the religion. "Cherokee's more of a center, back to the basket. He had a bunch of rebounds tonight. He can really get the ball out with the outlet pass. We just have to make sure that we don't allow him to be the only guy getting the rebound. That will probably be something we fall into."

One thing Krzyzewski vows Duke won't fall into is playing without desire.

"I think one of the misconceptions about maintaining hunger or whatever, it's about the fact we're not a pro team," he explains. "It's not the same team we were last year. So it's much easier to have motivation. We change. Kids grow more between eighteen and twenty-two than they do from twenty-five to thirty.

"Each year's different. I don't think there's a hunger to win a national championship right now. There's a hunger to have fun playing basketball. . . . If we're really good and we don't win, then we don't win. I just want to be really good. Then maybe we will win. Try not to make this like the invention of the atomic bomb or something more than it is. It's coaching basketball and having fun, and then developing a team. Then when March comes, it's a little bit different." March and April have come to be considered Krzyzewski's time. Each veteran on Duke's roster has been to the national title game every year of his college career. The last two senior classes got to the Final Four every season they played at Duke.

Krzyzewski is anxious to get on with shepherding the '93 squad to similar heights. "Coaching basketball is something I like. You wouldn't get tired of something you like. You get tired of doing things that take you away from something you like," he says. "Coaching basketball is not pressure. It's exciting. It's very fulfilling for me, so I love to do that."

This is Krzyzewski's eighteenth season as a college coach, the first five at his alma mater, the U.S. Military Academy, the rest at Duke. But, increasingly, the joys of Krzyzewski's professional life are compromised by offcourt demands that drain his time, attention, and energy. The Chicago native has become almost as popular as Valvano once was—beloved by the media, subject to strangers' frequent autograph requests, sought as a spokesman, called by coaching colleagues for advice, leadership, and job recommendations. In short, he's learning to deal with many of the demands that for decades have confronted—some would say warped—Dean Smith.

"That's pressure, is handling all those things. How do you get all that done? Do you need to get it all done? What do you need to get all done? That type of thing. What are your priorities? Can you prioritize? In so doing, in making those decisions, you get another tier of decisions based on the people's reaction to your first decision. In other words, if I have ten requests and I can do two, the eight requests that I haven't responded to or said no, they react. You know: 'Oh, I can understand.' Or 'He's a jerk.'"

After two national titles, Krzyzewski fears his prominence has begun to interfere with coaching his team, too.

"I'm not saying that pressure is just from media. It has to do with a countless number of things. Most of all, fan or charity, people requests that as a human being, you find yourself: 'How can you turn that down? You have to do that.'

"Like someone asks you, there's a person dying in the hospital. And he wants to see you. What if you're catching a plane? What if you're going to see your daughter in a dance recital? What if you have a meeting set up with Bobby Hurley? And what if someone else calls you up right after that and asks you to see someone who's dying in another hospital?

"I'm not saying that happens every day. All of the things you could have been doing were all good. But if you don't do that one, if you don't do one of them, you're a real schmuck now that you won. It's that type of thing. And I don't want that to happen. Because I'm sensitive to the media's needs, to charity's needs, and my team's needs. And hopefully I become sensitive to my own."

TODAY the hunters open their pouches and let the rest of us admire their catches. Well, not all the hunters.

This is an especially bitter time for the N.C. State staff, which thought it had all but landed Jerry Stackhouse and Jeff McInnis, North Carolinians rated among the top handful of players in the country.

Stackhouse is the biggest prize, yet another in a long line of players called the next Michael Jordan. He may come closer to the mark than most. At six-foot-six Stackhouse is strong, fast, polished, and fierce. He plays inside and out. As a junior at Kinston High he averaged 29.8 points and 13.7 rebounds per game and was on track to become the leading scorer in North Carolina prep basketball history.

"Stack" visited each of the Triangle's ACC schools on his own, engaging in offseason pickup games with team members. Duke, State, and Carolina, as well as Michigan and ACC schools Florida State, Virginia, and Wake Forest, made his short list. Yet Stackhouse's intentions remained unclear. Complicating matters, NCAA rules prevent college coaches from speaking with a prospect until July 1 following his junior year in high school.

That didn't keep recruiters from jockeying for position in anticipation. Each had his angle to play, his ins to exploit. Or thought he did.

"It's like a big game," Duke's Tommy Amaker says. "It's like the Final Four. You crank it up a notch."

But it wasn't only the coaches who cranked it up. By all accounts, Stackhouse is a savvy, self-possessed young man. So when virtually every coaching staff that recruited him thought it was in solid, you had to wonder who was manipulating whom.

"I think Jerry was smart enough and astute enough to tell people what they wanted to hear," recruiting handicapper Bob Gibbons says. "I think Jerry did a great job keeping everyone guessing. I don't know if that was by design or it just happened that way. I still haven't put it all together in my own mind."

Stackhouse told a member of Duke's staff in the spring he wanted to play there. He told an N.C. State assistant during the summer that, were it not for his mother's strict orders to the contrary, he'd commit immediately to the Wolfpack.

"We were given every indication he was coming," Robinson says, choosing his words with almost palpable care, "but I never put it down in ink."

A coach at Florida State insisted, however, that Stackhouse disdained joining N.C. State because "they play like pussies. They're soft." As a matter of fact, countered an N.C. State coach, Stackhouse's interest in Florida State "was just courtesy to his brother," who'd played at the Tallahassee school.

Coaches at three schools reported Stackhouse made disparaging remarks about North Carolina. A head coach insisted the youngster called the Carolina coaches "liars."

Rumors about the player's plans didn't include the Tar Heels. Instead N.C. State appeared to be the school to beat. The State staff wasn't convinced. "One week you'll hear one school, the next week you'll hear another school," Al Daniel said matter-of-factly.

Complicating the equation was Stackhouse's decision to transfer for his senior season to Oak Hill Academy, a nationally powerful prep school tucked away in Mouth of Wilson, Virginia. The move apparently removed Stackhouse from the influence of Florida State's best hope, half-brother Tony Dawson. It also took him away from peers in Kinston who might favor N.C. State or Wake Forest, which usually recruit well in eastern North Carolina.

But whom did it favor?

Dean Smith—whom Gibbons, the expert with his ear constantly to the ground, believed had "virtually no chance" of landing Stackhouse.

Dean Smith—who didn't go to see Stackhouse when the forward's AAU team played in-state in mid-July, and didn't phone until September. "He said, 'Dean Smith finally called me,'" recalled Buzz Peterson, N.C. State's point man in the recruitment and a former Tar Heel. "I said, 'Oh, Lord.' It's just a mystique to the kid: Dean Smith. It's Dean Smith."

Dean Smith—who wowed Stackhouse's mother, a minister and Jerry's closest confidant. "A lot of it was, they won the mother over in the home down there," says Steve Smith, the Oak Hill coach, who gets to play golf with the UNC coach.

Dean Smith—who has an ironclad rule against discussing recruiting with members of the media, serving to keep his moves and interests more subterranean than most.

Dean Smith—who clinched the deal on Stackhouse's visit to Chapel Hill. "Chapel Hill's a great place, a great school academically," Smith says. "[Players] know they're going to improve; we have a track record of them improving. And they know they're going to be a contender for the national championship. We hope top ten in the final poll."

Returning to Oak Hill, Stackhouse said his mind was made up. All along it was between N.C. State and UNC, he told Steve Smith. He's always been a Tar Heel fan. He could see the Heels have a better supporting cast. He was impressed with Dean Smith's track record preparing players for the pros, and with the way he advised Bob McAdoo, James Worthy, Michael Jordan, and J.R. Reid to leave college early when it suited their individual interests.

"I just had a good feeling about it being the situation I wanted to go into," Stackhouse says. He canceled upcoming visits to Florida State, Michigan, and N.C. State, and in mid-October announced his intention to attend North Carolina. "I was ready to get it out of the way," he says of the decision. "I was tired of the recruiting process and what-not."

Watching from afar, a recruiter from another league who's worked against Smith called the signing "the coup of America." "When I saw that, I said, 'Nobody should ever knock that man,'" he confides. "When he zeroes in, look out! He comes from nowhere. Ol' Les is getting a dose of Dean."

So is ol' Buzz, whose mother remains so fond of Dean Smith she keeps a picture of him in her bedroom. "Jerry thinks in the long run, it's the best thing for him. He gave us this pro spiel," Peterson says. "I said, 'There's nothing I can say. It hurts me.' He said, 'That's why I feel bad, because I told you I was coming.' I said, 'Yeah, we were counting on you.'"

Buzz Peterson admits the call left him feeling "really bummed out." It left his wife, Jan, in tears. "She was just hysterical," the young coach says. "I kept her involved in it. She knows how hard I worked at it."

Peterson, who's teased constantly by his N.C. State workmates about his Carolina ties, finds one consolation in the disaster. "I'm glad he went to Carolina if we didn't get him," he says. "They're really nice guys. It's hard to beat them rascals out." Further salve for Peterson's wounded feelings comes in the form of a handwritten note from Smith, who congratulates him on the fine job he did with Stackhouse and the notable lack of "mudslinging" by the Wolfpack staff.

But all the kind words in the world won't change the fact Stackhouse would have been a breakthrough recruit for a program trying to become competitive again with Duke and North Carolina. "They're still reeling over it," Gibbons says of N.C. State. "He told them, 'You don't need to recruit anyone else. I'm coming. You can count on it.' That's unfortunate. If he's going to mislead people like that, there's a flaw there that's going to come out down the road." Several coaches darkly hint that the Tar Heels, already eclipsed by Duke, simply couldn't afford to lose the state's best prospect in years, let alone lose him to N.C. State. "They pulled out all the stops," says an ACC coach.

Dean Smith bristles at the notion a single player could be so important to his program. "What do they think, we won't go to the NCAAs if we don't get him?"

Someone else insists the Tar Heels promised Stackhouse a starting job. "You know I would never say that," Smith states, laughing. "Ask Stackhouse. He'll laugh too."

Eric Montross, a comparably prominent recruit, says he certainly wasn't promised playing time or a starter's role. "Here it's not a game, it's a straightforward, 'Here's how we play if you want to come,'" he says. "Coach Smith is the best coach in the country. That's why I'm here."

But while Montross may have been content to wait his turn, many observers wonder how Stackhouse will adjust to chasing down loose balls, deferring to teammates, having his game redefined, and being forced to wait to drink at practice or to play in games. Beware the system, they whisper.

"I used to think it was funny," Smith says. "This system stuff is really getting ridiculous." The naysayers have become so persistent, Smith felt compelled to show Stackhouse film to assuage the player's fears. "That really bothers me," Smith repeats.

Top assistant Bill Guthridge, who's been with Smith since the 1968 season, concedes the subject of the system's limiting parameters has surfaced recently. "We don't hold people back," he protests. "People who use that against us in recruiting say you have to fit into the system. That's not true."

As evidence, Guthridge cites a common conception that Smith shackled Michael Jordan, who averaged twenty points in 1983 and in 1984 was national player of the year and led the ACC with a 19.6-point average. "It started up with Norm Sloan; he tried to get it going in the seventies," Guthridge says, referring to the former N.C. State coach who made little secret of his dislike for Smith. "Like he told Phil Ford, you have to pass ten times before shooting" at UNC.

Whatever. It's all part of the game within the game that makes recruiting so murky a business, so seemingly unsavory even when there's no real evidence of wrongdoing.

Once Stackhouse made his intentions known, it was only a matter of time before teammate and friend McInnis, a highly sought guard, followed suit. It will take McInnis months to get the necessary SAT score, but his commitment is announced anyway.

North Carolina's success is a vindication of sorts for Smith and Guthridge. Only recently they were dismissed as a pair of elderly white men from Kansas overmatched in the recruiting wars. Critics said Carolina missed the sales skills of Eddie Fogler, a city-wise New Yorker, and Roy Williams, his successor. This even as, during the latter half of the 1980s, UNC brought in high school All-Americas Reid, Scott Williams, Steve Bucknall, Jeff Lebo, Kevin Madden, Pete Chilcutt, and King Rice. Lebo and Reid were regarded in many quarters as the nation's top prep prospects when they arrived at Chapel Hill in 1985 and 1986, respectively. "Of those we can get, we've done pretty well," Smith said blandly at the time.

Then, with Phil Ford replacing Williams, the Heels landed their vaunted '91 freshman class. "Just because we had one at each position, everyone went crazy," Smith observes. Now come Stackhouse and McInnis, each a likely future starter. No one's calling Smith a recruiting has-been anymore.

While Carolina gets the Oak Hill boys, Duke brings in four players: A powerful, versatile, and pleasingly nasty post player from Canada, Greg Newton; Virginia's Joey Beard, a forward with a wide range of skills whom Mike Krzyzewski likens to former all-pro Bobby Jones; a heady all-purpose guard and son of a college coach in North Carolinian Jeff Capel; and a lightly recruited wing from Delaware, Carmen Wallace.

Capel, whose father formerly assisted at Wake and will become head coach at North Carolina A&T starting in 1993–94, is merely the fourth

North Carolinian to sign with Krzyzewski. The first, David Henderson, was a little-known but ultimately essential element in the five-member recruiting class of 1982–83 that transformed Duke's fortunes. This year's haul by the Blue Devils, like that group and many since, is rated among the best in the nation.

"They can read, 'We're not going to get this guy, let's move on to the next kid,'" Gibbons says admiringly of Duke's recruiters. "They're dealing with a very select group. What's the difference between a Stackhouse and a Beard? Stackhouse gets points for athleticism; Beard gets points for being six-ten." Mike Krzyzewski and staff certainly don't get all the players they pursue, but they come close. Moreover, they tend to get their men early, almost invariably during the early signing period. That frees recruiting point men Mike Brey and Tommy Amaker to spend the winter evaluating rising sophomores and juniors, getting a head start on many of their competitors.

Observes Gibbons: "They're the most proficient and efficient recruiters in the business. There's very little wasted motion. The thing that impresses me the most is their ability to assess their standing with recruits and know when to move on. No program in the last five years has done a better job of doing that." Duke recruits appear carefully fitted for discrete slots. One year the Blue Devils collect guards. The next year it's wings, or big men. Hurley, Thomas Hill, and Bill McCaffrey, all guards, arrived for the 1990 season. In '91 it was Grant Hill, Tony Lang, Marty Clark, and Kenny Blakeney, all wing types. In '92 it was post players Erik Meek and Cherokee Parks.

Rarely does Krzyzewski bring in more than four freshmen at once; the last time he had more than thirteen players on his roster was 1987. "It's helped us as far as establishing team unity," he says. "We're all on the same page, the players and the coaching staff." The pursuit of blend and contentment has caused a change in tactics since McCaffrey and center Crawford Palmer transferred two years ago. Now the Dukies consciously seek to leaven the mix of hotshots with low-profile recruits like Wallace and current freshman Tony Moore.

Duke recruiters attempt to come across as normal, natural people representing a school that's more than "playing basketball and going to chemistry class," according to Amaker. "We don't go through the song and dance of twisting their arms. I think we're very down to earth. We're very prepared. I think we come across as very sincere." And when a prospect comes to campus, he rarely leaves without making a commitment. "For all practical purposes, they're committed before they even go," Gibbons says. "Once a kid's there, it's like he's died and gone to heaven."

The experience isn't quite that dramatic for Beard, who comes to Durham prepared to resist pressure. "People were telling me, well, Duke likes to pressure people into making their decisions, and that was the last thing they did. They did not pressure me. I totally, I just felt this was the right place for me. They really didn't ask me once would I like to commit. I went to them and told them I'm ready to commit."

The news isn't really much of a surprise to the Duke coaches. "We should get him," Brey confided months ago. After all, though Beard grew up a Carolina fan, like many other youngsters in the ACC region, Duke has been wooing him since his freshman year at the same high school attended by Grant Hill.

"In a sense I did go there because of him," Beard says of Hill. "I saw what happened. I saw how he developed and how he became such a great player."

Beard also relies on Hill, a trusted friend, to help him decide between Duke and Virginia, for whom he'd be as important a recruit as Stackhouse was for N.C. State.

"I think that was the hardest thing about this, was telling Virginia that I decided I was going to Duke," he says. "I told Coach (Jeff) Jones straight up, 'I've decided Duke's the best situation for me.' And I thanked him for everything. He took it hard and I took it hard. It was hard to do it. It just made me feel I just wish I could've gone both ways."

SATURDAY, NOVEMBER 14

NO ONE appreciates Triangle basketball more than Leslie Gregory Robinson, who supped heartily at the table then wandered through the basketball wilderness for a quarter-century.

Arriving in Raleigh from St. Albans, West Virginia, during the Kennedy-Nixon presidential race of 1960, Robinson quickly realized he'd landed in an unusual place to play college basketball.

"I think the three schools, the proximity to each other, the airport, I always thought that was a novelty," he says. "When I came here from West Virginia, that was amazing to me. It's even more amazing to me now that they've all registered championships."

Making his mark as a defender, Robinson eventually worked his way from last among eleven guards to third in the rotation. "I was wild," he remembers. "Coach Case liked me, but not as a player." That became clear Robinson's senior year, when "The Old Grey Fox" invited him to quit playing and start coaching the freshmen.

Two games into the 1964–65 season Case retired, terminally ill. He was succeeded by assistant Press Maravich. Case died the following spring, but not before the Wolfpack won the 1965 ACC title, upending top-seeded Duke in the championship game.

Robinson, an easygoing, ursine man with country charm, served as assistant coach and chief recruiter at N.C. State through the 1966 season, then left when Maravich and his son, Pete, went to LSU.

The first stop for the new coach, his wife, Barbara, and two young children was Cedar Key, a small, untrammeled island off Florida's Gulf Coast. Though the school had only twenty-three boys, in two years Robinson's teams were 43–9. He also coached a six-man football squad from the island to a state title. "We got out of there because we were liking the place too well," Robinson says. "I wanted to do more than that in my career."

After a year as an assistant at Western Carolina, where he earned a masters degree in guidance, Robinson landed at The Citadel in Charleston, S.C. He remained there for fifteen years, the last eleven as head coach. Robinson's teams were noted for controlling the tempo and applying tough, disciplined defense. Despite severe recruiting handicaps, including Vietnam Era antipathy toward the military school, he managed the most victories in the program's history, including its only twenty-win season in 1979.

"I got to The Citadel and I found out that you don't always have talent," Robinson says. "You don't always run the stuff you want to run. But I think that was when I learned to coach, where you had to make do with what you had. We were very, very limited, and gradually I learned how to adapt and I guess that's where I developed my philosophy of coaching."

Those beliefs were sorely tested during five seasons at East Tennessee State (ETSU), where he took over a program rife with academic underachievers and about to go on probation. His second year, when the Buccaneers were 7–21, Robinson became athletic director too. By his fourth season, 1988–89, the team won twenty games, captured the Southern Conference title and gave Oklahoma a severe scare in the NCAA Tournament. His final year, ETSU was 27–7, again won the Southern Conference title, and lost in the NCAAs to eventual Final Four entrant Georgia Tech, led by future pros Kenny Anderson, Dennis Scott, and Brian Oliver.

Through the years Robinson kept an eye cast toward his alma mater, which, during the '90 season, was racked by turmoil surrounding the regime of head coach Jim Valvano. Robinson's interest quickened when Valvano told him in mid-December the job might soon come open. When it did, in April 1991, the alum leapt at the chance to return to his basketball roots.

"I know it's going to be a tough job, but there's no basketball position in America I'd rather have than this," Robinson said when he was hired, calling the N.C. State job his "secret dream." Robinson brought a losing career record (213–232) but an easygoing personality and a near-perfect graduation rate among his players. At East Tennessee, where he'd been able to recruit a better grade of talent, his teams employed man-to-man defense and an offense heavily reliant upon the three-pointer.

Robinson's strengths immediately came in handy at N.C. State. So did his realistic attitude, born in the game's more remote outposts.

The coach obviously had inherited an excellent starting five, including a sterling senior backcourt of Rodney Monroe and Chris Corchiani. So, adapting to circumstances, Robinson started the same players every game, and the Wolfpack won twenty and reached the NCAA Tournament. Throughout, though, Robinson warned that years two and three of his tenure—he signed a five-year contract—would be difficult ones.

Perhaps because an appeal to pride might lessen the sting of the blows to come, Robinson also immediately re-emphasized N.C. State's basketball tradition.

Raiding the cluttered basement of Reynolds Coliseum, Robinson championed the reinstallation of the wooden playing floor removed after the Pack won the 1974 NCAA title. The team returned to an old uniform design and to a dramatic style of player introduction, with the houselights extinguished and the recorded howls of a wolf accompanying the spotlighted appearance of each Wolfpack starter.

The nostalgic touches helped. When the lights went down, one could feel reunited with a glorious past marked by two NCAA and ten ACC titles, and more victories than all but sixteen schools in the country. "Everything and anything has happened in this arena long before I got here," Robinson says. (Still, envious of North Carolina, N.C. State seeks to build a new 22,600-seat arena well off campus.)

By 1991–92, the new coach's second season, nothing could hide the fact that N.C. State had fallen far off the pace set by Duke and North Carolina, its next-door neighbors. Today's practice, just four days prior to the season's first exhibition game, gives cause for concern about the quality of this year's squad too.

LAYING its first outside opponent, Duke cruises to a 105–81 exhibition victory, dismantling ill-named High Five America (a majority of the squad hails from former Soviet republics) with a familiar mixture of calm precision and arresting fire.

"To be honest with you, I'm kind of shocked at how well we played," Grant Hill says. There's a palpable sense of confidence in the Dukies' play, especially at Cameron, as though victory is less to be courted than conjured, all a matter of command. "I think they believe they're going to win, just like I think we've had that for some time," observes UNC's Dean Smith. "That's something that's hard to acquire, but it's nice to have."

Someone else may win the championship this season—no one pretends this year's Duke squad possesses the experience, depth, and power of '92—but supremacy won't be given up without a fight.

Hill leads the way against High Five, scoring two dozen points along with eight rebounds, five assists, and three steals. It's the kind of performance everyone expects from the wondrously gifted junior.

"I think Grant will emerge as one of the truly outstanding players," Mike Krzyzewski predicts. "Especially early, I want him to try things and make mistakes. Of commission, not omission. I don't want to hold back Grant."

To hear Hill speak, there's not much chance of that.

Hill and teammate Bobby Hurley served as practice fodder for the U.S. Olympic basketball team during the offseason, and returned to school with confidence greatly bolstered. Dean Smith speaks of the ego-battering that surely befell Eric Montross when his center faced pros Patrick

Ewing and David Robinson. (The UNC coach may have a point; other players on the developmental squad were unimpressed with the Carolina big man.) Krzyzewski, on the other hand, touts the value of the experience for his players, who agree wholeheartedly.

Certainly you can hear the change in Grant Hill's voice at practice as he demands the ball, or observe it in his manner against High Five.

"I feel confident and sure what I can do now. I have to just go out and do it," Hill says, a steely tone underlying his words. "That experience with the Dream Team, I was able to see how they are arrogant, at least on the court. It doesn't carry over off the court. You have to be a different person on the court." Such arrogance isn't a comfortable fit for Grant Hill, even if it's confined to the basketball court. Direct and animated, he is forever thoughtful, introspective, analytical.

"In high school I didn't want to be that demanding because I didn't want to be better than my friends, but I was," says Hill. "I didn't want any jealousies to occur in high school." Only now is he groping toward accepting a position as team leader and "go-to" guy, still a far cry from the sort of dominating presences he encountered on the Dream Team.

Truth be known, for all his intelligence, obvious skills, and natural gifts, little about basketball ever has come easily to Grant Hill.

The twenty-year-old mastered the game in part by studying it closely, learning moves from countless hours of watching tapes of other teams and players, particularly Georgetown during the Patrick Ewing era and North Carolina with Michael Jordan. He's watched up close, attending the Final Four for years with his father, Calvin Hill, an outstanding National Football League running back with Washington, Dallas, and Cleveland from 1969 through 1981. And of course he's gotten on the court and immersed himself in the game, reveling in the competition, the winning.

Yet, like teammate Cherokee Parks, Hill came to the sport as much out of a sense of obligation as of love.

"Why did I start playing basketball?" Hill replies to a question. "Because I was tall. If you're tall and you're black, people assume that you're either playing basketball or you're supposed to play basketball."

Not that he jumped at the opportunity to conform to expectations. "At first, I didn't like it too much," Hill says of basketball. "I remember, I started playing when I was seven. I didn't want to play. Then I saw the Carolina game (the Heels defeated Georgetown for the 1982 title) and started enjoying being a fan. But I still didn't want to play."

Instead Hill enjoyed playing music—piano, bass, trumpet. Athletically he was partial to soccer. "I was like, I want to be a soccer player. Soccer's my first love. But it was as if I wasn't supposed to play soccer—you don't see tall black kids playing soccer."

Hill's athletic orientation changed permanently at age thirteen, when he played well in AAU basketball competition against some of the top players in the country. "From then on, I really started to like the game and feel I had a future in the game," he recalls.

Hill was a starter from the outset of his Duke career, praised by Krzyzewski as a "special" player. (The coach employed that word so often, a local reporter wrote an article gently mocking him. These days Krzyzewski avoids calling anything or anyone special, and the favorite buzzword inside the Duke program is "internalize.") Roommates Brian Davis and Christian Laettner led the first two teams on which Hill played, pushing teammates on the court and keeping them together off it. They made it easy to defer, a comfortable choice for self-contained players like Thomas and Grant Hill (no relation), and Bobby Hurley.

Grant Hill and the senior co-captains compare this season's team to a 1991 squad that grew as the season progressed, surprising even itself by not only reaching the Final Four but upending UNLV and winning the NCAA championship. But while they speak of '91 they can't escape the shadow of 1992, when the major task was keeping sharp and the toughest adversary was more often injury than the opposition.

"I think last year we kind of knew who we were. This year we're trying to sort of discover that, and I don't think we've really found it yet," Grant Hill says.

"Although we did have a lot of fun last year, there was still pressure on us to do well and just stay number one and be number one and that was fine," says Hill. "This year is a little different. It's like, OK, we lost Christian and Brian; we're not the dominating team this year. So I look at it, it's just a lot more relaxed.

"And that's, I don't know if that's good or bad, but I just know in that sense it feels different. I think also with Christian and Brian, with them being leaders and being the way they were, they put pressure on all of us to try to do well and just to motivate us. With them gone, although we have leadership, it's just a different style of leadership. We're going to put that same pressure amongst ourselves."

MONDAY, NOVEMBER 23

No ONE reports the gunshot, though it occurs at supper time. Probably the other tenants of the Stroud Center—a motel long ago converted into housing for N.C. State athletes—are on campus across four-lane, forty-five-mile-per-hour Western Boulevard, going to class, hanging out with friends, enjoying the warm fall evening. Or perhaps people did hear the shot and dismissed it as an automobile backfire, or none of their business.

Whatever the reason, it won't be a neighbor who discovers the body of Tony Robinson on the bed in his single room. The reserve basketball forward has a hole neatly punched through his right temple about halfway between eye and ear, the work of a bullet from the .25 caliber pistol beside him, five of six charges unspent.

Robinson is found because he doesn't show up for a 7:30 P.M. exhibition contest against Brandt Hagen, a team from Germany. Standard game-day procedure calls for the squad to meet for supper four hours prior to tipoff. But Tony Robinson is missing when the team gathers.

Coaches and teammates assume Robinson is attending to business on campus. Occasionally labs, meetings with professors or other academic responsibilities keep players from attending team functions. But it's customary to inform the coaches in advance of such conflicts, and no one has heard from Robinson. A lack of discipline is unusual for the twenty-two-year-old who "always wanted to do the right thing," according to teammate Marc Lewis.

The son of a career Marine, Anthony James Robinson, Junior, resided on or near military bases all his life before coming to N.C. State. He lived the military life in Indiana, then Florida, Japan, England, California, Texas, and, from the time he was eleven until he went off to college, in Have-lock, hard by a Marine base in eastern North Carolina. One thing Robin-son learned from his indirect tour of duty was a military politeness, a strict adherence to rules and to the etiquette of a good soldier. Les Robin-son, whom the player jokingly called a relative though the coach is white and the player black, describes Tony Robinson as "mannerly," a word you don't hear much anymore.

Robinson also seemed unusually self-sufficient. He didn't need the close bonds of basketball to make friends; most of his buddies were mem-bers of State's swim team. And, unlike many athletes, Robinson valued being alone. During a break in classes two years ago he drove to the North Carolina mountains, some four hours distant, and spent the time hiking and sightseeing by himself.

Nor is basketball a consuming passion. Robinson liked to cook, to tin-ker with his Volkswagen, to work with computers. A fourth-year student in his third year of basketball eligibility, he told friends he had a postgrad job lined up with IBM. He fantasized about spending the summer of 1993 not in a gymnasium weight room, but in the sun at Venice Beach, Califor-nia. Robinson wanted to give surfing a try, rather an arresting thought given his shoe size (seventeen and a half), his stiff-legged manner, and his six-foot-ten frame.

It was his height, coupled with decent athleticism, that earned Robin-son a scholarship to N.C. State in 1989.

Jim Valvano, State's head coach at the time, had a fondness for collect-ing tall players and for bringing in more players than would get a chance to make meaningful contributions. Every year a few would get discour-aged and leave, including players who went on to start at other major pro-grams, like Sean Green at Iona, Andy Kennedy at Alabama-Birmingham, and Walker Lambiotte at Northwestern.

Recruiting experts flatly considered Robinson to be out of his league at the ACC level. But as Valvano struck out recruiting high-profile big men—like Shaquille O'Neal, who chose Louisiana State, Malcolm Mackey (Geor-gia Tech), Doug Edwards (Florida State), and Matt Wenstrom (North Car-olina)—and got commitments from two big men who predictably failed to qualify academically, the coach offered a grant-in-aid to the unheralded Robinson.

Unpolished and relatively new to the game, having taken up organized basketball in the tenth grade, Robinson hesitated before signing with the Wolfpack.

"I was a little scared at first," he admitted, "but then I said to myself that this is an opportunity of a lifetime that comes to only so many people, to go to an ACC school and play basketball in the ACC. When I was growing up, I'd always wanted to play for North Carolina, but then I decided that State was where I wanted to be." His first year at Raleigh, Robinson was redshirted, meaning he could work out with the 1989–90 team, even attend games, but not play. "He felt it would really benefit him academically and athletically," explained Valvano, who called Robinson "a project." That's coaching parlance for a big guy who might surprise you and become a useful player.

Robinson never got to play for Valvano. When Les Robinson took over following Valvano's ouster, Tony Robinson had yet to play a collegiate game and had all four years of eligibility intact.

Valvano drops by Duke's practice about the time the Wolfpack entourage takes note of Robinson's absence. Readying for a season-opening journey to Tallahassee to broadcast a game, the ex-coach has been to Duke Medical Center for a blood count and a biweekly dose of chemotherapy to treat a cancer of mysterious etiology that was discovered in his back.

For more than a decade the basketball careers of Valvano and Mike Krzyzewski followed strikingly parallel courses. Each was a playmaker in college near New York City—Valvano at Rutgers from 1965 through 1967, Krzyzewski from 1967 through 1969 at West Point at the U.S. Military Academy. Each returned to the New York area as a head coach for the 1975–76 season, Krzyzewski at Army and Valvano at Iona College. Each moved from there to the ACC for the 1980–81 season.

Valvano and Krzyzewski brought to the ACC a refreshingly collegial attitude, in distinct contrast to the distrust and downright hostility that divided the league's established coaches.

Early on, while Krzyzewski fought failure and criticism at Duke, Valvano flourished. In Krzyzewski's second season the Blue Devils lost seventeen games and landed none of the recruits they sought most avidly. Valvano developed a core of talent he inherited—eventual pro forward Thurl Bailey, shooter Dereck Whittenburg and his DeMatha High teammate, Sidney Lowe, one of the best point guards in ACC history—and won twenty-two games.

The next season, Duke again lost seventeen. Valvano won the national championship and ran headlong to embrace the aftermath.

Valvano was no ordinary coach. When he said coaching "isn't brain surgery," unlike his professional brethren he meant it.

An English major at Rutgers, Valvano loves to quote Shakespeare and Yeats along with Lombardi and Wooden. He prefers laughter to anger, freedom to discipline.

During his coaching days, Valvano didn't worry about arriving promptly at practice. Assistants and team managers could take care of that. He didn't thrive on instilling toughness or on running defensive drills. Not for him the standard coaching talk about enjoying practice and teaching above all. For him, then and now, the game's the thing. The game, and winning. Show Valvano a game and he'll try to master it, to learn the limits and figure a way to beat them.

He's no system guy, trying to force you to do things his way. He's a counterpuncher, adaptable, reading what exists rather than trying to impose order.

Nor was Valvano ever content with being simply a coach. He knew he didn't have to be, given his glib tongue, comic's timing, and a mind that dances like a water sprite. To be around him is to be endlessly entertained, to feel good. He's fun, the rare person who can make you think and laugh at the same time. It's an attractive quality, and marketable in any realm, especially recruiting. Join me, he told youngsters. Play for me, win with me, he told them as he hopped from Johns Hopkins to Bucknell to Iona to N.C. State and beyond in pursuit of his dreams.

That's the other thing that sets Valvano apart from most everyone. He's always moving on even amidst success, restless to the point it makes him uneasy. So many things to do. So many ideas, so many dreams. How to have them all? He wants to be rich, famous, loved. To be a TV sports commentator. To be an athletic director. To be a TV talk-show host. To manipulate real estate. Show him a game worth playing and he'll want to play it. Valvano sleeps fewer hours than most people. No time. So many appetites, so many schemes.

Before Valvano won the national title he was a small industry, a diversified sports corporation. Given national visibility, he parlayed prominence into a portfolio that included a cookbook, a signature clothing line, and a constant schedule of corporate motivational speeches. He tried game commentary in-season, tried commuting to New York weekly to share his throaty laugh and keen mind with millions of CBS morning viewers. He exploited other opportunities as well—when word of the book *Personal Fouls* reached Valvano, his first reaction to the supposed exposé of his program was relief, not anger, because author Peter Golenbock spared discussion of the coach's personal life.

Watching from down the road in Durham, Krzyzewski, a basketball purist and committed family man, made increasingly disapproving remarks about his colleague's conduct.

Duke began winning in 1983–84, the season it commenced an uninterrupted run of NCAA appearances that ranks second only to North Carolina's among major-college programs. From then until Valvano's 1990 departure from coaching, the Duke–N.C. State series was as heated, well-played, and dramatic as any in the ACC. Key to stoking the fires was the systematic Krzyzewski's distaste for losing, as he did more times than not, to an improvisor relying on loosely guided though gifted players.

Coach K and Coach V have remained friends of a sort since Valvano became another TV-commentating former coach. Now, Valvano's illness has drawn them closer, and after receiving his dose of therapeutic poison, Valvano comes by Cameron to watch Duke practice and to deliver a pep talk to Krzyzewski's confident Blue Devils.

He speaks of his passion for the game, encouraging it in others. He speaks of life, sharing his pleasure at simply being around to feel. "My goal," Valvano tells the Duke squad as, twenty-one miles away, Tony Robinson readies to embrace mortality, "is to be able to come back and talk to you next year."

Les Robinson met with each returning player soon after he replaced Valvano. Predictably, most were quick to seek increased playing time. Not Tony Robinson.

"One of the first things he told me was that he was a role player," the coach recalls, amused. "He was, like, saying, 'I don't expect much. I rebound and play defense.' Which, again, is a sign of a guy who hasn't played a lot of basketball. Guys who've been playing a long time, they don't do that. They tell you how good they are." Tony Robinson worked devotedly and was rewarded with a significant role in 1991, his first season of eligibility. True, the same five players started every game and there was scant reliance on the bench. But when the Wolfpack needed size, it turned to Robinson, who appeared in two thirds of the team's games for an average of 6.4 minutes.

"I'll never forget him for his smile and all the hard work he put in on the basketball floor," says Kevin Thompson, who arrived the same year as Tony Robinson and became a starter by his sophomore season. "He was always a very positive guy."

Robinson's second season, 1991–92, the team needed all sorts of help and struggled to a 12–18 record. Yet Robinson's appearances dropped to eleven, his minutes to a paltry total of nineteen.

The prospects for playing time aren't much better for the '93 season: against USA Verich, when he could have shown his stuff, Robinson plays four minutes while freshman frontcourt players get twenty-two, sixteen, and eleven minutes respectively.

Robinson is frustrated by the situation and telephones Shelly Marsh, his high school coach, to talk about it. "I tried to encourage him," Marsh recalls. "He was down then but after we talked a while he seemed to get himself together."

Les Robinson prides himself on being father and counselor as well as basketball coach. He remains convinced Robinson, the player who visits his office most frequently, is reasonably content. "Tony, really—from the standpoint of class attendance, attitude, effort on the court—he was a model," Robinson says while trying to come to terms with the player's death. "I would have said this a week ago if you asked me. And I have said it."

So, when the model player fails to show up for the pregame meal, coaches and teammates become concerned. "Tony had always, he'd always been everywhere on time," says junior guard Migjen (pronounced "mah-gin") Bakalli. "It just wasn't like him." When Robinson fails to show up for the pregame meeting too, concern changes to alarm. Phone calls to Robinson's room go unanswered. A team manager is dispatched to knock on the player's door. He gets no response. The door is locked.

Finally, as the Wolfpack prepares to take the court against Brandt Hagen, an athletic department intern secures the appropriate key, and goes to see what's wrong.

At halftime, he tells Les Robinson what he'd found, including a preliminary police conclusion the wound is self-inflicted. The instrument of death is found lying beside the nearly nude body on the bed. No signs of alcohol or drug use are noted. Later an acquaintance tells investigators Robinson bought the revolver recently for eighty dollars. "When asked why," the coroner's report states, "subject said need it when I have my suicidal tendencies." Les Robinson elects to keep the news to himself until the game ends.

Playing with far more intelligence than it did four days ago, the Wolfpack wins, 73–70, the key basket coming on a follow shot by freshman power forward Chuck Kornegay with 2.7 seconds remaining. Throughout the second half Les Robinson remains noticeably subdued on the sidelines. Later he recalls struggling to concentrate on coaching while a "sick feeling" overwhelmed his attention. "It made for a long twenty minutes, I'll tell you that."

Back in the privacy of a locker room enlivened by victory, the somber coach enters, accompanied by athletic director Todd Turner and several physicians, and the State players immediately sense something is amiss. "Everybody just kind of put their heads down because they knew it was something bad," Bakalli says. "I was telling myself it couldn't be before they said the words." Curtis Marshall recalls: "Coach came in, and he said he had some terrible news. Right then, I heard Migjen and Marc Lewis, they started crying right there. He said, 'Tony is dead.' I cried; everybody broke right there."

MANY Wolfpack players can't sleep in the wake of Tony Robinson's suicide.

Kevin Thompson decides not to spend the night in his room adjacent to Robinson's, but as he gathers some belongings inadvertently catches a disquieting glimpse of his teammate's lifeless body, rigor mortis setting in. Thompson and high school chum Donnie Seale go to the house of assistant coach Robert "Buzz" Peterson. There they talk well into the night. To lighten the mood the former UNC guard shows the players a tape of a 1982 win over LSU in which Peterson scored a game-high eighteen points, thoroughly eclipsing his roommate and fellow sophomore, an emerging talent named Michael Jordan.

When the nine-to-five world takes motion, Les Robinson heads to the basketball office. As he drives, he passes two female students engrossed in conversation and laughter, one standing, the other in a wheelchair. Robinson wishes he could show Tony Robinson this scene on campus, tell him how much he has to live for, how much he has in comparison with others.

Too late.

Consequently the coach's morning is occupied arranging counseling sessions for players, who drift in and out of the office alone or in pairs, and in meeting with the athletic director and coaching staff on how best to proceed for the immediate future. Two phone lines stay busy with incoming calls, including offers of assistance from clergy and mental health professionals. Tony Robinson's father and stepmother arrive in late morning. They spoke with Les Robinson twice last night by telephone.

Now they're here to enlist the coach's help in making arrangements for a funeral to be held in Raleigh.

Robinson readies to cancel the day's practice, but is advised to stick to routine as much as possible. Before heading the few yards to Reynolds Coliseum for the afternoon's practice Robinson also attempts to satisfy the public's curiosity, meeting with members of the media in a conference room a floor below his office.

Valvano had dubbed the space "The Room of Dreams," converting it, during his tenure as athletic director, into a multimedia marketing tool and recruiting weapon for Wolfpack basketball at a cost of about one hundred fifty thousand dollars. When Valvano left, the special effects went too, literally as well as figuratively. Now Robinson sits at the head of an unadorned, rectangular wooden table in the same room, answering questions and assuring listeners, as well as himself, that there were no warning signs, no missed opportunities that glare in hindsight.

"He didn't change his behavior from the first time I met him through Sunday," says Robinson, clearly trying to shake off inevitable second-guessing of his own conduct. "There were no signs."

Suicide ranks as the seventh leading cause of death annually in the United States, with between thirty thousand and thirty-five thousand people taking their own lives. Firearms are the method of choice, and are used by 70 percent of all male suicide victims. The suicide rate has seen a sharp rise in recent years among teenagers and young adults, a group that includes Tony Robinson.

Police discover a note in Robinson's VW in which he writes of failure to meet expectations and that "The hardest thing about life is living." For those who thought they knew him well, that's not enough. Probably, no explanation would suffice.

"You just look at yourself and ask, 'Why didn't I see?'" says Bakalli, voicing the survivor's guilty theme. "Why wasn't I looking for something?"

"Tony always kept to himself," Peterson says. "There was always a wall you couldn't get beyond." Whether the team was in an airport or locker room, Robinson preferred to sit a little apart, wearing headphones, in his own world. Still, his teammates saw him as upbeat and friendly, his coaches as a good soldier who accepted his role with equanimity.

"Why, why, why would he do something like this?" laments nineteen-year-old Curtis Marshall, who's never experienced the death of a person close to him. "There had to be a lot more than he showed. He covered it up pretty well."

Perhaps the seeds of alienation were sown early. Robinson's mother left when he was a preschooler. The youngster once confided to an interviewer that his father "was gone most of my childhood" and that the two were not especially close. "It's more of a friendship basis," Tony Robinson said.

In fact, Robinson wasn't particularly close to anyone. Teammates aren't sure if he has a girlfriend, leading eventually to speculation that Robinson was gay.

After practice his last night alive, Robinson headed to his VW to drive alone to the K&W Cafeteria, where the team was going for supper. Lewis insisted Robinson ride along with a group, and Robinson, accepting, playfully leapt upon his smaller teammate's back, taking a piggyback ride to the car. "He was just his normal self," Lewis says, a quaver in his voice. "He was a real independent guy, self-sufficient. He could be very playful." The dinner conversation was of basketball, girls, and school. Robinson was doing passably well academically and, though he sometimes seemed to go out of his way to take difficult courses, was on schedule to graduate in the humanities and social sciences curriculum.

"It was just totally unexpected," Lewis says in the wake of the suicide. "It's just kind of confusing. It's eerie, is the best way I can put it."

Worse, standing on the court at Reynolds prior to practice, undergoing the prescribed catharsis of speaking with others in hopes of gaining a measure of release, Lewis sifts back and finds disturbing reminders of what might have been.

He recalls Robinson saying several times that he needed to talk, and their mutual failure to follow through. And, come to think of it, Lewis recalls his friend's pain. "He probably did feel a big burden to live up to someone's expectations. I think he was pretty hard on himself, took things very serious at times, when it might have slid off someone else's back. I think the biggest thing is that he was searching for something. The bottom line is, I think he was searching for love. That's not unique to Tony."

Few of the N.C. State players or coaches feel much like practicing today. To give the players something to look forward to, and to create some private time together, Les Robinson invites the team and staff to his house for Thanksgiving dinner following practice.

Barbara Robinson, who often comes to practice and helps foster a family atmosphere in the program, cooks four turkeys and salts them with her tears.

"Maybe this is saying something, telling us something," offers Seale. "God doesn't put anything on you that you can't handle." He pauses, then seizes upon a basketball silver lining. "Maybe we'll end up in the Sweet Sixteen."

Peterson, usually upbeat, sees a darker picture.

Reviewing a span of less than a year in which the team lost eighteen games, Feggins was shot and seriously wounded, Valvano was diagnosed with cancer that's likely terminal, Thompson hurt his knee, guard Mark Davis broke his wrist and is lost for up to two months, and now Robinson has killed himself, Peterson notes, "It's like there's a black cloud hanging over this program."

Familiar echoes fill Carolina's Carmichael Auditorium, where Peterson was team captain when last the Tar Heel men's program called the place home.

Seeing the Heels in an exhibition game at Carmichael quickly rekindles memories of past glory. Not that starters Eric Montross, George Lynch, Pat Sullivan, Henrik Rodl, and Brian Reese possess the outstanding talent characteristic of many previous Carolina squads. But they do handsomely embody the corporate entity that once haunted this building. See this veteran squad and see the prototype in clear outline, retooled yet again according to variations in personnel.

The subliminal message is unmistakable: This is how Dean Smith teams do it. This is how they've done it in the past, this is how they'll do it in the future. The passing game. The jump-switch. The secondary break. Traps executed just so. Endless screens, set arms at sides. Fists raised to indicate tiredness. The bench rising and pointing in unison to the man who makes an assist.

The result, like the approach, is familiar. UNC uses a dozen players, leads High Five America by 55–32 at the half and wins going away, 121–74.

Players explain it's all a matter of experience. "Everybody knows what to do, more so than last year," Reese says. "That's what it is. We don't have to really stop and think: 'Am I goaltender?' You just do it from instinct. We're veterans. We've been doing this. Everybody that played last year is playing this year. And Donald [Williams] is stepping up.

"Especially in this system, there's so many things to learn. That's why so many freshmen don't play that much. Because you've got so many things to learn. You can't come out thinking you have all the time in the world. This is North Carolina. You play together. You play team defense.

You play team offense. Everything is a team. It ain't just set a screen for this one player; this one player is going to have eight plays. So, a freshman player, it's hard to come in here and really get used to all those things."

Unfortunately, the evening's least impressive performance is turned in by Montross, tabbed by many as the best center in the country. Such praise comes as something of a surprise to Smith. He's seen Montross develop for two years and knows how far he has yet to go.

Montross already holds a special place in the Smith formidable pantheon of players: He's the first whom the coach allowed to be listed at seven feet tall.

Smith perceived a psychological advantage in avoiding the expectations that went with such height, a view he picked up from Frank McGuire. Over the years, despite obvious evidence to the contrary Smith thus insisted various tall players were not seven-footers. This was taken to such an extreme that Warren Martin was listed during the mid-eighties at six-foot-eleven-and-a-half.

Now the Tar Heels have four roster members listed at seven feet or taller, making them perhaps the biggest team in NCAA annals.

Montross is especially imposing because he's not only tall but weighs two hundred seventy rather solid pounds. "He's the biggest human being I've ever seen," a Duke office staffer said after Montross visited the school. "He just filled the door."

As a youngster Montross was self-conscious about his inordinate size. "I finally realized, be proud of who I am. That goes for everybody," he says. He also found his stature attracted expectations like an open road attracts speeders. But Montross is a good athlete and a bright, quick learner. He harbors no illusions about being anything but a low-post presence. He's difficult to budge, and difficult to resist when he seeks to occupy a spot on the floor. He works hard to master a notably frill-less game, hustles at all times, and runs with surprising speed.

But against High Five he displays mediocre balance, falling down a surprising number of times. He appears mechanical in his movements and, as in the past, is plagued by foul trouble, finishing with four personals in twenty-five minutes.

Montross also continues to struggle from the free throw line, missing three of four attempts. Considering how often he's likely to be fouled, his 61.9 percent career foul shooting isn't acceptable.

Smith rarely criticizes players, especially in public. If he does it in private, it's off the record. And his assistants operate under standing orders to defer all discussion of the current team or individual players to Smith. "I think that's the way it should be," Bill Guthridge says. "I think there should be one voice talking about the program and that should be the head coach. I see so many assistant coaches talking, maybe they mean to say what the head coach says but it comes out a little differently." The ACC also has rules about talking: coaches aren't allowed to criticize game officials in public. Last season, irked by Montross's repeated foul trouble, Smith held his tongue—barely—and instead sent a taped compendium of what he considered poor calls to five ACC referees and administrators. All the copies reportedly were returned unopened.

Montross has learned to politely question officials about their calls—so he can learn from his mistakes, he says archly.

Still, the center feels he gets banged on a lot and unfairly burdened with touch fouls. "It's kind of like the bigger the better, or the bigger the more you can take," he explains. Montross has learned to retaliate subtly—a well-placed hip here, a quick elbow there—rather than employ showy fall-down tactics for which Smith's teams once were infamous. "I've never been accustomed to acting to draw a foul. I'm not going to act. I don't want to be seen as somebody who's fake, who's fickle."

Strangely, though, the player who shuns display appears to have gone out of his way to attract attention. Already the largest person on the court, Montross wears the unusual jersey numeral "00" (which Smith had in junior high) and a severely spare haircut that's bare on the sides and bristles on top, making him look very much like a classic thug.

Smith says Montross's hairstyle is now the 'do of choice among youngsters at North Carolina's summer basketball camp, supplanting the box cut common during J.R. Reid's years (1987–89).

Montross is not among the many ACC players who attended Smith's camps. But he had extensive tutoring in the basics before coming to college, including private lessons from former pro George Irvine. Montross also benefits from having basketball in his blood. One of his grandfathers was an All-America at Michigan and his six-foot-eight father, lawyer Scott Montross, likewise played at Ann Arbor.

Even now, father and son go one-on-one at home during the summers when the family's not off canoeing in Alaska or on photo safari in Africa. "He's still got a pretty good shot on him," says Eric. "I don't think dad wants to play me as much anymore. I still drag him out there."

Given his genes, Montross knew early in life he was destined to be quite tall. Yet it wasn't basketball the Indiana native loved while growing up. "Hockey was my first love and I played basketball on the side," he says. Montross played ice hockey from the time he was eight until he was about fourteen, or until "my feet got too big for skates."

Montross was a defenseman; one can only imagine what it would be like to see a man his size skating toward you, intent on smacking you into the boards. What Montross liked best about hockey was not the hitting, though. "I was always bigger than the other players, but I was fast," he says. "I liked the speed of hockey and how the game moved so quickly. It could turn around just like this and you always had to be on your toes."

Basketball provides a reasonable substitute because it too requires "fast movement and quick decisions," Montross says.

One decision he didn't make quickly was where to attend college. Montross's choice of North Carolina came as something of a surprise, even to Dean Smith. After all, the kid's other two final choices were Michigan, his father's alma mater, and Indiana, the power in his home state. "I had a lot of pressure on me," says Montross, who was booed when the Heels played in Indianapolis his freshman year. "People said that I was the ticket to the national championship and I was going to start every game."

What ultimately swayed the country music fan was the recruiting class UNC assembled that year—"You can have a great big man, but you have to have a great team around you," the junior explains with coach-like assurance—and Smith's success preparing contemporary big men Brad Daugherty, Sam Perkins, Scott Williams, and Reid for the pros. "I thought he was the best coach in the nation, and today I still think he's the best coach in the nation," Montross says in his deep, even voice.

MONDAY, NOVEMBER 30

TOMORROW the season starts. The games count. This morning, Tony Robinson's body is buried in Mount Hope Cemetery, in a predominantly black Raleigh neighborhood almost within sight of two outdoor basketball courts and an elementary school where children cavort happily in midautumn sunlight.

The gravesite is in a newer section of the Reconstruction-vintage cemetery, hard by a tall chainlink fence and a stand of young pines. More than a hundred people gather round the burgundy burial canopy, beneath which Robinson's body lies in a cream-brown coffin. Family members sit beside it on velour-draped folding chairs. Robinson's thirteen N.C. State teammates, who served as pallbearers, stand close to the minister as he intones words of comfort that are lost a few yards away to the sounds of traffic and cawing crows.

The crows, having chased a hawk from their territory, are shouting triumphantly from perches in the pines. The birds' black shapes and oddly mocking voices lend an appropriately sepulchral touch to the proceedings.

The casket is opened for a final viewing, and the majority of mourners file slowly past to gaze upon Robinson one last time. Later, several will comment on how good he looks.

Robinson's teammates, most dressed in ties and jackets, lead the mournful parade. They're joined by erstwhile teammate Bryant Feggins, still recovering from his gunshot wound. Much of the school's athletic hierarchy is present, including Todd Turner, the athletic director, and Kay Yow, the women's basketball coach. Les Robinson and a crying Barbara Robinson hold hands as they pass the body.

Tony Robinson's high school coach is on hand, as is Dick Stewart, a Valvano assistant who recruited Robinson for N.C. State. In fact, every Valvano-era assistant who knew Tony Robinson has called the basketball office to express condolences. But there's been no word yet from Valvano, who's getting plenty of media attention for a newfound sense of proportion in the face of his own mortality.

TUESDAY, DECEMBER 1

IT STILL feels like exhibition season, though this is the first game that counts.

The Canisius Golden Griffins act as if their visit to half-century-old Cameron Indoor Stadium is a privilege, a pilgrimage. They're so taken with the occasion that as each starter is introduced he trots to the Duke bench to shake Mike Krzyzewski's hand. This gesture isn't as simple as it sounds, considering Krzyzewski's pregame ritual includes crouching on one knee before his bench, back to the court. By the time the P.A. announcer finishes introducing the Canisius starters, three of whom have only known college ball with Duke as national champ, they've got Krzyzewski standing, waiting to accept their tribute.

Duke scores first, beginning the 1993 season the same way it ended its 1992 championship run—with a basket by Grant Hill.

Hill's final shot in the title game was a dunk. Tonight he opens with a fourteen-foot jump shot. By game's end, employing a wide array of moves, Hill has a career-high twenty-eight points on twelve of thirteen shooting. His only miss is a finger-roll that hangs on the front of the rim before falling off. Unfazed, he rebounds his own miss, draws a foul and makes both free throws.

"It's scary," Kenny Blakeney says afterward. "He can do whatever he wants whenever he wants. It's disgusting. I hate him. If he puts his mind to it, he can do whatever he wants." The smallish Grifs keep the score close for a while in new coach John Beilein's Division I debut, helped by Duke, which works harder on offense than defense. Most players prefer scoring to the hard work of stopping the other guy, especially when, like Canisius, the other guy is patient and well prepared. Still, these Blue Devils pride themselves on their defensive prowess. They aim to make their mark by disrupting opponents' plans, extending perimeter pressure more than Duke has in years. "We're a defensive team; that's our trademark," Hill says.

Krzyzewski can't like what he's seeing, but maintains his seat, chin in right hand and body tightly coiled as Canisius pulls within 32–24 with 8:44 left in the first half. Wearing a dark sport jacket and an equally dark expression, the Duke coach resembles a storm cloud gathering strength.

But the storm that breaks first is on the court. Suddenly the Blue Devils rediscover their defensive discipline and break the Grifs' poise, running off twenty-one unanswered points despite a pair of prophylactic timeouts by Beilein. "I think that you have a tendency sometimes to play a game like this and just play it offensively," Krzyzewski says afterward. "Once we got into character, I thought we played well at both ends of the court."

Duke leads 60–28 at halftime, finishing the period with a 26–4 outburst. Bobby Hurley already has ten points and six assists. The Grifs commit twelve turnovers and grab thirteen rebounds; Cherokee Parks and Tony Lang combine to match their rebounding total. And Grant Hill scores a third of Duke's points. "I was shocked," Krzyzewski says. "I looked at the halftime stats and he had twenty points . . . He does everything easy. He doesn't force anything."

With the issue decided, the remainder of the game becomes a warmup, an exercise. The Devils are well aware their next opponent is top-ranked Michigan, their victims in the '92 title game, so they work hard to stay on track. "It's a clinic every time they play," Beilein says.

Gradually, though, concentration wavers. Marty Clark, Duke's top reserve, finds he has an advantage in size and speed, and reverts to past form, driving to the basket almost every time he gets the ball. Once Clark grabs a defensive rebound and simply drives coast to coast; he winds up with more shots in fifteen minutes than Lang, a starter, takes in twenty-eight.

Later, Parks and Erik Meek start throwing sloppy outlet passes, converting defensive rebounds into scoring opportunities for Canisius, not Duke. This doesn't sit well with Krzyzewski, who refuses to grant his players excuses due to the early date or the overmatched opponent. "I don't think it should be understandable. I don't think it's understandable. We're trying to develop good habits." Krzyzewski isn't too thrilled with the Duke fans either.

For years he's assiduously cultivated student support, praising the

Cameron crowd as his team's "Sixth Man." Duke students sit in wooden bleachers that ring the playing surface. They had a reputation for creative rowdiness and intimidation long before Krzyzewski's arrival, but Krzyzewski has made certain they feel a part of what's happening. These days, when hundreds of undergrads camp out for preferred seating prior to big games, he buys them pizza and invites them inside for late-night pep talks and question-and-answer sessions.

The notion that Duke students and players are all part of the same team got Krzyzewski in hot water in 1990. A writer for the student newspaper, *The Chronicle*, wrote an article evaluating each player on the squad, awarding letter grades. None received lower than a C+. The team got a B+. Shortly afterward Donna Keane, Krzyzewski's administrative assistant, phoned to invite the paper's ten-member, all-volunteer sports staff to come by Cameron for a chat. The meeting took place in the Duke locker room, where it was recorded surreptitiously by one of the student writers.

With doors closed and his team and assistant coaches looking on, Krzyzewski proceeded to berate the writers in much the same manner he would address players who'd displeased him. That the setting, and the profanity, might constitute an act of intimidation never occurred to Krzyzewski, he said. To this day, in fact, Krzyzewski believes he was mistreated because his words were secretly recorded and his meaning publicly misconstrued.

The incident made national news, serving to awaken Krzyzewski to his high-profile status. But other than a few expressions of dismay, the outburst did little to undermine Krzyzewski's status as "coach-educator," as he was dubbed in ads for a stock brokerage firm.

Today the run-in is but a distant memory and *The Chronicle* tends toward an adulatory tone. After all, it is hard to criticize success, especially when the more Duke has succeeded—winning all but two home games over the past four seasons—the more famous its student-rooters have become.

For Canisius and this season's opener, though, perhaps bored at the prospect of witnessing a blowout, the "Cameron Crazies" don't even fill the bleachers. (Duke reports a full house, anyway.) Seeing this emptiness for the second time in three games (spanning two seasons) Krzyzewski uses a postgame press conference to scold the crowd as though it really is a part of his team.

"I was kind of disappointed that our student stands weren't filled. I couldn't believe that," he tells the media. "I hope we don't get up just for the Michigan game. That's not the proper attitude. I was very disappointed in that. This was our first game." A few minutes later, a writer in the Duke locker room asks Parks if he thinks it's appropriate for Krzyzewski to chastise the fans.

"You better say yes," mutters an eavesdropping Thomas Hill. "You've got no choice."

Virtually all of the country's better college basketball teams work out opening-night jitters by beating up on weaker opponents. It's as much a ritual of the season as buying a Christmas tree or eating turkey.

Occasionally though, the erstwhile basketball turkeys bite back. N.C. State's coaches fully expect to defeat UNC-Wilmington, a sister school from the coast that finished with a losing record last year in a mediocre lcague. Al Daniel says the Wolfpack should win by at least eight points, even if it's not playing well. The worst-case scenario would be "a Robert Morris," he says, a reference to a surprisingly close game two years back when a late free throw by Migjen Bakalli preserved a home win over a supposed patsy.

Daniel's assessment proves off the mark. UNC-W leads virtually the entire game before a stunned crowd at Reynolds Coliscum. The Seahawks lead 42–33 at halftime and win by a dozen points.

"Instead of us taking it to Wilmington, they took it to us," Daniel laments after the Wolfpack commits eighteen turnovers compared to twelve assists. "We were almost indifferent. That's disappointing to us."

But not surprising. Tonight the team unveils a new and unfortunate bit of uniform equipment—black bands on the left straps of their jerseys in memory of Tony Robinson.

Free throw shooting often provides a good indication of a team's concentration—N.C. State makes eleven of twenty against the Seahawks. Bakalli, who admitted after Robinson's death it would be tough to "get after it" on the court, commits three turnovers and misses six of nine shots, including five of six from three-point range. A wing player, he somehow manages to foul out. Marc Lewis, another player close to Robinson, misses both shots he attempts.

At their meeting prior to the game, the coaches discussed the possibility that Tony Robinson's death might have a lingering effect on team performance. Publicly, though, and to the team, they discount such an effect. "We were trying to fight that off as much as we could as coaches," Daniel says. "When people ask us, we try to play it down. But it's been a tough week."

The loss to UNC-W makes it even tougher. Worse, it has lasting repercussions of its own. Now, in order to stay on track to a successful season, the Pack must steal a victory somewhere against a stronger opponent. The surprise defeat also intensifies the air of uncertainty engulfing the team, which has two more games this week, including a home court matchup with Connecticut, a ranked opponent.

THURSDAY, DECEMBER 3

THE tent city continues to grow outside Cameron Indoor Stadium. Inside members of the media, many from out of town, sift through the corridors in a steady stream, seeking interviews and colorful snippets to bolster stories about the upcoming game with Michigan.

The sports section of *USA Today* features a piece on the game, detailing the number of television stations that have signed on to carry the syndicated broadcast (140), as well as the record-setting wave of media requests accommodated by Duke's sports information office. Raycom Sports, based in Charlotte, N.C., expects the largest audience for a syndicated game since 1968, when UCLA, with Lew Alcindor, had a forty-seven-game winning streak stopped by Houston and Elvin Hayes.

CBS reportedly is willing to pay in the neighborhood of a quarter-million dollars for the rights to Duke-Michigan, hoping to pair this reprise of the '92 NCAA title game with another heavyweight matchup on Saturday, Indiana versus Kansas.

Duke-Michigan dwarfs the other game in appeal. Mike Cragg, Duke's sports information director, has had plenty of experience slaking media thirst on such occasions and has arranged an afternoon press conference via telephone. More than one hundred media representatives tune in as Michigan coach Steve Fisher and forward Chris Webber, followed by Krzyzewski, Grant Hill, and Bobby Hurley, each spend about fifteen minutes answering callers' questions.

"It's a little like a UNC game, a home game against North Carolina," Hill says of the sense of anticipation on campus and around Durham. He and the other Blue Devils seem remarkably relaxed about the whole thing.

Seated in Cragg's office, a familiar hangout that adjoins the suite of basketball offices, Hill says: "Hey, I wish we could play more big games like this. That brings out the best in everybody."

Well, almost everybody. The Michigan players have a predilection for trash-talk, the sort of verbal posturing Muhammad Ali raised to an art form before they were born. But whereas Ali backed up his talk with titles, the young Wolverines have yet to win much of anything other than a preseason number-one ranking and a lot of media attention. They have yet to learn that their words can and will be used against them in a court of basketball.

Webber, a master of the less-than-bon mot, confidently predicts Michigan will celebrate on the Blue Devils' home court, and insists that he won't be bothered by the Duke fans' notorious taunting. The six-foot-nine forward has visited Cameron previously, as a spectator. Recruited by Duke, he sat behind the team bench for a 1991 game with Louisiana State in which the fans were relentless in their derision of Tiger center Shaquille O'Neal, who was outplayed by Christian Laettner as LSU lost in a rout.

"We've all played in parks and in the city," Webber says, "and I don't think anyone can say anything or chant or do anything to make me mess up."

In fact, a letter from two seniors printed in *The Chronicle* cautions fans against singling out any Michigan players for derision. Krzyzewski has noted in the past, the students remind their compatriots, that such tactics often inspire top players to transcendent performances.

As for the taunts, challenges, and posturings emanating from the Michigan players, Grant Hill voices the standard Duke line. "I kind of compare it to being an actor and having your character," he says in his normal, even manner. "They have their characters." Hill departs Cragg's office and immediately attracts two reporters, who trail in his wake like sea gulls seeking scraps from a passing trawler.

A few doors away, Pete Gaudet sits in his perennially unkempt office surrounded by stacks of newspapers (read and unread), game balls, videotapes, books, piles of personal letters, boxes of Duke shirts, and assorted other paraphernalia of the trade. "This team doesn't have an identity yet," he says of the team's groping process of discovery. "It's a different team. We don't know what it will be like with different leadership, different players, different freshmen. So the Canisius game was an important first step. Will this team dive for loose balls? Will they play together?

Will they like one another? Will they be fragmented? Will they be close? No matter what you do in the preseason games, this is for real."

As for the Michigan game, Gaudet says: "We'll tell our guys before they go out: 'It's a great opportunity to have Michigan in here. Let's just really not be awfully nervous. Let's be gunned up to have a fun game and to do our stuff, to showcase yourselves and the program.' That's how we'll treat it."

Just to make sure the players attain the proper emotional level, the program's master of videotape prepares a little feature on the Wolverines to be shown prior to tomorrow's practice.

The tape begins with TV hype about great groups—the Beatles (or "Fab Four"), the Jackson Five, Michigan's Fab Five. There are clips of Michigan players spouting off about meeting Duke. The tape then uses old game footage to review strategic pointers Gaudet gleaned from a November trip to watch the Wolverines play an exhibition game.

Finally, there's Michigan center Juwan Howard telling an unseen ESPN interviewer, "I just have pity for Duke." Actually, it appears he's saying, "I just have the pity for Duke." It's easy to follow the words closely, since on Gaudet's tape Howard repeats his putdown three times in staccato fashion like a boxer with a quick jab.

Today's motivational ploy, discussed at the daily coaches' meeting, also is standard coaching issue. If Krzyzewski detects a lack of intensity, he'll seize the players' attention and underline the seriousness of the task at hand by dismissing them from practice. The workout is designed to focus on defense first, assuring important drills have been covered should Krzyzewski angrily abort the late-afternoon practice.

But no one is tossed out. Interviews completed, the Dukies enjoy their most inspired and hard-hitting practice of the year.

UNC-Asheville is considered a classic "bop," an automatic victory purchased with a handsome piece of the gate proceeds at 12,400-seat Reynolds Coliseum. UNC-A has lost its previous nineteen encounters with ACC teams; N.C. State has won the previous seven meetings between the sister schools by an average margin of 29.7 points.

Tonight, after blowing an eleven-point halftime lead, State recovers its poise sufficiently to eke out a three-point victory, though not before having to survive a botched chance by Asheville to tie the game at the buzzer.

As in the UNC-Wilmington game, the Pack is carried by Curtis Marshall, who finishes with eighteen points and a few key defensive plays, and a healthy Kevin Thompson, who leads all scorers with twenty-one points. Thompson sees the ball sparingly in the second half, taking four shots and making them all.

Obviously shaken, Les Robinson puts a coach's positive face on an ugly evening. "If we turn around this year, we have to thank UNC-Asheville and UNC-Wilmington. They were perfect for us to play. Our players were able to see we're not that good. They gave us the message."

Of course, the Wolfpack players supposedly got this message after losing their opening exhibition, as Robinson well knows. "We've got a long way to go on this journey," he confides ruefully. "A long way to go. Longer than I thought. I thought it was cross-country. It may be halfway around the world."

His accompanying laugh is not a happy sound. How much unhappier he would be if he knew his team will never again reach the modest plateau on which it now resides, with as many wins as losses.

FRIDAY, DECEMBER 4

Two games, two victories, two one-hundred-point performances by North Carolina.

First the eighth-ranked Heels hosted Old Dominion at the Smith Center and won, 119–82. The Monarchs, a disciplined, pressing squad, will win twenty games by season's end. South Carolina, tonight's opponent in the opening round of the two-day Diet Pepsi Tournament of Champions, doesn't do anything in particular and loses even more decisively, 108–67.

Nothing about South Carolina matches North Carolina on this occasion.

Fan loyalties in the Charlotte Coliseum are clearly evident when the Tar Heels are introduced; the roar is comparable to any at the Smith Center, two hours' drive distant. "Charlotte's always amazing when we come here," a pleased Smith says afterward. "That's some neutral court." The game is equally lopsided, with the Tar Heels using superior size, depth, intelligence, and teamwork to seize immediate and permanent command.

It's already apparent this is Smith's most formidable squad in years, even with Derrick Phelps struggling to regain his wind after being sidelined for weeks with a leg injury. North Carolina players are confident and aggressive at both ends of the court, in contrast to recent seasons when they groped uncertainly for long stretches. They seem to be playing the game, flowing with it, rather than transparently running Smith's system like so many interchangeable cogs in a changeless machine.

"I think we know we have the potential to be very aggressive, and successful being aggressive," explains Montross, a dominating force against South Carolina.

Montross is persistent on the boards and crisp in his offensive movements. He haunts the low post. He releases his shots quickly and generally sticks with layups, dunks and short jump hooks. He conveys the ball with a sense of purpose, a change from his previous, overly deliberate manner. He's less prone to bring the ball down within the reach of smaller defenders. And he has a newfound control that helps avoid fouls.

There are many pro scouts in attendance tonight, and rumblings among them suggest Montross should leave school following this season, when draft pickings are projected to be slim.

"I've heard rumors about that," Montross says evenly. "I'm not concerned about that right now. I'm here to win a national championship." He admits, though, such talk "is a great compliment" and that he's trying "not to think about it too much."

Donald Williams plays well again tonight, too.

Williams came to Chapel Hill from Garner, a suburb of Raleigh, where he'd won All-America honors, recognition as North Carolina's 1991 high-school player of the year, and a reputation as an outstanding shooter. Les Robinson's N.C. State staff eagerly wooed the local hero, and surely would have ensconced him at second guard to replace the departed Rodney Monroe, the Pack's all-time leading scorer. But Williams had his heart set on wearing Carolina blue.

Privately skeptical of Williams's abilities, Smith immediately anointed the freshman a point guard and parked him on the bench, where he languished through most of his first year. "He really didn't understand how Coach Smith wanted him to play defense and move without the ball," Pat Sullivan says. "He had to relearn the game, just like all of us."

Though Williams won't admit it publicly until his sophomore season ends, and despite the fact that, from the first, the coach encouraged him to shoot, Williams, like many freshmen, was disillusioned by the way Smith used him. "Sometimes I pass up open shots," said Williams, who led ACC players in 1992 by launching a shot every 1.8 minutes played. "He keeps telling me to relax and shoot it." As often happens, the discouraged freshman considered transferring, though Williams apparently didn't put it that way when he spoke with Smith. "He came in and said, 'People keep bugging me, my friends,'" the coach recalls. "I said, 'Well, are you strong enough to handle it?' He said, 'Yeah.'"

Williams, an only child, chose a school in the Triangle so his parents could readily see him play. In his time of doubt he drew strength from his father, a truck driver who insisted Williams avoid being a quitter. "Once I stopped thinking of transferring, I started working hard to improve," says Williams, who with his wide face, low voice, quick words and retiring manner has the public demeanor of a spooked deer. "He's real quiet," Brian Reese says of "D." Yet Williams isn't all that retiring, having formed a bond with New Yorkers Reese and Phelps, both a year older and more world-wise than Williams. "He's real funny," Reese says. "He's like, down to earth. He definitely fit in real quick. We're the type who get along a lot because we're to ourselves a lot. We're cool." The veterans help ease their buddy's adjustment to UNC; Reese especially had, and is still having, difficulty accepting the Carolina Way.

"You just don't know if you're good enough anymore," Williams recalls of his season of doubt. "You just have to listen to the other guys on the team who have gone through this and believe them when they say things will get better."

Besides, there was little rational basis for Williams to expect extensive playing time in '92.

There was simply nowhere to put him. He wasn't and never would be a playmaker, certainly not compared to Phelps. "He sees somebody; he's got a shooter's mind," Smith says. "The guy is wide open, and he's not . . . But you watch Donald on the ball defensively," the coach says, changing directions in midstride, "he's really good this year. Off the ball he's still struggling."

There was no room for Williams at second guard last season either. That spot belonged to senior Hubert Davis, now with the NBA's New York Knicks, who attempted and made nearly half of UNC's three-pointers. Davis's 21.4 points per game was tops by a Tar Heel since Charlie Scott registered 27.1 in 1970.

"Usually that means, when you have a high scorer, that's a sign of a weak team," Smith admits. Davis was so central to North Carolina's attack, opponents often geared their defenses to stop him, daring the rest of the Tar Heels to make them pay. The tactic wasn't a bad one—the other Heels hit 28 percent from the bonusphere, less than a break-even rate, and UNC lost ten times in 1992.

Understandably, then, one of the biggest questions about the current Tar Heels is how they'll replace Davis's outside shooting. Williams, one of several options, struggled early during the preseason, prompting Smith to say, "I think it's people saying, 'Hey, now Hubert's gone, you're going to get your crack.'" But Williams eventually relaxed, and is a regular at second guard. He doesn't start, of course; Henrik Rodl, a senior, merits that honor. No matter. Williams still leads all scorers with twenty-three points coming off the bench against South Carolina. Included are five three-pointers in eight attempts.

Equally important, the muscular sophomore plays hard, does a good job guarding his man, and seems comfortable handling the ball himself, his training at point guard standing him in good stead. "He seems like he's been playing for years," an NBA scout comments admiringly.

For all that, the highlight of tonight's rout is neither the play of Montross nor that of Williams. Rather it's the contribution by North Carolina's deep reserves, who score on virtually every possession as the game winds down.

All fourteen Tar Heels get in the game and score. The benchwarmers' most memorable basket is registered by senior Scott Cherry, whose presence on the squad is in part Dean Smith's way of thumbing his nose at experts who make a living identifying and handicapping high school prospects.

Mindful of the need to minimize expectations for the numerous blue-chippers he signs, Smith delights in pointing out the successes of unheralded prep players like 1989 NBA rookie-of-the-year Mitch Richmond, or his own Hubert Davis, a first-round draft choice whom Smith tried to discourage from attending UNC. Cherry was so overlooked, "Nobody had him on their list," Smith said happily upon signing the slender guard from upstate New York.

Cherry came to Smith's attention via a videotape sent by an employee of a Rochester television station. Long ago, the same amateur scout steered Smith to Schenectady's Dick Grubar, who became a key member of the coach's first Final Four teams in 1967, 1968, and 1969.

The six-foot-five Cherry achieves no such prominence, remaining a third-stringer for most of his career. He plays almost exclusively in mop-up situations, the Smith Center crowd screaming for him to shoot when he touches the ball.

Now, though, injuries and Cherry's experience and senior standing result in increased playing time. He appears in both halves against South Carolina; Smith customarily gives players a taste in the first half if he expects they might play a role in the second. Cherry's big moment comes with two minutes left and UNC leading by thirty-three. He deflects a lazy

Gamecock perimeter pass, runs it down, races ahead of the field and slams the ball home.

Cherry's teammates erupt from the bench in laughter and applause, and throughout the next Gamecock possession Cherry is unable to wipe a broad grin from his face. "I've done it in practice before," he says afterward of the dunk, "but this is the first time in a game. I've been waiting for that."

Smith points out yet again that Cherry is a good athlete. "He didn't make any of the recruiting lists," the coach repeats.

SATURDAY, DECEMBER 5

TODAY'S Triangle basketball hors d'oeuvre is served up at noon on ESPN. Connecticut, a top twenty-five team from the Big East, visits Reynolds Coliseum. Such exposure is old hat for Duke's Blue Devils, waiting to play Michigan tonight, but it's a special occasion for members of the Wolfpack. "It was our first national TV game," Curtis Marshall says afterward. "There was a lot of hype. Everybody's been talking about the game all week. The students, our friends." So it's easy to imagine how Pack players feel when they fall behind by thirteen points before scoring, commit more turnovers in the first half than they produce field goals, and trail 49–29 at halftime against an opponent missing two starters.

"They were scared shitless, and for no reason," Les Robinson says of his team. "It was sickening. What you hope is, if you're just bad, you're not capable, you just say you've got to practice, you've got to do this and this. But you've got to be a team before that. You've got to be functioning to be coached. We weren't even functioning." And to think, Connecticut coach Jim Calhoun tried for much of the summer to get this game canceled.

The Huskies play a physical, aggressive defense that aims to trap ball handlers. The last things you want to do against a trap are pick up your dribble without a plan, take the ball into the corner, or throw weak passes toward midcourt. Despite forewarning, State's inexperienced guards do all three. They seem overwhelmed, like small boys trying to wade into heavy seas.

"The first half we were just a little intimidated. A lot, really," Marshall murmurs. "I just wasn't into it. My head wasn't in it. For some reason I just wasn't into it. That's probably the worst half I've had in my career. Including high school." Marshall's brainlock is especially regrettable since he, rather than Seale, has become the point guard. Seale, who continues to fixate on attacking the basket regardless of the wisdom or feasibility of the task, is at small forward in Mark Davis's absence.

But playing Marshall at point has its drawbacks. The sophomore is small, only five-eleven, one hundred sixty pounds. He's more comfortable as a scorer—his team-high twenty-seven points in the loss to UNC Wilmington were a career best.

Marshall also came to college with little grasp of the game's nuances. Playmakers Bobby Hurley of Duke and Derrick Phelps of North Carolina hail from the New York area, their games honed on inner-city playgrounds where basketball is as much a tradition as toughness. For them, running a team is second nature. Marshall comes from Omaha, Nebraska, hardly a basketball hotbed. A friendly fellow with a narrow mustache and heavy eyebrows that give his face a darkly soulful look, Marshall knows how to play, not how to direct a team. He's unusually quick, though, and Robinson and staff, scrambling to assemble a competitive recruiting class in the sour aftermath of Valvano's departure, offered him a scholarship without ever seeing him in a high school game.

In Marshall, State got an alternately timid and uncontrolled guard who, midway through the '92 season, finally accepted a subordinate role. Now, as the Pack troops to the locker room trailing UConn by twenty at halftime, Marshall knows enough to recognize he's had a miserable half. "It's one of the worst feelings if you can't get control of yourself and make the right decisions," he says. "Some of those passes, as soon as I threw them, I knew." Les Robinson's address to his stunned players is light on instruction and basketball fine points. Instead he appeals, often loudly, to the players' pride.

"You guys are here because you wanted to play in the best basketball conference in America the last four years. That's a goal. That's an opportunity. I feel like that as a coach. . . . We owe it to everybody to give it our best. You came here because you wanted to play against the best, and you're not doing your best."

There's no reference to Tony Robinson, whose open locker has been converted into a modest shrine within which hang an N.C. State uniform and a photo and plaque honoring the player who wore it.

Nor does Les Robinson hint at his own doubts or pain. "You lead the parade. You've got to be strong; you've got to be tough," he admits. "I try to see things with a positive attitude. I can't say it hasn't been tough at times. . . . November was a tough month, the toughest I've ever had."

Robinson is no stranger to death. Since he's been at N.C. State both his father and stepbrother have died. His best friend and jogging buddy at The Citadel dropped dead one day too. But Robinson's alarm today is more about the athletic version of mortality. The pain of Tony Robinson's death may be easing, but the State squad appears in the process of following his example, delivering a devastating, self-inflicted blow to its season. "Those first two games, they jolted us. Forget about all the other stuff," says the coach. Already his aspiration for this squad—sixteen or seventeen victories and an NCAA bid—"sounds like a joke."

Connecticut hasn't won yet, though. The Wolfpack responds to Robinson's call to pride by opening the second half with a 13–4 run. The guards play with purpose. Turnovers are cut to three for the period, while UConn has seven. Passes flow with regularity to post players Kevin Thompson and Chuck Kornegay, who crash the boards as well. Thompson, the senior, finishes with thirteen points and a dozen rebounds. Kornegay, a six-eight freshman, has twenty-one points and nine rebounds.

The Connecticut lead is down to single digits with twelve minutes to go, down to five with 10:58 remaining after a Lakista McCuller three-pointer. It's down to 59–56 with 9:43 left as Migjen Bakalli hits a three-pointer. Reynolds rocks, the sound deafening, one of college basketball's best, and least recognized, home court advantages coming into play.

"In the second half, when we started taking care of the ball, look what happened," Marshall says later. "We came all the way back." Well, not quite all the way. The Pack spends the game's final eleven minutes within two baskets of the Huskies, but there are too many mistakes, too many forced three-pointers and ill-advised passes. The result is an 81–74 loss. "Even though we lost, I felt we made a lot of progress in the second half," says Seale, sounding a theme common in State's locker room. "For the first time, people seem to feel we're going to be all right," adds Thompson.

But there's still the matter of that execrable start, which Seale attributes to an emotional daze that's gripped the team since Robinson's death.

"It's been kind of rocky, due to what happened," Seale says. "It kind of confuses the players, because they really don't know what happened. We were close to him, and we don't know. We don't want to blame our whole season on that. We don't want to make that the scapegoat for us. We're trying to get over it. We want to keep on going and win, no matter what happened. That's what he would want for us."

Amidst the confusion and gloom, at least one person is smiling and upbeat. "I'm just excited to be here and be on the team," freshman Marcus Wilson says. "It's just a blessing that I'm out here. Sometimes it's hard to believe I'm out here. I'm enjoying it. I'm not complaining about anything right now."

Finally, the early season's big moment: The third meeting in twelve months between the champion and the chief pretender:

Krzyzewskiville, an emptied tent city spreading into the darkness.

Thousands of students waiting in the cold to cram into Cameron Indoor Stadium. First arrivals get the best seats—opposite the scorer's table and the TV cameras, where everyone at home can see them.

An electronic card reader placed on the sidewalk, checking student IDs to make sure they're valid before bearers can pass.

The guard in the student lobby exclaiming, "Here they come!" The students streaming through the turnstile almost two hours before game time, then racing for the bleachers in a scene like the running of the bulls at Pamplona, the student pep band providing spirited musical accompaniment.

Two guys in Domino Pizza shirts getting ejected by the police when they try to bluff their way in.

Fliers cast upon the bleachers containing a mock version of Michigan's fight song, calling the school at Ann Arbor "the cesspool of the West."

Banners. Placards. Noise. Heat. Painted faces. Painted chests (men's).

An end to the waiting. Number one visiting number three. Kenney Brown, Duke's walk-on (the months of preparation having been amply rewarded), shooting around with Michigan's superstuds before the other Blue Devils are in evidence. Joe Brown, Kenney's father, seated behind the scorer's table, blue clothing having replaced the red he wore this afternoon while cheering N.C. State.

Duke signees Joey Beard and Jeff Capel by the bench, along with Keith Booth, possibly wavering in his intention to attend Maryland.

Michigan taking the court four minutes before tipoff, Duke immediately afterward. Mike Krzyzewski appearing last, preceded by a vanguard of student-managers.

Introducing the Michigan starters first: Chris Webber. Ray Jackson. Juwan Howard. Jimmy King. Jalen Rose. The Duke fans saying "Hi" to each, along with his first name.

Then the Blue Devils: Grant Hill. Tony Lang. Cherokee Parks. Thomas Hill. Bobby Hurley.

Krzyzewski crouched before the bench, back to the court. As each starter rises from his seat, the coach greeting him by firmly bumping fists, Duke's private symbol for playing as a unit, five fingers merged to form one unified hand. Krzyzewski remaining on bended knee throughout the Blue Devil introductions, awaiting his players' return for final instruction.

Parks winning the opening tap against Webber, one of the few jumps Parks wins all year.

Grant Hill scoring the first basket on a follow of a missed shot by Thomas Hill. The crowd's response a massive roar, electric.

Trading baskets. Duke building a five-point lead on a Thomas Hill dunk, a six-point lead on a Parks dunk.

Chris Webber drawing a second personal foul at the 15:28 mark, terribly early, on a charge taken by Grant Hill. Removed from the game for more than three minutes, Webber plays more cautiously upon his return.

Michigan tying the score at 23–23 just past the midway mark in the first half on a short jumper by Jimmy King. Hurley responding with two free throws. King hitting another jumper. Hurley hitting a three, putting Duke ahead for keeps.

Lang getting whistled for his third personal barely a minute later. Krzyzewski protesting, disputing almost every call as the action grows more heated.

Exchanges on the backboard furious, frenzied, big bodies muscling for position and possession. Krzyzewski's first words to reporters after the game: "The court seemed small, didn't it, with all those big guys?" And later: "It was a battle tonight, not to get into those coaching terms, military/coaching terms." Thomas Hill posting up taller defenders, stalking the basket deliberately but inexorably, backing in, a patient hunter, curling toward the basket for short layins or elevating for quick jumpers. "It felt good," says T. Hill, a low-post player in high school. "I like going down low and mixing it inside with guys like Webber." Hill leads all scorers with thirteen first-half points and twenty-one at game's end. His basket puts Duke up 40–33 at halftime.

The indefatigable Hurley, smallest man on the court, directing the offense with aplomb, keying perimeter pressure that forces a dozen turnovers in the opening period and prevents the Wolverines from exploiting advantages inside. "With Duke you start with the defense," says Steve Fisher, Michigan's coach. "They played solid, smart, pressure defense the whole game."

Hurley scoring a dozen points in the first half, more than Rose, more than Webber and Howard combined. "Hurley was Hurley," Krzyzewski says later. "He always makes me look good." Duke extending its lead early in the second half, showing superior poise, the residue of experience.

The crowd loud and emotional, nearly as wired as if Carolina were in the house. Subdued in its derision of the Wolverines. "I want to thank our crowd for being so positive for Duke," says Krzyzewski, who ripped the student-fans only four days ago. "It always makes me proud to be the coach at Duke when the sixth man performs at that level."

The Blue Devils continuing to build their lead, moving it to fourteen, Grant Hill dazzling with a dunk off an assist from Hurley.

Suddenly here comes Michigan, scoring six straight points inside. Duke calling timeout. Grant Hill whistled for a charge, his fourth foul, on the following possession. King making a layup to cut the lead to 58–52 with 8:35 to go.

TV calling for its next-to-last obligatory timeout, Duke in possession. The Blue Devils running something for Hurley when play resumes, a maneuver Duke's had in its repertoire for years, the guard hitting a three off the inbounds pass. "That three-pointer, I thought, was the biggest basket of the ballgame," Krzyzewski says.

Duke trying to rest on offense, to run time off the clock, drained by emotion, battered, playing long stretches without G. Hill and Lang, both saddled with four fouls. Neither team playing with precision, Duke unable to complete the kill, Michigan unable to pull closer than five.

Hurley scoring a layup, leaping in the air in exultation as the buzzer sounds, Michigan's verbal slights paid back in full. "It seems like they would have learned from last year," Hurley says of Duke's two previous wins. "When you talk like that, it gives a team extra fuel. When you're beating them down the stretch, you're thinking about all the things they said about you. It's just fun to look back on it and know we've beaten a team three times in a row, three times in the last two years. I'm sure the next time we play, they'll talk again and I'll laugh at it again."

Duke 79, Michigan 68.

Smiling teammates rushing to hug Hurley, the Dukies running together off the court, index fingers held high, the crowd screaming its approval. "They said we could bring Christian back from the Timberwolves and they'd still beat us," Hurley proclaims in the locker room. "Then they'd celebrate. No one does that on our court."

Krzyzewski, face flushed, manner composed, tie neat, sport jacket on, informing the media, "We told our guys we haven't won anything. We're 2–0."

"They have a very good team that's rock-solid in every aspect of the game," Fisher says. "All your blemishes show against good teams." He mentions especially weakness shooting free throws and boxing out.

Both coaches lauding Cherokee Parks, coming through with fifteen points, three rebounds and a powerful presence inside where Duke is weakest. "People thought that our team was made up of Bobby, Thomas, and Grant," Parks observes. "I think there's a lot more to our team than people think."

Quite a lot more, declares Grant Hill: "This showed Michigan and everybody across the country that even though we lost two great players, the beat keeps going. We're still here. All those doubters out there, beware."

SUNDAY, DECEMBER 6

THE air of expectancy, the crush of humanity, the TV trucks and students' tents, all have vanished like stars in daylight. As though the cold had indeed accompanied the Michigan team, it's much warmer, too, more appropriate to late fall in North Carolina.

Inside Cameron, which officially seats 9,314 but probably held more than ten thousand spectators last night, there are a dozen onlookers, not counting the pair of pigeons that dart among the rafters and rows of commemorative banners.

A perpetual electric buzz emanates from the overhead lights, filling Cameron like a chorus of crickets on a summer evening.

At the west end of the building, near Duke's game bench, shafts of sunlight flood through the windows, falling golden and warm on the wooden floor where Krzyzewski has gathered his squad for a twenty-minute review of the Michigan game.

"Learning to play at that level is a habit," the coach tells his team. "That's why we schedule those games." Throughout his talk, and the few demonstrations he adds for emphasis, Duke's eleven players lean forward in their molded-plastic chairs, unwaveringly attentive.

Krzyzewski commends the team for some things: following the scouting report, treating the officials with respect, utilizing shot fakes, playing aggressively, taking advantage of mismatches, handling the endgame with poise. "End of game situations, and how we think and react in situations, is how we won those banners," the coach says, barely glancing upward.

He chastises his players for some things, too: Grant Hill for forcing penetrating moves that got him in foul trouble, Thomas Hill for taking thirteen seconds, three more than the rules allow, to get off his free throws.

Krzyzewski also reinforces lessons and beliefs while the taste of success is fresh and strong.

"How did you feel when you got a loose ball?" he asks. "The main thing about it is, you feel good about it." And, he points out, the feeling arises from the players pleasing themselves, not from satisfying their coaches. "That's what the whole fucking game is all about, feeling good about what you're doing." Taking note of Michigan's four-of-eleven free throw shooting, Krzyzewski suggests it might be the result of not practicing foul shots the way Duke does—after the players are tired.

He tells Grant Hill to get used to being hit on the elbow when attempting jumpers, and commends him for drawing the key early charge against Webber.

And Krzyzewski reminds Bobby Hurley to get even wisely, by employing the full gamut of his skills, from taking charges to dishing assists.

Hurley hung out with Webber while both were members of the Olympic developmental squad. Thus Hurley was particularly stung when Webber made denigrating pregame comments comparing him to his Michigan counterpart, Jalen Rose. "Bobby, Rose scores on you, I know you want to get back at him," Krzyzewski says. "I don't want to take that away from you. I want you to understand there are other ways to get back at Rose."

Krzyzewski's final admonition is that it's time to move on. "Let's create new war stories tomorrow," he says, referring to an upcoming game with Northeastern.

THE total lunar eclipse is not visible in Roanoke, a city of eighty thousand residents in the mountains of central Virginia. Too cloudy.

In fact, it's those clouds that are the big news here, rather than the eclipse or the U.S. Marines landing in Somalia to the camera's white glare. Forecasts of freezing rain around Roanoke change before dark to predictions of snow, perhaps as much as four inches. The precipitation isn't expected before midnight, plenty of time for the Tar Heels to flee town and head back down Highway 220 toward Chapel Hill.

First, though, there's the matter of capping the celebration of George Lynch Day.

Lynch's hometown gives him a key to the city at a luncheon in his honor. Accompanying the senior is Phil Ford, representing the coaching staff. The assistant coach touches the customary athletic-testimonial bases, saying he hopes his one-year-old son grows up to be like George, and that he'd want George with him if fighting his way out of an alley. Presumably Ford would have mentioned that Lynch is a better person than he is a player, but forgot that part of the catechism.

Lynch is in fact something of an exemplar. True, he's gifted with good hands and quickness, considerable strength, and the best speed on the Carolina squad, as well as a six-foot-eight, 220-pound frame. But few things have come easily to Lynch, born two months premature and weighing three pounds.

Lynch learned the game playing against bigger boys, became a star at Patrick Henry High in Roanoke, then made the highly unpopular choice of transferring away his senior year to play in a more nationally-oriented prep program. "It was very difficult to leave," Lynch recalls. "I had a lot of friends. But I had a lot of friends say, 'George, you have to do what is best for you.'" A high school All-America at Flint Hill Academy, Lynch made another unpopular choice with folks back home when he decided to play at Chapel Hill, where his divorced mother had moved, rather than at the University of Virginia.

Lynch played more as a freshman than any member of the current UNC squad, making his mark as a rebounder. "He just loves to compete," Dean Smith says. "He tries hard every play." Lynch went on to lead the Tar Heels in rebounds as a sophomore and junior. He also proved suitably responsive to instruction, as Smith demonstrated prior to the '91 season. Women's access to locker rooms was at issue and Carolina had just adopted the use of terry cloth robes to shield players' anatomy. When Smith wanted to show the new garb to members of the media, he dispatched Lynch. The player—who once told a reporter he'd jump off a building if told to by Smith—unquestioningly hustled off to fetch a robe. "He's so coachable," Smith said, laughing. "That's why everybody wants him on his team."

Such willingness to toe the line, augmented by what Smith calls "the heart of a lion," helped Lynch become a solid defender and team leader. "He's always been very well respected by the other players because he works so hard," Bill Guthridge confides. "As Coach Smith says, he comes to play every day, and what more can you ask from somebody?"

Yet Lynch is frustrated. The senior wants to play small forward. He's wanted to play small forward throughout his career. But he remains stationed inside. "We need another Lynch, we let him shoot it outside, we need another Lynch to be on the boards," Smith explains.

"I never really got over it," Lynch concedes. "I still go out and work on my jump shot, but there is a time when you have to let things go."

That time has not yet fully arrived, though, as the Tar Heels travel to Roanoke.

Like many coaches, Smith routinely schedules a game in or near the hometown of an upperclassman as a combination salute and reward. Last year's honorees were Matt Wenstrom, a Texan who enjoyed a homecoming in Houston, upstate New Yorker Scott Cherry, whose family and friends got to see him at New Jersey's Meadowlands, and Henrik Rodl, for whose benefit the team played a Christmas-break exhibition in Germany. (With a stop along the way in the Canary Islands.) This year it's Lynch's turn. "A Virginia Tech at Roanoke can be tougher than a top twenty team at home," says Smith, knowing that's not true this season. As for the over-matched Hokies, they're willing to come out of the deeper mountains of Blacksburg in exchange for an attractive date on a sympathetic court against a high-profile opponent.

The Tar Heels are not at full strength, however. Donald Williams, sud-denly important, is on the bench, wearing a decidedly non-basketball suit while he nurses ribs bruised during a 104–68 rout of Texas in the Tourna-ment of Champions title game. And starter Brian Reese, though dressed for action and a participant in warmups, won't play due to a sprained right ankle. There are plenty of experienced players primed to take their places. But subtracting Reese and Williams makes the North Carolina squad far less athletic and creative, and far more reminiscent of its plod-ding recent predecessors.

Many head coaches remain in the seclusion of their locker rooms until shortly before the start of a game; the conclusion of the national anthem is usually the equivalent of the all clear. Smith, however, likes to watch the opposition warm up. So he sits for more than twenty minutes studying the Hokies as they go through their pregame routine, presumably look-ing for tendencies an assistant's firsthand scouting report and in-house video study might have missed.

Virginia Tech starts the game in awe, commits four turnovers in the first two minutes, and quickly finds itself trailing 14–0. The worst having been realized, the Hokies play on essentially even terms after that, meaning North Carolina retains untroubled command but never puts the game away.

Lynch appears off-stride. Perhaps he's trying too hard to impress the home folks, who've filled all but the upper reaches of the Roanoke Civic Center. Perhaps it's that nagging desire to show he belongs on the perimeter. His early shots are off the mark. He commits two traveling vio-lations far beyond the top of the key. He fails to block out on rebounds. He draws three personal fouls in the first half.

Even so, the level of competition is such that Lynch finishes with eigh-teen points and eleven rebounds. Afterward Smith lauds another "All-American-type performance" by the senior.

With the game less than gripping, Smith has time to attend to other matters. Throughout the first half he's bothered by the presence of a writer seated at the end of the scorer's table, a vantage point from which the interior of the Carolina huddle is visible. (Though the vigorous efforts of the Virginia Tech pep band make eavesdropping quite difficult.)

Finally, during the first timeout of the second half, Smith has Ford take a position that blocks the writer's view. "Coach, sit right there," he commands.

Not that Smith is altogether disdainful of the writer's presence. Near game's end he briefly challenges official Lenny Wirtz over a clearly correct call of a backcourt violation. Then Smith turns to the writer and gives a quick wink.

THURSDAY, DECEMBER 10

EVERYTHING seems right with the Duke basketball world. The Blue Devils are 3–0 and back atop the polls. They proved against Michigan they're capable of playing with the best. School demands have eased now that fall semester exams are over. The first road trip of the year, to play Rutgers on Saturday in New Jersey's Meadowlands, should be a successful one.

Mike Krzyzewski takes a different view. He's worried and skeptical. "Being number one, there's no way," he says, an air of protest in his voice. "I don't know who is, if anybody is the so-called number one. Like, for us to be number one right now, then it's a weak year, man."

Assistants marvel at their leader's capacity for remaining fixed upon his team, ever attuned to greater truths, individual components, technical flaws, and undercurrents of emotion. "He's definitely not one of those guys who adhere to the philosophy, 'If it ain't broke, don't fix it,'" Mike Brey says. "He's always working to improve, even if it's rolling along."

And Krzyzewski sees plenty to improve on, beginning at this afternoon's practice, number twenty-nine of the season.

"You tell the truth to yourself too," he says. "Like, are you placing too much emphasis on offense? Are you not concentrating enough about defense? Are you signing too many books? Are you doing too many interviews? Are you? Are you? And then, why didn't you see that you're not getting the ball to the outside enough on offense? . . .

"Why weren't you thinking it, dummy? So, see, what a player, what I would hope my players understand is that I do that to myself. Like, if I am going to call Thomas Hill a knucklehead, I've called myself that. That's not a problem. If you are one, then you are." As Krzyzewski sees it, among the first orders of business today is adjusting the team's inner rhythms, starting with the older players, who work hard but tend toward an impatience that approaches haughtiness.

"The fact is that we've won, and they've been through it," Krzyzewski explains. "So they believe they can do it again. That's good. Now what we have to remind them to do is that, 'Remember, we took fifty-three steps, or whatever, to get there. You guys can't go to step fifty right now. You still have to hit one through fifty.' And you know what? This team needs seventy-six steps. Or maybe it only needs forty. We don't know how many steps, but we have to touch bases or whatever analogy you want to make. You still have to go through those things. And those steps or bases that you have to touch are different for every basketball team. Absolutely different." Touching "whatever" is an especially delicate balancing act with the current squad, Krzyzewski continues. Even as Duke returns four upperclass starters, it's also incorporating into the lineup a sophomore center and a half-dozen unproven reserves. "The attention to detail might wane with the veterans. But, see, then you have a group on the same team that needs unbelievable attention to detail. So you have one group ready to swim the channel and the other group that's doing their laps width-wise across the pool." The pace of learning is less important than the will to excel, and there too Krzyzewski and staff detect a problem. Some players see themselves as lesser lights. Which is accurate and perhaps even unusually honest, but self-limiting. Accepting secondary status can cause slackening of effort, settling for less than the best, ceasing the challenge to the starters that forces one's own development.

"Everyone wants to know roles," Krzyzewski says of his reserve players. "I don't know what roles—make your own roles. Brian Davis didn't have a role, he made his role. Thomas Hill didn't have a role, he made his role. We can get into that thing where you stop competing and you just want someone to tell you, 'This is the amount of effort I want from you.'"

No such information is likely to be forthcoming. Not today, not ever. Not from Krzyzewski.

Especially not today. Today, with exams over, the coach expects his student-athletes to be introspective and a little satisfied. "Well, it's like all of us," he explains. "When we get through with something, before the next something there's like a mental release. 'I don't have to think about anything, thank God!' There's a joy there." So he's come prepared to light some fires, to force players' attention to the basketball task at hand. "As much as any habit that you can develop in practice, as much as a dribble, a shot, a pass, a defensive assignment," Krzyzewski says, "the habit of competing each time out is the most important habit. That's what we need more of." To get there, the coach believes a little verbal pressure is in order. "It's not like you're browbeating them," he explains. "I mean, I don't do that every day or whatever but, if you never do it, I'm not sure if . . . you know, for us, the way we do things, if we're ever going to become real good."

The day's practice plan, hand printed by Krzyzewski, shows no sign of such an agenda. The fifteen-minute "Pre-Practice" period is devoted to individual work: "Check on Grant," "Talk to Bobby, Kenny [sic] Brown," and "Check on Warmups-Bags." Then, after fifteen minutes of "STRETCH," come nearly two hours of drills, chosen to accent certain teaching points, one drill building upon another, subsets into sets, revealing a formula for breaking a 1-2-1-1 press or for running "Our #12." Offensive drills predominate. Two respites are built in—at 4:15 and at 4:45. Each break includes shooting free throws.

Cameron is closed for this afternoon practice, as for most Duke practices. Doors from the lobbies to the court are locked. Team managers politely motion to interlopers to leave, and are meet with near-total compliance. Occasionally athletic department personnel stroll around the edges of the court on their way to various offices in the building, or stop by to sit and watch practice.

As usual, the coaches wear some article of Adidas clothing. Krzyzewski's active intervention varies from practice to practice. What rarely changes are his postures: standing with arms folded and ample hips wide, or roaming the sidelines, resembling a bird of prey with his long nose, straight black hair, and intent gaze. From time to time he also crosses the court to the scorer's table for a sip of Gatorade from a Coke cup, or to glance at notes lain atop a folder fat with papers.

"Most of the time I'm watching my guys," he says of his thought process. "I watch how Kenny [Blakeney] is competing against Thomas. Not just technique-wise, but try to get a feel for his . . . why is Tony Lang quiet today? Can I do something to get him to not be quiet? In other words, you try to get to know your players." Krzyzewski's ideas about leadership coalesced in college. An all-city player in Chicago, he'd hoped to attend Creighton or Wisconsin on a basketball scholarship. Then the chance came to attend West Point to play for Bob Knight. By his own admission Krzyzewski had an "unbelievable" temper in those days, and wasn't enamored of submitting to military-style discipline and sexual segregation. But his parents, who often spoke Polish between themselves, were thrilled at the idea of their elder son gaining so prestigious an honor as an appointment to the U.S. Military Academy. Obediently, Krzyzewski went.

To this day, he admits it was a struggle. But, he says, "I learned many things at West Point, many, many things because you're with different kinds of people in stressful situations where you have to cooperate to get over obstacles."

Training in command, five years as an officer, and a personal dream of returning to civilian life as a high school math teacher and coach honed Krzyzewski's thinking about leadership. The reality of diversity helped inform it. Krzyzewski didn't know any non-Catholics until, as a plebe, the Army had him room with an Episcopalian ("I never heard of an Episcopalian, it could have been a disease") and a Baptist ("I'm now married to a Baptist"). Eventually Krzyzewski came to appreciate that, to coin a phrase, in diversity is strength, a strength far more flexible than a military-type structure might suggest.

"The incredible human being—you name it, it can do it," he says. "Man can do it. Figuring out how to make him do it is part of what makes it interesting." Therein lies a great challenge and reward of coaching. "I'll tell you what: When you can get them all going, it's pretty exciting. It's very exciting. And you don't have to win everything."

Krzyzewski's Blue Devil squads are more diverse than is generally recognized, since Duke students are stereotyped as rich white kids, predominantly from the Northeast. Five of Duke's dozen players are African-American. Eight come from outside the ACC region, but only Bobby Hurley is from the Northeast. About half come from families of moderate means.

What's more, Krzyzewski encourages limited self-expression by his players, in games and off the court. He wants them to mature as quickly as possible, and knows such growth comes from within.

"We're demanding excellence, so maybe you have to go through more," muses Gaudet, Krzyzewski's longtime assistant as well as his successor as head coach at West Point in the early eighties. "Maybe you're doing a better job if you're bringing out more of the problems. Maybe that's better because they're growing faster."

Duke coaches must then spend considerable time trying to know their players, to anticipate and manage problems. Krzyzewski especially values having players come to speak with him about the team and teammates, not to squeal but to discuss, to keep him and his brain trust abreast of currents that might affect cohesion and performance. "Things aren't the same every game emotionally and physically," Gaudet says. "It's like the soap opera 'As The World Turns.' Things aren't always the same."

So Krzyzewski's always watching, most especially during practice. "I think I'm fairly intense. I think I'm capable of giving the things I'm responsible for full commitment. If that's what intensity means."

This afternoon Krzyzewski watches as Marty Clark starts practice wearing his jersey white-side out along with the five starters, a telltale sign of approval. Not that it's terribly significant—whites and blues are in greater flux than usual today. The shifting sides are accompanied by increasingly fierce activity: Clark, sporting a black eye from last week's practice, accidentally clobbers Grant Hill from behind; Cherokee Parks scatters heads as he clears space with swinging elbows; Hurley leaps for a Blakeney shot fake and goes cartwheeling over Blakeney and crashing to the floor. The coaches surreptitiously gasp, but make it a point not to react with alarm to the sight of their All-America playmaker plummeting to earth. Hurley—tough, resilient, sleeked down and stronger this season—is on his feet in an instant, easing the coaches' anxiety almost before it takes hold.

That leaves plenty of opportunity to pursue the day's sub rosa agenda.

Afterward Krzyzewski confides: "I started saying things early on in practice, one, to get their attention, to get them angry, get them to spark some emotions. Whatever those emotions are, and then to see if we could carry ourselves through. It worked somewhat." The first salvo hits as the Blue Devils attempt to trap in the corners. The defense isn't particularly effective. There's little chatter among the defenders warning of picks and the ball's location, essential behavior in executing things the Duke Way.

Disappointed, Krzyzewski looses a verbal barrage at the players. "You're being a piece of shit today!" he yells angrily. "You're being selfish. You guys are missing something a good team has—you're missing a sense of urgency."

Later, when the scrimmage concludes and the players take seats at the visitors' bench, sucking water from individually labeled plastic squeeze containers, they receive a longer blast.

"Fear has left you," Krzyzewski informs them. "Cockiness and complacency have taken over." The players are "immature." Not only is there "no way" they're the best team in the country, they're not even among the top ten. And they're riding for a fall. "You're not preparing to win on Saturday. I'm telling you right now." This is followed by calm talk of travel times, the road dress code (sport coat and tie or coat and sweater), the need to pack extra shoes and sweat suits. The importance of packing tonight, practicing well tomorrow. A reminder that "the key thing about trips is flexibility."

Then, inevitably, the remonstrative emphasis repeated throughout the season: "Duke doesn't beat Duke!"

The traditional players-only huddle ends the day's formal activity. At State such huddles break with a chant of "Go Pack!" At Carolina they end with "Go Heels!" At Duke the word is simply "Win!"

SATURDAY, DECEMBER 12

A STORM labeled one of the century's worst flails the Northeast. Coastal neighborhoods flood from New Jersey to Massachusetts. Snow falls from Virginia to New England. There are high winds, beached whales, downed power lines, National Guard call-outs, more than a dozen fatalities.

Back in Raleigh, removed from the storm's path, Les Robinson expresses hope that the Blue Devils, in New Jersey to play Rutgers tonight, are "washed out to sea until April. I'll bet," he adds, laughing, "Dean would like that even better than me."

N.C. State will journey to the Meadowlands next week to take on Princeton, the basketball antithesis of a storm. Robinson greets the prospect cheerily. He'd play Princeton ten days in a row if he could, the way you'd take "castor oil," he says. "They make you better." And N.C. State will have to get a lot better, and fast, to beat Princeton.

"We've got a long way to go, a long way to go," Al Daniel laments. "I get so frustrated at times, but I forget who we've got playing. I forget, because they're not a veteran bunch." Recollecting that truth helps, but doesn't banish the impatience that eats at the thirty-four-year-old. "I want to be down the road, but it's not there," says Daniel, who came to Raleigh when Robinson did. This job is Daniel's big break, his chance at the big time after a decade at Furman, and he dreams of having a squad that plays tough defense, that applies the lessons he longs to teach. "I've read Krzyzewski. I've read Knight. I know about quadrants on the floor, I know all that stuff."

Sometimes, Daniel admits, he thinks about attending a Duke practice almost as a professional restorative, "because they know how to play defense."

Diverted from Newark due to the storm, the Dukies flew into Philadelphia yesterday, and bused several hours to the Meadowlands. The Rutgers players are anxious to take Duke's measure, according to Bob Wenzel, their coach. "For them, it's really a big, big, big thing," he says. "The kids are fired up. I've got some competitive guys."

Wenzel is impressed with the Blue Devils, and has been voting them number one in the *USA Today* coaches' poll. "I just think, if you have the guys who have been there already, and they have been, you have the best shot. You've got the best point guard, so you can control things. And you've got the two Hill guys. There may be guys who are as athletic as the Hills, but not on the same team." If Wenzel's team is to beat Duke, and he concedes "it's really going to be hard for us to compete with them," then it will have to take advantage of the Devils' pressure defense. That means beating Duke off the dribble and crashing the offensive boards when its big men leave the low post to cover for teammates in "help" defensive situations.

Rutgers competes, but Duke wins far more handily than the 88–79 score indicates. Grant Hill leads both teams with twenty-three shots and twenty-six points, and has ten rebounds. Thomas Hill has nineteen points. Tony Lang gets in foul trouble but has what will prove a season-high eleven rebounds. Hurley has sixteen points, eleven assists, and seven rebounds in a homecoming appearance.

Also receiving a rare portion of playing time is Kenny Blakeney, the only veteran who failed to appear against Michigan. The third-year sophomore (he sat out his freshman year at Duke to catch up academically) is strong, plays good defense and can run the team, but recently corrected knee problems have sapped his confidence and athleticism.

Blakeney has yet to find a playing niche, in part because he's among the players whose willingness to accept a supportive role most irritates Krzyzewski. "He gets real upset with me when I say, 'I've got to wait my turn,'" Blakeney reports. "He actually gets pissed at me."

Blakeney wonders if Krzyzewski even knows what it's like to ride the bench, to go from being a high-school hotshot and D.C. playground legend to a college afterthought. For his part, Krzyzewski has difficulty understanding Blakeney's attitude. "If you don't play in a game, and you feel you have paid the price to play, then you should be angry about it," he says.

Then, abruptly, against the Scarlet Knights Krzyzewski plays Blakeney for three minutes in the first half, six in the second. The first time Blakeney is dispatched into action, the six-foot-four guard is stunned and elated.

"As a matter of fact, I think I was at the end of the bench laughing at that time," he admits. "I was more than shocked. I think when I got to the scorer's table, I was laughing I was so happy I was playing."

Blakeney does well enough, providing solid play at both ends.

"I do a game by feel," Krzyzewski explains. "I don't have minutes, like he's going to get six minutes. I don't do that. I've never done that. So, if you haven't done stuff to put it in my 'feel,' then you are not going to play unless we're ahead. Against Rutgers I put Kenny in because I had seen a couple of things in practice that gave me a good feel for Kenny. And so, he had to be shocked when he was put in against Rutgers. And I didn't do it, I didn't plan, 'Well, I'm going to put Kenny in just to shake him.'"

One player manages to shake Krzyzewski, though.

Since arriving at Duke, and before that at summer all-star camps, Tony Moore has had trouble accepting that his future is inside rather than at a wing. Duke coaches want Moore to concentrate on moves around the basket. But after practice Moore, whom Krzyzewski calls a likable "baby," persists in shooting three-pointers.

Moore attended a Maryland prep school where ten of the eighty students were on the basketball squad. At six-eight he was by far the biggest and most athletic member of the team. At Duke, his adjustment has been predictably slow, as it's the first time he's faced players every bit his physical equal, not to mention far more polished.

But while Moore's adjustment is understandably difficult, in Krzyzewski's estimation it provides no excuse for his action shortly after entering the Rutgers game with 2:21 remaining.

The first time Moore touches the ball at the offensive end he flings up a jumper from the wing well beyond the free throw line. The shot has no relation to what anyone else on the court is doing. Moore's form is lousy. The shot doesn't even hit the rim.

It does, however, hit a nerve with Krzyzewski, who berates the freshman as soon as the team reaches the locker room. This after the coach scolded the team at halftime for what he regarded as self-centered play.

"He took one of the worst shots of the last decade of Duke basketball," Krzyzewski says of Moore. "Someone said, 'Well, you're up by seventeen points or whatever, what's the difference?' Well, it makes a lot of difference. Because if he takes it and drop-steps and charges, I have no problem. But the shot he took was never, ever, ever acceptable. And it was reverting back after a week of really good practice, and so Tony Moore has to understand that as long as he's on the court, it's never garbage time.

"As long as I'm coaching a team it's never garbage time. So, if he reacts that way, then he's telling me he's garbage. Because I'm not reacting that way.

"'So, well, you tell me, are you garbage? You're not? OK, well, let's get going. Let's work together and let's get better. There have to be certain things that aren't acceptable, and that is not acceptable. If that's who you want to be, then you're not acceptable. If you want that to be acceptable, then you're never going to be very good.'"

Krzyzewski pulls the Hills aside and asks them to reinforce the message. But they, too, have felt the lash of the coach's displeasure tonight.

"Isn't it sad that in our society, that the truth is tough?" Krzyzewski asks later. "Like after our ballgame Saturday night and I was displeased with a number of things, my players didn't just clamor around me. They weren't like, 'Hey, Coach.' There was a distance there.

"And it was because they knew that the truth had been spoken and they didn't want to hear too much more of it. They had heard enough. And I understand that. Like the popularity poll would not have been at an all-time high at that point. So, do you trust your relationship enough with your players to do those things?"

For the Duke coach, there's only one answer to that question, just as there's only one standard to which players should aspire.

"We get back to that thing, do you go up to the level of your best, or down? We have to always be looking at, we better keep going up. That's what I always tell them: The train is moving. The train is not stopping, just doesn't stop. It keeps moving, and if our best guys are keeping it moving fast, you'd better skedaddle, you'd better pick up speed. And if you do, you're on the train, man."

FRIDAY, DECEMBER 18

THE worst start to a season in almost half a century. The lowest scoring total in three hundred thirty games.

50–41. So much for playing Princeton.

Given the circumstances Les Robinson prefers to talk academics. First semester grades are coming in, and the team's overall grade-point average is around 2.4, the best in the three years Robinson has been N.C. State's coach. "I didn't think we'd get this high this fast," Robinson admits, "but I thought we'd be better basketball-wise. So I was wrong on both counts." Best of the students is center Todd Fuller, a computer-science major. He's recorded a perfect 4.0 in his college academic debut. "He's following in my footsteps," Robinson says, defying fact.

The six-eleven, 235-pound Fuller has found a way to avoid following in anyone's footsteps. Six years ago, at age twelve, Fuller began taking pilot's lessons. By now he's accumulated ninety hours in the air, more than enough to qualify for a license. "I haven't flown in a good while because of college and basketball," Fuller says. But all that remains is to take his FAA check ride—"a road test," Fuller calls it. Beyond that, perhaps he'll pursue a career in aeronautics.

Then again, another path seems increasingly possible. "It all depends on basketball, of course, and school," he explains. "I have some people telling me that there's a chance to have a career in basketball. God's blessed me."

Fuller is not only the best student among State's three freshmen, he's the biggest. He's also the most polished, with good form on his shots and a firm understanding of his position. He runs well if not swiftly, catches

and passes the ball without slipping gears, and seems devoted to
improvement.

The big lefty was a bit of a steal for Robinson and staff. "It's remarkable," says Bob Gibbons, who produces a well respected recruiting
newsletter, *All Star Sports Report*. "I mean, this kid suddenly changed
from being a nice high school big man to being a very aggressive,
advanced, top-fifty player in the country." Through his junior season at
Charlotte's Independence High, Fuller was considered a mid-major
prospect at best. Then the soft-spoken straight-A student transferred to
Charlotte Christian Academy, coached by former all-pro Bobby Jones.
Jones played at North Carolina from 1972 through 1974, then enjoyed a
twelve-year pro career, mostly with Denver in the American Basketball
Association and Philadelphia in the NBA. Quick and disciplined, Jones
was a ten-time selection to all-defensive teams in the pros, led the ABA in
field-goal percentage twice (1975 and 1976) and led the NBA once (1978).
He's the ACC's fourth most accurate shooter of all time (.608).

Besides playing for Jones, Fuller got to play against him, going one-on-
one with the coach after practice. "He gave me a lot of honest opinions,"
Fuller says appreciatively. Suddenly, thanks to an alum of its bitterest rival,
N.C. State had a solid big man who could apprentice under Kevin Thompson and then step into his place.

Thus far, Fuller's role has been as modest as expected, just as, predictably, freshman Chuck Kornegay has started every game. As for the
third freshman, Marcus Wilson, he played even more sparingly than Fuller
until the Princeton game. Against the Tigers, the slender wing with the
big dreams played nineteen minutes and paced the Pack with ten points.
Included was three-of-three accuracy on three-pointers.

Wilson is the most vocal player in practice. Typically, this afternoon he
exhorts teammates during a defensive drill: "Don't let anybody score!
Yeah, White! Don't let them score, baby! White, don't let them score."

Last week, Robinson noticed the hardworking Wilson seemed more
relaxed and receptive during practice. "I told the team, 'Coaches are
always saying we watch you in practice, we watch you in practice.'" Proving he meant it, Robinson announced prior to the Princeton game that
Wilson had earned extended playing time.

Wilson's response to the opportunity encourages Robinson. "He delivered. He played very well. Now, he will still make the same mistakes that
Donald Williams and Cherokee Parks made last February, but the differ-

ence is, we're playing him out of necessity." With Oregon State coming to Reynolds tomorrow, and the Pack playing at Kansas two days after that, Robinson is further heartened by Mark Davis's return to practice this afternoon. "He's a guy that showed great leadership last year as a freshman," Robinson says. "Just his being out here at practice, you feel a little better." The wing with the healing wrist is held out of the roughest drills. Noted for his three-point shooting as a freshman, Davis makes his first shot and seems comfortable. "It's not really sore, it hasn't hurt in about two weeks, I would say," Davis does say of his right wrist. "I feel pretty good. I'm not in game shape right now." Davis's time away from basketball hasn't been ill spent. He's worked out as much as possible, and compiled a 2.7 GPA in an engineering curriculum last semester.

Little of Davis's time is ill spent.

"I'm always, I'm thinking about how to improve on something," says Davis, nineteen. "I don't settle. I think perfection can be achieved. I believe in perfection. Or, either, if you can't achieve perfection, the more you pursue it the closer you'll get. So I'm always thinking of ways to improve different things and improve myself, whether it be personally, academically or athletically, it doesn't matter. I'm always thinking of ways to improve myself, the world, and things around me."

Davis, who chose N.C. State for its prowess in civil engineering as well as basketball, hails from Utica, Mississippi. A town of one thousand residents near Jackson, the state capital, Utica is described by Robinson as so small it doesn't have a stoplight. "It has plenty of stoplights," protests Davis. "It's peaceful, it's in the country. It's nothing like Raleigh, the inner city."

Davis didn't even grow up in Utica. His home was in the countryside, down a dirt drive well off the beaten path. From the first, his mother was his mentor.

"She always stressed academics, and I'm thankful for that," Davis says. "She said academics comes first. If you can't do academics, you can't do basketball. Plus, I love school. I love to go to school. I was taught when I was younger that school was the only way to go, and that was the only way that you were going to ever be anything." Teammate Donnie Seale received the same message from his mom, yet he struggled in school. In contrast, Davis was an honor student throughout, and culminated his senior year as class valedictorian. Also unlike Seale, Davis learned basketball from his mother, a small forward in her high school days. Davis's father wasn't around to do much teaching—he was shot and killed when his son was eight.

Davis began playing basketball at age three. "I guess I got fascinated with the game," he says. "Anything that dealt with the mind I was fascinated by, and basketball is a mind game. You have to think while you're on the court, and I think a good thinker and a decent basketball player can be a great basketball player. Because he can think, he knows what to do on the court." In fact, when playing Davis shares an odd kinship with Todd Fuller. "When I'm out here playing basketball, I feel like an airplane pilot flying a plane," he says.

Davis, whose heroes are Julius Erving and Magic Johnson, didn't make his school team until the eighth grade. His first game he was the high scorer. Later in the year, while high jumping, he tore an anterior cruciate ligament in his knee. Following an operation, the knee healed sufficiently to allow Davis to return to basketball. Over the years he also suffered a cracked thumb and a cracked wrist. But he persevered, and by the tenth grade had caught the attention of recruiters.

Interest picked up Davis's senior year. By then he was six-five and weighed one hundred ninety pounds. The best ball handler and tallest player on his team, he served both as inside defender and point guard, displaying a tenacity and range of skills that intrigued coaches from Tulane and Southern Cal, as well as N.C. State.

Once at Raleigh, Davis quickly emerged as the most productive and well rounded of the team's four freshmen. Though unpolished in the game's finer points, he was a better scorer than expected, and most especially a better three-point shooter. Davis attempted more three-pointers than any freshman in N.C. State history, and hit 41.3 percent, tops on the team and fifth-best among ACC leaders. Reynolds fans dubbed him, "MD, Doctor of the Three." This season Davis expects to build on his debut, which was marred by poor ball handling and execrable free throw shooting. But his wrist injury in the first exhibition has kept those efforts in abeyance until now.

SUNDAY, DECEMBER 20

ERIC Montross could, perhaps, have chosen to play this contest at Purdue or Indiana. Certainly there's no court from which Dean Smith would shy to take a North Carolina team (assuming the visit was reciprocated with a trip to the Smith Center). But the choice is up to Montross, it's his homecoming game, and he's chosen Hinkle Fieldhouse on the campus of Butler University in Indianapolis. "I told him it's up to him to explain how tough Butler is," Smith says.

Butler isn't all that tough this year. The Bulldogs reached the NIT last season but lost their top player and are struggling with a freshman point guard. They're quick, but there's no way they match the Tar Heels in experience, depth, or size.

Smith continues to downplay the Heels' size, but he's not fooling opponents. Only three Butler players weigh more than two hundred pounds, compared to nine for North Carolina, and only one is taller than six-foot-nine. "They're huge," says Barry Collier, the Butler coach, echoing the comments of Houston's Pat Foster after he lost a week ago at Chapel Hill. "They're a wall of flesh inside and they keep coming after you."

Not that the basketball detail matters much today. Montross hasn't brought his mates to Butler for competitive reasons. It's the fieldhouse that's lured him, the 1928 arena with residential streets adjoining, with windows near the roofline along the north and south sides and a raised floor that, from courtside, makes players look like mythic figures floating on air.

This was the home of the ABA's Indiana Pacers, of a Billy Graham crusade, and a Sonja Henie ice show. It's where the climactic state championship sequence was filmed for the movie "Hoosiers." And from its earliest days, when it was called Butler Fieldhouse, the building has hosted the wildly-popular Indiana state high-school playoffs.

That's how Montross came to know and love the hangarlike structure with its brick outer walls, its 1925 and 1929 "national college basketball champion" banners, and its old-fashioned glass and wood trophy cases lining the hallways. "The major starting point for me is the tradition that it holds, the place, it's the center of Hoosier basketball," says the graduate of nearby Lawrence North High, which he led to a 1989 state high-school title. "And the fact that I played here seventeen times."

Typically, though, Montross's affection for Hinkle is as much visceral as intellectual. He's been called "Nature Boy" by teammates amused at his outdoor orientation. Montross says it's "a distinct smell" that immediately charms him upon entering Hinkle, soothing his pregame jitters. "It's got a natatorium kind of smell. It's just old. I can't really explain it."

Collier, the Butler coach, is pleased with the present, with the honor of hosting North Carolina, even after his team falls behind 50–26 at halftime and loses, 103–56.

Collier cites three major influences on his basketball thinking. The first is Mike Montgomery, whom Collier assisted at Stanford before returning to his alma mater in 1989–90 to become a head coach. The second is Don Monson, for whom Collier worked at Oregon.

The third major influence? Collier reaches into a briefcase propped on the floor beside his office desk and extracts a battered copy of a 1982 book, *Basketball—Multiple Offense and Defense*. The author is Dean Smith. "I really like what he does," Collier says, "but I like the way he does things even more."

Among the things Smith does best is remember. "His memory is unbelievable," Bill Guthridge agrees. Smith can recall with remarkable precision scores, opponents, and game situations from nearly forty years in coaching. He also has a knack for remembering faces and names, not to mention past slights and the alma maters of writers covering his teams.

Smith's facility with names surpasses any trick of recall. Supposedly, the human brain retains some trace of all the information it processes, most of it filed randomly and therefore only marginally retrievable. Smith's mind, in contrast, is uncannily organized, as if he keeps a mental file on everyone he meets, cross-referenced by name and face and any other relevant information. This data is kept instantly available, enabling the ever-mindful Smith to offer a personal comment from congratulations on the recent birth of a child, to a challenge over a critical remark, to inquiry about a spouse's continued fondness for pizza.

Without doubt, this gift enables Smith to easily disarm most people, placing the discussion on safe, controlled ground.

So it is with Collier, who worked as a counselor at Smith's basketball camp in Chapel Hill during the mid-seventies. Collier has seen Smith only once since, and he's still talking about it.

The meeting occurred immediately after Smith won his first and, thus far, only national championship. "When they won the whole thing in '82 in New Orleans, at about 6:20 that morning in the New Orleans airport, I just passed him in the concourse, my wife and I," Collier says. "I had literally not seen him in eight years, and even when I saw him I was one of forty or fifty counselors in one week at his camp, and the camp went for four weeks. We passed him, and I was certainly not wanting to bother him, but I wanted to acknowledge the title. I said, 'Congratulations, Coach Smith.' He said, 'Thank you. Congratulations, Coach Collier, on your season.'

"That really floored me. I understand he has a really good memory. That's an illustration, though, of a guy who's a legend, yet he's got time."

For the third game in a row Pat Sullivan starts in place of Brian Reese, though Carolina's pregame notes give no indication this will occur. Butler's sports information director, Jim McGrath, is surprised at the absence of this information, and is even more surprised when he scans UNC's seasonal stat sheet. Unlike most others, by Smith's edict his program doesn't list the number of games a player has started or how many minutes he's played, on the theory that everyone's contribution is important. Likewise, virtually alone among major programs, Carolina's stats list players alphabetically rather than by scoring average, highest first. Smith believes too much emphasis is placed on scoring.

In fact, Smith keeps his own arcane set of statistics for internal use that includes points per possession and a generous way of crediting assists that recognizes good feeds either botched by teammates or converted into free throws.

The game's conclusion leaves Smith tied with Phog Allen at fourth all-time in Division I career wins. Smith routinely protests the attention coaches receive, as well as American society's fixation on judging by quantity rather than quality. So, predictably, he tells the media he'd rather not discuss his place in history.

"I don't deal with that," Smith says. "I never had gotten into coaches' numbers. I'm interested in each team's numbers. I'm interested in those six wins. That's six wins closer to the NCAA Tournament."

A RED-coated Ohio State usher blocks the path of a young man holding four cups of clear liquid. No drinks allowed on press row, the usher pronounces.

"These drinks are for Dick Vitale," the young man calmly replies. A second usher moves close, having overheard the exchange. "Let him go," he tells his colleague. "It's OK." The first usher steps aside. "Well, if they're for Vitale," he says as the young man walks past, "let's piss in them first." Anger at Vitale, and his return to St. John Arena, receive more attention in central Ohio newspapers than the arrival of fifth-ranked North Carolina, appearing on the Buckeyes' home floor for the first time since 1966.

Twice during the '92 season, Vitale offended Ohio State stalwarts with comments about the actions of Lawrence Funderburke, the Buckeyes' forward. This led to breathless charges of collusion between Vitale and Indiana coach Bob Knight, whom Vitale regularly praises in the most gushing terms, and from whose program Funderburke fled. "I've never been in a situation during my fourteen years at ESPN that has hurt me more," Vitale says courtside in Columbus.

The remark that most alienated OSU fans was uttered when Vitale thought he was in private conversation with ESPN broadcast partner Mike Patrick during a commercial break. While watching a replay of Funderburke's mean intentional foul of Indiana's Damon Bailey, Vitale spiced his disapproval with a touch of profanity. The comment was made off-air, but was picked up via satellite and suddenly Vitale went from hero to villain in large portions of Ohio.

The *Columbus Dispatch* weighed in with an editorial denouncing

Vitale's "vicious tirade" and condemning his "big mouth." Neither Vitale's repeated apologies, nor gracious public responses from Funderburke and Ohio State coach Randy Ayers, stanched the flow of hate mail and opprobrium. "Some of the stuff that was written to me blew my mind," says Vitale, who confesses the incident heightened his sense of vulnerability. "I always like to have fun. Now I even watch myself on the phone from hotels, airports. Now, you can't even fool around anymore."

For all his fretting, Vitale has been greeted warmly in Columbus as he prepares for this rematch from last year's NCAA Southeast Regionals. Ohio State won the '92 meeting, but the Big Ten champs have since bid adieu to four starters, including Jimmy Jackson, the league's most valuable player. Vitale keeps hearing the Tar Heels are likewise a team transformed. "Everyone says they look so much quicker," he repeats, perplexed, to the few North Carolina media folk in attendance. "Why? It's the same players." The answer, simply, is experience, knowing why and where to go in Dean Smith's complex system. But the media in Ohio remain more interested in Vitale's appearance at yesterday's OSU practice and his amiable chat there with Funderburke.

The potentially-hostile focus leaves Vitale edgy as fans fill St. John Arena, a chilly grey building at the edge of campus that sports an impressive array of banners, including one for the 1960 NCAA title. "I'm sitting here, I don't know what to expect," Vitale says. "I wouldn't be surprised if they boo me today. I wouldn't be surprised if they yelled profanities at me today. I can handle that. As long as nobody gets physical, as long as nobody throws things." The heckling proves sporadic, inconsequential. The capacity crowd of 13,276 is far more disapproving of an ACC officiating crew of Dick Paparo, Edwin "Duke" Edsall and Chuck Pitts. The trio quickly display a fondness for making closely-guarded (five-second) calls against Ohio State's young guards, loosing a cascade of boos from the wooden seats in the 36-year-old building whose steep sides bring to mind Shakespeare's Globe Theatre.

Yet, despite the officiating and discouragement from a decisive loss at West Virginia in its previous outing, Ohio State leads 38–35 at halftime.

The Heels commit thirteen first-half turnovers against the Buckeyes' press—they committed nine straight against Houston's full-court pressure, but were far ahead at the time. Brian Reese looks uncertain in his first start in two weeks; he's bothered by the pinky on his shooting hand, hyperextended at Butler, and attacks the OSU defense out of phase with his teammates. Derrick Phelps plays smothering defense, forcing several five-second calls, but his shot remains as unreliable as Wal-Mart's claims that it buys American. George Lynch has ten first-half rebounds en route to sixteen overall, but commits turnovers on consecutive possessions and rushes shots. Dean Smith is up repeatedly during the half to wave his offense forward—faster, faster—like a third-base coach waving a runner home, but he also is repeatedly taken aback by plays like Phelps's alley-oop to Eric Montross, which thumps wildly off the backboard and straight to the Buckeyes.

Smith envisioned exactly this sort of trouble after watching the team struggle during a light workout upon arrival in Columbus.

First, as always, the players worked on fundamentals. Then they practiced their press offense, but with an imprecision that so distressed Smith he began shouting on every possession, his scolding voice filling a modest gymnasium on the Ohio State campus.

Smith grew so perturbed, he stopped coaching and ordered a manager to scan the handful of onlookers leaning unobtrusively against the gym walls. "If you don't know anybody, throw them out!" he yelled. Two young Tar Heel fans from Ohio were duly discovered, and politely rousted.

The hunt for interlopers wasn't over. At the conclusion of practice Kevin Salvadori settled onto a metal bench beside his father, Al, and began discussing the workout. That brought Smith hurrying over. Also on the bench was a writer whom Smith had introduced to Al Salvadori, and to whom the coach had given permission to attend practice.

Writer and father had chatted intermittently throughout the ninety-minute workout. Tall, curly-haired Al Salvadori attended South Carolina during the sixties, playing for Frank McGuire. He also was recruited by Smith at UNC. A quarter century later, the North Carolina coach visited the Salvadori home in Pittsburgh to woo Kevin, and instantly dazzled the dad with his standard flourish. "He recalled the homemade bread my mother made for him twenty-five years before," Al marveled. "Without any prompting at all. That was amazing. He thought it was a treat, but we were so poor we had to bake our own bread." Now, though, the coach was in a different mode. He ordered the writer to leave, explaining he didn't want any interference with the father-son chat.

"I haven't talked to Kevin," the writer protested. "I don't even want you commenting on the weather," Smith replied.

As always with Smith, there was more to the exchange than met the eye. The coach knew his admonition to the writer would make it clear to "Sal," and any watching teammates, that he frowns upon airing family matters in the presence of media members. The lesson is especially timely for Salvadori, a lightly recruited late-bloomer who was a pleasant surprise his first two seasons but is unhappy his playing time hasn't increased this year.

Out in the hall a few moments after practice, full-length leather coat covering his blue sweat clothes, Smith sarcastically lauded his team for a great workout. Asked to elaborate, he groused, "That was a terrible practice, full of foolish mistakes that mean you're not concentrating."

When similar play characterizes North Carolina's first half at St. John Arena, Smith is disgusted. "I was a disappointed old man at halftime," he admits afterward. "I thought we looked like the inexperienced team."

Smith tells his players they're not playing "Carolina basketball." They're too selfish. They're letting the Ohio State press dictate their offensive tempo, forcing quick shots, the very failing North Carolina prides itself on producing in opponents.

"I was beginning to wonder if I had been working with these guys for the last six weeks," Smith says. "First, I asked who they were. Were you the same guys we'd been working with back home? Because they were going on their own. We were going one-on-one. We don't play that way at Carolina."

He's especially irked by Reese, who is so eager to score he barges into the clutches of the waiting defense. "In the first half, Brian may have been aggressive, but he didn't have any direction," confides teammate Henrik Rodl. "I begged him never to do that again," Smith says.

Only Montross, Donald Williams and Pat Sullivan, Smith's eternal favorite, draw praise for their first-half play.

Message received, the Tar Heels score six unanswered points to open the second half. All come on interior jumpers. Ohio State rallies to forge a few quick ties, but UNC responds with an 18–4 run that decides the outcome and leaves the energetic crowd booing.

The last tie is at 45–45 with 16:48 to go. In short order, Phelps pulls a favorite stunt, beating the defense in transition with a layup; Williams gets the ball alone in the corner on the secondary break and sinks a three; and Montross dunks on a feed from Dante Calabria and makes a free throw to boot.

"It's a good road win," a cheerful Smith says after securing an 84–64 victory. "That's why you play these games in December." Montross has nine rebounds, five offensive, and twenty points. He makes all eight shots he attempts and does a fine job denying Funderburke the ball or a clear look at the basket in the second half. Funderburke becomes so frustrated, he talks a steady stream of trash as the game winds down. Montross, a primary recipient of the barrage, struggles to keep a straight face until he's in the locker room. "It gets to be quite humorous," he confesses with a grin.

Smith calls the overall performance Montross's best to date, but adds, "Eric, I hope you're not seeing the real Eric yet." No one stops Smith before he departs the interview room to ask how he feels about surpassing Phog Allen's career victory total. Members of the Ohio media apparently aren't interested, and the North Carolina writers are too tired of dismissive answers on the subject to broach it again.

Smith does share his thoughts on the subject with Woody Durham. "Dr. Allen was a very motivational-type coach," he says. "He was a great after-dinner speaker. He was a great football coach. He did that too. But he was a great motivator, and we spent three hours a day on fundamentals. Almost to where I was fundamentally sound, but I sure wasn't happy with it. But certainly Kansas had great tradition. He wasn't quite as much into the Xs and Os as I enjoy being, but certainly I picked up many things from Doctor Allen and Dick Harp."

TUESDAY, DECEMBER 29

MIKE Krzyzewski raises his voice. The zigzag drill stops. Tony Moore, dribbling upcourt against Thomas Hill one-on-one, has lost the ball. It rolls toward another pair of Blue Devils engaged in the same drill along the opposite sideline. Hill and especially Moore yell "Ball! Ball!"

This is standard shorthand when drilling at a quick pace, simultaneously sounding a warning to teammates of a hazard underfoot and a demand for a replacement ball from a manager. But Krzyzewski seizes upon the incident in order to rebuke, instruct, and prepare for the future. He's about to lose the services of Tony Lang for a couple of games, possibly longer. With so few inside reserves, the nation's top-ranked team may need to throw Moore into the breach.

Not that Lang's absence means the loss of a major force. He hasn't scored through the first seven games the way his coaches had hoped, hasn't expanded his game to include the perimeter jumpers he displays regularly in practice. In fact, Lang seems off-stride offensively: During Duke's three victories in Hawaii he was four for fifteen from the floor. On the year he's hit 36.4 percent of his shots. Lang also has been foul-prone, leading the team in personals. He frequently plays in foul trouble, limiting his effectiveness.

Yet, even with his shortcomings Lang's a solid contributor. He performs well many of the complementary player's duties— screening, playing defense, rebounding. And he's been perhaps the most consistently vocal and upbeat of the upperclassmen.

The Mobile, Alabama, native has been especially helpful with freshmen Moore and Chris Collins, giving the latter rides on occasion and accompanying him to Cameron to get in extra shooting. Lang feels he's passing on a favor done for him by Christian Laettner and Brian Davis, who befriended Lang his first year. "I really appreciated that," he says. "They told me exactly what to expect. Not growing up in the ACC, I didn't know what to expect." Such help wasn't always manifest by Krzyzewski's upperclassmen. Duke's breakthrough freshmen in 1982–83 were offered scant support by seniors who rightly saw their playing time threatened, a source of yearlong tension Krzyzewski admits now he was too inexperienced to counteract.

Lang doesn't only help freshmen. At practice one day, Kenny Blakeney, Lang's scholastic classmate, is having trouble hitting outside shots. Blakeney stays after practice to work on his jumper with Mike Brey, who amiably feeds him pass after pass, interjecting occasional comments and pointers. Brey and Blakeney have a special relationship, a bit like guardian and ward. Both attended DeMatha High and played for Morgan Wootten. Brey coached Blakeney for a time at DeMatha, and helped convince Duke confreres the kid was worthy of a scholarship. From the first Blakeney has been a bit of a personal mystery. An outgoing person with a fondness for wearing a variety of ballcaps, he says the right things yet leaves a listener with a sense of doubt he really means it. Since he's also been known to be less than self-disciplined, he comes in for close attention by Brey. "I'm on his butt more than anybody," concedes the assistant, "because I sold Mike that he's going to be good for us. I'm happy about him so far, but I'm watching him like a hawk. I don't want him going into cruise control."

Even with Brey's ministrations, Blakeney can't hit his jumper with any consistency one afternoon. Finally, frustration reaching a boil, he fires the ball off the backboard, a sound like thunder in the quiet gym. Almost as the ball ricochets into Blakeney's waiting hands, Lang turns to offer a soothing, good-natured word from an adjacent basket.

Later, Brey says of Lang: "He just gets along with everybody. He's really got a knack for moving guys around. He's really been the glue."

Lang is a third-year Dukie. As a freshman he was eighth or ninth in the rotation, playing about the same amount as Crawford Palmer, who transferred to Dartmouth following the '91 season. Last year Lang became a starter, moving in at post forward through the final eighteen games. That means he's had time to master the intricacies of Krzyzewski's particular brand of basketball ballet, from the coach's ideas on spacing to his preferred inbounds plays, including the way he wants the ball slapped once, like a spanked bottom, before it's put into play. Equally important, Lang is seasoned, toughened by the amalgam of excitement, fatigue, pain, fear, and instant challenge that only game action provides.

Duke's starting lineup is rich in such players, a key, underappreciated advantage over less experienced squads. "We won the second national championship game because we know how to play tired," Krzyzewski says. "In the last seven minutes against Michigan, we were both tired. We scored twelve straight times. If you can only do things when you're fresh, it isn't going to happen." But, just today, Duke's coaches learn from school medicos that they've lost a portion of that advantage. Lang has a broken bone just below his right eye and will be sidelined, unable even to exercise, for about a week, possibly longer.

Lang's face sprouts a swollen black and blue pocket where a bone cracked after taking a blow from the elbow of Brigham Young's Jared Miller—the dirtiest of a physical crew, says one Duke coach. According to several members of the Duke entourage, Miller gratuitously battered Bobby Hurley and Grant Hill in loose ball situations in the finals of the Maui Invitational, precipitating an angry oncourt admonition from Krzyzewski.

"Don't do that!" the coach yells when Miller goes after Hill more than the ball. Krzyzewski implores BYU guard Ryan Cuff: "Tell that guy to knock that shit off."

"They were dirty as shit, I thought," says one Dukie. "They had a couple of hatchet fouls. There's a fine line between being tough and being dirty; they crossed it a few times." Still, at the time Lang was hit, no one thought the blow intentional. Now, the player admits, "the more I look at the tape, the more I wonder."

Lang, who suffers from sinus trouble and a deviated septum, didn't immediately realize the extent of his injury. "When I got hit, I knew something was wrong. At the time, you're in the game, you don't think about it." But in the locker room after Duke routed Brigham Young 89–66 to capture the Maui title, Lang made a startling discovery. He blew his nose and his right eye instantly, painfully swelled with blood and air. "It was ugly," recalls Lang, an ardent boxing fan who watches tapes of prizefights in his spare time. "It closed completely shut. It was scary, real scary." The injury isn't considered serious, but fearing further damage or an infection that would be difficult to treat, Duke doctors advise Lang to avoid all strenuous activity while the bone mends. "I can't sneeze. I can't breathe deep. I can't do anything," Lang laments.

As a result, he won't be available for an expected cruise to victory over Boston University tomorrow. Even if he's cleared for play in about a week following a CAT scan, Lang won't be in normal playing shape for a potentially difficult matchup with Oklahoma.

Lang's absence thrusts Marty Clark into a starting role for the first time in sixty-five appearances as a Blue Devil. The red-haired, apple-cheeked junior has been increasingly efficient; Krzyzewski lauds him at practice as second-best on the squad after Hurley at getting the ball to the post, a highly valued though little-recognized offensive skill.

Lang's absence also increases Tony Moore's importance, especially in those instances when rebounding becomes key. Moore performed better in Hawaii than he did at Rutgers, but is he to be counted upon? Krzyzewski wants to hasten the day when the answer is yes, so he stops the zigzag drill to chasten Moore for contenting himself with yelling "Ball! Ball!"

Employing one of his favorite phrases, Krzyzewski strides across the court and exclaims, "We need to have a sense of urgency!" With exaggerated force, he demonstrates by taking a ball and rolling it across the floor, then vigorously chasing it down. He stoops low, grabs the ball and scuttles back to the spot where he started.

Point made, Krzyzewski orders the drill resumed. The other point emphasized in more than two hours of practice is the need to remain "focused," a favorite Duke buzzword.

The subject arises during a review of the team's performance at Maui, where on consecutive days Duke defeats DePaul, Louisiana State, and BYU by an average margin of twenty-three points.

Krzyzewski concludes: "We've got a pretty good thing going, and we need to stay focused." He tells his players it's important to maintain that single-mindedness of purpose until it becomes habitual, giving Duke another edge over opponents.

North Carolina loses to Michigan by a point at the buzzer in the semifinals of Honolulu's Rainbow Classic.

George Lynch has perhaps his worst offensive game of the season, forcing up shots and missing thirteen of eighteen. As usual he finds a way to compensate, getting sixteen rebounds, more than twice as many as any Wolverine. Derrick Phelps, too, shoots an inordinate amount and has more turnovers than assists. Brian Reese throws the ball away seven times, a personal worst, and has a single assist. (Lynch set the team's turnover standard for the season with nine against Houston.) Still, the fifth-ranked Heels play sixth-ranked Michigan dead even.

The Wolverines, playing without injured starter Ray Jackson, take a one-point lead in the final minute after Chris Webber catches and dunks Jalen Rose's long, missed jumper as the shot clock is about to expire. North Carolina calls timeout with twenty-five seconds remaining. As usual, Smith has husbanded all his timeouts for late-game maneuvering. (It's rare for Smith to call more than one first-half timeout per season.)

Shortly after play resumes the Tar Heels get the ball to Donald Williams, who drives the lane and puts up a jumper that bounces on the rim and falls in.

The Tar Heels lead by a point. Thirteen seconds remain. With a veteran unit on the court Smith is confident UNC can stop Michigan on one possession. Michigan's Steve Fisher has expended all his timeouts, and Smith would rather not stop the clock and allow Michigan to regroup. What's more, Smith has anticipated the situation and his team knows what defense he wants played.

The Wolverines race upcourt, and against UNC's pressure Juwan Howard comes within an eyelash of traveling with the ball near his own free throw line. The ball makes it to UNC's end. A closely guarded Jimmy King forces a jump shot from the right corner over Lynch and Eric Montross. Phelps and Reese miss a box-out on Rose in front of the basket. The ball caroms off the rim directly into the six-foot-eight guard's hands. Rose's follow shot goes in as the final horn sounds, giving Michigan a 79–78 win.

The Tar Heels have lost their first game.

Smith is perhaps the only coach in Hawaiian tournament history to wear a jacket and tie throughout games. Now, in keeping with that sense of decorum, he walks the court amidst the strutting, celebrating victors, graciously shaking hands before departing for the UNC dressing room.

Tomorrow night the Wolverines will win the Rainbow Classic title, defeating second-ranked Kansas, the team that supposedly runs Smith's system better than he does.

NO CONTEST.

Last season Boston University put up a good fight on its home court, where the Blue Devils' appearance attracted the largest crowd (4,108) in BU history. Those Terriers finished 10–18, their second losing season in a row under Bob Brown, whose recent predecessors include Rick Pitino (Kentucky) and Mike Jarvis (George Washington). This year's crew is even worse, the "weakest opponent on our schedule in two years," confides a Duke assistant.

BU arrives at Cameron with a 1–5 record, having lost five straight. The Terriers provide less of a challenge than Duke's intrasquad scrimmages. The visitors trail 16–2 when beleaguered Brown takes his first timeout less than four minutes into the game. Even with Duke making liberal use of its meager bench, the margin at halftime is 55–16.

The Terriers, unable to run their offense, whatever it might be, and physically incapable of beating the Blue Devils one-on-one, commit two dozen turnovers in the first half, 50 percent more turnovers than points. Remarkably, BU achieves this dubious feat while failing to record a single assist.

Duke wins 106–62.

Krzyzewski, recently named *The Sporting News* "Sportsman of the Year," manages to praise both teams for playing hard. Brown says of his Terriers, "I think there are some positives we can gain from such an experience, but I'm not sure what they are tonight." The margin is as close as it is only because Duke goes to its bench extensively throughout the second half.

Krzyzewski expresses pleasure with the second unit's effort. All is not well, though. Only one bench player proves himself ready for prime time. In general, the subs make mistake after mistake, and are outscored by BU over the final fourteen minutes.

The sole bright spot among the reserves is soph Erik Meek, who plays fluidly, confidently, and efficiently, and finishes with a team-best nine rebounds and twenty-one points in twenty-six minutes. "He's been playing like that in practice," Tony Lang offers. "Sometimes he's practically unstoppable in practice." Meek, one of the unnoticed members of last year's squad, is interviewed by a few reporters following this game. The attention causes him to linger near his dressing cubicle longer than usual, a fact that elicits teasing comments from teammates and Pete Gaudet. With little to note about the game itself, game stories and headlines will focus on Meek.

The blond from Escondido, California, bears a scar nearly the length of his left calf, testament to the trauma that leveled him following his senior year in high school. Jogging along the side of a road, Meek was hit by a vehicle operated by a drunk driver. The six-foot-ten center suffered injuries severe enough to make him attend his graduation in a wheelchair.

As a freshman Meek played sparingly, hesitantly and with minimal athleticism. Leaping was especially difficult because his left leg couldn't flex. A Duke physician confides that scar tissue in Meek's calf made the simplest movement painful, often leaving the big man in tears. "My mind was really messed up because of the accident," Meek says. "It was really difficult to concentrate." Prior to this season Meek underwent an operation to clean out a mass of scar tissue eight inches by four inches, restoring much of his leg's flexibility and leaving an angry red line down the back of his calf. Tonight's performance seems an important marker on the road back.

A few spaces closer to the door, Kenny Blakeney remains largely unnoticed. Blakeney struggled more at Maui than any other reserve, and struggles against BU. After the game, someone mentions that the light's not working in the ceiling panel above Blakeney's locker, and teasingly asks the player if he's shot the lights out. "Yeah, three-of-eleven," Blakeney moans. He also commits four turnovers, compared to a single assist.

Blakeney does manage seven rebounds, second only to Meek, continuing the trend of prominent rebounding efforts by Duke's perimeter players.

The freshmen also struggle.

Tony Moore plays thirteen minutes, mostly in the second half, collecting four points, four rebounds and four fouls. He's active, he hustles, but he moves spasmodically, especially on defense, and obviously remains unsure of himself.

Chris Collins—who shined in Maui, earning his father, Doug, the former all-pro and NBA coach, plenty of TV time where he sat watching from the stands—has one assist in half a game against BU, and misses eight of ten field goals and two of three free throws. "I've never seen him miss that many shots at all," says Lang.

Dressed in a tan suit and unaccustomedly seated near the end of the bench, Lang offers the freshmen the solace of a peer's experience. "They're taking their bumps and bruises," he explains.

Typical of an inexperienced playmaker, Collins ventures into the lane with no idea what he'll do when he gets there. He forces shots, attempts things he's not good at. The confidence and creative freedom enjoyed by Bobby Hurley surely hasn't eluded his notice, though mastery of it far eludes Collins's grasp. The freshman calls home and cries to his dad, who counsels patience.

"I just tried too hard," Collins explains glibly after the BU game. "I feel I'm one of the better shooters we've got on this team, if not the best. I get real mad at myself when I don't make open shots, because that's something I work real hard on trying to contribute to this team.

"Yeah, you're down a little bit. You've got to just keep playing, and play out of it. You can't let this be a turning point for the down side because I feel I played real well in Hawaii. I'm looking forward to continuing to get some minutes. Everybody's going to be counted on because Antonio Lang's out."

Gaudet, ever the devil's advocate, sees things a bit differently. "With freshmen sometimes, it's two steps forward and one step back. Because they want to be somebody else. Because they did something one night, so they think they can do it again tonight." Freshman, senior, star or sub—many among tonight's Cameron faithful don't seem to care. Most Duke students are away on semester break, creating a rare opportunity for the general public to purchase tickets (at eighteen dollars apiece) to see the Blue Devils. An hour after the game about one hundred such visitors, mostly preteens, remain camped near the Duke locker room in search of autographs.

Some players, like Moore and Kenney Brown, emerge to eagerly raised programs, posters, hats and pens, but few murmurs of recognition. Thomas Hill's appearance elicits a chorus of welcome: "Thomas! Thomas!" Muttering, "Oh, no," Hill patiently wades forward to accommodate the wave of voices and hands that splashes across a restraining rope.

Mostly, though, it's Hurley the fans want. "Is Bobby coming?" they ask teammates. Finally, growing impatient, they chant, "We want Bobby! We want Bobby!" The chant soon changes to "Hurley! Hurley! Hurley!"

But their hero has departed, slipping away through an unwatched exit.

SATURDAY, JANUARY 2

FOR the first and only time, Les Robinson starts what he considers his best lineup—four guards and center Kevin Thompson. Mark Davis is back in the lineup. Chuck Kornegay had been starting, but was late for the pregame meal, giving Robinson a convenient excuse for making a change he'd been contemplating recently.

"In the beginning, I can remember from the first day, he said he wanted to start four guards," Thompson says. "It really worked well." N.C. State defeats Iona College 88–66, an outcome welcomed with open mouths and arms by the estimated crowd of seven thousand that half fills Reynolds Coliseum. The fans are supportive, lively, and apparently ready for the Tar Heels, the team's next opponent. They cheer happily when a first quarter score from the Peach Bowl is announced, reporting the UNC football team trails Mississippi State.

Iona goes eight minutes without a field goal, allowing N.C. State to build a seemingly safe and certainly comfortable 42–27 halftime lead. That's the same score by which Kansas led the Wolfpack two weeks ago, and only the second time in seven games State has led at intermission. "That was a good feeling for us," Todd Fuller says. So, too, is being the dominator. "This is the first win, literally, where we didn't have to come from behind."

Migjen Bakalli leads all scorers with twenty-two points, hitting half his ten three-point tries. The bench outscores the starters. All twelve eligible roster members play in each half. Three players have five assists each, including Thompson, reflecting successful relocation passes from the post to open three-point shooters. As a team the Pack enjoys its best bonusphere bombing of the season.

"Tonight was what I envisioned on December first," Robinson says as N.C. State raises its record to 3–4.

MONDAY, JANUARY 4

THIS is almost unthinkable.

At Cameron, up by twenty points in the second half, Duke displays ineptitude reminiscent of N.C. State at its worst. As in the sort of dream in which you suddenly, shockingly, inexplicably find yourself gasping for breath or unable to move, the Devils are reduced to feverish longing for nothing so much as escape, which they manage only after being taken to overtime by Oklahoma.

Tuned and rested, the ACC season just around the corner, top-ranked Duke comes into the game 8–0 and the team to beat until someone proves otherwise. The Dukies carry a confidence born of surpassing success, the aura of a flourishing tradition, one that defines the current peak of college basketball: Two straight national titles. Five straight Final Four appearances. Twenty-one victories in a row. Thirty-three straight wins at Cameron, a streak in its third season. Seventy-six consecutive wins at home against non-ACC teams, a streak dating to the '83 season, when the catalytic recruiting class of Mark Alarie, Jay Bilas, Johnny Dawkins, and David Henderson were freshmen.

But while Oklahoma is not to be feared, it's not to be overlooked either. Tenth-ranked and 10–1, Oklahoma might be the quickest team Duke will face this season. The Sooners start five upperclassmen, three of whom were on the squad when Duke came to Norman in 1991 and broke OU's fifty-one-game home court winning streak.

Duke and Oklahoma might have met at Maui, except the Sooners blew a lead and self-destructed in the first round against Brigham Young. Many took this as fresh evidence of Billy Tubbs's inferiority as a coach. Imagine their surprise when, against Tubbs's Sooners, mighty Mike Krzyzewski's Blue Devils nearly succumb to a similar collective collapse.

There's trouble from the start as the normally accurate Blue Devils miss their first four shots and their first two free throws. Bobby Hurley makes a three-pointer, then the Dukies again misfire on four straight shots. They miss threes, they miss jumpers in the lane, they miss layups. In fact, they miss layup after layup.

Meanwhile the Sooners take advantage of Duke's defense in much the manner employed by Rutgers, crashing the boards for nine offensive rebounds in the first half, twenty-six in the game.

Duke has other problems. It's hot, nearly seventy degrees earlier today, and the Devils find they are the ones a bit out of competitive shape. Tony Lang has been cleared to play, but his stamina is absent after a ten-day lay-off. Thomas Hill (whose father is an assistant athletic director at Oklahoma) is in a funk offensively. And playmaker Hurley twists his right ankle about eleven minutes into the game, initiating a chain reaction that sends him hurtling backward in development to midway in his sophomore season, when his lack of emotional maturity constantly threatened his oncourt concentration.

Hurley always has been painfully self-critical, perhaps because he so much wants to live up to the standards set by Bob Hurley, his father and high school coach. "My dad taught me a lot about basketball," he said his freshman year, when his father critiqued his play via telephone after every game. "Growing up, that was my first interest, really. Basketball has always been a big part of my life." Hurley the Son arrived at Duke a bit out of control, not only in the breakneck pace at which he played but in the way he allowed his emotions to get the better of him. Faced with adversity in his first visit to Chapel Hill, he tied a Duke single-game record with ten turnovers against a single assist. UNC's King Rice got under Hurley's skin for two years with verbal taunting.

Hurley became so well known for moping and whining when things didn't go his way, he became a favorite target of derision on the road in the ACC, engendering chants of "Hurley! Hurley!" that echoed the "Ferry! Ferry!" that once greeted another outstanding Duke competitor and complainer, Danny Ferry.

"I may have been a little bit more of a front-runner my freshman year than a perfectionist," Hurley recalls. "I couldn't turn it around my freshman year. If I had a couple of bad plays in a game, I wasn't able to turn it around and do some positive things. It would just turn out to be a totally bad game for me. The last two years if I made a couple of mistakes throughout the game I would still be able to turn it around and do a lot of positive things." Hurley's path to maturity was speeded by viewing one of Pete Gaudet's masterful highlight tapes, this one an embarrassing compilation of his prize pouts. The point guard finished the '91 season in grand style, recording forty-three assists versus ten turnovers in the NCAAs, and hit the key three-pointer in an upset of Nevada-Las Vegas as Duke went on to capture its first national title.

These days he's considered a lock to make the NBA and is likened to all-pro John Stockton of Utah. But against Oklahoma the ankle sprain slowly shifts Hurley's mental equilibrium. "I was able to run, but I lost a step," he says afterward. "I couldn't get by my man. That was very frustrating."

At first, the injury has no discernible effect. Possessing a warrior's pride, Hurley wills away a limp, and within seconds of getting hurt hits a three-pointer to give Duke its initial lead of the game, 28–26, at the 8:22 mark of the first half. Barely a minute later he hits another three, helping fuel a spurt that puts Duke ahead, 40–29.

But just when the Blue Devils appear to have righted themselves and restored order, another old emotional habit surfaces to haunt them. Mike Krzyzewski draws a technical foul. Aided by two free throws and an extra possession, Oklahoma runs off ten unanswered points to pull back into contention.

Trouble with game officials is nothing new for Krzyzewski, who chronically is at or near the ACC lead in incurring technical fouls. In part, this simply reflects Krzyzewski's competitiveness. Against Oklahoma, his team struggling, the former Army captain wants to lead the fight.

"The fact is, I ask for their attention in the game," Krzyzewski explains. "It's not so much working the officials. 'What the hell does that mean? You didn't call two straight traveling violations. Are you going to call travels tonight? What are you looking at?' . . . really, I'm not up that much in a ballgame. I like to sit and analyze." But Coach K undeniably applies verbal abuse for effect in the manner of Bob Knight, his college coach. Hoping to ensure a fair break and perhaps more, he's apt to pick on one official in a crew almost from the opening buzzer. Like a wolf culling a herd, he usually chooses the least experienced ref, or one whom Krzyzewski considers somehow undeserving of full respect.

Tonight's target is Steve Gordon, the junior member of a crew that includes Dick Paparo and Duke Edsall. Gordon, a sales representative from Virginia with a bum knee, is in his sixth year in the league.

The Duke coach isn't terribly popular with ACC refs. He, Florida State's Pat Kennedy, and Maryland's Gary Williams are considered the league's most obstreperous sideline second-guessers. (Dean Smith is equally active in his jockeying, but prefers sarcasm to profanity. Once, before a game, Smith apologized to Paparo for how poorly the Tar Heels played the last time the ref saw them. Paparo assured the coach he didn't even recall the game. Smith replied that Paparo should review the tape. "You didn't have a very good game, either," Smith said.)

Tonight's game is barely five minutes old before Krzyzewski starts yelling at Gordon.

Though coaches' bench conduct can be a significant part of a game, television tends to steer clear unless the behavior is comic or blatantly offensive. Perhaps it's to avoid showing grown men, supposed role models, employing intimidation tactics and foul language. Or maybe the game's purveyors simply prefer to avoid revealing in a bad light the stars whom they promote.

Whatever the reason, the camera's selective eye misses Krzyzewski being warned to cool it by Paparo. Then Gordon whistles Grant Hill for a charge near Oklahoma's bench on a drive with 4:33 left in the first half. Krzyzewski explodes, leaping and hollering. Paparo calls a technical; Krzyzewski is still yelling at Gordon as Oklahoma's Jeff Webster makes the two resultant free throws.

The sniping goes on throughout the game, though at a reduced level in the second half, which Duke begins leading 44–41. Two bench technicals automatically mean the coach's expulsion from the game, as Tubbs knows from personal experience at the 1991 NIT. But it takes real guts to eject a head coach, especially the coach of the national champs on his home court.

Krzyzewski has learned when to cool it, though. He's been privately chastised in the past by Duke and ACC officials for his sideline behavior. He also recognizes he can become distracted by officiating, a bad idea tonight because, whether or not the officiating is at its best, Duke certainly is not. The Blue Devils fail to score on their first three possessions of the second half, the time he wants them to pounce, as Hurley misses a three and a layup and Marty Clark steps on the sideline with the ball.

Then, magically, the accustomed Duke reappears, running off seventeen unanswered points while the Sooners miss seven straight shots and commit five turnovers. With 14:40 left, Duke leads 61–41. This is more like it.

Just as suddenly, the magic vanishes. Duke scores once in a dozen possessions, with five turnovers, as the Sooners pull within eight. Along the way, Thomas Hill picks up his fourth foul and goes to the bench.

Hurley hits consecutive jumpers, pushing the lead back to thirteen. Then Grant Hill's elbow catches the Sooners' Bryan Sallier just below the left eye, flooring him and opening a gash that requires rubber-gloved treatment and a considerable delay.

When play resumes, Duke is back in a funk. The Blue Devils score six points in the final 8:43 of regulation. During one span they miss eleven straight free throws. Enjoying 72.3 percent accuracy prior to facing Oklahoma, the Blue Devils wilt when forced to make free throws that count, and finish fifteen of thirty-one.

Perhaps the most disconcerting aspect of Duke's evening occurs down the stretch when Hurley, the college game's consummate master of clutch playmaking, nearly comes apart.

Over the final five and a half minutes of regulation play, Hurley forces a bad shot, misses two of three free throws, and commits three turnovers—one on a foolish crossover dribble against a double-team, the others on seemingly unfocused forays into the lane. He also dribbles into traffic on the final possession of regulation and gets tied up, resulting in a jump ball.

The one free throw Hurley does make comes with 1:15 left and Duke's lead reduced to two points. The shot bounces twice on the rim and falls in, after which Gordon halts the proceedings and orders a platoon of young, towel-wielding "ballpersons," as their T-shirts put it, to wipe a wet spot on the floor. "Don't do that again!" Krzyzewski yells at Gordon.

Clearly irked, Hurley complains, too, then tosses one of the towels. And misses the second free throw. "That was ridiculous," he says later. "There were a lot of stop-actions that kept you from concentrating."

Oklahoma's Angelo Hamilton ties the score on a three-pointer with thirty-three seconds remaining. Duke calls a pair of timeouts and T. Hill gets off a baseline jumper to beat the buzzer. There appears to be contact—perhaps even initiated by Hill—but nothing is called. Krzyzewski stands with hands on hips and yells, "He got him with the body, Gordon!"

The official's reply is inaudible across the court. The coach's is not. "Bull-shit!" he says.

In the overtime, Duke plays with great poise. Tony Lang scores two baskets, one in traffic in the lane, the other on a long drive from the wing that takes Oklahoma by surprise. Grant Hill scores twice in-close on passes from Hurley. Cherokee Parks dominates the defensive boards. Duke converts six free throw in six attempts, the last four by Hurley, to seal an 88–84 win.

The coaching spin on the two-and-a-half-hour game is that both teams played very hard; Duke ran its half-court offense poorly because its players didn't work together; and the close escape, under conditions difficult to simulate in practice, is healthy. "If you don't win by 'X' amount, you're horrible," Krzyzewski protests. "You've got to be careful so winning is always fun. Not perfection. That's what our success has done."

It turns out Hurley set the school single-game record for assists tonight, with fifteen. "I almost set the turnover record too," the senior grouses. Actually, he has eight, two shy of the mark he set in 1990.

Asked if the sore ankle bothered Hurley, Krzyzewski replies: "The ankle has nothing to do with your head. If it is bothering you, you should compensate with better intelligence." Perhaps, the coach muses, Hurley needs to learn not to take so much on his own shoulders.

Later, in comments that might serve for himself as well, Krzyzewski adds: "Bobby is very critical of himself all the time, and that's what makes him Bobby. The thing is, he doesn't take it on to the next play. He has to understand, it may have a negative impact on his teammates. Some of that should be kept inside more. A leader can't wear his feelings on his sleeve all the time. He has to keep them inside more."

While the first flush of pregame activity rustles through Cameron, over at N.C. State the Wolfpack practices six against five and seven against five in preparation for facing North Carolina's trapping, pressing defense. "I used to do that at The Citadel a lot," Les Robinson explains. "It's the old overload principle." Even with six defenders, Kevin Thompson drives easily to the basket. So, too, does Donnie Seale. "This is five on six!" Robinson remonstrates.

Coaches' voices are raised far more frequently than usual this evening. Players are cautioned to stay out of the corners, to avoid unnecessary dribbling, to not pick up their dribble, to play smart, look smart, feel smart.

"Men, an open man is an opportunity!" Robinson shouts. And later: "Have a second plan in mind when you go inside, men!" Marcus Wilson— he of the long face, long body, long limbs, long fingers, long waist—is exceptionally emotional and vocal tonight. "Playing sorry, White!" he shouts to his mates during a drill. "Let's go! Let's go! Get up!"

Sometimes, as Robinson says, Wilson looks lost on the court, "like there were two games going on out there, the game he's playing and the other game." But, mistakes and all, the freshman is having a blast. "It's fun," he says of the long, tough practices. "I just like to play. That's all there is to it."

Seale, wearing a red T-shirt with cutoff sleeves beneath his practice jersey, complains to a coach when he's pushed by a teammate. "I can tell you, they're going to push you," Robinson says of the Tar Heels. "They push like that." On the sideline Curtis Marshall and a team manager laugh over the exchange.

WEDNESDAY, JANUARY 6

CLEMSON, undefeated in nine games, comes to Cameron and loses 110–67. The ACC season, part two in a three-act play, has begun.

Tony Moore outscores Grant Hill, Duke's leading scorer, who complains he's tired all the time and wonders if he's sick. Marty Clark leads Duke in rebounding and has a dozen points, and is featured on Mike Krzyzewski's weekly television show. Walk-on Stan Brunson, a six-foot-six soccer player who's joined the squad for the second semester, plays two minutes and has both shot attempts stuffed. "We played real well," Krzyzewski says. "Everybody played real well. Tony Moore. Kenny Blakeney. Stan tried to head one in."

The game is especially satisfying for Cherokee Parks, who rises to the challenge posed by the Tigers' top player, center Sharone Wright. Parks makes eight of eight shots, scores nineteen points and grabs seven rebounds. During a decisive 21–5 run he scores six points on a follow shot, a power move inside, and a turnaround jumper. He also screens for Bobby Hurley on a three-pointer at the top of the key.

Parks does a good job defensively as well, fronting Wright and denying him post passes from his guards. Frustrated, Wright fouls out with more than a quarter of the game remaining, scoring ten points and grabbing nine rebounds. "Cherokee got better that game," Pete Gaudet says. "There's no doubt he turned up his defense a notch to play with the other big men in the ACC."

Duke appears vulnerable tonight, though. Hurley remains a bit off-stride. The college game's active assist leader misreads cuts, throws an alley-oop to nobody, and has more turnovers than assists. But he also scores twenty points to lead Duke, shuts down Clemson playmaker Chris Whitney, and spearheads a defense that forces nineteen turnovers and fuels a devastating fast-break attack.

Grant Hill tries an early jumper and misses. After that, with the game under control he contents himself with a strictly supportive role, taking only seven shots and scoring seven points. "He still sees a miss as a mistake," Gaudet laments.

The ten-year Duke assistant confides Hill is the best long-distance shooter he's coached at Durham, but that's only in practice. In games, Hill shies from the bonus line as though it's a cliff. "It didn't come with Laettner until his junior year, until he had to do it with Shaquille O'Neal. After that he took everybody outside," Gaudet says a bit hopefully. "They can get psyched too. They're only young kids. They're not like Michael Jordan." Tonight the flaws hardly matter. Clemson, its record fattened by an unchallenging nonconference schedule, comes unglued midway through the first half and is totally out of sync thereafter. Cliff Ellis's club commits fourteen turnovers and misses virtually every jumper it tries in the opening period.

The Tigers trail 57–23 at intermission. Until the last, it appears they'll score fewer points than either Canisius or Boston U.

Following the game the coaches take turns meeting with the media in Duke's Hall of Fame room, a carpeted enclosure just off the playing floor where the walls are hung with retired basketball jerseys and dozens of drawings of past Blue Devil athletic luminaries, including sportswriters. A bust of Eddie Cameron, the coach and athletic director for whom the building is named, looks out from a backlit alcove. On the reverse side of the same wall, out of sight except to those en route to a bathroom tucked in a corner, are mementos of Duke's football greatness, none more recent than the 1960 season.

The winning basketball coach—Krzyzewski all but twice since the 1988 season—speaks first. Before the Duke coach finishes his opening remarks about the Clemson game, a South Carolina writer interrupts to ask what purpose is served by playing so lopsided a contest.

In the past, comparable questions regarding overmatched opponents evoked angry outbursts from Krzyzewski. But the coach has worked to improve his patience with the media, and though emotion colors his voice his reply is measured and polite.

"Well, I'm sorry I took your question first, because that's a really bad question," he says. "I used to say that's a dumb question, now I say it's a bad question. Because this is an ACC conference game. We're playing a team that's 9–0 and we played our butts off. I don't know—in the newspaper business, does your Tuesday column not mean as much as your Sunday column? I would hope not. Because we're playing, and it means a lot to us."

Once Krzyzewski finishes answering questions he hustles out through a back door, SID Mike Cragg leading the way like an icebreaker. The Duke coach is not one for schmoozing with the media, retiring immediately to the privacy of the coaches' locker room. Soon he and his staff will reassemble at Krzyzewski's house in Durham's newish northern suburbs to review tape of the Clemson game while impressions are fresh.

THURSDAY, JANUARY 7

An ACC assistant who's come to Reynolds Coliseum to scout the Wolfpack scans the four-paragraph press release. N.C. State starters Chuck Kornegay and Donnie Seale, and seldom-used sub Jamie Knox, have been declared academically ineligible for the spring semester, and are unable to play tonight against North Carolina.

"Holy shit!" the scout says. "I might as well go home." Certainly this latest blow in a parade of woe settles the outcome and North Carolina cruises to a 100–67 win. Only once, in a series dating to 1913, has UNC won by a larger margin.

No one is surprised. Even prior to the suspensions, interest in the game is at a modern low. Area newspapers spend little space hyping a contest that was so keenly anticipated just a few years ago, the most powerful TV station in eastern North Carolina carried the game at the cost of pre-empting a live presidential State of the Union address.

Now the Wolfpack is more an object of pity than interest among fans in general, though its loyal followers remain convinced victory is just around the corner.

"I've had people tell me, we need to get an exorcist in there, with all the problems we've had," says Julie Hendricks, a former team manager now employed in the basketball office. "I still say we're going to surprise some people. People look at me and say, 'Be quiet.' I have to stand by my team. People say we don't have the caliber of players the rest of the ACC has, but I beg to differ. We're capable of competing in the ACC. It's not going to be smooth sailing, but we're out of the rapids now."

But without Seale's ball handling and Kornegay, the Wolfpack is swamped inside and out. UNC, which routed Cornell 98–60 earlier in the week, has almost twice as many rebounds as State, with a near-equal number coming on the offensive and defensive boards. Even when Derrick Phelps is lost early in the second half due to a mild concussion, the Tar Heels maintain intense defensive pressure, forcing fifteen turnovers.

Prior to the game, Buzz Peterson studies hours of tapes and scans old notebooks for clues on how to beat his former team. He comes away impressed with the Tar Heels, and with how impressed he believes Dean Smith is, too.

"I think when he's trapping more like that, he thinks the defense is better," Peterson says. "I think they've got one of the better teams they've had in a while. I look back to the early eighties. The last four or five years, this is the best team they've had. They're really playing well."

To defeat UNC, Peterson believes N.C. State must ignite its eagerly supportive home fans, including students close to the court on all sides, who make Reynolds every bit as tough a place for visitors as college basketball's more acclaimed venues, including Duke's Cameron Indoor Stadium. "You go man-to-man, it's tough for us to beat them," Peterson says. "You have to go on emotions. You have to hope the shots are going in." But N.C. State quickly falls behind and, eager to rally in one big gulp, rushes its shots, exactly what Dean Smith's defense tries to make opponents do. The result is predictable. The Wolfpack makes fewer than four in ten field-goal tries, including misfires on twenty of twenty-seven attempts from three-point range.

Besides producing points in a hurry, Robinson's trademark long-range attack has an emotional component, energizing players, deflating the opposition, and inspiring fans. Conversely, shooting failure as abject as tonight's leaves the Reynolds crowd repeatedly raising its expectations, only to buzz into neutral as shots clang off the rim.

Worse, as often as not, when the Heels catch the long rebounds of Pack misses they instantly convert them into fast-break opportunities.

"I think Carolina is a better team this year," Curtis Marshall, the N.C. State point guard, says after committing five turnovers and missing seven of ten shots. "They're a lot quicker, it seems like. They have more of a team concept."

However weak, even crippled the opponent, this victory is especially satisfying for North Carolina.

Smith spends little time telling players about upcoming opponents; he rarely shows them tape of the other team in action. The emphasis is on playing one's best, playing the course rather than the opponent. But UNC coaches are not above recalling past slights as a motivational tool, rallying pride in defense of The Carolina Way.

So this year's team not only adopts the standard North Carolina goals—a twenty-win season, first place in the ACC, an ACC title, a trip to the NCAAs, a national championship—but harbors an appetite for a few paybacks as well.

"I think going over there, and in general just playing N.C. State this year, is going to mean a little more for us because we lost to them twice last year," Henrik Rodl says prior to the game. "I think we'll be really up for the game, and it's going to mean a little more than it's just a game."

Mission completed, the Tar Heels savor the moment. "Last year put a sour taste in our mouths," says Eric Montross, who helps smother State center Kevin Thompson, "and now it gets a little sweeter."

The air is somber in the Wolfpack locker room at the other end of the basement hallway in Reynolds. Losing to North Carolina is painful, no matter the circumstances, just as beating the Heels can expunge many frustrations. Beverly Sparks, the administrative secretary in the basketball office, has a save-screen computer program that sends the scores of last season's upset victories against UNC floating endlessly across her view, still soothing and satisfying almost a year after the fact.

"It seems like each team wants to beat Carolina for some reason," says a perplexed Marshall, the Nebraska resident. "Our fans would rather have us beat Carolina than Duke any day. I don't know what it is. When you walk in the gym, you can feel, I don't want to say hatred, but it just seems crazy. You can hear them yelling vulgar things and stuff at the Carolina fans." It reminds him of the Nebraska-Oklahoma football series.

The Reynolds crowd rushed the court after last year's surprise win over UNC, emotions stoked by a three-point barrage spearheaded by Tom Gugliotta, who finished with thirty-six points. The result left State's record at 9–6 and its confidence high. But the win apparently lent the team a false sense of security; it proceeded to plummet to nine consecutive defeats.

Then, just when things were bleakest, State traveled to Chapel Hill on a warm late-February afternoon and shocked the Heels, 99–94. That time Kevin Thompson had twenty-nine points and Mark Davis had his coming-out, hitting seven three-pointers, the last putting N.C. State ahead to stay.

"To beat them is just an incredible feeling, I can't even describe to you how those last two victories have felt," says Migjen Bakalli, who grew up near Charlotte. "It's great. That's why you do it. That's why you get out and practice every day." Les Robinson is relying on that intensity of desire, as well as the regimen of rugged practices between semesters, to elevate the Wolfpack's play against the Tar Heels. Then, like a boomerang tossed and forgotten, vestiges of the Valvano years return to deliver the crushing blow that eliminates Kornegay and Seale from the lineup.

Robinson informs his players of the loss just prior to pregame warmups. "I told them we can't feel sorry for ourselves," he recalls. "I've got that talk down."

Seale, given the choice of retreating to his room or sitting on the bench, opts to be alone with his brother, who's come to town for the game. "I was totally in shock," Seale says. "It was hard for me to operate, really. To take a game like Carolina from a player . . . take any other game, but not that game. I wanted to put my jersey on anyway. I'm not saying we would have won, but me and Chuck would have helped a lot."

Instead Seale watches the game on TV, and squirms with embarrassment. "If they wanted to see my grades, I wouldn't mind showing the world," he says. "People look at you different. I knew they would. I know they do. Because they don't know the whole story." Seale supposedly has done everything possible to expedite the appeal of an incomplete grade; prospects appear good he'll be reinstated eventually. Meanwhile, the precious days of his N.C. State career fly past, a career already halved by academic deficiencies during his high-school years.

"I thought after the Iona game, and the practices before that, we had been playing real well," Seale says. "Everybody was starting to get the same idea of what was going on. We all were on the same page. Everybody was playing defense. Kevin and Chuck were in there fronting like we always wanted them to do. The guards and everybody else were playing real well. We were about this close away from getting that definition of team unity that we wanted.

"And, all of a sudden, here comes a fist, here comes another blow to the season. All the ambitions we had at the beginning of the year seemed to go down, one by one. Everybody says we're going to be all right, you learn from this.

"But nobody wants to ever go through this type of ordeal on a team. It's hard on the players who are playing, and on the players that's not playing. Everybody says, 'Well, there'll always be next year.' You don't want to hear that."

The abrupt personnel loss stuns the already-shaky Wolfpack. Not even the crest of feeling engendered by playing North Carolina can overcome the here-we-go-again sense among the Pack. Even Robinson has the look of a dog that's been boxed around the ears as he takes his place on a bench where occupants in ties and jackets outnumber those in basketball uniforms.

Ironically, it was almost exactly a year ago that Seale became eligible and took Lakista McCuller's spot in the starting lineup. McCuller, too, had run afoul of higher academic standards imposed by faculty vote subsequent to Valvano's departure. McCuller missed three games while his appeal was processed, and never regained either his playing form or his starter's role last season.

"I think a little bit we're getting hit with some of the old," Al Daniel says on the very day *Sports Illustrated* goes on newsstands with a Valvano cover feature minimizing his controversial legacy at N.C. State. "Three kids ineligible at the end of first semester. My God! My first reaction would be, 'Are you guys watching them over there, or not?'"

During Valvano's decade N.C. State coaches routinely assured eligibility by steering players to courses with sympathetic or easy-grading professors, a practice employed to various degrees at virtually every school, Duke and North Carolina included. "It ain't that hard," explains a former ACC assistant now scouting for the pros. "Sit in front of the classroom. Do a little PR. Get a C." Valvano also insisted players be treated as adults rather than be subject to demeaningly close supervision, or threatened with deprivation of basketball privileges for academic failures. But the persuasiveness of his arguments was undercut by their conveniently self-serving character, as his nonsupervisory role neatly fit a hectic schedule of in-season speeches and other business ventures.

Problems arose as Valvano turned increasingly to basketball mercenaries, players only marginally interested in attending class. One, Chris Washburn, proved a sociopath as well, and was arrested at the end of his first semester on campus for stealing a schoolmate's stereo equipment. When court documents at Washburn's 1985 trial revealed he'd been admitted to N.C. State with a 470 combined score on the SAT, with 400 a given, a firestorm of criticism engulfed Valvano's program.

Just as the death by cocaine overdose of Maryland's Len Bias intensified public consciousness of drug abuse, so Washburn's academic weakness highlighted abuses rife in big-time college athletics. The heightened scrutiny, and continued recruitment of marginal students, forced Valvano and his basketball staff to become more active in lobbying professors and manipulating the system.

Valvano privately held that acquiring a college education wasn't necessarily synonymous with earning a degree. Rather, he argued persuasively that exposing a youngster to a broad range of people and experiences was of more lasting value than anything to be gained by merely grinding through the classroom system. But, finally, to satisfy the rising tide of rectitude over athletes' academic performances, and to pre-empt mandates from outside, the coach/athletic director voluntarily imposed higher scholastic standards on the basketball program.

(In interviews and a book he wrote after leaving N.C. State, Valvano avoided mention of his politically incorrect educational philosophy or that a central life goal was to become a millionaire.)

Upon Valvano's departure in the spring of 1990, N.C. State adopted higher academic standards for all students wishing to compete in extracurricular activities. The new eligibility requirements include grade-point averages higher than needed under NCAA standards. Similar standards regarding adequate progress toward a degree are expected to be adopted by the NCAA for the 1994–95 academic year.

Unfortunately for N.C. State basketball players, appeals of first-semester grades are initiated during semester break, a time when professors are likely to be out of town and the school is in bureaucratic hiatus. Even parking tickets are difficult to come by between semesters. Meanwhile the basketball season proceeds, and if there's a delay in processing appeal of a grade, a player may be declared ineligible.

"We have absolutely no contact with anybody," Daniel insists. "That's the way it should be. We have no qualms about that." He pauses. "You just hope you get cooperation." A fellow N.C. State coach is more blunt. Academicians should understand that recruiting restrictions, a depleted squad, and the school's sullied reputation put Les Robinson at a disadvantage from the moment he took over. The appeals process must be speeded up. Otherwise, like rules in many areas of public life, from zoning regulations to fishing limits and NCAA standards, N.C. State's unbending academic posture may prevent abuses, but to the detriment of innocent bystanders.

"Don't they get it, that they have a person who's responsible, who's accountable?" the coach asks in exasperation. "Les is a man you can put your trust in. You know what he stands for. He believes in having standards. He believes in academics. He believes in growth as a student. If you have a person like that, give him a chance."

For his part, after the game Robinson says he's "just sort of really numb." If he feels anything at all, it's regret that Seale, Kornegay, and Knox appear like "dummies" when they're not.

Mark Davis sags on a stool in front of his locker, eyes downcast. "I don't think anything else can happen," he says after missing most of his shots and fouling out with eight points. "Only good things can happen now, it should be. We've taken some blows, definitely, this year. Out of all the bad, eventually there has to be some good. We definitely deserve some good."

SATURDAY, JANUARY 9

AMILIAR stirrings emanate from drizzle-draped Chapel Hill: The Master Craftsman is conjuring another masterpiece. A decidedly ill-advised time to venture into the Dean Dome, as Gary Williams knows.

The unseasoned Terrapins opened the ACC season at home, and were routed by Georgia Tech. Now their first road trip takes them to "Blue Heaven," along what cliché-mongers call Tobacco Road, a term long obsolete, the tobacco markets and most of the farmland having long since vanished. (Not to mention that the Erskine Caldwell novel, "Tobacco Road," from which the name derives, was set in Georgia.)

The Terps enter the Dean Dome near midafternoon. By suppertime they've been boiled, shelled, chewed up and discarded, 101–73.

The game essentially is over by halftime, when North Carolina leads 53–31. The Terps make a brief run in the second half but never pull closer than fourteen points. "For this point in the year, they're the best team in my four years," Williams says. "But it's only January eighth."

The date may be a bit elusive for Williams, but the shape of North Carolina's victory is not. Tar Heel traps disrupt everything Maryland tries to do. Superior size, strength, and discipline enable the Heels to dominate the boards. They pound the ball inside on offense and punish the defense with three-pointers when it tries to cheat toward the interior.

"We are more experienced," Henrik Rodl explains. "I know that is a cliché, but we really are. That makes us more confident on the court. We're not cocky, but we are more comfortable when we play."

Maryland finishes the game with more turnovers than assists, makes just 41.7 percent of its shots, and is outrebounded 50–30. Kevin Salvadori and Eric Montross, each bigger than anyone on Maryland's roster, combine for eleven blocked shots. The Heels get thirty-three points and twenty-one rebounds from the inside tandem of Montross and George Lynch.

Gary Williams comes away particularly impressed with Montross. "I think he, really, his timing's better," Williams says. "It seems when he moves it's not wasted." The Maryland coach, who played for the Terps against Smith during the mid-sixties, also marvels at Montross's ability to catch the ball in traffic. "He's got great hands. You don't notice it until you play him. He doesn't drop it."

More notice has been paid Montross's abilities than Williams realizes. Pro scouts at the UNC–N.C. State game were abuzz over the Tar Heel big man. With rumors of an impending salary cap for NBA rookies, there's growing speculation Montross will go for the gold following this, his junior season, as Heels J.R. Reid (1989), Michael Jordan (1984), James Worthy (1982), and Bob McAdoo (1972) did before him.

No way, Montross says, eyes burning in deep sockets. "There's nothing in my mind right now that would tell me to do that. I think that I'm here for the four, I know that I'm here for the four years. I'm having too much fun, and enjoying this team and Coach Smith, to consider that right now."

What about after the season? a questioner persists. Will Montross, whose family is quite prosperous, consult then with Smith about going pro? "I think that *no* is no," Montross states flatly.

The mammoth Montross, with hands the size of frying pans, isn't the only Tar Heel gaining wider attention. The media also flock to today's leading scorer, Donald Williams. When teams "double-down" on the big men, it's up to Williams to find an opening and spot up for three-pointers, or penetrate from the wing and draw defenders to him. He's done his job quite well against the Terps, hitting five of eight on three-point attempts in a twenty-point performance.

Williams is quick to note he draws strength from Smith's encouragement that he shoot, which in turn reassures teammates. "When they see me open, they get me the ball," says the soft-spoken sophomore.

Especially days like today. "At times you have that feeling that you can't miss," Williams says, grinning shyly. Come to think of it, he adds, "I think that every shot I take is going in." Montross recalls being "astonished" by Williams's shooting ability when the guard joined the program. Still, a groping freshman performance made Williams a bit of an enigma entering this season. Says Montross: "We always knew he could shoot, but we didn't know how he'd handle the pressure of coming on, everybody thinking that he had to replace Hubert, he had to be the next Hubert Davis instead of the next Donald Williams. He really has done an excellent job."

So, apparently, has Smith, and he's done it according to his own often-maligned methodology. Start inside on offense and work outward. Don't take the best shot available, *work* for the best shot achievable. Accent man-to-man defense. Force dribblers baseline, then trap them before they retreat. Place team before self.

The personalities change, as does the shape of victory. But the parameters of Smith's perpetual formulation remain constant, producing that remarkable consistency that is his greatest legacy. It's as if a quarter-century ago Smith hit upon basketball's "Om," the Sanskrit sound that's said to tap into universal consciousness, and he's been adjusting squads to reproduce it ever since.

"We do change each year, contrary to what people say," insists Smith, whose predictable answers are mimicked in press rooms throughout the ACC. "We still have a philosophy of playing very hard, playing smart and playing together. But other than that it does change."

Yet listen to Derrick Phelps discuss this year's offense and, with a few name changes, you might be listening to any one of a dozen Tar Heel playmakers through the years.

"I think teams always worry about our inside game all the time, because we have Eric Montross and George Lynch down low that are exceptional players that can get the ball and score easily," Phelps says. "And, once people try to jam inside all the time and try to stop us from getting the ball inside, we've just got to refocus.

"OK, I think the main thing is to get the ball inside, but if we don't have that we try to run things for other players. You know, easy ten-footers or an open three-point shot. I think we adjust real well with other things we're doing, and I think we have the players that can adjust to the type of style that people play against us." The formulation has shifted this year, perhaps most noticeably in the team's approach to shooting three-pointers.

Since the advent of the shot in '86–87 Smith has assigned players green, yellow and red "lights" from long-range, basing the level of freedom on the evidence of a thousand threes attempted by each during practice. Under that or any system, Donald Williams would have a loose rein. Recently, though, Smith decided more marginal bombardiers were overemphasizing the importance of achieving green-light status, to the detriment of other parts of their games. So he's done away with all but red lights for big men.

There's been another recalibration as well, albeit a subtle one. "We made one major change that nobody has really picked up on, I don't think," Smith confides. "I'd be surprised. Something that's different from what I've done for thirty-one years."

"Want to tell me?" prompts an interviewer. "No. You're the one who's writing the book." Whatever Carolina's up to, it can't be executed to Smith's satisfaction without the presence of a playmaker like Phelps. As a matter of fact, like Phelps several of Smith's best playmakers have come from New York City. That was the case with Eddie Fogler (1968–70), Jimmy Black, who as a senior piloted the Heels to the 1982 title, and Kenny Smith (1984–87).

Kenny Smith was an inspiration to Kenny Anderson, perhaps the best guard ever from the city. But despite Smith's encouragement, the playmaker signed prior to the 1989–90 season with Georgia Tech. Anderson said he spurned the Heels in part because the UNC system "handcuffs" players and he didn't want to be "just another horse in Dean Smith's stable."

Phelps had no such misgivings. He'd been a supportive player on a team at Christ the King High School in Middle Village that included another prep All-American, Khalid Reeves, now playing at the University of Arizona. Thus, while Carolina players routinely report an adjustment period of a year or more until they feel comfortable with Smith's system, Phelps says he fit after about two weeks. "I think it was easy for me because I'm the type of person that likes to play defense," he explains. "That's what Coach Smith likes. I really fit in well in what he wanted and I just felt comfortable with it."

Phelps possesses a quick laugh and an easy, outgoing manner. His talkative nature, as well as his role, makes him a leader on the court. But Phelps also is one of the team's more thoughtful members. Asked a difficult question, he's apt to lean back in a chair, delicately place his long, finely boned fingers to his forehead, and contemplate before answering. More uncommon, the mustachioed twenty-year-old is sufficiently confident to occasionally admit he doesn't have the answer.

"I just want to go out there and help the team and just basically win," Phelps says of himself. "I've always been like that. In high school, I didn't care if I scored, either, as long as we won the game. If I had the worst game ever, if we came out winning I was happy. That's the type attitude I have. I'm the type of person, I don't get down too much on things, especially with basketball. It's just a game. We've just got to go out there and have fun and just play ball. It hurts when you lose, but I ain't going to get depressed about it." This notably healthy attitude may well trace to lessons imparted by Emanuel Phelps, a former college shooting guard who taught his son the game. For years the two went to a nearby park in East Elmhurst and played one-on-one. Later the son brought along a friend, and the two youngsters took on the elder Phelps with no change in result. "He used to kill us," Derrick Phelps recalls.

Finally the equation changed when the son reached high school. Yet, rather than drop the competition once he began losing regularly, Emanuel Phelps persisted. "He just took it in stride," says Phelps, who clearly has benefited from the example.

Phelps benefited, too, from his uneven success directing the Tar Heels during the '92 season.

Given extensive opportunity at the helm—he was the only Heel to start every game last year—Phelps now has reached that level of understanding, of integration with the thinking of Dean Smith, that Carolina point guards traditionally strive for and cherish. The point guard, after all, is the manifestation of Smith's will on the court, the one charged with calling the offensive and defensive plays in his intricate system. Finally, after years of study, the time inevitably comes when a playmaker is so attuned to Smith's preferences their thought processes converge, and the player finds himself instantaneously anticipating the coach's directives.

"It's been happening a lot this year, I think I'm having a good feel," Phelps says, clearly pleased. "It's funny how we start to, not think alike, but have the same type of feel for the game and how it should be played.

"And the way Coach Smith's mind is, you know, I'm starting to get a good feel for what he wants on the court and what plays he wants me to run at particular moments. It's funny because Coach Ford used to always tell me he used to do the same thing. He used to say something, and Coach Smith would tell him something, and he'd tell him he'd already called it. And that's the same thing that Coach Smith and I are going through, because I'm calling plays that he tells me after I called it."

Today against Maryland, Phelps makes his usual contribution, playing more minutes than any Tar Heel while contributing solid defense and directorship. He also chips in seven rebounds and six assists.

But the stat sheet reports six turnovers and three of twelve shooting, perhaps reflecting the lingering effects of a concussion suffered two days ago at N.C. State, when Phelps's head inadvertently met the shoulder of the Wolfpack's Lakista McCuller. "I know one moment I was playing defense, and the next thing I remember I was on the bench, you know, talking to the trainer, Marc Davis," Phelps recalls.

A dizzy Phelps was led to the locker room at Reynolds, but made his way back to the bench. That's as far as he got, sitting with an ice pack pressed to his skull, head drooping like a sunflower overladen with seed, before being escorted back to the locker room for the duration of the game.

Taking such blows, sometimes intentionally, is nothing new to Phelps, one of the tougher guards around. "He's a finesse player, but he can be very physical," Montross says.

During a 1992 game with Wake Forest, the 184-pound Phelps willingly took a charge from rock-solid, 235-pound Rodney Rogers. "It was like a train hit me or something," Phelps said afterward. Woozy from the blow, he retired to the bench. Soon he was back in the game, only to collide with Wake forward Trelonnie Owens, ten pounds heavier than Rogers. Again Phelps sat, then returned, directing the Heels through the last minutes of a successful twenty-point, second-half rally.

"I love playing defense, you know, I just love taking big collisions like that against big guys of that size and that strength," Phelps says, laughing. "It's kind of crazy to stay in there and take a charge when the person is six-eight, two hundred and like sixty-something pounds, to stay in there and take a charge, but I'm trying to sacrifice my body, just to do anything to win a game."

Virginia arrives at Reynolds Coliseum as one of four undefeated teams in the country, along with Xavier, Kentucky and Duke. It's Virginia's best start since 1984, the second and last year a Cavalier squad reached the Final Four under Terry Holland.

But unlike North Carolina, Duke, and many other national powers, Virginia hasn't played a tough schedule. Rather, very much like Clemson it has built a delusive record by beating a succession of plug-uglies, pretenders, and puny neighbors. To its credit, coach Jeff Jones's squad has beaten the best team it's faced thus far, Florida State. Now it's come to N.C. State for only its second road test in nine starts.

The Wolfpack is anxious to bounce back from its thrashing by the Tar Heels, and sniffs a chance at redemption against the chimerical colossus from Charlottesville. Playing with unaccustomed confidence, the Pack takes a 29–27 halftime lead and runs to the locker room accompanied by a warm ovation from a crowd estimated at 11,800.

"N.C. State did a good job of slowing things down a little bit, keeping us out of any rhythm," Jones says. "I think it made them much more efficient defensively."

Les Robinson has a simpler explanation: "Seeing us on television against Carolina, they probably weren't expecting much fight in the game from us."

The players might have thought that, but Virginia's coaches didn't, says an assistant.

"We were worried, and we did, I think, as much as we could without overstating our case to warn our team. N.C. State has been through a lot of adversity, but they have a lot of pride and tradition, and they weren't going to roll over," insists Tom Perrin, like Duke's Gaudet a so-called restricted-earnings coach whose future is unsettled by NCAA fiat. "This is what people do when they get their backs to the wall—they get angry."

Actually, the getting-angry doesn't come for State until after it loses. Through the first half, the signs are generally positive, the mood upbeat. The offense runs as designed. Perimeter players succeed in getting the ball inside to Kevin Thompson, who has ten shots and ten points in the period. Curtis Marshall does a good job holding down the Cavs' exceptional playmaker, Cory Alexander. Mark Davis is more active, more confident.

Perhaps best of all, Todd Fuller makes an impact, the game's "silver lining," according to Les Robinson. The freshman's previous rebounding high in a game is six against Iona. Against Virginia, a far superior opponent that has players about his size, Fuller has eight rebounds in the first half alone.

Reynolds fans have more than basketball to watch, tonight and every game. Above the court, placed where those in nonstudent seating can't miss it, an electronic message board flashes a constantly changing variety of color ads—for a bank, an air conditioning firm, a real estate development company, a radio station. Commercials crowd one after another, fast-breaking into consciousness.

So what if there's a game going on? So what if this is a public facility on the campus of an institution of higher learning? So what if the red score-board shows more ads and less game information than any other in the league? And so what if the game information it does share is difficult to read?

As long as you can read the score. And the ads. Tonight the score shows N.C. State expanding its lead to 35–29 early in the second half.

"I thought we were rolling," Marshall admits. "We were up six. I don't know. Everything just changed. They became more aggressive. They were coming at us."

Virginia's improved defensive play causes the impatient Pack to stray from its game plan. Soon three-pointers are flying a bit faster, and then faster still, not a good sign on a night when State misses its first nine attempts from long range and finishes two for twenty.

"I don't understand why guys started shooting the threes," says Marshall, one of the primary culprits along with Davis and Migjen Bakalli. "In the second half we got back to our old style, jerking up the threes. The three wasn't there tonight. We just have to realize that. Sometimes the three is there; sometimes it's not.

"For a while, I thought we were there. For a while. Then all of a sudden we were back to our old style, everyone out there lacking confidence, not knowing what to do."

Pack players squander numerous opportunities by failing to recognize their limitations. Compounding the problem, the players' desire to make amends only adds pressure when they do get good shots. Bakalli's judgment is especially skewed, and he's benched with eight and a half minutes remaining.

Overall, N.C. State shoots 29.7 percent from the field. The Wolfpack's last lead comes with 12:22 remaining thanks to the second of consecutive three-pointers by Marcus Wilson. By the time the Pack scores again five minutes later, Virginia has an eight-point lead. State never gets closer than six points the rest of the way as Virginia wins 73–56. In what's become a familiar sideline pose, the cheerleading Robinson can't help occasionally bowing his head and putting his face in his hands in dismay.

Afterward Robinson talks disappointedly about his team's lack of toughness and its poor reaction to game pressure. But he also sees progress. "I thought we substituted well tonight. We looked more like a basketball team. We adjusted to the new team. Again." But Robinson can't help but glance back, if only for a few moments. "That team against Iona I believe could have beaten Virginia," he says. "I believe that team could have taken it across the line against Virginia just as sure as I'm sitting here. That team that night. We could have beaten them, and should have beaten them."

A loser again, Robinson makes his way courtside to greet the last well-wishers and gather up his waiting wife and adult children. Unlike his Triangle colleagues, Robinson doesn't mind hobnobbing in public after games, though tonight Reynolds is nearly empty by the time he leaves the locker area.

Virginia's Jones is among those who stop by to say hello. The coaches are asked to pose together for a photograph. Both smile. "Guess which one has the real smile, and which grin is false," asks Robinson.

SUNDAY, JANUARY 10

WHEN it's over, when Marty Clark's meaningless three-pointer is counted and Duke's aura of invincibility has dissipated into Atlanta's low clouds and cold drizzle, Mike Krzyzewski and Georgia Tech's Bobby Cremins hug at midcourt.

Duke is in an opponent's arena for the first time this season, and like a worn cloth examined in bright light, the weaknesses revealed are integral to the fabric of the team. But it's still a good, hard-fought game that goes to the wire.

Certainly it's no surprise that the tenth-ranked Yellow Jackets are up for the game. Everyone gets up for Duke. If you can't get inspired to play a team that's won twenty-three games in a row, you're not much of a competitor. But this is different. Bobby Cremins, Tech's visceral leader, invests his teams with his own special feeling for playing Duke. He respects the hell out of Mike Krzyzewski and what he's accomplished, and therefore wants to beat him badly.

"God forbid we were chasing the same girl, we'd kill each other," Cremins says. "How can I put this? Mike has always been gracious to me, but at the same time I really believe Mike would take my head off in a game if he could. I feel the same way." From 1982, the season of Cremins's arrival in Atlanta, through 1990 each program won eleven games in the series. Duke beat Tech in the 1986 ACC title game. Tech beat Duke twice in the semis en route to ACC titles, including 1990 when both reached the Final Four.

While not exactly friends, Cremins and Krzyzewski are longtime acquaintances. They first met on the basketball court during the 1969

National Invitation Tournament at New York's Madison Square Garden. During a timeout, South Carolina coach Frank McGuire switched from a zone defense to a man. "He said, 'Cremins, who do you have?'" the ex-guard recalls. "I said, 'I have the guy with the big nose whose name I can't pronounce.'

"And," Cremins continues, "Mike always shoots back, 'Yes, but who won the game?' And he's right, Army won the game.'" Recently, the balance between Tech and Duke has shifted dramatically in the Blue Devils' favor. The Devils have won five straight and eight of the last nine in the series, a change Cremins ascribes to his adversary's maturation.

"In a way, I look up to Mike, simply because I've seen him go through the bad times and then I've seen him take his program to number one in the country. I love his coaching philosophy. I've said this many times: His defense is always the best. To beat them is always a special thing. That's why I was so excited at the end of the game."

Knowing Georgia Tech will play inspired ball only whets Duke's appetite to defend its undefeated status. Most coaches would play down an unblemished record this early in the year. Not Duke's. "It means a lot," Pete Gaudet says. "I don't know how to explain it. It's a feeling of maintaining a certain level of excellence." Still, he'd rather concentrate on winning one more, thereby setting a school record for consecutive victories. "People keeping talking about undefeated, undefeated. You'd almost rather have them talk about the streak—what's happening, not what hasn't happened." But streaks and records quickly become of secondary interest. Graphically revealed in this afternoon's game is what's present and what's missing from this Blue Devil squad. The two coincide in the area that's to prove most crucial—inclusive court leadership.

The players regard the '93 team as belonging, in a sense, to co-captains Thomas Hill and Bobby Hurley. The two seniors see it that way as well, having paid their dues while Christian Laettner and Brian Davis dominated discourse. Yet neither Hurley nor Hill is particularly outgoing, or prone to be solicitous of teammates' feelings, essential qualities in Duke's personally oriented, leadership style.

"You can talk about it forever, but if you're not comfortable you won't do it," Krzyzewski explains. "They're not talkative people, and it's not in their nature to be complimentary people. They don't say it and they don't need to hear it as much."

What Hill and Hurley do best is shout at teammates, as they were shouted at by their elders. Hurley is normally so quiet, he stunned everyone at halftime of the '92 title contest when he screamed at Laettner, who'd committed seven first-half turnovers. "I think at times people need to get yelled out," Hurley says. "The way we were playing wasn't up to par. I was upset because people would die to play in a national championship game."

Today, everyone's playing hard. But from the first the Blue Devils need somebody to rally around as they face the team from Atlanta. Hurley is distracted by the crowd of ten thousand, which boos every time he touches the ball. "It seems that I concentrate a lot better when I have the fans against me and everything else," Hurley says. "But initially in the Georgia Tech game, just not dealing with it for a long time, it did affect me a little bit." Alexander Memorial Coliseum rings with mocking chants of his name, the sound almost plaintive: "Hurley! Hurley!" They tease him about his drunk-driving arrest during the offseason: "D-W-I! D-W-I!" Hurley glances at Krzyzewski with a wounded, uncertain look, as if to say, What now?

What now, indeed. The question first arose several weeks ago, when Krzyzewski was asked about Duke's leadership in the absence of last year's vocal captains. "I'm still the leader of the team," Krzyzewski said. "Christian and Brian were really good players, but the coaching staff leads the team."

True enough, as far as it goes. But amidst competitive adversity someone must seize emotional control on the court as well.

The last few years, in fact throughout the careers of most everyone on Duke's roster, that meant turning to Laettner, whose absence fills this team like a tree is filled by the spaces between its leaves. Laettner was the lightning rod, the designated target for much of the hostility directed toward the tough, successful Devils, as Krzyzewski warns his team in anticipation of the trip to Atlanta. Laettner was like a pro wrestling villain—booed, vilified and feared. He seemed bigger than life. And there was an edge to him, an air of difference that raises anxiety and bloodlust in the mob.

Laettner fed the animosity by cultivating a public image of smugness and ambiguous sexuality, the latter trait bringing out homophobic bigotry on courts around the country. Worst were the chants of "Homosexual!" hurled his way at Louisiana State, gay-bashing that CBS announcers, in keeping with television's nonjournalistic bent, were too gutless to expose on-air.

More important than Laettner's public presence was his cohesive influence on the team. He had his own ideas about how he and Davis should manage "their" team, and wasn't afraid to implement them. As Grant Hill puts it, "We miss the toughness and leadership that Christian and Brian gave us, even if they were dicks sometimes." Laettner had an especial knack for calming Hurley. Sometimes the volatile playmaker—whom teammates believe is babied by his coaches—is overwhelmed by emotional fogs, whether precipitated by an official's call, a twisted ankle, or a teammate's shortcomings. Laettner wasn't reluctant to bring Hurley back to his senses by whatever means necessary, even if it required firing a ball at him or shouting in his face.

"To play with Christian Laettner is to play with a guy who wants to win every night," says Hurley, accustomed to similarly harsh treatment from his father, who was also his high-school coach. "He was the guy who helped me more than any other player I've played with, as far as helping me develop."

Here at Georgia Tech, Hurley and teammates confront the next phase in their development—banding together in new ways that stretch them personally—and fall behind by a dozen points in the game's first three and a half minutes.

By the first TV timeout at 15:12 the score is 14–5, Duke's points coming on a three by Hurley and a pair of free throws by Parks.

Following the break the Jackets score five unanswered points on a follow shot and another three by Best. Grant Hill responds with eight unanswered points within a minute and a half, putting Duke within 19–13.

Tech quickly regains a double-figure lead. Proud Duke isn't about to concede anything. After missing twelve of their first sixteen shots the Devils make two in a row for the first time, a fast-break layup by Hurley and a three-pointer by Marty Clark with just under four minutes remaining in the first half.

Malcolm Mackey, the Tech big man who romps across Parks as though he were a meadow, pushes the lead back to 42–30 on an inside thrust. At that, Duke clamps down defensively and moves within 44–37 at halftime.

That Duke is so close is remarkable considering it was outrebounded 21–10, outshot 58.8 to 36.4 percent, had twice as many turnovers as assists, and only four points from its big men. Duke opens the second half with jumpers by Parks and Grant Hill, who already has sixteen points. Tech calls timeout. There's a bit of machismo in the use of timeouts— forcing a rival to expend one is a small victory of sorts in coaching circles.

Cremins worries less about appearing like a sideline genius than he does about controlling his team, so he tries to stem the rising Duke tide with 18:47 left and the lead down to 44–41.

The Jackets build their lead back to eleven, only to experience a scoring drought that lasts nearly five minutes, allowing Duke to pull within 57–54 on a Grant Hill layup. His lean-in jumper over Forrest gives Duke its first lead, 60–59, with 9:20 to go. Again, Cremins calls timeout.

"I thought we were choking," Cremins says. "I thought we were throwing it away. I called a timeout and I challenged them. I just told them, 'You played so hard, and now you're just giving them the game.' I could see the look in their eyes. They got mad, and we really showed tremendous guts."

The teams are dead even with five minutes left. Tech breaks the logjam with an 8–0 run, all of its points coming in the lane. Duke pulls within 74–69 with 2:21 remaining and calls timeout.

When play resumes, the Yellow Jackets' Martice Moore beats the defense on a fast break off the inbounds. Grant Hill hits an acrobatic shot inside. Tech freshman Drew Barry—who's stripped the ball several times from Parks and chips in eleven points and five assists—throws away a pass. Grant Hill is fouled. He's been chagrined by his free throw shooting, and working to improve it. This afternoon he makes thirteen straight at the line before finally misfiring, leaving Duke four points shy at the 1:49 mark.

Barry misses a layup. Thomas Hill misses a jumper, part of a three for thirteen shooting performance on the day. Duke controls the rebound. Grant Hill tries a three and misses, but Clark follows. It's 76–74, and it appears the Blue Devils are about to pull one of their familiar escapes. Cremins calls timeout.

Georgia Tech designs a play for Forrest, who attacks Grant Hill along the baseline. Hill is called for a foul, Krzyzewski leaning back in his seat in distress. Forrest makes one free throw.

Hurley misses a three, Thomas Hill misses a three. They finish the day a combined nine of thirty from the floor, four of sixteen on three-pointers. That they're responsible for nearly half of Duke's field-goal attempts, transforming the Blue Devils into a jump-shooting team, is testament to the seniors' desire to win. But the more they shoot, the less involved other teammates feel.

"At times you get caught up in the whole thing where you see guys who are in my position scoring thirty points a game," says Thomas Hill, who admits to sometimes taking jumpers to impress pro scouts. "You feel, well, I need to do that to be up there with them. It isn't necessarily the case . . . there have been times where I've said, yes, I'm going to shoot this shot right now, right here, like this because I think I need to do that, which is wrong."

Hurley's control problem is of a different sort. "If you get too emotional, at times you get, 'All right, I have to make it happen now,'" he says. "'I have to make the big play, the big three.' You get caught up in that mentality and it's not productive all the time. Sometimes it's real good, it goes real well. But there are other games when it's just not there and you're forcing it a little too much."

One who doesn't have to force anything today is Grant Hill. He scores twenty-nine points, a new career high. He can't shoot, though, while Tech has the ball.

To get it back Hurley fouls Mackey with twelve seconds left. Earlier in the game, the center leveled Hurley with a pick, knocking the guard momentarily unconscious. Mackey, a 61.4 percent free thrower, hits both ends of the one-and-one opportunity. Five seconds later Hurley hits a running jumper with his foot just inside the three-point arc.

Down three, Duke calls timeout with six seconds on the clock. Tech's self-described "Thriller Dome," a round arena just off Tenth Street at the edge of the school's downtown campus, is bright, hot, and very, very loud.

A second after the Jackets put the ball in play, Hurley fouls Mackey. It's Duke's tenth team foul, giving Mackey two tries.

A single point will put the game out of reach. The excited crowd falls silent as Mackey shoots. A national audience looks on via CBS—the game is the network's answer to NFL football, and wasn't set until late December so it could be scheduled for maximum counter-programming effect.

Mackey, an erratic senior who's never won Cremins's full trust or admiration, badly misses the first free throw. The game hangs in the balance as he steps away, then toes the line and tries again. The shot goes in.

Clark's three-pointer, his fifth field goal in five attempts, completes the scoring. Georgia Tech wins, 80–79. Cremins leaps to slap hands with fans who swirl everywhere as the celebration begins.

MONDAY, JANUARY 11

JUST when it seems things can't get worse, they do. N.C. State journeys tonight to Davidson College, which ceased to be a basketball power more than two decades ago. The Pack hasn't lost to the Southern Conference school since 1944, a run of thirty-three games. The Wildcats last beat an ACC team during the 1982 season, besting Mike Krzyzewski's worst Duke team.

Last season's floundering State squad beat Davidson by twenty points, raising expectations of a similar, welcome result among Wolfpack veterans. "I thought it would be a blowout, to be honest with you," Mark Davis says.

Instead, the Wolfpack totters throughout the game on the brink of defeat.

They hold on for a 63–58 victory, improving their record to 4–7. But any good feeling is short-lived. With less than two minutes to go Migjen Bakalli forces up a running one-hander, which goes in. As it settles through the net, Bakalli crashes to the floor. He limps off, right foot injured.

Subsequent X-rays reveal the foot is broken. Bakalli has a metal pin surgically inserted to facilitate healing of his fifth metatarsal. He'll miss six to eight weeks, essentially the remainder of the regular season.

Pending the reinstatement of Kornegay and Seale, the loss of Bakalli reduces the Wolfpack to eight active players. "It'll be easier to call out who's not starting each night, rather than who is starting," Robinson offers.

"We don't have any more good news, do we?" asks Beverly Sparks, Robinson's administrative secretary.

There is some solace amidst the seemingly ceaseless flow of misfortune. As if a spike had been driven into a rock flaw, the bad times cause a stream of commiseration to burst forth. Much of it is offered kindly, and eagerly accepted. But there's also a taste of opportunism in the mix. Some callers to the basketball office solicit the purchase of books and courses on positive thinking. Others insist Robinson must heighten his religious devotion.

Among the friendly voices is that of Duke coach Mike Krzyzewski, who recalls his own tough times and marvels at the parade of pain endured by the '93 Wolfpack. "He said you all have had more (misfortune) than the rest of the conference put together, all eight teams. He was trying to be comforting. . ." Robinson recalls, voice trailing off.

Robinson cannot help thinking, though, that Krzyzewski and Duke are at the opposite end of fortune's continuum, atop a crest even as the Wolfpack wallows in a trough. "When it gets like that, it snowballs," Robinson says. "And the way it snowballs for us, it's snowballing for them in the opposite direction."

Living in the Triangle, it's impossible to escape constant reminders of that gap. Robinson hears radio ads for coverage of Duke's quest for a third title while driving to work in the mornings. "That does make it that much more challenging," he admits. "It quickly puts you in place. If they were out in Colorado or something, I wouldn't be hearing a commercial like that on my way to work on a Raleigh station."

While N.C. State fights for a win at Davidson, about an hour's drive north a bench-clearing brawl ends a game in Greensboro between North Carolina A&T and Morgan State.

The Aggies and Bears grapple with 1:55 left in the first half. The spark is a fistfight between two players. The conflagration eventually engulfs both benches, and results in the ejection of all but three players from each team.

North Carolina A&T once was the state's African-American version of North Carolina State. Among the school's alumni is Jesse Jackson. Greensboro was also the site of a 1960 Woolworth's lunch counter sit-in that helped spark the civil rights movement.

Like other Southern states, North Carolina was taken to court by the federal government to speed integration of its public university system.

Today, its historically black schools—A&T, North Carolina Central in Durham, Winston-Salem State, Elizabeth City State, and Fayetteville State—are better funded but remain overwhelmingly African-American. And the state's superior black students are increasingly drawn to predominantly white schools with funding geared to speed integration.

Most of North Carolina's traditionally black schools belong to the Central Intercollegiate Athletic Association, now lost in the ACC's shadow but once a thriving if unsung league.

For decades North Carolina's best black players either went to CIAA schools or left the South. Those who left include New Bern's Walt Bellamy (Indiana) and Greensboro's Lou Hudson (Minnesota). The CIAA produced Hall of Fame players like Earl "The Pearl" Monroe (Winston-Salem State) and Durham's Sam Jones, as well as Hall of Fame coaches John McLendon (Durham) and Clarence "Bighouse" Gaines (Winston-Salem), the man with more wins (828) than any college coach in history except Adolph Rupp.

Since integration in the late 1960s, African-Americans have gravitated to the ACC with nary a second glance at the CIAA or the Mid-Eastern Athletic Conference, to which A&T belongs. From North Carolina alone, the talent drain includes Michael Jordan (Wilmington), David Thompson (Shelby), Phil Ford (Rocky Mount), James Worthy (Gastonia), John Lucas (Durham), and Bob McAdoo (Greensboro). Prominent in-state blacks among the ACC's current players are Wake Forest's Rodney Rogers (Durham), UNC's Donald Williams, and N.C. State's Kevin Thompson.

Yet, for all the prominence of such players, ACC integration remains remarkably superficial and rarely discussed.

For the eleventh straight season a distinct majority of ACC basketball players are African-American, and each program sports at least one black assistant coach involved with recruiting. But there are no African-American university presidents in the nine-member league, no black athletic directors, sports information directors, or fund-raising directors.

The number of black assistant athlete directors among the league's dozens of school athletic administrators can be counted on one hand. There are no black assistant sports information directors. Duke has no blacks in positions of athletic authority except a few assistant coaches. Among the twenty-one assistant athletic directors at UNC and N.C. State, there are two African-Americans, both at Chapel Hill. The Triangle's three ACC schools list four female athletic executives.

When Gene Corrigan was hired in 1987 as the ACC's third commissioner, faculty and administrators who chose him asked no questions about either minority hiring or gender equity. Corrigan currently has a single woman or African-American, Dee Todd, among six assistant commissioners.

The only black among forty-six basketball coaches in ACC history was Bob Wade, hired at Maryland in 1985. (Maryland also was the first ACC school to use a black player—native son Billy Jones during the 1966–67 season. Two years earlier, Dean Smith, an active civil rights advocate, recruited a potential breaker of the ACC's color line. But Willie Cooper quit basketball to concentrate on his studies after playing on UNC's freshman team, and it wasn't until the 1967–68 season that Charlie Scott played for the Tar Heels.)

So there's a certain understandable tension between some at North Carolina's historically black schools and their counterparts elsewhere in the state, who appear to be skimming the cream while the black community does much of the milking.

As it happens, perhaps the most vocal among the outraged is A&T president Edward B. Fort, a long-time fighter for racial justice within NCAA councils. Fort is upset when the brawl between A&T and Morgan State, the second in three years involving the Aggies, makes national TV. His frustrations lead to an unfortunate overstatement.

"I wonder," he says, "whether ESPN would have run the tape of the fight if it occurred at Duke University. I doubt it. Black institutions have to be purer than Caesar's wife." Fort's faulty news judgment is quickly dismissed and does nothing to focus attention on larger issues.

Thanks to debate at this week's NCAA convention in Dallas, ACC athletic poobahs even now are grappling with issues of gender equity. But nothing has yet come along to spark similar discussion about racial inequality within the conference.

Some small change is occurring within the league's coaching ranks. Jim Caldwell is hired by Wake Forest, and becomes the ACC's first African-American head football coach. Several black basketball coaches are named in speculation about a possible successor to Cliff Ellis (who ultimately survives at Clemson), though there's considerable doubt such a move would be accepted in South Carolina, birthplace of the Confederacy.

A rung lower, students at ACC campuses are agitating with increasing vehemence and success for more attention to minority issues.

Within the last year students at UNC, including football players and basketball's Brian Reese and George Lynch, have pushed for creation of a freestanding black cultural center. Chancellor Paul Hardin (a Duke grad) appoints a panel to study the issue, and it quickly recommends approval of a new building.

Perhaps seeking to circumvent similar militancy, N.C. State increases its commitment, financial and otherwise, to issues important to the 12.6 percent of its student body classified as minorities.

Duke, like UNC, was the site of angry demonstrations by black students during the late sixties and continues to fall short in its institutional commitment to hiring African-American faculty. To its credit, since 1988 Duke has hired nineteen black professors. But only five remain, and black students are growing restive, including a few who came to Duke to play basketball.

Among them is Grant Hill, a member of Duke's Black Student Association. He follows what's said, done, and not done to improve attitudes and conditions at Duke, and speaks vaguely of getting involved to "make some changes" once the school's black community "find out what we're going to do."

"A lot of people don't realize that we are aware of these things going on on campus," Hill says. "Although we are black student-athletes and we might get special treatment, we realize that there are problems going on, racial problems going on on campus and in this community."

Hill is aware that filmmaker Spike Lee has criticized athletes, including Jordan, for not speaking out in support of what's perceived as "their people." Certainly Hill is more able to speak his mind without serious repercussion than most college players—he's almost certain to become an NBA millionaire in a year or two, his parents are well-off, he has a glowing public reputation, and he won't have his scholarship revoked by an angry coach at this point in his career.

But Hill is still feeling his way personally, grappling with his role-model status and the need, reinforced by former athletes like his father, Doug Collins, and former pro wide receiver Lynn Swann, to be aware of life after sport.

"People expect us to be role models and really I don't think we are role models," Hill protests. "I know that I've been placed in that position and I have to live up to it. But I tell kids they should have their mother and their father or themselves, they should be their own role models. I have my dad as a role model, but not because he played football. For other reasons. I have my mom and those people close to my family as role models. People look up to Michael Jordan and Magic Johnson, I don't think that's right. It's unfortunate, but we do that as a society and as a race."

Hill isn't sure where he's headed as a person, let alone as a role model, spokesman or freedom fighter. "I think right now I'm like most under-graduates, I don't know exactly what it is I want to be, but I know that in time I'll be able to find out what it is. I just know, I think of my father, I saw how it was tough for him to leave the sport, and you just have to be real about it.

"It's funny. If you asked, if you were to go to a school and ask kids two years ago who they'd rather be, Magic Johnson or Will Perdue, everybody would say Magic Johnson. Now if you were to say that, they would all say Will Perdue (a reserve center on the Chicago Bulls). So you have to be real about it and just understand that one day it can all be over.

"I like to think I realize that, but I know that one day I'll be putting the game down. Right now I don't really think about it. But, you know what I'm saying. It's scary. It really is."

ACONSTANT mist bathes Durham, where a Crayola sampler of tents sprouts on a small lawn in front of Card Gymnasium. Semester break is over. From now through February third, students will maintain their tent encampment just yards from Duke's basketball headquarters in the ivy-covered, granite battlements of Gothic Cameron Indoor Stadium.

Approaching Cameron, Kenney Brown overhears a female student in conversation "talking about how, after we lost, all of her friends were picking on her," he says. "She said 'we.' We do play for Duke, but we represent the students . . . when we're all in Cameron together, it does feel homey. Everybody has their cheers together. I think it's really good support. It feels like pulling an all-nighter, studying with a group."

As one freshman says to another prior to a game at Cameron while the band bays, dancing girls strut and sway, basketballs pound and fly, and the crowd buzzes: "This is why I came to Duke." National studies show otherwise, but at Duke, basketball success has had a measurably positive effect on the fortunes of the university as a whole. "The sport does wonders for the place. It provides us with the opportunity to say that academic and athletic missions can coexist well," says outgoing Duke president H. Keith H. Brodie.

Basketball success does more than that. University fund-raising nationwide has slackened in recent years, but not so at Duke. Since the Blue Devils became regulars at the Final Four in 1986, nonathletic gifts and contracts have doubled, increasing every year, standing at $127 million for fiscal 1991–92, the last year for which figures are available. During the same span, applications for undergraduate admission increased 14 percent. While no direct relationship can be proven between prosperity on the sports and academic sides, Brodie believes there's a definite link.

Income from licensing agreements also has burgeoned—sales of Duke memorabilia have become a multimillion-dollar enterprise.

Moreover, basketball's visibility makes Mike Krzyzewski the most prominent representative of the university. "I have a feeling that comes with the territory," Brodie says. "I have a feeling that if you asked somebody to name someone associated with the University of Indiana, they'd name Bob Knight. It is the case that Mike is an excellent ambassador."

Ambassadorship is on Krzyzewski's mind as he cleans up the damage from the loss to Georgia Tech and prepares for tomorrow's game at Wake Forest. Duke's oncourt welfare isn't the exclusive focus of his thinking, however. Today Krzyzewski also is attuned to his role as an ambassador for the nation's major-college coaches.

Following the Wake game, Krzyzewski will fly to Dallas, where the next morning he'll address the NCAA Convention, a rare opportunity for a coach. The topic of his remarks will be basketball's upcoming reductions in men's scholarships (from fourteen to thirteen) and coaching staffs (creating an ill-compensated "restricted earnings" position).

Krzyzewski intends to be respectful but firm. Previously, he's struck some presidents as presumptuous. But ill-informed rule-making irks him even more than reporters' ill-formed questions, and he remains fixed not only on fighting specific recommendations but on articulating a role for coaches at the decision-making level, on bridging what he calls "the moat" separating those who work daily with student-athletes from those who make the rules.

Meanwhile, on Coach K's own team, a little bit of real-world consciousness could prove quite beneficial for the walk-on, Kenney Brown.

Last season, Brown fulfilled his work-study obligations by serving as a student-manager for the women's team, enabling him to earn up to twenty-two hundred dollars toward his educational expenses. The average annual cost of room, board, tuition, and fees at Duke is just under twenty thousand dollars. Brown and his parents, who are split and putting his sister through law school, must make up the difference through loans and other earnings.

Since joining the basketball team, time demands have forced Brown to give up his work-study job in the equipment room at Card Gym. He doesn't have a car, and moves from an apartment to a dorm to be closer to Cameron, where his presence is required twenty hours per week for basketball, not to mention for other team activities.

Every one of the other eleven players on the squad is on full scholarship. That leaves unused three of Duke's allotted measure, enough to award Brown a grant-in-aid, if only for the spring semester. Yet the subject wasn't broached when the sophomore joined the team, and hasn't come up since.

"I haven't brought it up because I guess it's not my place to bring it up," says Brown, who works hard in practice and seeks nothing more than to be helpful to the team. "When I think about scholarships, I think it's up to the coach to decide. He has to evaluate my play." Such subservience is common among major-college athletes.

So is the sense, as Brown discovers, that many fans regard athletes less as people than as objects.

When Brown goes to the movies, he finds he's no longer anonymous, especially if wearing a Duke shirt. "I wear Duke stuff because that's mainly what I have," he says. "But sometimes I don't wear Duke stuff. You can get negative reactions, different looks." The responses are more intense at game sites, even hundreds of miles from the Triangle. "For example, I'm leaving the Georgia Tech game, people are giving you the finger, yelling 'Duke sucks!'" Brown recalls. "It's just different; the relationship a fan has to a fan is different than a player to a fan."

The loss at Georgia Tech is the first defeat Brown has experienced as a member of the Duke program. "I just didn't like the feeling of losing, and neither did my teammates and coaches," he reports. "People were really quiet at first. Our locker room was really quiet. I'm sure everyone in hindsight wondered what more they could have done. Coach is very positive about things, but we were very moody. Just like when we beat Oklahoma."

Recognizing those wounded feelings, and smarting himself from his team's subpar performance, Krzyzewski conducts tough, intense practices after losing to Tech. Physically, the workouts focus on correcting kinks in individual games. Mentally, in the Duke manner, much criticism is shared.

Hurley is reminded not to freeze out teammates who botch a pass or mishandle the ball, and not to let a hostile crowd affect him adversely.

Thomas Hill, who's missed two thirds of his field-goal tries over the past three games, is reminded to find his shots within the offense rather than on his own. His coaches also wonder how to get Hill back to the form he demonstrated at Maui, when he was perhaps the best player in the tournament. Teammates wonder if Hill has become too enamored of his pro prospects, to the detriment of Duke.

Then there's the more predictable dissatisfaction with Tony Lang and Cherokee Parks, who combined for nine rebounds and six points at Georgia Tech.

"We need Tony Lang to improve back to where he was at the end of last season," Gaudet says on the eve of the Atlanta trip. But Lang continues to look nothing like the tough, confident, aggressive forward who started for Duke in 1992. His malaise may in part trace to the effects of the antibiotics he's been taking for three weeks, since he was injured at Maui. For the past week he's been getting sick to his stomach.

Yet Lang struggled prior to breaking his cheekbone, so the deleterious effects of the antibiotics provide a partial explanation at best. Equally germane, according to a teammate, is the fact Lang and Parks don't work as hard as other members of the squad. At least, some of their more experienced teammates don't think they do.

Remarkably, the point is well taken by Parks. "The older guys come out and they play hard all the time," he observes. "It seems like some of us, not the veterans, we'll have our moments. We should be ready to play all the time."

Parks also is quick with *mea culpas* following the Tech defeat. "I was playing intimidated," he says. "I wasn't looking to get the ball. I made a couple of passes that just weren't there. I wasn't rebounding. I was traveling. Whatever could go wrong . . . I shot myself in the foot.

"It would be like a test you've studied all week for, and you just bomb it," Parks explains. "It's hard to understand, especially if you've been getting A's all year."

The sophomore isn't about to fret over the bad showing, though. He's heard from coaches and teammates, seen taped lowlights of his performance. "That happens. Move on," he says. "I'm not going to sit here and ponder over it."

That doesn't stop others from pondering how to move Parks. "Nobody knows what motivates him," says a member of the program. "It's not the hype. It's not the crowd. It's not the game. It's not the school."

DEAN Smith's forehead is bathed in sweat as he takes a seat at the cloth-draped table in the corner of the Smith Center press room.

During a game, if Smith perspires heavily he says it's a sign he's not totally focused on the task at hand. If, however, he's on his game, the perspiration bursts forth afterward in a palliative lather, the way an accident victim stoked by adrenaline reacts to danger when it's past.

Tonight's outcome was certainly not guaranteed, and Smith has sweated only at the last. But fifth-ranked North Carolina's 80–67 victory over eighth-ranked Georgia Tech is predictable. Bobby Cremins's teams tend to ride tides of emotion. Coming off a win over Duke, with only two days to prepare, the youthful Yellow Jackets are not apt to conjure the fire necessary to scorch the veteran Tar Heels in Chapel Hill.

Recognizing that likelihood, Cremins's game plan is to stay close, then make a run at a crucial juncture. The first part of the plan works. The Tar Heels lead for all but one first-half possession, yet are unable to sustain a double-figure advantage until the game is three-quarters gone. Tech can't find the wherewithal to close the gap, anyway.

Smith more or less anticipated this scenario a month ago. "It's more interesting who you play after a big game," he offered abstractly. "You know, a team gets up for us over the years when we were playing well. Now it's probably going to happen to Duke. Who has them after that game, it'll affect the regular season." Sure enough, Smith finds himself answering questions with a winner's ease, as he's done following three quarters of the games in which his teams have competed over half his lifetime. He doles out praise in heaps to vanquished Georgia Tech, a team he rather generously calls "excellent" and "tremendous." The coach also has plenty to say about his own 13–1 squad, which now has won five straight since the one-point loss to Michigan. "It's been remarkable what they've done," Smith comments, insisting his team "is much farther along" than he'd anticipated.

"They came out real hungry," Tech's Ivano Newbill says admiringly of UNC. "I think they came out hungry because we were coming off a win against Duke."

Everything goes smoothly until a reporter from the *Daily Tar Heel*—the school newspaper that's been an incubator for half the North Carolina press corps—asks Smith how he's kept his players from looking ahead to the Duke game on February third.

Certainly the Smith Center faithful have Duke on their minds. They cheer lustily as their heroes dispatch the conquerors of the hated Blue Devils, and when the outcome is assured and Smith clears his bench in the final seconds the chant rings forth: "We want Duke!" Much about the Smith Center atmosphere is synthetic, forced, like the air that rustles the thirteen honored, tablecloth-sized jerseys hanging from the roof. The crowd here accepts instruction from electronic message boards along two mezzanine facades: "CHEER!" or, to the accompaniment of clapping cartoon hands, "ON YOUR FEET!" But tonight's enthusiasms are uncharacteristically spontaneous and genuine, and the chant at the last reveals a startling truth: Duke basketball is now the standard of excellence, and having a team good enough to beat the Blue Devils, not the Tar Heels, is the ultimate measure of success in the Triangle, the ACC and the nation.

Smith is neither ready to concede Duke's pre-eminence, nor willing to fixate on beating the Blue Devils. "Beat Duke this year? Well, what about the other teams? I say, we beat Duke twenty-five out of the last twenty-six years. What's the big deal? Let's try to get better."

Nor will Smith countenance indulgence in long-range thinking that distracts from more immediate concerns—like the five games between now and UNC's journey to Durham.

"Where've you been?" Smith asks the student reporter. "We're trying to have a good basketball team, and our next game is at Clemson. I hope [the players] haven't even watched a Duke game yet. We can't do anything about what somebody else does, we've got to worry about ourselves and that's getting ready for Clemson. If I thought for a minute . . . we'd be a lousy team if they were looking ahead to one date."

Clemson is a tough place to play, yet there's little doubt North Carolina will make short work of the disorganized Tigers, who journeyed to Virginia tonight, fell behind 24–3 at the outset, and lost handily. Clemson's ball handling is suspect, a condition exacerbated by recent backcourt injuries.

Not a hopeful sign when facing the Tar Heels. Especially these Tar Heels.

Prior to Georgia Tech's visit, Smith frets about applying pressure to point guard Travis Best. Sure enough, Best, a strong and able ball handler, largely retains his composure. But his teammates readily succumb, starting with inconsistent Malcolm Mackey, who has six turnovers and gets in quick foul trouble. James Forrest, the ACC's leading scorer entering the game, is held to a season-low nine points.

"They rattled us," Cremins says afterward. "They took us out of our offense." The Yellow Jackets often act as though they're suffocating, caught like insects in waving webs of white and blue. More often than not, their passes out of traps seem aimed at nothing so much as escape.

"We love to see another team mess up like that or get flustered, because then we know that we're doing something well," confesses Eric Montross, who again dominates the lane. "I think when we do that, it lets us feed off of our defense and our defense creates our offense. And that's something we pride ourselves in."

For years, ACC coaches have confided pleasure at Smith's insistence on employing traps—double- and even triple-teams designed to force dribbling mishaps, bad passes, or at the least an offensive tempo quickened beyond what's comfortable for an opponent.

The strategy remained quite successful against weaker teams. But, increasingly, coaches of disciplined, athletic squads compensated smoothly when Smith's defense trapped according to ancient rote. Worse for Carolina, because recent Tar Heel teams haven't been especially quick, either, they've left yawning gaps as they raced crosscourt to cover areas left unguarded by their "scramble" and "jump-switch" tactics. This frequently produced easy scoring opportunities and contributed to double-figure losses by UNC in two of the past three seasons.

Smith's insistence on sticking with the traps despite their apparent loss in effectiveness was taken as evidence his thinking had calcified. Not surprisingly, Smith sees it differently. He points out that, if the traps are so easy to beat, you'd expect opponents to shoot better against UNC than the 43.4 percent accuracy they achieved last season or the 39.8 percent so far this year. "We're gambling a little more and still have low field-goal percentage defense," he says.

As for the Heels being too slow, he notes: "Everybody gives up something. Size presents a problem to some other teams. But there's a life's-full-of-tradeoffs type of approach. You're not going to be as quick. I could put a quicker team on the court. Apparently I don't think it's better."

This season, though, the Heels seem quicker. And they surely haven't lost any size. It's enough to leave Cremins wondering whether the ACC's balance of power is starting to shift back in Smith's direction. "It's starting to go the other way, maybe," he says. "We'll see. He's got Donald Williams, the Stackhouse kid coming in. When Duke loses Hurley and Grant Hill, will the next great player be at Duke or North Carolina?"

Now that Duke's been defeated, the questions spring up like antiaircraft fire, coming fast and furious. Most revolve around a central question: What's wrong?

The Dukies have an answer, and they intend to deliver it tonight at Wake Forest.

They also have a few private incentives. "One of the things we talked to our guys about is the two teams that have won national championships, never won in Winston-Salem," Mike Brey says.

Then there's Dave Odom's contribution to a compendium of articles for "USA Coaches Clinics." As prelude to discussing Wake's defensive philosophy, Odom cites his teams' recent success against the Blue Devils. "We've been fortunate enough to beat Duke on our home court for two straight years," Odom declares. "Yet Duke has not lost a game outside our league over the last two years. People ask me where ever [sic] I go, 'How did you beat Duke?'" Then Odom proceeds to tell how it's done.

The Blue Devils also bring to Lawrence Joel Memorial Coliseum an ongoing experiment in leadership. Mike Krzyzewski wants Bobby Hurley to unleash his feelings, to lead by the incandescence of his desire for victory. But loosening the bonds is a messy business. Hurley struggled earlier in his career to learn how to play with feelings in tow, how to be daring and aggressive without losing control. Asking him to let go opens an emotional Pandora's box, and risks experiences like the one at Georgia Tech, where mockery got under his skin.

"I'm somebody who can be a spirited player, a guy who can be emotional," Hurley explains. "It's just that with me, when I tend to be too emotional in a positive way, I tend to be emotional negatively, too. That's why in the last couple of years I've tried to be very even and let Christian do a lot of the emotional stuff." For a half tonight at Wake Forest, the fans again disconcert Hurley. But only for a half.

Duke jumps to a 13–4 lead but Wake comes back to forge a 33–33 tie at halftime. Serenaded with chants of "D-U-I! D-U-I!" ever time he goes to the foul line, Hurley, ordinarily an excellent free thrower, misses two of three attempts.

There's a twenty-minute delay at halftime while one of the basket supports is repaired. Duke players find the wait frustrating. Krzyzewski has them stretch and keeps things calm. His team has done a good job containing inside power Rodney Rogers; Tony Lang seems less intimidated by Rogers than he was by Georgia Tech's James Forrest. The guards have controlled outside threat Randolph Childress.

"Let's not lose your concentration." Krzyzewski tells the team. "The defense is coming. You're wearing them down. They only have so many guys. Childress hasn't gone off. Rodney is tired."

Just before the team retakes the court, Krzyzewski says to Hurley: "You're a great shooter. When you have your shot, look for it."

Ever coachable, Hurley obliges. What's more, the crowd's taunting suddenly proves a source of powerful motivation. It's just like times in high school when Hurley had to endure heckling because he was the smallest player on the court, because he was the coach's son. He rose to the challenge then, and in vintage fashion he does it again with devastating effect against Wake Forest.

Duke starts the second half with a 14–0 run. Half the points come from Hurley. Following a TV timeout and a few baskets, Hurley strikes again. He hits a three-pointer, strips the ball from Wake playmaker Charlie Harrison, and feeds Grant Hill for a layup. Then he steals the ball again and drives for a layup.

Hurley's basket gives Duke a 56–39 lead with 12:11 remaining. Wake already has eight turnovers in the period, with Hurley spearheading the pressure. Odom calls timeout before matters get entirely out of hand.

Hurley exchanges an exuberant high-five with Chris Collins on the way to the bench, a rare display from the senior playmaker. When he reaches the sideline, he points an imaginary gun at the Wake fans and shoots a few choice words too. Hurley is so excited, teammates and coaches report he's fairly vibrating. Krzyzewski grabs him by the hand and speaks soothing words. "My intensity and my enthusiasm just reached levels that I don't think I've ever reached before," Hurley says.

"Bobby just let everything go in the second half," Lang observes. "If you see that much emotion in Bobby, you know that everybody on the team can do it."

The lead reaches thirty before Duke coasts to an 86–59 victory. Since Joel Coliseum opened during the fall of 1989, Wake has lost here by a greater margin only once—against Duke in 1990.

Hurley finishes with twenty-five points, twenty in the second half as Duke makes 60.6 percent of its shots. Lang has a dozen points and a team-high seven rebounds. Cherokee Parks is the only starter who fails to score in double figures, and he has only three rebounds.

Duke's defense forces the Demon Deacons into twenty-five turnovers and 33.3 percent shooting. Hurley has four steals, Grant Hill four blocked shots.

"I love Bobby, I've said that," Krzyzewski says again. "How many ways can I say, 'I love you'? His grit and determination are at the top degree, and certainly his talent level is way up there. He wanted to win so badly tonight. I'm looking forward to watching the tape and kind of focusing on him for five or six minutes at a time. Because he was great tonight. He wasn't just real good, he was great."

THURSDAY, JANUARY 14

Les Robinson is hoping to speed the recovery for struggling Mark Davis and his entire team by again adjusting to circumstance. Given N.C. State's lack of depth, size, experience, and success, that means reverting to the deliberate offensive style Robinson employed nearly two decades ago at The Citadel, a style he calls "two notches" slower than the reduced pace employed against Princeton a month earlier.

"That's the only way we can survive with eight players, and I knew that, we were moving that way even with Migjen," says the coach, his words interspersed with a persistent cough he gets midway through every basketball season. "Then, when Migjen went down, I decided riding back on the bus after Davidson that's the only possible way we can survive and not just have a farce. No way we can run with anybody in the conference. So we have to really slow it down, play tempo. Basically, we just want to shorten the games."

First, though, Robinson must sell his team on the new strategy. A coach can order players to do something, herd them into line. But it makes for a happier and more efficient crew if they believe in what they're doing. That's why coaching changes often aren't successful until a new coach gets "his own" players, as Krzyzewski's early Duke experience demonstrated.

Robinson continues: "So what I did when we got back from Davidson, I said, 'I want you all, over the next twenty-four hours, I want to make you the coach for a night. You're the coach against Florida State. You're preparing the team. You are the head coach.' I said, 'I'm not asking for who's starting. Not that kind of thing, but what you would do to win the game.'

"I didn't want to paint it, give them any hints as to what I was wanting. I said, 'I want you to look at it defensively, changing defenses, offensively, the overall thing. Just use your imagination. Don't ask anybody. Your thoughts—you can't be wrong. There's no wrong in opinion. It is an opinion.'"

Sure enough, the players are nearly unanimous in suggesting a throttled-back approach. Robinson leafs through a yellow legal-sized pad and reads off synopsized versions of their remarks.

"They all said the same thing, worded differently," he concludes. "Then I came back the next day and I was happy and said: 'All right. This is what we were thinking too, the coaching staff. By coincidence we're all on the same page. That's a great start.'"

At the NCAA Convention in Dallas, Mike Krzyzewski finds that he and his audience are definitely not on the same page.

The coach and his listeners, most nonathletic types, are in fact worlds apart, ignorant of the constraints, economic and otherwise, that shape their separate realities. What the groups do share is a sense of pursuing a right-minded agenda, an attitude that always carries with it a whiff of intransigence.

Of course, given the lack of communication between university presidents and the income-oriented athletic administrators they've increasingly come to distrust, the agendas of the two groups are quite dissimilar. In many instances, they're mutually exclusive.

The assemblage at Dallas's Loews Anatole Hotel spends considerable time dealing with the severity of the economic crisis facing American higher education. This strain includes serious cuts in faculty at many schools, reductions in library spending and facility upgrading, and in some cases the elimination of whole academic departments.

Within that context, representatives of schools large and small, from all three NCAA divisions, grapple with downsizing their athletic enterprises, cutting sports, grants-in-aid, and coaching staffs. They also discuss the position of "restricted-earnings coach" as a way to increase opportunity for graduate assistants in football and hockey as well as basketball.

Then, following a speech by Kentucky athletic director C.M. Newton on the supposed complexities of coaching basketball, Krzyzewski enters the ballroom. Speaking on behalf of the National Association of Basketball

Coaches, he addresses the delegates about restoring a scholarship and retaining a third fully paid assistant.

Subsequent response to Krzyzewski's arguments includes some snickers, causing him to return to the microphone to chastise the group.

"I must say it hurts me when people joke about the number of coaches, and to hear laughing and clapping," he says. "I implore you to have a better relationship and a better understanding of what's going on with coaches. We are trustworthy. We are teachers. And we're your closest link to why we are here—the student-athlete. If you don't at least listen, that's wrong. You don't have to agree. Just listen. That's all we ask."

The view is decidedly different from the other side of the podium, where Krzyzewski's proposals are soundly defeated.

"Mike kind of barged in and he says, 'The game's going to fall apart without a fourth coach, a fourth full-time coach.' People just didn't take it seriously," says Jeffrey Orleans, executive director of the Council of Ivy Presidents, the equivalent of commissioner of the Ivy League.

Orleans says he and others are sympathetic with the need for improved communication and further involvement by coaches in NCAA decision-making. But he wonders if Krzyzewski is well served by those who advised him, since pleas for what seem to be spending increases in a time of austerity come across as "simply not credible." Also, through little fault of Krzyzewski's, a certain air of theater, even comedy, accompanies his appearance before the convention. "He gets up to leave the room at the end of his speech," recalls Orleans, "and 90 percent of the people in the front row get up and troop out like ducklings."

In the lobby, the media ducklings surround Krzyzewski, whose feathers are clearly ruffled. "I am more disheartened and disappointed today than I was after Georgia Tech beat us," he says, displaying a laudable sense of perspective.

SATURDAY, JANUARY 16

REPORTERS swarm Bobby Hurley like sweat bees around a bean picker at noontime. This is juicy stuff. Tomorrow the image of Hurley frozen in a pose of anger and exhaustion before his locker will appear in word pictures in newspapers throughout the six-state ACC region. The senior's private emotional roller coaster has left him at a jagged edge, from which he denounces the officiating in this afternoon's hard-fought 65–56 victory over Iowa.

"I've never—never in my four years here have I played a game when the officials were so bad," Hurley says of a Big Ten officiating crew that accompanies the thirteenth-ranked Hawkeyes to Cameron. "You're wondering if they had a date after the game and didn't want to blow the whistle. Maybe they were Big Ten football officials out there instead of basketball officials."

The game *is* rather physical. Bodies fly frequently when the ball goes inside. Players get clobbered and nothing is called. Of those fouls called, though, three-quarters go against Iowa.

"It was a very physical game, one of the most physical I've been involved in my career," says Iowa forward Chris Street, who will die in an Iowa City traffic accident three days after this game. "They were almost as physical as we were. They got their share of hacks in, too. But I didn't feel there were any cheap shots. It was actually a pretty clean game. You're going to find that when you play a big ballgame."

The Dukies come to the game ready to trade blow for blow.

Near the end, even-tempered Grant Hill comes close to mixing it up with Iowa's Kevin Smith, who's whistled for a flagrant foul against Hurley.

That leads to a heated exchange between Hurley and Street, one of four Hawkeyes who at various times draw verbal fire from the Duke guard.

Lang and Street engage in a brief confrontation, pleasing Duke confreres who yearn to see Lang cut a tougher figure. Lang has one of his best showings in a superheated atmosphere in which each basket is a small, hard-earned victory.

Duke takes command in the final six minutes of the nationally televised game, the killing blow a quick drive by Lang, who sweeps in from the right, soars by Iowa center Acie Earl and emphatically dunks on the bigger man. The unexpected suddenness of the move, the savage finality, cause the crowd and Duke bench to erupt in cheers. Cherokee Parks races over to hug Lang, who converts a free throw as well, putting Duke ahead by eleven with 1:51 to go.

"The thing that I admire about Duke," Iowa's coach Tom Davis says, "is that they are able to make the big plays when they need to."

Lang finishes with eleven points, five rebounds and three blocked shots. Parks holds his own inside as well, contributing eight points, eight rebounds and three blocks while keeping Earl in check.

Thomas Hill thrives, too. Fired by the occasion, he contributes one of his finest performances. He leads both teams with twenty points, makes most of his shots, and lays a defensive blanket on Iowa guard Val Barnes. Hill even blocks a shot by Earl, who's half a foot taller. And the senior tries to lead with emotion, shouting at his teammates in good moments and bad.

Hurley is equally intent upon providing leadership, though he continues to grope for a methodology compatible with his playing style. "What I think he's doing now, instead of trying to do things by himself, he's become very emotional," says Kenny Blakeney, Hurley's understudy. "The first thing he said when he got into the locker room was, I don't know what got into me tonight." Progenitor of this fiery spirit is Mike Krzyzewski. Smarting from the loss at Georgia Tech and his reception at the NCAA convention, the coach is keyed to a fever pitch for a weekend that offers home games against a pair of top twenty squads within a twenty-four-hour period. And, as Krzyzewski goes, so goes Hurley.

"The week has been a little trying I think for both of them," Mike Brey says. "And those are guys that are extremely competitive anyway. Extremely competitive. So I think they were, I'm trying to think of a word, very wired for this weekend." Few coaches and playmakers are linked as closely as Krzyzewski and Hurley. The two are much alike in their competitiveness, their willingness to work in order to succeed. They're both the products of inner-city, working class families.

"I know Mike sees a lot of himself in Bobby, and Bobby's been great here because he's been able to relate to Mike so well," Brey says. "It's been a very close bond. I agree that I think at times Bobby will really take the lead from Mike, and that can even be maybe in a negative way. If Mike's getting after an official, maybe just to make a point, maybe he's under control but he's trying to make a point. I think Bobby sometimes can get it in his mind that maybe Coach is right, maybe we are getting a raw deal here and I need to complain too since I'm captain.

"There's been times when we've said as a staff, 'Hey, let's stay off the officials because then the kids kind of take the lead from us.' And certainly Bobby, being the most fiery and emotional of the guys on the floor this year, he figures if Coach can get on them, green light for me to get on them too."

That symbiosis is manifest during the first half against Iowa.

Krzyzewski persists in challenging officials' calls, his comments liberally laced with profanity. (Probably not the best way to impress Duke's newly selected president, Nannerl Keohane, late of Wellesley, who's in attendance this afternoon and seated across from the Blue Devil bench.) The coach finally goes too far during a TV timeout with 7:34 left in the first half, and incurs a technical foul from ref Art McDonald.

Throughout the interchange Krzyzewski uses Hurley, the team captain, to convey his complaints to the officials, who wisely stand at a remove from the bench. Later the coach rues his conduct. "Instead of getting my team to adjust to the different style of play, I was trying to impact on the officiating," Krzyzewski acknowledges. "That's stupid."

The repercussions are greater than loss of concentration by Krzyzewski. The coach sets off his playmaker.

"They're both very poised," Marty Clark observes. "Lead by example. But when something irritates them, anything, they'll go off." Two minutes after the technical is called on Krzyzewski, Hurley drives to the basket, only to have his shot blocked by Earl. Hurley responds by yelling in McDonald's face. Showing remarkable restraint, the official chooses not to call a second technical.

For the remainder of the contest Hurley is attuned to the officiating. He's irate, "negative" emotions triumphant. Thus, his well-chronicled outburst and physical and emotional exhaustion following the game.

"I don't feel like moving right now," he tells reporters. "I may just sit right here until tomorrow."

Florida State's Sam Cassell puts it well, if strangely. "That's the most frustrating game I've ever been a part of since playing basketball," Cassell says after facing N.C. State's new, very-slowdown tactics. "I would have rather watched a Spanish soap opera."

Just as Les Robinson envisioned.

"This game plan will blow their minds," he says in anticipation. "What I'm hoping is that they get itchy, gamble. And we handle it, the pressure, and get some easy ones. And they shoot quickly. If we come out and don't execute it'll be a long night." The Pack runs its high-post delay, draining the 45-second shot clock to the dregs, looking for backdoor cuts, employing that Princeton patience. There's extensive use of the triangle-and-two defense installed over Christmas break.

"To beat Florida State will take a perfect game," Les Robinson says beforehand. "We'd have to play perfect." That doesn't happen. The Seminoles survive their frustration and ennui to dispatch the Wolfpack, 70–54. Guard Bob Sura takes over, scoring twenty-three points.

"It was frustrating," Curtis Marshall says. "I mean, the style worked. The players, you could see it on their faces. They were talking to each other and saying, 'Let's play basketball! Let's play basketball!'"

The Pack commits seventeen turnovers against FSU's pressure defenses, hits only three of ten from three-point range. Mark Davis misses seven of eight shots and scores two points. The slow pace and heightened importance of each possession makes the team's flaws all the more glaring.

A small rally falters near the end of the first half when Marcus Wilson blows an easy layup. Wilson otherwise has a good game, finishing second to Kevin Thompson in scoring and rebounding.

Another burst pulls N.C. State within 48–38 with 13:20 remaining. But with the Tallahassee crowd chanting "Bor-ing, bor-ing," the visitors commit four turnovers and miss five shots in their next eight possessions.

Speaking of eight, that's how many healthy players are on the Wolfpack squad. The new number nine, long jumper Neil Chance, doesn't make the trip. Doesn't make the team, as a matter of fact.

NCAA rules strictly govern situations in which a player on scholarship in a "non-revenue" sport like track moves to football or basketball, a "revenue-producing" sport (revenues are not profits; most Division I-A football programs claim to lose money). In such circumstances the grant counts against the allotment for the squad the athlete joins. But the NCAA interpretation given N.C. State is that it already has fourteen players on scholarship, so it can't take a Chance.

Fourteen? There are the eight healthy players, the three on academic suspension, the two sidelined by injuries, and Tony Robinson. Yes, a player who died before the first regular season game occupies his scholarship all year.

"Just our luck," Les Robinson says. "The one guy we picked out of twenty-eight thousand students can't play for us."

Things start ugly and stay ugly. Forty-five fouls are called and five players are disqualified. After North Carolina registers an 82–72 win at Clemson, raising its record to 14–1, both Dean Smith and Cliff Ellis send taped highlights to the ACC office detailing their complaints about the officiating.

The players are less circumspect.

Take Clemson's Sharone Wright. He enters the game as the nation's shotblocking leader and the ACC's top rebounder. Against the Tar Heels he fouls out with 15:51 remaining in the game and only five rebounds, three blocks and two points to his credit. Playing with four fouls, Wright tries to take a charge against Eric Montross. The shot succeeds, the big men fall and no foul is called. But running back upcourt, official Larry Rose whistles Wright for a technical foul due to "unsportsmanlike conduct." That also counts as Wright's fifth personal.

"I feel like I was being cheated all night, but what the heck," Wright says. "I didn't say anything. I might have made a gesture, but I didn't say anything. I blocked three of his shots"—Montross, that is—"and they didn't want me making the All-American look bad. They had to get me out of there."

Montross has his own complaints, starting with a play in the first half on which he grabs a rebound, is knocked to the floor by Clemson's Kevin Hines, yet is called for the foul. Consistent with his somewhat tongue-in-cheek practice this season, the UNC center asks official Gary Wall to explain the call.

"I really wanted to know," Montross says. "I might have learned something. I mean, maybe there is a way for me to keep from falling out of bounds when I get pushed in the back."

Focus on the fouls and thirty-nine turnovers obscures several important facts that Clemson's defensive approach reveals about the Tar Heels.

"We wanted them to pack it in and make them beat us from the outside," guard Chris Whitney says. "It wasn't a matter of us thinking they couldn't beat us from the outside. We wanted to test them. We know they like to pound the ball inside, but we wanted to make others beat us from the outside."

The Tigers employ a zone designed to clog the lane. The tactic varies when Donald Williams enters the game. His appearance causes Clemson to switch to a box-and-one, with four men guarding the lane and one assigned exclusively to Williams. Playing with a brace and protective pad on his right knee, which was bruised against Georgia Tech, Williams makes more than half his shots. But he only tries seven, laudable restraint that's reciprocated rather too well by his teammates.

"A lot of times they were backing all the way off you," Brian Reese explains. "In our offense, you don't take the first open shot. You try to do the things that we've been doing, and you're kind of, like, 'Should I shoot it? Shouldn't I shoot it?' A lot of times I think a lot of us are hesitant on our shots. We're so wide open. The defense was so sagging off it was ridiculous." Ridiculous, perhaps, but effective. The Heels never get into an offensive rhythm, never find the proper balance between caution and aggressiveness. They commit eighteen turnovers, miss three quarters of their three-pointers, and shoot 42.9 percent from the field, 34.4 percent in the first half. Not the sort of performance that pleases Dean Smith.

"He said take it like a loss," Reese reports. "That's like a loss to us personally, because we played so poorly. But, in a way, it's a good sense; we played so poorly and won."

SUNDAY, JANUARY 17

IN THE balcony seats at Cameron Indoor Stadium, in a direct line with the midcourt end of the visitors' bench, Jamie Krzyzewski, age eleven, snuggles for solace in mother Mickie's arms as Duke loses, 77–69. Other fans in the upper deck head for the exits with just under a minute left and Duke trailing Virginia by thirteen. "That's one of the worst feelings I've had," Mike Krzyzewski later says of the exodus. "I'd like to see everyone face to face and say, 'You're such a jerk for walking out.'"

On the floor-level wooden bleachers, students cheer on. But they've had minimal effect. Virginia's coaches preach that Cameron is a great, fun stage upon which to play, and neither the students' chants nor their attempts to bother free-throw shooters with the eggbeater, the hop and whoop, the moaning sea grass, or the sudden shout, deter the visitors from maintaining their poise.

On bleachers near Duke's bench, parents of virtually every player on the squad make outward peace with disappointment while their sons choke down defeat. Among the moms and dads is a trio of fathers prominent in athletics—Calvin Hill, Doug Collins, and high-school basketball coach Bob Hurley, his St. Anthony's program a perennial national power.

Calvin Hill, who rarely claps, cheers or changes expression, watches son Grant's shots repeatedly rim out as he struggles against similarly sized Cornel Parker, a fine defender. The elder Hill sees Hurley recognize a mismatch at a key juncture late in the game and get the ball to Grant in excellent scoring position, only to have his son slip, fall painfully on his elbow, and get called for traveling. Hill chews gum to the last, his thick, dark mustache pumping rhythmically with each bite, a battered blue baseball cap pulled low over his eyes.

Bob Hurley's St. Anthony's High School team is 11–0 and coming off two victories in two nights despite the graduation of Rodrick Rhodes, Kentucky's impressive freshman. But tonight Hurley stands and grimaces, a grayed mirror of his elder son. Bobby's shot is not falling; his passes are just a tad off, and he can't contain forays to the basket by Virginia guards Cory Alexander and Doug Smith. The senior's emotions again seem at the edge of control, his personal failures shaping his demeanor, short-circuiting the air of leadership he's cultivating.

Doug Collins—the second former pro player and coach to send his son to play for Krzyzewski, after Bob Ferry sent Danny—concentrates on being supportive. He's just seen Chris play a modest role in the first half, then force needlessly off-balance jumpers like his older teammates in a futile foul-and-fire catch-up run at the end.

Watching his son in action, Collins confesses "is great joy, and yet at the same time your stomach is in knots because all you can do is sit back and watch. You try to enjoy it. It's hard."

Also in the seats at Cameron are player-agent David Falk and two associates sporting the dark-shirt, no-tie, sportjacket look. They've come to meet Bob Hurley, Sr., but decide to write off the trip, reluctant to approach on so sour an occasion.

Along press row, opposite the Virginia bench, sit John Feinstein and Bill Brill, writers who cover the Blue Devils while unabashedly bleeding their alma mater's royal blue. Rare for both, they will not chirp much in the press room today.

On the court, as the final buzzer sounds Virginia's Doug Smith moves happily with the ball, shouting: "Yes! Yes! Yes!" Nearby, orange-clad teammates Parker and Ted Jeffries leap to exchange very high fives.

Eleventh win secured, the Cavaliers remain the only undefeated team in Division I. They own the nation's longest winning streak, going back to a five-game march to the 1992 NIT title. Having beaten Duke on ESPN, U.Va. is assured its first top-ten ranking in recent memory.

It's also Virginia's first victory at Cameron since the 1982–83 season, a year after coach Jeff Jones concluded his playing career.

This is all very strange to the Dukies. Last Sunday at Georgia Tech they saw a twenty-three-game winning streak snapped. Today a thirty-six-game home court win streak ends, a run equaled in ACC history only by N.C. State's great David Thompson-led teams of 1973–75.

For all but two Blue Devils, this is the first time they've experienced defeat at Cameron.

"It seemed very empty," says Marty Clark, a junior. "It wasn't like anything I've ever, ever experienced. Not that we didn't see it coming in the back of our minds. We're not the teams of last year and the year before. We're still in the process of finding out about our team, especially in the big games."

The loss prevents Duke from regaining the top spot in the polls, since both number-one Kentucky and number-two Michigan lost earlier in the week. By now, though, such acclamation is no big deal. More important today is showing Duke's trademark toughness. And it's not quite there.

"I was ashamed," Krzyzewski confides. "We didn't play tired. We didn't execute tired."

The players remain uncertain how to react and where to turn in difficult circumstances. "It's agonizing," Clark says. "Coach used the analogy 'big brother' the other day. We don't have a big brother on this team, no one who assumed the role. I just think Christian did it so well, and played so well. Who knows if anyone can do that?"

The Blue Devils simply look leg-weary playing a second defense-oriented opponent within a twenty-four-hour span. They fumble passes they'd normally dart to grab. Their jumpers repeatedly fall short.

"Their legs look like mine felt," says sympathetic N.C. State scout Ed Conroy. Due to the Wolfpack's reduced numbers, the twenty-five-year-old assistant has been forced to participate in defensive drills at practice.

Virginia's tenacity, combined with Duke's fatigue, brings out the worst in the stressed Blue Devils, who only sporadically have the patience to run their half-court offense. "The team that deserved to win, won," says Krzyzewski, who's so unaccustomed to taking the loser's turn in the Cameron press room he makes a premature trip to the door, only to return moments later.

Duke's only significant bench contributor is Clark. A moderately-rated recruit with moderate talent, Clark has lingered in other people's shadows his entire career. Now the six-foot-six wing is eager to make the most of his chance.

"Guys have told me to step up," says the player nicknamed "Charlie" by teammates. "You can tell that in practices and games. It's what you want most." Clark's coaches fret about his commitment to defense, and dislike how quickly he loses confidence if he misses his first shot. But Clark plays well offensively against Virginia, contributing thirteen points, third-best on the team, before fouling out near the end.

No other Blue Devil has a good offensive showing. Exactly as happened in Atlanta, Hurley and Thomas Hill combine to make a measly nine of thirty field-goal attempts. They miss the vast majority of their three-pointers. The team again hits less than 40 percent from the field.

Krzyzewski points out that, as in Atlanta, Hurley's attempts to lift Duke on the strength of his scoring lead him and the team astray. "He knows that it's not me being selfish, it's me trying to win," Hurley explains. "I just think that I need to get back to my role and what I do really well. My first and greatest skill is to give people the ball, get people involved. My shots has always been a secondary thing. It's been too much of the focus for me the last week."

Yet failure, too, is part of Krzyzewski's winning formula. During his first ten years Duke finished atop the ACC regular-season standings just once, in 1986, and won the ACC Tournament twice (1986 and 1988). Early on, the Blue Devils simply weren't good enough. More recently, Krzyzewski's teams have been geared for the longer haul, for the NCAAs, for peaking on spring's doorstep.

Duke's success the past two years, when it was perhaps the strongest team in ACC history with Christian Laettner, Brian Davis and most of the current crew, obscures a curious fact. Prior to 1991, the Blue Devils routinely experienced late-season stumbles—losing three of their last four regular-season games in 1990, two of the last three in 1989, three of the last four in 1988, and two of the last three in 1987. They nonetheless reached the Final Four in all but one of those years (1987).

Krzyzewski at times appears to court defeat, willingly pausing from ACC play to visit dangerous locales such as Oklahoma's Noble Center, Arizona's McKale Center, Michigan's Crisler Arena, UCLA's Pauley Pavilion. More to the point, like the game's senior coaching giants, Dean Smith and Bob Knight, the man whom friends call "The Captain" recognizes the value of difficult nonconference play in toughening a squad to face any circumstance.

What's more, Krzyzewski uses games with unfamiliar opponents to challenge his own judgments about the Blue Devils. He particularly wants to see how rivals break down Duke's weaknesses and attack them. Usually he schedules such games late in the season. This year they've been front loaded.

Krzyzewski also prefers to build in a quick turnaround weekend such as this, though playing a pair of veteran, defense-oriented opponents like

Iowa and Virginia on consecutive afternoons may have been a bit much. Duke trails throughout against the Cavaliers; two years had passed since that happened in any game. (Virginia was the winner on that occasion too, though on its court.)

"Basically, out of the back-to-back games, I wanted to put our team in a situation where we would improve," Krzyzewski says. "And my whole goal is to improve. We're not an old team. We have a lot of youth on our team, especially in tough situations. This was a tough situation this weekend.

"And hopefully we learned, one, that we will play hard all the time, and two, some of our needs. We'll evaluate what those needs are. One of them is more mental toughness in running a half-court offense. It takes that mental toughness to do that. I think it showed today and parts of yesterday that we don't have that. That doesn't mean we won't, but we didn't have it today."

Krzyzewski is determined to maintain that long, dispassionate view in public. Questioners' gentle probes won't elicit signs of the disappointment and distress he feels.

"I think we can improve on just about everything," he offers. "I would hope I don't have to remind you our team has played well this season. So, I mean, there are a lot of good things our team has done. I'm not down on my team. I put them in a difficult situation against two outstanding teams and we fell short. I felt going into the weekend we were capable of winning two or losing two. Not that we're happy losing today. But we understand the big picture. It's January seventeenth. There's a long time to go, a lot of development to go."

Back at his house, Krzyzewski also plays the realist with his assistants as the foursome reviews tape and discusses the team.

"We don't want to do anything drastic here," Krzyzewski says. "We've got to look to use the bench more, to get Bobby a little more rest so he doesn't play as many minutes, and Grant. That's what we've got to do, now how do we do it and who do we do it with?"

WEDNESDAY, JANUARY 20

JEFF Jones has known North Carolina basketball firsthand for fifteen years, first as a guard, then as an assistant coach, and, for the past three seasons, as head coach at the University of Virginia.

Jones comes away from this year's meeting quite impressed with the latest edition in the Dean Smith basketball anthology. "North Carolina is a very good team," he says after Virginia is overwhelmed 80–58. "If they play aggressively like they did, they're as good overall as any Carolina team I can remember."

North Carolina is expected to win handily, the point spread is in the mid-teens. Yet there's reason to wonder just how good this UNC ballclub is. The Tar Heels have played fifteen games, just more than half their regular season quota, and their only true test has come against Michigan, which beat them.

Since returning from Hawaii, UNC has played three of five games at home. Cornell was a mismatch. A young Maryland team making its first road trip produced a scare for a single, brief stretch early in the second half. Georgia Tech arrived fresh from overcoming Duke and was emotionally spent, proof of its "flatness" underlined by a subsequent home defeat at the hands of John Cresse's College of Charleston club.

As for UNC's road trips, they've been to the home courts of ACC weaklings—N.C. State, on the very night it had two starters suspended for academic reasons, and Clemson, beset by its own little soap opera of misfortune, miserable play, and mismanagement that's recently earned a two-year NCAA probation. The Clemson game wasn't exactly an unmitigated triumph, either, as Smith scoldingly reminds his players.

Virginia may finally present a serious challenge. The Cavaliers rank higher in the polls than at any time in a decade and are fresh from a confidence-boosting win at Cameron.

The Tar Heels miss six of their first eight shots and Virginia slogs to a 6–5 lead.

Then the Carolina shuffle begins, igniting a thirteen-point outburst that puts the Heels ahead to stay.

This North Carolina squad, not Alabama, should be nicknamed the Tide. The Heels come at you in waves, a substitution per minute, nine players receiving quality minutes, the team constantly changing looks, changing bodies, changing styles, changing defenses. "They wear you down," says Virginia assistant Tom Perrin. "And the talent level doesn't drop when they go to the bench."

Barely three minutes into the game, Smith replaces Reese with Pat Sullivan, junior for junior, six-foot-eight for six-six, a technically superior performer replacing a more creative but uneven one. Half a minute later, Smith reverses the flow by introducing Donald Williams—creative, a physical defender, a feared outside shooter—in place of Henrik Rodl, a taller, slower senior who makes few mistakes.

Forty-five seconds after that, even as television demands its first time-out, here comes Kevin Salvadori to bump Eric Montross from the lineup. The trade is seven-footer for seven-footer, resoluteness replaced with mobility and UNC's best per-minute shot blocker since the 1986 season.

Sullivan starts the 13–0 run with a three-pointer from the top of the key. Montross replaces George Lynch, giving Carolina a towering advantage inside.

Williams scores on a drive, is fouled and makes the free throw. Rodl replaces starting playmaker Derrick Phelps.

With Montross drawing most of the defensive attention, Salvadori scores consecutive baskets on a dunk and a turnaround jumper. Between them, the junior giants block eleven shots on the night, get eighteen rebounds and score twenty-five points.

Rodl drives the lane and makes a layup. Reese replaces Sullivan, Lynch takes Salvadori's place inside, Phelps comes in for Williams. Almost magically, the starters all are back on the floor.

Reese goes inside, is fouled and makes one of two free throws to push UNC's lead to 18–6 at the 11:51 mark. Ten points in the run have come from bench players.

Here the Tar Heels stumble, though, scoring once in seven possessions while Virginia enjoys a 10–2 rally. Typically, the Dean Dome crowd, which cheers lustily when things go well, grows quiet when they do not. This doesn't change despite the peppy posturings of seventeen cheerleaders and exhortations from the message boards until the Heels again punch ahead, Lynch working inside while Rodl hits consecutive three-pointers to rebuild a 30–18 advantage.

Again, prosperity is short-lived, and Virginia closes within 32–25 at halftime.

The first half is almost a replay of Clemson. The Heels shoot just 39.4 percent from the floor. Montross takes three shots, scoring just before halftime for his only points. Phelps misses four shots and fails to record an assist.

"We were very frustrated in the first half," Dean Smith says. Asked later what particularly bothered him, he snaps, "Next question." Listeners assume he's irritated at the officiating.

Smith's second-half solution to his team's offensive constipation is predictable. "We just decided to force-feed Eric inside." For a time, the smaller Cavs cope by sagging into the lane. Gradually they lose control of the boards, start fouling. They also fall prey to Carolina's traps; they finish with eighteen turnovers, nine in each half.

A 10–0 outburst midway through the second period puts the game out of reach. UNC coasts the rest of the way. Long before the game ends, fans pour from the building. The booster section is half empty by the final buzzer. "That's Dean's eleventh national title in January," John Feinstein declares in the press room when it's over.

Carolina hits nearly 57 percent of its shots in the second half and outrebounds Virginia almost two to one. Five Heels finish in double figures. Montross and Lynch have a dozen points each. Lynch also has eleven rebounds, six on offense. Donald Williams misses seven of eight shots but has five assists.

"Their intensity tonight was unbelievable," says Virginia assistant Dennis Wolff. "Again, some of it I think was us, our own errors. And other teams too—we watched the tape of Georgia Tech and it was the same thing."

Someone asks Wolff why the Cavs, particularly Cornel Parker (six turnovers), persist in dribbling to spots on the court where Carolina loves to trap. "Rest assured, for like three days we told them not to take the ball into the corner, and the fucking thing ended up in the corner. Why is that? Could you tell me?"

Postgame, Smith can't resist commenting on the performance of several Cavalier reserves. "We taught Doug Smith well," he says of tonight's leading scorer for Virginia. "He was in my camp for four years. Chris Havlicek, we didn't teach him so well. He was in my camp." Havlicek, son of Hall of Famer John Havlicek, fails to score, missing two field-goal tries and two free throw attempts.

Down the carpeted hallway in the UNC locker room, which will close to the media twenty minutes after Smith emerged for this press conference, reporters now ask what Dick Vitale asked courtside observers a month ago in Ohio: Why does North Carolina seem so much quicker than last year with virtually the same players?

Tonight Phelps gives his version of The Answer. "I think people are just more experienced," he says, words rolling fast-forward, propelled still by the evening's ebbing emotion. "I think that's the main focus out there. I think with Hubert last year, everybody always looked to him. This year I think everybody is trying to combine everybody's game, go all around together, because that gives us a better chance."

Nearby, Montross calmly denounces the Cavs' defensive tactics. "Virginia's game is to hit you as you come down the floor, hold you as you cut," he says.

"I can remember, playing and coaching, it seems like there's always comments about how Virginia plays defense," says Jones, who arrived at Charlottesville in 1978. Jones no more likes the charge now than he did when he first heard it. "People don't think of North Carolina as being physical. They just punish you. People say we're physical, and we try to be. But they're just as physical."

Jones readily notes the current Heels are an order of magnitude stronger than his squad. Still, he wonders if they're strong enough. "Do they have somebody like Jordan or Al Wood before him in that intermediate range?" Jones asks. "If the outside shot isn't going and the other team is packing it in the way we did, who can have a big night? Brian Reese, I think, can be that kind of player." So do the folks at Carolina. Yet tonight is a nadir for Reese, who plays only eighteen minutes, despite starting.

The season thus far has been a huge disappointment for the Brooklyn native, a wonderfully versatile midrange performer. Reese has an explosive first step, a deceptive stride that makes him appear to glide across the floor, and a good shooting touch. He also wants to improve, and has ever since he discovered during a pickup game at age thirteen that he could dunk.

He came on well enough last season to lead Smith to predict he'd become "an excellent basketball player." Encouraged, Reese stayed in Chapel Hill much of the summer, working on his game with buddies Phelps and Williams. It was quite a sacrifice, considering the resident of the Castle Hill projects in The Bronx finds Chapel Hill a social backwater.

Then, during the second preseason practice in November, Reese slipped on a wet spot, did a split, and pulled a leg muscle. After that came a sprained ankle and a hyperextended pinky on his right (shooting) hand. Reese's first two years, he lacked stamina. The leg injuries only exacerbate the problem.

"He's in bad shape," Smith says. "When he's sitting out of practice, it's hard to get better."

Reese often speaks of a desire to get better. An avid baseball player, he came to basketball only when prevailed upon to participate in a neighborhood game. He recalls he "got destroyed," which served as an impetus to master the game. "There's always room for improvement," he says. "I never was the person, the type of guy that'd be like, 'Yeah, yeah, I could dunk. I'm this. I got All-American.' You come to my house, I've got so many trophies it's ridiculous. I've got over one hundred seventy trophies or something, and plaques all over the house."

Reese became so promising a prospect, Bobby Cremins made him the singular object of Georgia Tech's recruiting attentions in the fall of 1990, hoping to pair him in the backcourt with Kenny Anderson. Cremins's preference for Reese caused him to quit recruiting Duke's Grant Hill and Arizona's Khalid Reeves, Phelps's high school teammate.

Reese made a verbal commitment to Tech, then changed his mind after attending a North Carolina practice. (Recruits sit courtside, not in the upper deck.) The youngster was impressed by the businesslike atmosphere of the workout. "Everybody was working so hard, it was like everybody's together, grabbing each other up," Reese says.

The choice of schools also enabled Reese, the youngest of five boys and five girls, to stay close to a brother in Roanoke Rapids, N.C.

From the first, though, Reese discovered he needed a lot more improvement than he'd anticipated. Usually he can discuss the subject calmly, with studious appreciation.

"You do tend to get a lot of bad habits in high school," he said during such a moment earlier this season. "Like I said, I never hardly ran back on defense, things like that. You don't always play hard. You come here, you learn those things.

"I think he [Smith] breaks you down in that aspect. You know, first thing he wants you to do: Always be competitive. Always work hard. Always run and try to do the best you can while you're out there. So that's one of the things he teaches you before he teaches you any type of skill.

"Next thing is basically, try to learn everything before you go out there, and just show him that you have. Things like that. I mean, he breaks you down in that aspect. He doesn't try to take nothing away from you that you have. You know, like your abilities. Like my abilities, penetrating and dishing and things like that." Reese reports a third key component of Smith's regimen. "He tries to build you up mentally also, because he always says basketball is a mental game. So that's all he's trying to do, prepare you and make you mentally strong."

Recently, though, that oversight and mental prompting have become a bit onerous because Reese is not entirely in his coach's good graces. "Anything you do, good and bad, whatever it may be, anything you do in the game, they've got it all on tape," Reese says, irritation clear in his voice. "You're going to see everything we did—from running on the court slow to running off the court slow, you'll see it."

Clearly, what's shown up lately on tape hasn't entirely pleased the coaches. Reese is anxious to play for more extended periods, and Smith keeps telling him he's not ready.

When will he be ready? Reese is asked.

"It all depends on what Coach says," he replies a bit sullenly. "Whatever he says. If I'm out of condition, I'm out of condition." And how will Reese know when he's in condition? "I guess he'll tell me when I'm in condition," he replies. "I'm working hard. I can't do but so much in practice."

Even when he does play, Reese hasn't been passing muster.

"We have to get Reese playing better," Smith says. "Basically we have to get him more aggressive."

Prior to last week's Georgia Tech game, Smith confided a key area of concern was Reese's work on the boards. "We'll see how he rebounds tonight," the coach said. "I worked with him yesterday, boxing out better."

Reese played twenty minutes and had a single rebound.

The next game, at Clemson, he played twenty-five minutes and had zero rebounds.

Tonight Reese plays good defense and scores ten points, but has only three rebounds, two on offense. His ball handling also has been questioned; against Virginia he has four turnovers and two assists.

THURSDAY, JANUARY 21

NC. STATE'S first mistake is the route it follows to reach Durham.

Before his death in 1965, Everett Case arranged to be buried in a cemetery overlooking U.S. Highway 70, which in those days was the main thoroughfare spanning the twenty-one miles between Raleigh and Durham. The longtime Wolfpack coach further directed that his head be laid to rest facing the road so he could forever "wave to the team when it goes to Durham to play Duke."

But on this rainy night the Pack gets a late start from Reynolds Coliseum and Les Robinson pays scant attention to the route. "It was so dark out there, I don't even know where we were," he says. "We had so many things going on."

Whichever way the bus driver chose to travel, it was not on Highway 70.

N.C. State's second mistake is in showing up in Durham at all. This certainly is not a propitious moment to face the Blue Devils, who've spent days chastising themselves and each other for the loss to Virginia and the way they've been playing.

Bobby Hurley is particularly distressed by the mortal breath of defeat, largely absent from his oncourt life until the past two weeks. "I didn't even want to go out to eat with my family after the game," he says of the Virginia loss. "I was embarrassed . . . it's like you want someone to slap you across the face a couple of times and get you going."

There's only one person in the program who responds as bitterly to defeat, Hurley says. "I think me and Coach K are nearly on the same page as far as hating to lose."

Krzyzewski gives the team a day off following the Virginia loss, then works it hard in subsequent practices and meetings. Almost every player is seriously critiqued, and practices are spirited, with bodies colliding, balls slammed and tables kicked in anger.

"Just concentrate on getting better, that's all I'm asking for," Krzyzewski tells his team. "We have blinders on. We're not worried about anybody else."

The Dukies work hard. Everyone is told to concentrate on rebounding, and Cherokee Parks is given explicit orders to look for his shot when fed the ball in the low post.

After a few days of this, the Blue Devils are predictably eager to dismantle an opponent. "I'd hate to be playing Duke next," UNC sports information director Rick Brewer notes idly. "Who are they playing next, anyway?"

Who else but star-crossed N.C. State?

"We kind of expected it; we kind of expected Virginia to win the way our luck has been going," Pack point guard Curtis Marshall says. "We're catching Duke at a bad time, I guess. But it could be a good time, if they're not playing like Duke. Hopefully they won't come out of their slump on us."

N.C. State intends to stick with the slowdown style that so annoyed Florida State. Marshall admits it would be "the biggest upset in college basketball" if his team beat Duke. But his read on the game is that the Pack has what it takes to defy convention: "We're just going in, nothing to lose. No one expects us to win except us. No one thinks we have a shot. We're just going to go in and play, try to relax, and play basketball. I think that the big key is to survive the first five, six, seven minutes, because they're going to try to come out strong. They're going to try to show everybody they're still Duke; they're still the top team in the nation."

Robinson, the progenitor of N.C. State's wishful thinking, says: "I think we will survive the first five, six, seven minutes. I'm confident of that. Because of our style. I'm more confident than I was last year." Of course, the previous year N.C. State lost at Duke by thirty-five.

The way Robinson sees things, or wants to, the pressure is on Duke. "For people not to say they've fallen off, they've got to beat us badly," he says. "They want to win big. They're mad and they want to win big. If we can hang in there, they may think, 'If we can't win this game!' . . . they can't have a lot of respect for us."

Meanwhile State's players speculate appreciatively about the greeting they'll receive from the Duke students. Marshall guesses "they're going to try to joke us about academics" and about losing games. "They're going to say something like, 'UNC-W, they're real tough.'"

In fact, as the teams gather for the opening tap the Dukies raise the chant "Start the bus! Start the bus!" standard for the moment a game is in the bag. Then they launch into a favorite that dates back at least to Case's day: "If you can't go to college, go to State!"

The Wolfpack controls the jump and gets the ball to Mark Davis, who's fouled by Tony Lang as he drives the lane. Les Robinson removes his jacket (under which he's not wearing his customary red sweater), rubs his face, and loosens his tie. Davis steps to the foul line.

The game is seventeen seconds old. N.C. State has peaked. Davis misses both free throws. (The Pack will make seven of fifteen on the night.)

Parks hits a jumper to open the scoring for Duke.

The game is not yet three minutes old when Robinson calls timeout, already trailing 9–0.

Duke's total reaches thirteen before State scores. Eight minutes into the game, Duke leads 21–3. "Put them all in!" the students chant, eyeing the three reserves on the State bench.

The disparity reaches 32–9 and the fans chant, "Thomas has got eleven, State's got nine!" They yell "Double digits!" when Davis hits a follow shot to make the score 38–11.

At halftime Duke leads 55–20. "This is humiliating," says a member of the modest contingent of spouses and athletic department personnel seated behind the N.C. State bench. Most members of the group wear red—on their ties, sweaters, jackets, and faces.

Things are little better inside State's locker room. "They were whipped puppies at halftime," Robinson says of his players.

Once again, Robinson appeals to the team's athletic pride to spark its competitiveness. Once again, that's a good button to push.

The teams play to a standstill in the second half. When the game officially ends, the score is 92–56.

Robinson considers it his worst humiliation as a coach since 1983, when his team at The Citadel played another defending national champion. North Carolina won that game 81–36, led by Michael Jordan and Sam Perkins.

SUNDAY, JANUARY 24

THE scoreboard makes it a four-point play, wishful thinking. The actual score, 89–88, is sufficient. The three-pointer that Byron Wells makes, from in front of the Florida State bench, in fact from a spot near where the reserve forward normally sits and watches others play, is good enough to sink Duke for the third consecutive Sunday.

Duke has one more chance after Wells's shot, calling timeout with 2.7 seconds remaining in overtime and the length of the court to travel. Though the situation seems hopeless, the Blue Devils are buoyed by memory of Christian Laettner's score in similar straits to defeat Kentucky in last year's NCAA East Regional final.

The circumstances differ in several notable respects, however. This time the inbounds pass is guarded. Grant Hill has fouled out, so Tony Lang makes the throw. And the intended receiver is not Laettner but Bobby Hurley, stationed near midcourt where he can call timeout, make a pass, or quickly dribble toward the top of the key for a long shot.

Lang's toss is tipped and FSU's Charlie Ward intercepts to end the threat. Asked after the game to detail his strategy, Krzyzewski crosses himself and makes a joke about putting through a quick call to Minnesota and Laettner.

Game's end brings a rush of fans onto the court, as well as a shower of precut confetti that exemplifies the staged feel of the afternoon's proceedings at the Tallahassee–Leon County Civic Center.

Interest in basketball is still a sometime thing in this small-townish state capital hard by the Georgia border. "Yes, we are still a football school, and that's never going to change," basketball coach Pat Kennedy says.

Durham's population is about the same as Tallahassee's 124,773. But Duke's hometown has a far more urban flavor. Force-fed by Reagan-era growth and undergirded by the national industries and institutes at Research Triangle Park, Durham sits within a far larger metropolitan area. That urbanized feel helps Duke recruit in every area from basketball to brains to bucks, but also has overwhelmed and virtually banished the agriculturally oriented culture that built Durham and Duke University.

In contrast, Tallahassee, despite its status as the capital of the nation's fifth most populous state, has largely eluded the stampede of Florida's despoliation. Once you escape the clotted inner-city traffic, a drive quickly takes you out of town to palmettos, pastures, and natural springs; to swamps, rivers, and bays where cypress, alligator, duck, anhinga, and manatee reside; into quiet communities like Sopchoppy, Panacea, and Carabelle, and to uncluttered vistas of the great Gulf of Mexico.

From his first day, FSU's Coach Kennedy, who'd spent years with Jim Valvano before succeeding him as head coach at Iona College in New York, accepted the need for glitz as well as excellence in order to build interest in what was a near-moribund program. That approach has remained a constant. Even as Duke pulls into town on a balmy afternoon, billboards around Tallahassee extol Kennedy's crew. "Welcome to Seminole Air," reads one sign along Capital Circle. "Direct Flights to the Sweet 16 and Points Beyond."

Kennedy's program acquired additional sparkle when the school entered the ACC for the '92 season, bringing to town heavyweights Duke and North Carolina. "We're more legitimate as a basketball program, being in the ACC," Kennedy says. "We're not the best basketball job in the ACC, obviously, but we're still ACC. . . . And that's made all the difference for me."

Fans took notice too.

Duke's 1992 arrival occasioned the largest crowd in Florida State basketball history. This year's game attracts the second-largest crowd ever—13,333—and, according to FSU ticket manager John Sheffield, is as tough a ticket to acquire as any football game with Florida or Miami.

Still, the game has more the air of a concert than an ACC contest. Students at other league schools may camp out for days to get into big games; FSU's undergrads make news by showing up several hours prior to the Duke game. If they're of age, students join other fans in stoking up on beer, a beverage not sold in ACC arenas as a matter of league policy. (This became an issue when FSU joined the conference, but quickly got buried when decision-makers realized the financial impact of banning beer sales at the public facility.) And, for all the excitement, it's not Florida State the fans come to see, as Jim Valvano points out. "People come to see Duke play," says Valvano, in town to do color commentary on ABC's telecast of the game. "You've finally made it when people come to see you play, not the opponent."

Valvano is wan and weak and in constant pain that makes it difficult to stand upright. He's still trying to do two games per week, as well as go to ESPN headquarters, in Connecticut, Monday through Wednesday. But his white blood cell count has shot up, and he's receiving debilitating chemotherapy more frequently. Fresh from six hours of treatment at Duke Medical Center, Valvano arrives in Tallahassee the day before the game and drags himself to both teams' practices.

"He's afraid to lay down, so he's pursuing this vigorously," a longtime friend says of Valvano's TV career. "He's doing a great job, but he's failing fast."

Prior to the telecast a steady stream of reporters, autograph seekers, and well-wishers approach Valvano as he sits courtside studying notes and marshaling his energies. He talks about his illness if asked, though he keeps specifics to himself. "When you're facing what I'm facing, there's two ways to handle it," Valvano explains. "And those of you who know me know there's one option I won't choose. That's to go into a corner and bemoan my fate." Instead he's joined the fight to fund more cancer research.

TV's presence feeds the circuslike atmosphere, as does the lingering smell of elephants from a recently departed show. There are other special touches for the occasion—new gold uniforms donated by FSU alum and former running back Burt Reynolds, whose name also graces a dorm near the football stadium; the halftime ceremony in which coach Bobby Bowden and the entire football team are paraded onto the court to delirious applause to receive their Orange Bowl trophy; and the pregame press conference announcing a Fred Flintstone lithograph honoring the football team's first ACC title.

The game itself possesses an intense, frenzied, athletic pace that's a bit of a tonic for the Blue Devils, who play hard and sometimes well. Once in each half Duke builds double-digit leads. Both at the end of regulation play and at the end of overtime, Duke has the ball when a single score will decide the outcome.

This showdown has come against a team Kennedy believes is his best in seven years at Tallahassee, better than last year's squad that surprised the ACC with six road victories and a Sweet Sixteen finish. Florida State boasts a gaggle of players with pro potential, from postman Rodney Dobard to swing forward Doug Edwards to guards Sam Cassell and Bob Sura.

Charlie Ward, the point guard, also is the starting quarterback on the football team, and a leading candidate for the 1993 Heisman Trophy. Strong and exceedingly quick, Ward came to Florida State on a football scholarship from nearby Thomasville. He walked onto the basketball team in 1990 after several years away from the game, and quickly transformed FSU into the Metro Conference champion. Ward again ran the show for Florida State during the '92 season. This season he resumes basketball following the Orange Bowl, and almost instantly has a selfish, struggling group working in unison.

Ward has a dozen steals in five games prior to facing Duke, and a stunning ratio of thirty assists to seven turnovers. Against the Blue Devils he has five steals, the last coming against Grant Hill with the score tied and time running out in regulation play. "I wished I had eyes in the back of my head sometimes—he's that quick," says Duke's Bobby Hurley.

Playing all forty-five minutes, Hurley has twenty-two points, five assists and three steals. But he also has four turnovers, the last coming with about fifteen seconds remaining in overtime and Duke trying to enlarge a two-point lead.

On the play, Duke runs down the shot clock and Hurley gets into the lane. He has an open shot, but once airborne decides to pass. Neither Tony Long nor Cherokee Parks steps out to make himself available for a dish-off, and Hurley throws the ball into heavy traffic, where his pass is intercepted.

Florida State calls timeout and sets up a play to go for the win. Two weeks earlier, in an overtime triumph at Wake Forest, Kennedy put the ball in Cassell's hands at the top of the key in similar circumstances and let him create. Wake tried to stop him with one man, couldn't, and lost the game. Afterward Wake coach Dave Odom says he should have double-teamed, forcing Cassell to pass.

That's Duke's intention too. Krzyzewski's modus operandi, after all, is to attack at both ends of the court. One of the most damning things he can say to a player is that he's "playing safe." In this case, Duke's aggressiveness makes its actions predictable. FSU expects a double-team on Cassell. "Look pass first," Kennedy tells his premier one-on-one player. "If everyone's covered, then you have to take it like you did in the Wake game."

Play resumes with fifteen seconds left. Hurley checks Cassell's penetration. Cherokee Parks comes up to help, and Wells, left momentarily alone, pops out to the corner. Cassell gets the ball to Wells, a fifth-year senior, who lets fly as the six-foot-eleven Parks leaps at him. "He only got it off by about two inches," Kennedy says.

The shot hits the rim, bounces high, hits the backboard, returns to the rim, perches, and falls through the net.

Kennedy proclaims it his biggest win at FSU.

Krzyzewski calls it "a great basketball game" and casts a resolutely positive light on the proceedings. "We're disappointed in the loss," he says after his team drops to 13–3. "I'm not disappointed in effort and competitiveness. I thought it was a step up for us."

A Florida reporter makes reference to Florida State's lack of standing in the polls. "The only Pole I pay attention to is my mother," Krzyzewski says to general laughter.

His last words before departing the press room echo what he said the previous week: "I'm pleased with the way we played. I'm not pleased we lost. It's important to keep things in perspective, that this is January 24."

There are definite signs of improvement. Grant Hill is a force for the second straight time. Defensively, he does a fine job against FSU shooters Cassell and Sura and, later, Edwards. Meanwhile he scores twenty-five points, has eight rebounds, four steals, and four assists without a turnover.

Duke's inside game shows improvement too. Parks has a dozen rebounds, all but one on defense, fourteen points, and five blocked shots. An aggressive Tony Lang has ten points and eight rebounds. Marty Clark comes off the bench to score ten points and record three assists.

But there's also a dark side, only some of which is publicly visible.

This is a game that recent Duke teams, certainly the repeat-championship squad of '92, would have won. Key scoring opportunities are botched when the game hangs in the balance, with players making mental errors.

Grant Hill fouls out early in overtime, foolishly contesting a Dobard fast-break dunk because he wants to keep the crowd from getting too excited. (Displaying rare oncourt emotion, Hill flings his gum at the press table after he realizes the ramifications of what he's done.)

Duke's post defense is porous. Disgusted by the ease with which FSU operates inside, Thomas Hill yells at Parks during a timeout. Parks says "Fuck you!" and walks away. At halftime, while Krzyzewski stays on the court to hector officials, T. Hill enters the locker room and throws a towel at Parks. The two exchange more harsh words.

Following the game, Hill complains, "We're not tough enough." Though he won't name names, he adds, "Right now I take nothing for granted with this team. What we did last year was totally different. But there are a few guys on this team who are taking things for granted. They expect to win just because we're here, and that's not going to cut it. They expect things to get done magically; that's why we're not playing well."

Previous Duke players have publicly vented their spleens in similar fashion, most notably guard Phil Henderson after Duke lost to Georgia Tech in a 1990 ACC Tournament semifinal. Krzyzewski chose to put a positive spin on that outburst, in which Henderson called his teammates "babies," and the Blue Devils rallied to reach the NCAA title game.

The coach says nothing to the older Hill about his comments at FSU. But they're not well received by teammates, who find Hill increasingly difficult to play with.

Hobbled by a twisted ankle, Thomas Hill again forces shots, missing nine of eleven. Teammates don't expect him to pass them the ball much anymore. They do expect Hill to yell at them, though, a habit that's less effective, and less tolerable, when he's playing selfishly. Says Mike Brey, "Thomas, even in practice, he can just get on guys to the point, you almost want to tell him to calm down. Everything's a mission with him."

The team has another potentially divisive problem.

Hurley plays every minute against the superquick Ward and Cassell, just days after the coaching staff decides he needs more rest during games. Kenny Blakeney, the player most likely to provide that relief, never leaves the bench. He arrived late for the bus that takes the team to the airport to fly to Tallahassee.

Blakeney is late because he was waiting for a ride from Hurley. Krzyzewski angrily complains that, given the senior's drunk-driving arrest during the offseason, suspending Hurley for tardiness will only rouse suspicions he's been drinking again. You've put me in a bad position, the coach scolds. Hurley, whose sweat sometimes reeks of beer during pregame warmups, is reduced to tears.

Hurley is not punished, reinforcing long-held irritation among some teammates that he receives preferential treatment.

* * *

About a thousand miles away, in Hurley's home state, North Carolina out-lasts Seton Hall at the Meadowlands, 70–66.

Dean Smith complains before the game that he'd been scheduled to play Villanova, but instead is forced to face the Pirates, a top ten squad. In fact, the matchup was made with Smith's expressed consent. "The whole connotation is that they were duped into the game," says someone famil-iar with the negotiations for the nationally televised contest. "That's not true."

Not that the challenge is beyond UNC's capabilities, even after a first half in which it makes fewer than a third of its shots. Play is very physical. Eric Montross misses all five field-goal attempts, most within easy reach of the basket, and appears bothered by similarly sized Luther Wright.

"Eric had trouble catching the ball; we had trouble getting the ball to him," Henrik Rodl says.

The Tar Heels' win anyway, a testament to their defense, their relentless assault inside, and their continuing ability to adapt. "We're a borderline tremendous defensive team," Smith says after UNC ends Seton Hall's nineteen-game home winning streak.

George Lynch, often maligned for his shooting touch, carries the load in the first half with fourteen points and finishes with a game-high twenty-five. Montross resurfaces as an offensive force down the stretch, chipping in a pair of three-point plays and two free throws.

Derrick Phelps scores a dozen points, most in the second half, includ-ing the clinching basket on a long lead from Lynch. The point guard also directs the offense so efficiently, the Heels commit a mere nine turnovers.

Most important, Phelps spearheads a defense that forces twenty-three turnovers, fourteen in the first half. He thoroughly dissects Bobby Hur-ley's younger brother, Danny, who is booed by his own fans.

"That's typical Derrick Phelps," Brian Reese says. "He loves defense. He's smiling. I've never seen somebody smiling so much and be so happy to be playing defense."

The Tar Heels are 16–1 and look like the nation's top team.

WEDNESDAY, JANUARY 27

THIS is how legends are made, or burnished in Dean Smith's case. North Carolina's 9 P.M. game with Florida State appears to be over midway through the second half. It's clearly not North Carolina's night.

Things start badly when good buddies Brian Reese and Derrick Phelps are tardy picking up Donald Williams. In Williams's car. The trio arrives at the pregame meal two minutes late. As punishment Phelps and Reese don't start. (Williams isn't a starter, anyway.) Upperclassmen Scott Cherry and Pat Sullivan start instead, and combine for a turnover and air-ball three-pointer before being yanked.

While North Carolina is tight, eager to pay back Florida State for two defeats last season, the visitors are loose and confident. The FSU squad sings in unison in the hallway before bopping onto the Smith Center court, and dances to a quick early lead. The advantage grows to 45–28 by halftime.

"I think the first half, our defense was the worst it's been in a while," Eric Montross says. Certainly it doesn't impress Florida State's Sam Cassell, who tells teammates in the locker room: "Man, they've got Rodl guarding me. That's an insult, man; that's an insult to me."

Pat Kennedy's approach is far more cerebral, similar to the one he employed in defeating North Carolina in his ACC debut, an event celebrated on videocassette and sold via 800-number soon after FSU returned to Tallahassee. Florida State uses a spread offense that makes players more difficult to trap and freer to attack the basket one-on-one. It passes the ball crisply and with a purpose. Defensively FSU negates UNC's size advantage with rhythm-busting traps and a zone that essentially dares the Tar Heels to shoot from outside.

Florida State's cause is helped considerably when Montross picks up his second and third personal fouls less than five minutes into the game. Rodney Dobard blocks five shots in the first fifteen minutes, further disrupting the Heels' normal flow. Susceptible all year to rushing offensively, Carolina misses more than two thirds of its shots in the opening half.

"They chose to give us anything we wanted, and we didn't handle that very well. And that's my fault," Smith says afterward.

By jumping on top early and staying there, FSU prevents the crowd from becoming a factor. UNC fans ache to avenge Cassell's cuttingly accurate remark characterizing them as a laid-back "cheese and wine crowd." Growing frustrated as Florida State's lead grows, students near one basket begin chanting "Bullshit!" as FSU attempts a pair of free throws. Smith jumps from the bench to stop the unseemly and unsportsmanlike refrain.

Florida State greets the second half as they did the first, with song. Confidence and swagger growing by the minute, it builds a twenty-one-point edge with just under twelve minutes to go. Even a brief flutter of activity by UNC—including its first three-pointer in fifteen frustratingly touchless tries—only brings the Heels within 71–51 with 9:36 to go.

Then, as if an alchemist had suddenly hit upon the proper formula, some balance shifts in the Smith Center universe and odd things start happening.

9:23—Henrik Rodl, one of the team's most demonstrative and emotional players, hits a second three-pointer. The crowd roars.

Up in a radio booth at the mezzanine level, engineer Paul Boone scrambles to recalibrate the master board used by the Tar Heel radio network. For the first time ever, the ambient sound emanating from the Smith Center throng is so loud it's distorted going out over the air.

9:21—Smith calls a timeout, an uncommon occurrence with so much game time remaining. Ordinarily Smith regards timeouts the way connoisseurs regard the cherries on ice-cream sundaes, saving them for last. He's especially loath to call a timeout during a televised game, since two-minute commercial breaks are built in at regular intervals.

Observers and rival coaches often bitch about the way Smith extends the endgame to interminable lengths even in hopeless situations, using timeouts, ceaseless substitutions, and strategic fouling to buy his team time to rally. Yet that habitual refusal to accept the inevitable may be the Heels' ultimate salvation; at least once each season a Smith team engineers an improbable comeback.

Rallying is so much a part of Smith's program that three pages of the press guide are devoted to "A Carolina Specialty: The Comeback Victory," as Pat Kennedy notices while perusing the publication hours before tonight's game.

Last year's great escape was engineered against Wake Forest from twenty-two points down, twenty in the second half. That rally culminated when Brian Reese scored on a rebound basket at the buzzer.

Perhaps the most famous escape of all time, not just at North Carolina but in college history, came in 1974, when the Tar Heels won in overtime after trailing Duke by eight points with seventeen seconds left in regulation play.

Smith knows things look hopeless as he instructs his team how to overtake Florida State. But Smith is known for his ability to mask anxiety in such circumstances. Sometimes he reminds his players of the game's unimportance in life's larger scheme. Or he'll do as he does now. Recalls Montross: "He just smiled at us when we first got in there and said, 'This is going to be fun.' He was very calm. I would have had my jacket off and my shirt ripped open."

Smith says: "I just thought at that time to let Florida State know, 'Uh, oh. Here we come. Timeouts.' I don't think it probably bothered them. And I wanted our players to know, OK, now we're in catchup, and we're really going to get after them. And [there's] plenty of time. Plenty of time. I brought up the Wake Forest game, when they came from that far back. And they believed, I think. If they didn't believe, they believed when we got to ten."

8:51—Ten seconds after a follow shot by Doug Edwards, George Lynch hits his first three-pointer of the year. The last time he hit one was during last season's rally against Wake.

8:43—Charlie Ward commits one of his ten turnovers on the night, getting whistled in the backcourt for a charge against Derrick Phelps, who falls convincingly to get the call.

8:37—Donald Williams, who's been struggling from the field for four straight games, hits a three-pointer. The score is 73–60.

8:33—The crowd is loud. The Tar Heels are pumped. Kennedy calls timeout. He's looking to stave off a protracted run, as he did against Duke by calling a pair of timeouts early in the second half.

8:06—Perhaps tired, perhaps losing its composure, Florida State abandons any semblance of an offense against UNC's scrambling defense. After Ward fires up an errant three-pointer—six of FSU's last nine shots are from the bonusphere—Rodl again finds himself open against a zone. He calmly hits another three as more than twenty thousand fans leap in unison toward the ceiling, arms and voices raised in exultation. FSU 73, UNC 63.

Prior to the game, Kennedy attempts to identify the improvement in this year's Carolina club, and settles on its defensive play. "They are playing in much more of a frenzy, and they're doing it for an extended period of time," he says. "That's a trait of the good North Carolina teams— they're always coming at you and at you and at you."

7:41—Rodl intercepts a crosscourt pass and feeds an equally emotional Phelps for a quick layup. The FSU lead is down to 73–65.

7:37—The Smith Center is as loud as it gets, so loud neighbors have to shout to be heard, so loud it's almost like being back in Cameron or Reynolds. Kennedy calls another timeout. Montross returns to the lineup after a protracted absence.

7:09—Following a turnover by Bob Sura, one of eight by Florida State subsequent to Smith's timeout, Montross gets the ball in the lane and is fouled by Edwards, his fourth. Kennedy wants a traveling call on Montross, who fires the ball to his bench as he falls to the floor. Instead referee Lenny Wirtz calls a technical foul on Kennedy, whom he's previously warned to tone down his vociferous bench-jockeying.

Kennedy stands with mouth agape as Donald Williams makes the two technical free throws.

6:52—Williams hits a short penetrating jumper as Carolina keeps possession due to the technical. The deficit is down to 73–69.

5:21—Cassell makes two free throws, pushing the lead back to 75–69. His team will score only once more in its final nine possessions.

2:56—Playing inspired defense, UNC traps at every opportunity. Unlike earlier, Florida State's players respond by taking the ball where their coaches warned them not to—into corners, on drives along the baseline, along the sideline. Edwards blunders into a trap and escapes only by calling FSU's last timeout.

Kennedy attempts to rally his team, but he has the stunned look of a man being sucked through a hole in an airliner. Nearby, Dean Dome ushers stand smiling, clapping, and slapping each other's hands.

2:28—Edwards scores after rebounding a missed three-pointer by Cassell. FSU's lead is only 77–74. Edwards's basket is the only shot in his team's last five that's not a three-point try.

1:59—North Carolina is running its regular offense now, growing more confident with each tick of the clock. Montross hits a hook to pull his team within a point. "They hit the threes and I had to pull us out of our zone," Kennedy explains. "With that, it kind of evened the game up . . . they do a good job of taking full advantage with their inside big people."

1:40—By now Florida State is near panic. The cockiness, crisp passes, and sharp cuts that fueled it earlier are nowhere to be seen. Ward beats a trap only to throw a looping crosscourt pass toward Sura. Lynch, who later smilingly likens himself to a defensive back, intercepts the ball near the scorer's table and drives for a dunk, elevating the screams from twenty thousand throats to a pitch that becomes a physical presence.

The steal is the two-hundredth of Lynch's career, a school record. UNC leads, 78–77.

0:03—North Carolina holds an insurmountable 82–77 lead. As it did in last year's rally against Wake, the ball ends up in the hands of Reese, who flings it toward the light blue rafters. The horn ends the game before the ball returns to earth.

Fans mob the floor. Many North Carolina players join the celebration. Kennedy and company, as well as members of the media, sort carefully through the tumult to reach safer haunts. In the hallway leading to the FSU locker room, Kennedy engages in a brief verbal joust with a taunting Smith Center worker and walks off muttering about "that Carolina class."

A few moments later Kennedy tells the media cuttingly, but with a smile: "I was a little amused at the response of the crowd after the game. I never thought a North Carolina crowd would respond that way to beating Florida State in basketball." He also complains the celebration "was a little dangerous" and that he "had to bang four or five students off of me trying to get to the locker room." Phelps, standing away from the crush at the inner door to UNC's locker room, says the Tar Heels "knew we could come back," but admits, "It's incredible what Coach Smith can really bring out in a team."

Rodl, standing awash in the swirl of reporters, beaming all the while, says happily, "I don't know if we can come back, down twenty every night."

The outcome, which pushes UNC's record to 17–1, only intensifies the bitterness of some fans, especially Dukies. Even before FSU comes to the Triangle, they grumble about a Sunday-Wednesday conspiracy masterminded by Dean Smith. "Duke softens them up, and then they roll over like dogs in heat for Carolina," is how one Duke fan puts it.

Smith is amused by the notion he's manipulated the league schedule in his favor, but catches himself before making a retort that would stoke rivals' competitive fires.

Still, there is an odd symmetry to the schedule. Georgia Tech beats Duke on a Sunday, then follows with a Wednesday visit to Chapel Hill, where it loses. Virginia beats Duke on a Sunday, then follows with a Wednesday visit to Chapel Hill, where it loses. Florida State beats Duke on a Sunday, then follows with a Wednesday visit to Chapel Hill, where it too loses.

N.C. State gets blitzed at Georgia Tech. The start is nearly identical to the Duke debacle. This time Marcus Wilson is the player who's fouled on a drive to the basket and misses both resultant free throws. Ed Conroy likens the game to "a bad dream," rather a strong statement considering the Wolfpack's luck thus far.

The Wolfpack's arrival occasions a familiar rehash of its troubles in the *Atlanta Journal-Constitution*. Again, Les Robinson uses the portrayal of his team as hapless victim to adduce a psychological advantage. "I thought they'd be thinking, 'There's no way this team can beat us,'" he says of Georgia Tech. "But they came ready to play." He's also aware that his close friend, Bobby Cremins, starts three underclassmen whose impatience might be exploitable. So Robinson's plan is to again throttle back his offense, reverting to the delay-like "road tempo" he used at Florida State.

"Gradually I'd like to be able to turn the switch on and the switch off," Robinson says. Chuckling, he adds, "As we make our tenth change of the year. The players have gotten pretty adaptable." But the stratagems don't work. Georgia Tech leads at halftime by more points (twenty-two) than N.C. State scores in the entire period (twenty-one). The Pack has just six points midway through a first half in which it misses more than three-quarters of its shots. "I've never seen us miss so many shots like that," Curtis Marshall says. "We came in thinking we could win. It ain't like we quit. It just snowballed."

The margin is a bloated thirty-six when Cremins clears his bench in the second half, something he rarely does. That charitable act enables N.C. State to make a run that closes the final margin to a respectable 85–74.

The Wolfpack remains the only ACC squad without a league win. "I'd like to say we made a gallant comeback at the end and popped back, but although the score may indicate that, [Tech] had more to do with the situation out there," Robinson notes.

A few numbers tell the story of N.C. State's tenth loss in fourteen games: Georgia Tech's three underclass starters—Travis Best, James Forrest, and Martice Moore—make all but two of their twenty-six field-goal attempts. So much for N.C. State's defense. Conversely, starters Wilson, Mark Davis, and Kevin Thompson miss all but five of their thirty-seven field-goal attempts. So much for N.C. State's offense.

Davis brings up the rear with two-for-sixteen shooting, just a day after both he and Robinson confidently predicted the player was on the verge of ending his slump.

"He's just a shadow of the player he was last year," comments a coach at another ACC school.

"He's trying too hard," Robinson confides. "I've talked to him. I've tried different approaches." Some ascribe Davis's struggles to a sophomore jinx. His coach doesn't buy that reasoning, though he believes Davis came into the season with an inflated idea of how he'd perform and is now grappling with the less pleasant realities of his limitations.

For his part, Davis is worried not only about his shooting but about a math test scheduled for early Thursday morning. The team takes a midnight flight back to Raleigh, and while others sleep, talk, or listen to music, Davis studies. "I look at myself as being a student first," he says. "My mom, she beat that into my head when I was young. Basketball can be taken away from you like that." He snaps his fingers. "Me breaking my wrist has never affected me in the classroom."

The sole bright spot for the Pack against Georgia Tech is junior forward Marc Lewis, who has a career-high twenty-five points and fifteen rebounds. The performance is totally unexpected—through State's first thirteen games, Lewis had scored a combined twenty-three points. His previous career highs were eight points and four rebounds.

Robinson says Lewis has earned the right to start the next game. It will be the second start in three seasons for the six-foot-eight forward.

Lewis was ignored by ACC schools despite compiling good grades and starring on a very successful high school team in Greensboro, N.C., where the league offices are located. "I felt like at times I was overlooked, and it was kind of depressing," Lewis said. He received only a smattering of Division I scholarship offers.

Robinson had recruited Lewis for East Tennessee State, then lost interest due to the player's limited athletic ability. But when he took over in midspring at N.C. State, Robinson faced severe recruiting constraints and a charged atmosphere in which the academic standing of his players was under intense scrutiny. Scrambling to fill out a roster, he grabbed Lewis and hoped for the best.

"It was a political signing," said an ACC recruiter, noting Lewis's 4.0 grade-point average.

"He's one of those kids who finds a way to win," a head coach from a lesser league observed approvingly. "I don't know if that's going to be good enough in the ACC."

The thick-legged Lewis lived down to expectations during his first two seasons, appearing for brief stretches in about half the team's games. He shot and rebounded sparingly and recorded nearly twice as many turnovers as assists. On the other hand, he was disciplined, doughty, and wily. And he accepted his subordinate role without complaint.

"He's strong and I look for him to give us some quality minutes," Robinson said charitably on the eve of the '93 season. "I think he's capable of doing that."

Then things started going wrong. Lewis is currently one of only two upperclassmen on the roster, and among the few bench reserves. Early in the year, Lewis was instructed to avoid taking risks offensively, like trying to dribble the ball. Just convey the ball to the scorers, he was told, rebound, and play good defense. Now he's encouraged to do whatever he can, however he can.

Against Georgia Tech he plays more than half the game, often against fellow second stringers. He does everything, even making the first three-pointer of his career. His rebound total is the highest by a Wolfpack player to date.

"That's the way it goes," Lewis says with the same even tone he brings to his play. "Some guys step in and play. Others, you have to wait your turn. I appreciate the opportunity. I just tried to do what I could do and it just came. I didn't do anything out of the ordinary."

Half a dozen of Lewis's relatives are in attendance in Atlanta, and when he exits the locker room his father leads the greeting party. "I want your autograph," he tells his son.

FRIDAY, JANUARY 29

DONNIE Seale, dressed in a red N.C. State sweat suit and black knit cap, sits on the floor outside the closed locker room door, not wanting to interrupt while the squad watches film, not sure anymore of his place in the basketball universe. His academic appeal has been denied—his D grade in cultural anthropology cannot be changed to an incomplete.

The door opens and members of the team troop past on their way upstairs to practice, slapping Seale's proffered hand as they go. The coaches too pause to say hello. Then Seale goes into the empty room, sits on a couch and contemplates his fate. He says the instructor admits mistakenly giving him zeroes for missing class before he enrolled in the course; an appeals board says his grade can't be converted to an incomplete. Seale says his parents may hire an attorney to pursue the matter. Seale doesn't know what to do.

"I broke my neck to get here for a year and a half," he begins. "I went to school. I gave up what I wanted to do the most, play basketball, for a year just so I could get here." He recalls spending last summer taking twenty-seven hours of credits so he could enroll at N.C. State. "I did all that just to come here, and when I get here I'm raped, so to speak. My pride, my respect for the school is gone. I don't want them to give me any breaks. But what's right is right.

"It's a dream to be here. I explored some things that I didn't know I had in me to get here. I didn't think everything was going to be a rose garden when I got here. But I did expect to be treated fairly."

The words come out in a torrent as Seale attacks a piece of gum, keeping his goateed face in constant motion. "The coach asks me if I'm going to practice. It's nothing personal to the basketball team, but if I get hurt out there nobody cares. I'm risking my body for somebody who doesn't even care about me. That's the bottom line . . . they just don't care. They just don't care . . . I've just been thinking about this for a month. It's taken its toll on me. I'm not going to quit basketball. I love it. But it's just made me tired. I just want to get away from it for a little while . . . now it's become such a moral issue kind of, so to speak. This decision could have been made so much earlier. Of course I'd want to come back. But morally the system is so terrible."

What Seale doesn't mention is that he had problems in several courses, and was twice warned during the first semester to get his academic house in order. Yet he let matters slide, just as he did in high school, as if there's a part of him fighting against maintaining his eligibility, fighting against the dream, the shared dream that so pleases his father.

"I feel bad for him; we all do," Les Robinson says of Seale. "What bothers me about it is, it's not his first time. It's not the first time he's been left out in the cold."

For Seale, the disappointment of again falling by the wayside brings old frustrations to the surface.

Last season he was among the best point guards in the ACC—everybody said so, Seale recalls. Pro scouts showed interest. He worked to hone his game for his last college season, the season he'd awaited all his life, only to be shunted aside while the team's "little guards," Curtis Marshall and Lakista McCuller, were installed at the point.

"It was almost like an insult," says Seale, insisting he holds no grudge against Robinson. "I worked hard to get here, and I thought I deserved that spot . . . not taking anything away from anybody, they're all my friends, but I just think I didn't get a fair shake . . . if one of the scouts thought I had a decent chance of going to the pros and playing the point, then why couldn't I play it here? That boggled my mind."

Even if he remains dedicated to his class work, Seale will complete the academic year eighteen hours shy of graduation. After that he's uncertain if he'll come back or try for a professional basketball career. "I don't know how the situation is going to turn out," he says. "I don't know what to conclude." For now, he decides to put on a uniform and join the squad for practice.

The Pack players are acutely aware that Clemson's visit two days hence may provide the best opportunity for an ACC win and a chance to turn things around.

Following practice, a freshly showered Marshall insists the team hasn't lost its competitive spirit. But the little point guard knows the team is edging closer to despair. It's already lost four straight, and if it doesn't beat Clemson could well go on to lose nine in a row before facing a breather against UNC-Greensboro. Such a prolonged slide would match the school record set by last year's squad. "That would just set the whole season off, top it off," Marshall offers gloomily.

(Above left): Duke coach Mike Krzyzewski shouts instructions from the sidelines. *(Ron Ferrell, Duke Sports Information Department)*

(Above right): North Carolina State head coach Les Robinson. *(© 1993 Bob Donnan Photography)*

(Left): Dean Smith celebrates his second national men's basketball championship by cutting down the net. *(Hugh Morton)*

(Above): Duke University students begin pitching tents outside of Cameron Indoor Stadium *(right)* days before home games in an effort to get front-row seating. *(© 1993 Bob Donnan Photography)*

(Below): Members of the ever raucous student body at N.C. State cheer on the Wolfpack at Reynolds Coliseum. *(© 1993 Bob Donnan Photography)*

(Above): Although he was then no longer coach at N.C. State, the memory and legacy of Jim Valvano remained ever present. *(© 1993 Bob Donnan Photography)*

(Below): A horde of young Duke fans waits outside the locker room, hoping to get autographs from their favorite players. *(© 1993 Bob Donnan Photography)*

(Opposite, above left): Cherokee Parks celebrates a dunk against Canisius. *(Ron Ferrell,
Duke Sports Information Department)*
(Opposite, above right): The effects of a
long season take their toll on N.C. State
coach Les Robinson. He is flanked by assistants Al Daniel *(left)* and Buzz Peterson.
(© 1993 Bob Donnan Photography)
(Opposite, below): Bobby Hurley fields
questions from reporters. *(© 1993 Bob Donnan Photography)*
(Above): Donald Williams shoots a wide-
open jump shot as Virginia coach Jeff Jones
looks on. *(© 1993 Bob Donnan Photography)*
(Right): Donnie Seale directs the N.C. State
offense. *(© 1993 Bob Donnan Photography)*

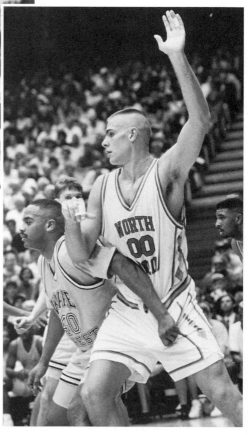

(Above, left): Grant Hill shoots over Michigan's Jalen Rose. *(Duke Sports Information Department)*

(Above): Eric Montross posts up against an aggressive Trelonnie Owens of Wake Forest. *(Hugh Morton)*

(Left): Antonio Lang laughing in front of the camera. *(© 1993 Bob Donnan Photography)*

(Above): Derrick Phelps is wheeled from the court on a stretcher after suffering an injury in an ACC Tournament game against Virginia. *(© 1993 Bob Donnan Photography)*

(Below): The 1993 NCAA Champion North Carolina Tar Heels celebrate their victory by raising the championship trophy on national television. *(Hugh Morton)*

GAME SCORE	DEFENSIVE AWARD	ASSIST/ ERROR	OFFENSIVE REBOUNDS	DRAW CHARGES	SCREENER AWARD	GOOD PLAYS 1st to loose Balls Savvy Draw Fouls	BLOCKED SHOTS	DEFLECTION
BLUE 89 W / WHITE 69	LYNCH	LYNCH	MONTROSS	CALABRIA	MONTROSS	LYNCH	WENSTROM	PHELPS
UNC 121 W / HIGH FIVE 74	RÖDL	LYNCH	LYNCH	MONTROSS SULLIVAN WILLIAMS	SULLIVAN SALVADORI	SULLIVAN	SALVADORI	LYNCH RÖDL
UNC 103 W / HISTORIAN All-Stars 75	LYNCH	CALABRIA	LYNCH	REESE	MONTROSS	LYNCH	MONTROSS RÖDL SALVADORI WENSTROM	LYNCH
UNC 119 W / Old Dominion 82	RÖDL	RÖDL	SALVADORI	WILLIAMS	—	RÖDL	SALVADORI	LYNC
UNC 108 W / North Carolina 67	MONTROSS	PHELPS	LYNCH	LYNCH WILLIAMS	REESE	LYNCH	SALVADORI	LYNC
UNC 104 W / TEXAS 68	PHELPS	PHELPS	WENSTROM	SULLIVAN PHELPS	REESE	PHELPS	SALVADORI	PHELPS
UNC 78 W / Virginia Tech 62	PHELPS	PHELPS SULLIVAN	LYNCH	—	LYNCH SALVADORI	CHERRY	SULLIVAN MONTROSS	RÖDL
UNC 84 W / HOUSTON 76	PHELPS	PHELPS	LYNCH	PHELPS	LYNCH	PHELPS	RÖDL	PHEL
UNC 103 W / BUTLER 56	PHELPS	CALABRIA	LYNCH	REESE CHERRY	WENSTROM	PHELPS	MONTROSS	LYNC
UNC 84 W / OHIO ST. 64	PHELPS	SULLIVAN	LYNCH	REESE PHELPS	MONTROSS	RÖDL	SALVADORI	PHEL
UNC 80 W / SW LOUISIANA 59	PHELPS	RÖDL	LYNCH	PHELPS	SULLIVAN	PHELPS	SALVADORI PHELPS	PHELP
UNC 78 L / MICHIGAN 79	PHELPS	SALVADORI	LYNCH	PHELPS	MONTROSS	RÖDL	MONTROSS	PHELP
UNC 101 W	PHELPS RÖDL	LYNCH	PHELPS CHERRY REESE RÖDL	MONTROSS	SALVADORI	SALVADORI	PHE

(Above): George Lynch addresses the UNC fans gathered for the victory party inside the Dean Dome. (© 1993 Bob Donnan Photography)

(Below): A wall in the North Carolina locker room records per-game leaders, as determined by the coaches after grading film. There is no listing for high scorer—an attitude characteristic of the entire North Carolina program. (Courtesy of Robert Crawford)

SATURDAY, JANUARY 30

THE aura of invincibility, once such familiar garb for Dean Smith's teams, apparently hasn't been tailored to this year's squad. Three days after the Tar Heels stage one of the great rallies of Smith's tenure, apparently clinching ascendance to number one in the polls, the stitches unravel, the chalk lines are smudged, and the seams burst.

North Carolina's weaknesses are exploited admirably by an intelligent, disciplined Wake Forest team. Benefiting from an uncanny three-point barrage by guard Randolph Childress, the Demon Deacons delight the fickle home fans in Winston-Salem by routing the Heels 88–62. That matches the largest margin of victory ever enjoyed by the Deacs against UNC in a series dating to 1911.

The triumph is just Wake's second over the hated Heels since handing Smith's 1982 national champions one of their two defeats. Predictably, the blessed event precipitates an oncourt celebration by hundreds of screaming students. Their sentiments are ably expressed by Wake center Derrick Hicks, a twenty-two-year-old Raleigh resident. "Being a North Carolina native and growing up here all my life, I feel like crying," the junior college transfer says in Wake's locker room. "It's probably the biggest high I've ever had in my entire life."

Just down the hall in the press room Wake coach Dave Odom steps from behind a curtain, takes a seat at a cloth-draped table, dons glasses to peruse a stat sheet, and addresses a bank of cameras, microphones, tape recorders, and faces. "Well, obviously we're overflowing with joy," he says, his sober manner directly contradicting his remark. "To be able to play that way against anybody in the country makes a coach's day. But to be able to play that way against what I consider the best team in the country on any given day, is almost inexplicable."

Not all that inexplicable, really. Wake has a cleverly tailored game plan. Helping its cause, the Tar Heels are on the road against a first-division league team for the first time, and are emotionally spent and a bit cocky after their FSU rally.

Perhaps, too, they're looking ahead.

As a Duke assistant puts it: "Everybody is thinking over there, 'This is the game we've waited for for five years. The sun's going to be out, it's going to be in the nineties, all the flowers are going to be coming up, and Carolina's going to be number one.'"

Now that his third-ranked team has dropped to 17–2, Dean Smith is asked how he'll ready his team for Duke, its next opponent.

"Whom do we play next?" he asks facetiously. "Oh. Defending national champions on their home court. And certainly having a great year, I think . . . I really think they're a little better defensively than they were a year ago because Parks is in there to block shots."

The prospects are hardly grim for the Tar Heels. This remains UNC's best start since 1987, when it was the last ACC squad to go through the regular season undefeated in league play. Over the four seasons prior to this one, Duke has suffered two defeats at home in fifty-seven games, and both were to UNC. And one mustn't forget Smith's eternal reminders that it's more dangerous to play a proud team that's just been throttled, as his was, than one that lost a close game.

Mike Krzyzewski isn't giving ground easily in the psychological war. Before Wake and UNC tip off, seventh-ranked Duke defeats Maryland at Cole Field House in College Park and Krzyzewski starts talking up the Tar Heels. "We know who they are, and we know who we are. It would be a big upset if we beat them," Krzyzewski says.

Krzyzewski is apt to grow snappish when someone wonders if his gaze has wandered from the task at hand. Yet while deep in the throes of facing other teams he's developed quite an informed view of UNC.

"I think Carolina's probably the best team in the country right now, and they may end up the best team in the country," Krzyzewski says. "What they have is a balance of outstanding talent and experience. Talent's nice, but when you add the experience factor, then you become a great team. Of course, Dean is as good as there's ever been in the game of basketball."

Duke meanwhile is refining the lessons of a month in which it's played twice at home against ranked nonconference opponents, on consecutive days against ranked squads, and on the road against ranked ACC teams at a time when Krzyzewski thinks ACC ball is the best in the country. (Five league teams are ranked among the Associated Press's top twenty.)

Duke's midseason tuneup begins at Cameron with a 117–73 rout of a good San Francisco squad. The entire Duke bench corps gets playing time. Near game's end the less-than-full student section bids San Francisco adieu by chanting: "Start the trolley! Start the trolley!" Then the Blue Devils win 78–62 over what Krzyzewski calls "a very determined and very spirited Maryland team."

Duke hasn't lost at the airplane hangar–style campus arena at College Park since 1985, surely a boon to the dominant D.C.-area recruiting that's brought current Blue Devils Grant Hill, Kenny Blakeney, and Tony Moore; alums Johnny Dawkins, Danny Ferry, Tommy Amaker, Billy King, and Brian Davis; and 1993–94 signee Joey Beard.

Thirteen of Duke's final seventeen points come from Grant Hill, who isn't sure he'll play until pregame warmups. Hill's left ankle is sore, having swollen shockingly following practice two days ago. X-rays taken upon arrival in Maryland reveal no apparent problem.

Hill's injury enables him to wear worn-in white sneakers rather than new black ones that match those of his teammates. Of course both sets are made by Adidas, to Hill's mildly vocal displeasure. Ostensibly, players may wear whatever shoes they choose. In reality, though, as at most prominent basketball programs, Hill wears the athletic shoes supplied gratis as part of his coach's endorsement contract.

Comfortably shod and tightly taped, Hill plays twenty-five minutes against Maryland. He scores fifteen points and leads Duke in rebounds and steals.

Thomas Hill also reinjures the ankle that's bothered him periodically all season, and Cherokee Parks jams the ring finger on his right hand. All are expected to play against North Carolina.

Tony Moore will not be available. Ignoring advice to the contrary, he borrowed Kenny Blakeney's scooter and crashed, injuring his knee. Moore, now called "Scooter" by teammates, is expected to be healthy in a few weeks, but hasn't endeared himself to coaches who once thought he could help address their rebounding needs.

Nationally, Duke has stepped off center stage.

Yet the coaching staff expresses pleasure with the team's progress.

Sure, this isn't a dominant team. The coaches never thought it would be. But, so what? There's no other dominant team in the nation, either, according to all evidence. Unless maybe it's Carolina.

"We're in the process of maturing as a basketball team," Krzyzewski says. "Last year we were mature on October 15, and ready to go. And that's unusual, but then we were an unusual team last year. This year we got off to such a great start, I think a lot of it had to do with based on past success and enthusiasm and whatever. And then reality sets it and maturity has to come in."

A student of his own teams, Krzyzewski tests them, sees how they react by placing them in tough situations. Then he adjusts and fine-tunes for postseason play. Because this squad is less experienced than the past few, he's embarked on the annual shakedown cruise in January rather than February. Now he has his answers.

"We needed to find out earlier," he confides. "People study you to see what they can do against you. They start taking things away from you. An older team will adjust to that quicker. Every team faces those adjustments. A more experienced team makes those adjustments quicker in January. We haven't been able to do that as quickly as we have the last couple of years, but we're making them."

The results are impressive, even if the public perception has Duke struggling. "We've been trying to get the team on a level where we're a team and not five individuals," Pete Gaudet says. "Our system is pretty much in place now."

Two of Duke's losses on the road were by a point. The third, against Virginia, came less than twenty-four hours after facing Iowa. Hurley has found a better emotional balance. Grant Hill has become more consistently assertive (though he's still oh-for-eight on three-pointers). Perhaps as important as anything, Parks has emerged as a reliable performer respected by his older teammates, his poor showing at Georgia Tech a solitary blemish on an otherwise solid record.

The sophomore has a friendly competition going with Grant Hill to see who gets more rebounds and blocks. To date both have exactly one hundred twenty three rebounds, 6.8 per game. Parks has rejected more shots, and ranks third in the league in that category. He's also the ACC's most accurate shooter at 66.7 percent, though he hasn't made enough field goals to qualify for the official standings.

"Cherokee's at a point where I feel he'll play against anyone,"

Krzyzewski says. "We can depend on Cherokee now for a good performance."

If Krzyzewski has any regrets, they're over how well he's anticipated his team's failings, manifest in execution in late-game situations and out-of-bounds plays and, more generally, the quality of oncourt leadership. In every case, lack of experience is a shaping factor.

"The main thing is, I don't know if you can ever realize the level of experience and maturity you have on a squad," he says. "I think that this year's team in the last two weeks has really developed better than what they'd done for the previous six weeks. I'm not going to get into a whole bunch of details. I think maybe I could have helped a little bit more if I would have known, if you could predict just where your team was at as you start practice." He continues: "That's what the tough stretch was about. See, too many times everything is placed on the players. You know, when you evaluate . . . what we did is I evaluated our team and we're on the team, the coaching staff. And I think we needed to make some changes. And only going through those tough situations I think would have shown us that. That's good. So that's why I'm very enthusiastic about our team and our future.

"Hey, our kids have really played hard all year. There's never been an attitude problem, not one. They've played hurt. We don't publicize our aches and pains, things like that. Our kids play with no excuse. Hopefully we'll always do that. So that's what I meant. It's not Lent yet and I'm not doing. . ." Krzyzewski pauses. "You don't know about that," he says to a non-Catholic listener.

"I've heard," the listener replies.

"All right," says Krzyzewski. "I'll explain it." But not now.

SUNDAY, JANUARY 31

FOR N.C. State's long-suffering team, on the receiving end all season, there's a certain inevitability in having its game with Clemson come down to a final, open jumper by the Tigers' hottest shooter.

The afternoon is sixty degrees and sunny, the sort of day that makes winter in North Carolina easily bearable. Still, more than eight thousand diehards shun the sun and come to Reynolds to root on the outmanned Wolfpack, which responds by playing some of its better ball of the season.

Prior to the game, Les Robinson says: "Our theme now is that we can't just think about our record, that people will look and say if we don't win, we're not going to win this year. That's so much pressure. We're working to improve individually and collectively."

Practices in preparation for Clemson genuinely excite both Robinson and Ed Conroy. "If we run our offense like we did today," Robinson says the day before facing the Tigers, "we can beat some teams. Tennessee. Wake at home."

Robinson has learned not to anticipate victory, however. He tells each player to find triumph where he can, to concentrate on what can be gotten from this season in terms of future basketball. He further notes that "in the big picture" there are more important things than how many basketball games a team wins.

The coach's attempt to finesse what he calls "that big goose egg," a winless ACC season, doesn't relieve the tension for his players, though.

"I think there was a lot of pressure because everyone knew that we could win this game," Curtis Marshall says after facing Clemson. "It was very winnable. Everybody expected us to win. Plus it was at home. I think there was a lot of pressure because you heard all week that 'You guys should win this game, you guys should win this game.'"

Last in the league in virtually every major statistical category, from scoring to rebound margin to three-point percentage, the Wolfpack decisively out-rebounds the taller Tigers, makes half its shots, and cans nine of twenty-one from three-point range (42.9 percent). For only the third time in fifteen games, both Marshall and Lakista McCuller score in double figures.

In fact, for the first time all year N.C. State has four players in double figures. New starter Marc Lewis contributes a dozen points and Kevin Thompson chips in eleven, along with a game-high nine rebounds and a career-high seven assists.

"The key was, I think, everybody hung together, being on the same wavelength," Marshall says. "Everybody thinking, 'Yeah, we can win. We can win this.' Not doubting each other. Looking for the open man and not being afraid that he's not going to hit the big shot. That's the way it was. Against Maryland, I don't think we had that."

The only starter who's not in double figures is Mark Davis. He continues to struggle, moving with the resolute imprecision of a badly tuned automobile. Davis looks hesitant on offense and a tad slow on defense. He misses four of five shots from three-point range, has just two rebounds and in thirty-five minutes commits a pair of turnovers without a balancing assist.

"I think I played a smarter game than I've been playing," says a subdued Davis, who takes only eight shots. "I'm clearly not shooting the ball well, but I'm not going to let it get me down or anything." Then he adds what by now has become his standard refrain: "I'm definitely going to get back. It's going to come back. I'm not worried about that anymore. It's going to come back. And it may be tomorrow, it may be Thursday, it may be a year from now, but it's going to come back. I'm not going to give up on it."

Marshall and McCuller openly encourage Davis during the game. It's a new experience for the sensitive sophomore, who finds he wants to make shots to please his teammates as well as himself. "We did something we hadn't done much this year—that is, we went and had fun playing together," Davis says.

But the pleasures of that camaraderie quickly fade as the blundering, blustering Tigers make a comeback, trying to avoid their twentieth consecutive ACC road loss.

Says Marshall: "We get out; we're up by nine with like two minutes to go and they come back. And it comes down to the last shot. The way our season's going, it seemed like the shot should have went in, really. Maybe this is the turnaround to the season, that missed shot right there."

The troubles begin with the Pack up six and Marc Lewis on the line. Lewis has attempted ten free throws all year, making nine. But in less than two minutes he misses three of five. Still, N.C. State leads 67–59 with 2:09 remaining.

Immediately Clemson guard Chris Whitney drives through the defense for a layup, and is fouled by Lewis long after his shot is off. He makes the free throw. The lead is down to five.

The Pack desperately tries to run time off the clock. But Marshall, the team's best foul shooter, doesn't dominate the ball. Instead it winds up in Thompson's hands and he's fouled.

By now, each foul costs two free throws. Predictably, Thompson, a poor foul shooter, bricks the first shot hard off the back of the iron. The big man makes the second, but Whitney races upcourt and responds with a three-pointer.

Timeout, Clemson, trailing 68–65 with 1:07 to go. Three seconds later, Lewis is fouled again. The defender fouls out on the play, and while his sub checks in Clemson's huge center, Sharone Wright, bombards straight-arrow Lewis with a string of profanity. "Marc Lewis probably learned ten words he'd never heard before," an N.C. State assistant says, laughing.

Les Robinson calls Lewis over and virtually orders him to make the free throws, trying to jolt the player into refocusing. It works. Lewis makes both.

But Whitney scores again, a layup, cutting the lead to three. More scrambling as State tries to burn time, its passes just barely adequate to avoid interception.

Forced to foul, Clemson wisely gets Thompson. He makes one, misses one, but gets and converts a third chance due to a lane violation. Robinson takes a seat on the bench, smiles, and claps. Then, as if remembering what team he's coaching, he immediately resumes a vigilant crouch on the sideline. He's well outside the coaching box, and has been much of the game though nobody seems to notice.

A five-point lead shrinks to two as Clemson's Bruce Martin immediately hits from long range, his third three-pointer of the afternoon. Twenty-three seconds to go. Again Marshall doesn't hold on to the ball, but gets it to Davis, who's fouled.

Before Robinson thinks to call the player over for a dose of shock treatment, Davis steps to the line and misfires twice.

"I felt great about the free throws," Davis says later. "I knew, I knew that I could make them. The first one looked like it was going in. When it went long I think I was so overwhelmed by that, I let that throw me off of my thinking. I just didn't concentrate at all. I felt pretty bad about missing, especially if he had made that shot."

"He" is Martin, who gets the ball on the left wing after Whitney again penetrates the lane. McCuller, who's helped cut off Whitney's drive, now races toward the wing. Martin deftly ducks as McCuller flies past. Then he gathers himself and, with his foot on the three-point line, fires away.

"I was like, 'Please don't let it go in,'" says Davis, who long after the game has the look of someone who's narrowly survived an auto accident unscathed. "Because that would have been another game that I affected, that I had a real impact on losing the game."

"Truthfully, I thought it was going in," Marshall says. "I really did. He got a really good look at the basket."

It's the shot Clemson wants too. "An inch a little bit to the right or the left on the last shot, we go home a winner," says Cliff Ellis, his team now tied for last with N.C. State. But Martin's shot hits the rim and bounds off. The crowd cheers as happy State players run off the court, and Robinson and Marc Lewis are led to the press table to be interviewed live on the ACC TV network, almost twenty years to the day since N.C. State won the first nationally televised ACC game on another Super Bowl Sunday.

Today Robinson cites N.C. State's rich tradition as a saving grace, keeping Reynolds two-thirds full of fans. "That was earned in the past," he says of such loyalty. "Sort of money in the bank. That's what we're living on, kind of our inheritance." Privately, Robinson says the Pack's fifth win in fifteen games has left him feeling "a little bit relieved" and his fragile squad momentarily numb.

"I think they're a little stunned," he says. "I don't know how they feel. They probably don't know how to feel. It's been that kind of year. There's so few of them. You almost have to tell them to be happy."

No one has to tell Robinson.

After most reporters depart, Robinson flushes a covey of young autograph seekers and obligingly signs whatever is proffered, making small talk all the while. Then he poses for a photo with a teenager, joking as he does that a nearby writer is his bodyguard. "He probably believed me," Robinson says later.

Approaching the playing floor where his family awaits him Robinson is stopped by a little girl and her mother. The child asks the smiling coach to sign one of the "3" placards that fans waved each time the Wolfpack hit a three-pointer.

Robinson signs. Literally making small talk this time, he tells the girl she should keep the placard as a souvenir. She says she will. He asks her age.

"Four," she replies, growing less shy.

"You're awfully big for four," Robinson says flatteringly.

He asks where the girl lives. Her mother names a town. "I live in a blue house," says the girl.

"It's not Carolina blue, is it?" Robinson asks.

"No," says the mother, joining him in laughter, "it's grey."

WEDNESDAY, FEBRUARY 3

AFTERWARD, when he's played his first important role in a Duke–North Carolina game, Donald Williams is almost in tears. It's his fault, he keeps telling himself, his fault Duke wins 81–67.

The game has no single, defining moment, no surpassing individual performance that will fix it in common memory. But the Tar Heels will remember open shots taken and missed, thirteen of fifteen that don't connect from three-point range, nearly two thirds of their overall field-goal attempts unfulfilled. "We'll shoot better on open threes than we did," Dean Smith vows.

Donald Williams will remember this game most especially. The score is close deep into the second half. The shots are there. And Williams misses. He misses eight of nine tries in the second half, misses six of six three-pointers, misses three of four shots in the final four minutes with the outcome in the balance.

"I was open more than I thought I was," Williams says. "Instead of relaxing, I tended to rush my shot. I know teams are going to be charging at me when I'm free, so I rushed my shot. I've got to keep shooting, settle down, and it will fall." Privately, though, Williams's reaction is less dispassionate.

"He's crushed," says a member of the Carolina crew. "He's devastated."

This is the eighth ACC game for both Duke and North Carolina. They're halfway through the league season. Two months' worth of games finished, two months left until the Final Four.

Play is rough, concentration rarely flags, and defense is foremost. There's none of the woofing that went on in 1990 and 1991 when UNC's

King Rice verbally accosted supersensitive Bobby Hurley each time they took the court. Talk after the game is respectful. Both sides take the long view: Just another game, just another regular season.

Sure. The same way Bill Clinton defeating George Bush was just another election.

"They say you'll never know what it's like until you get in that game. You may see it on TV, but you won't know," Chris Collins says. Unlike many players on Triangle teams, Collins is a lifelong basketball fan who kept abreast of the sport's full panoply via satellite dish at home. "I don't know how to really explain it. The emotion was much higher. You can feel intensity when you're playing. In the Carolina game it's just higher."

The game's special meaning to the participants is immediately apparent to Dante De Benedetti, a twenty-nine-year-old Italian who's spending the year studying American college basketball. He's been allowed near-total access to Duke's program, and upon entering the locker room prior to the game notices a transformed atmosphere.

"The faces of the people were different," he says. "The faces of everybody. The faces of the coaches, the face of Coach K, the faces of the people around the program—emotion, tension, expectation, hope, desires to win. All blended together.

"And at the end of the game the satisfaction was more. At the end of the game you saw relaxation, joy, real joy. Not because they killed someone but because it was important."

Carolina-Duke always has been a big game for fans, too. Cameron rooters point toward it all season, chanting "Go to hell, Carolina, go to hell" from the first game to the last. Even in the final seconds of a national championship triumph in Minneapolis in 1992, the chant went up, irrelevant to the action but the ultimate in nose-thumbing.

Because the quality of competition is so good and the emotional stakes so high, coaches in both programs use the meeting as a measuring moment, a gauge of progress in the season's quest to perform well at the highest level of competition.

More recently, Duke-Carolina has grown into something more: American sport's best and hottest rivalry.

Other rivalries boast similar intensity, tradition, and public interest. But none involve teams perched longer at the peak of their sport. And none involve programs more evenly matched as they slug it out for neighborhood and national supremacy.

Since 1986, when Duke began its remarkable run of six Final Four appearances in seven years, the Blue Devils have averaged thirty wins per season. They've also won two national titles, three ACC titles, and finished first in the ACC regular season three times. They've remained in the top twenty in the polls without interruption since early in the 1987 season.

North Carolina has remained just a half step behind. The Tar Heels have advanced to the Sweet Sixteen or beyond for a record twelve consecutive years. Since 1986, they've averaged twenty-seven wins per season, reached the Final Four in 1991, won two ACC titles, and twice finished first during the ACC regular season. UNC has finished in the top twenty in the polls in all but one season (1990) since 1971.

Yet, while both Duke and North Carolina have sustained excellence over a longer period than any two contemporary rivals in any other sport, neither can get a grip locally.

Prior to tonight's Cameron clash the teams have met eighteen times since 1986. Each has won nine. They've each won four games at home during that span and three at the other guy's place. They've met four times in the ACC Tournament final, with each winning twice.

From 1989 through 1992 the Blue Devils lost twice in fifty-nine games at home; both defeats were courtesy of the Tar Heels.

In 1986, 1989, and again in 1992, an undefeated and top-ranked Duke team suffered its first loss of the year at the hands of North Carolina.

The stakes are not so great for the first matchup of 1993. Duke has lost three times, Carolina two. The sixth-ranked Tar Heels are coming off a resounding defeat. The fifth-ranked Devils have won two in a row over outclassed opponents.

Yet the game is sufficiently lustrous to attract a handsome representation of national writers and to rank as the week's college headliner. It's also telecast nationwide—of sixty regular season games played by Duke and UNC, all but eleven are either on regional or national TV. Top ESPN mike-master Dick Vitale, fresh from doing a Subaru commercial and a UCLA game in Los Angeles, is in Durham to do the honors.

The student encampment draws the customary media crowd, though few reporters or TV types ask the obvious question (as Krzyzewski does, to his credit): Isn't a month's time and effort expended waiting for a basketball game a bit excessive? Not that this upperclass version of homelessness is without its comforts, including electricity. The campers don't even have to sleep in their tents. When the last few nights grew quite chill, Krzyzewskiville's tent-dwellers were invited to sleep in Cameron.

The night before Carolina arrives, Krzyzewski shares with the students his dismay at the public setting he and his squad confront this season. "I've experienced more hate and jealousy this year than I have in my whole life," the coach says. "I'll get my ass out of here" if the situation doesn't improve, Krzyzewski adds. "There are people who follow us who are very spoiled, and they don't make it much fun . . . I get paid a lot of money to do what I do, and the main thing I do is provide an environment that's great.

"This year has been my toughest year providing that environment by far. Not even close. The reason for that is, people want these kids to be perfect. I hate that."

The comments elicit barely a ripple of notice beyond Cameron.

Meanwhile, as it has for a generation, Carolina-Duke captivates fans. "It's really unbelievable how excited people get about these games, how really nice people get extremely hostile in the stands," UNC's Henrik Rodl says. "For some of our fans it seems sometimes that the object of the season is to beat Duke, not to win the NCAA title or the ACC Tournament."

You do suffer if you lose, though, and exult if you win.

"It is definitely more intense than any other game we play, for me personally," Bobby Hurley said in 1992. "A lot of other guys have said it's just another game. But for me, it's more intense. You're just into it so much more. The two teams play at such a high level. The fans are going crazy.

"My freshman year in the Dean Dome, I had no idea the type of game Duke-Carolina was. Once you're in it, you know what it's all about. That's why you have to experience it." Grant Hill finds the bitterness of the rivalry affects relations between players. He and Tony Lang encounter Brian Reese, Derrick Phelps, and Donald Williams during a social tour of Chapel Hill, and Hill at least feels snubbed, a experience he uses as personal motivation.

Rodl concedes the level of excitement "makes the games be more fun," particularly in contrast to his native Germany, where basketball is largely ignored. But this Duke–Carolina thing just isn't that big a deal, he insists. "You don't die right after you lose to Duke, and you don't go to heaven right after you beat them." But De Benedetti does see deep meaning in the event. "I can figure it out because I'm from Italy," he explains. "I know history. I can see the Colosseum in Rome, the Forum. I think Venice is a part of history like the Duke-North Carolina game is part of basketball history."

The aspiring coach finds himself gazing rapturously at the scoreboard early in the second half, the 44–43 score in Duke's favor etched permanently in memory.

"I thought about the years and years of UNC and Duke games," he says. "You feel like you are in the history of what is happening now . . . I don't know that something can exist more than this. To turn and see Dean Smith on the other bench is just great. I'm afraid I can't describe, I'm afraid I will not be able to describe it as well as I will describe it when I get back to Italy. I can become a great coach—I hope so—but no game can be like this."

De Benedetti smiles each time he recalls the "unbelievable" atmosphere in old Cameron. Crowds in his country tend to cheer more against the opponent and the officials than for their own team, he says. For all the occasional boos and chants of "Sit! Sit!" to Dean Smith or "Ugly! Ugly!" to Rodl or "Asshole! Asshole!" to Montross's shouting father, Scott, De Benedetti finds the Dukies refreshingly positive.

"The greatest thing, I think, is that all the ten thousand people there were having emotions—the Carolina people, the Duke people. Even to feel bad after a game like this is good because of the emotion. That's what makes it worthwhile to play, to coach, to cheer."

And cheering is something the Duke faithful know all about. The Cameron fans maintain their usual standards, mocking Carolina's designer uniforms with a chant of "K-mart! K-mart!" and taking note of a striking facial resemblance between official Frank Scagliotta and Michael Dukakis.

The word "legendary" is applied in sports about as often as fireflies blink in a spring meadow. After "end of an era" it may be sports' most common cliché. Therefore, to say Cameron fans are legendary neither does justice to the reality, nor communicates much. Suffice it to say, few crowds anywhere are as well known or as widely and fittingly acclaimed.

The Cameron crew is creative, intimidating, and entertaining. They're loud, close to the action, and acutely aware of their potential to affect a game. They're also the bearers of a proud tradition of insolent and abrasive behavior tied to a studious appreciation of others' foibles.

Thus, after N.C. State guard Clyde Austin acquired a car under questionable circumstances during the late seventies, he was greeted with rattling keys when he attempted free throws at Cameron. The year State's Lorenzo Charles accosted a pizza delivery man, he was greeted with sailing pizza boxes, just as Chris Washburn's theft of a stereo met with tossed album covers, record jackets and LPs. Condoms and panties thrown at an accused sex offender playing for Maryland drew widespread condemnation and an admonition from Duke's president; the following game students replaced their "Bullshit!" chant with "We beg to differ!"

Visiting players often engage in repartee with the crowd, sometimes before a game, sometimes during. Pregame exchanges usually have a kidding tone, student to student. Midgame talk is usually profane and one-way. That was the case when Carolina won here in 1990 and Rice mocked both Hurley and the crowd.

Today's interplay is confined to the court, where many of the participants rise to the occasion with superior efforts.

Eric Montross is back after struggling for several games, leading everyone with twenty-two points and thirteen rebounds. "You're not going to stop Eric," says Cherokee Parks, who tries. "They know how to use him so well."

Parks replies with fourteen points and nine rebounds, and contributes a decisive blow with a three-point play off an offensive rebound. "I thought it was very physical down low," Smith observes. "I thought it was a very physical basketball game. Very physical. Maybe we can learn from that."

Grant Hill sparkles as always—hitting the offensive boards, scoring fifteen points, helping to neutralize Reese and Williams. Typically for a big game, Thomas Hill, too, gives a solid, productive effort.

Hurley provides his characteristic daring and killing threes, partially reflected in twenty points and seven assists. He's only modestly impeded by Phelps, who has bruised ribs and can barely raise one arm, yet still plays twenty-eight minutes.

"He's the most dominant player in college basketball," announcer Bucky Waters says of Hurley. "Exclamation point."

George Lynch has seventeen points, eight rebounds, and three assists. Across the ball, Lang comes off the bench to yield ten points, five rebounds, and an inspirational play to break a 40–40 tie, scoring after taking a rebound from Montross's hands.

Duke coaches have resisted benching anyone, burned by the media stigma that attached to Brian Davis when they demoted him. But at various times they've considered using that bit of leverage to light a fire under Lang, Parks, and Thomas Hill. "Playing time is a great motivator for a coach, always has been," Pete Gaudet explains.

So Marty Clark starts against Carolina in Lang's stead. Clark is ineffective. But Lang responds as hoped, a fact that, Gaudet cautions, doesn't necessarily mean much. "Tony's been hot and cold, and hot and cold, and hot and cold. Let's give it another game and see what happens, because Tony can be a great player for us."

More important than any individual results is Duke's mastery of a late-game situation, something it has rarely managed this year.

A central component in Carolina's success has been its ability to wear down the opposition. Duke turns the tables, using its bench more than usual, figuring an advantage can be gained in the end by forcing the Heels' big men to run. Sure enough, UNC falters down the stretch. The Blue Devils score on their final dozen possessions.

"Instead of making passes that go way from the bucket, we attacked," Krzyzewski says. "They were thinking. Bobby was a lot more alert tonight than he was in the last week and a half or so." The Heels are within 57–56 with 4:19 remaining after a basket by Montross, but score only three points in their next six possessions. They make only 34.2 percent of their shots in the second half.

Duke, by contrast, follows Montross's short jumper by having five different players convert on its next five possessions. Hurley feeds Lang for a fast-break layup, feeds T. Hill on an alley-oop, then hits a three-pointer himself to give Duke a 64–58 lead with 2:35 left. Parks scores next, rebounding a Lang miss and making a free throw to build the edge to 67–59 forty seconds later.

The center's score causes the Duke bench to erupt with glee and Smith to erupt with dismay, striking the back of his head to indicate an offensive foul, hitting his grey hair first with his left hand, then right, then left, then right again as if patting on hair cream.

"I just think we made some demoralizing plays," says a pleased Hurley, who shakes hands with Smith following the game. "This was the way our team last year would have finished off the game. Everyone had big plays. Everyone contributed. That's what makes it special. We need to bottle it up and keep it."

SATURDAY, FEBRUARY 6

THE little band boards a bus and embarks from Raleigh at 11:45 A.M., bound for the heart of Carolina blue. No one comes behind Reynolds Coliseum to see off the bus with GO WOLFPACK scrolled on the message board above the windshield. Nor will there be a pep band or crowd of well-wishers awaiting the Pack's return, as happened last season. Forty-six-point thrashings don't do much for school spirit.

Most of the two dozen passengers have seats to themselves. Eleven on board are players, eight of them healthy. The coaches joke that, given the group's small number, they should have rented a pair of limousines and arrived in style. "Probably would have saved money, too," Les Robinson says.

Few beyond this bus, and probably on it too, expect N.C. State to win. There may never be a good time for the '93 Pack to play anyone of UNC's caliber, but this happens to be an especially bad time. The Heels are eager to banish the taste of two straight defeats, to silence the echo of '92 contained in errant perimeter shooting that creates fissures of self-doubt.

Since the Wake loss, Smith Center practices have been closed more tightly than usual. No media members allowed; a dissatisfied Smith wants the freedom to yell at his players without anyone overhearing. He's not quite as upset after the loss to Duke. "I thought we played well enough to win at Duke," Smith says. "On the road, against quality opposition."

During this past week, each Tar Heel also has had a personal session with the coach, reviewing film of his own recent performances, one of a series of such meetings held throughout the season. Players admit they sometimes approach these audiences with the patriarch with the sweaty palms and nervous reticence of students sent to the principal. But they also know they can question their playing time or bring up other concerns once inside his sprawling office, where little adorns the wood-paneled walls except composite black-and-white photos of past and present Tar Heel players.

"Coach Smith is very open," Derrick Phelps says. "If you don't feel something is right, he wants you to come and talk to him about things, see how you feel about things. He'll sit there and listen. That don't mean he's going to change it, but he'll sit there and listen. He'll give you consideration."

Smith, in a revealing slip of the tongue, calls the get-togethers "counseling" sessions. "I've heard some crazy things over the years," says Smith, who is married to a psychiatrist and plays golf regularly with another one. "I want them to be honest." The meetings not only further Smith's teachings, but strengthen bonds that link coach and players long after playing careers end. The potential for such relationships attracted Smith to his profession long ago, and helped sway him against attending medical school despite the encouragement of his Kansas coach, Phog Allen.

"I always wanted to coach," says Smith, whose father, Alfred, coached high school football, basketball, track, and baseball in Emporia, Kansas. "Dad always seemed happy. The players were always coming around the house. When they came back from World War II, their first stop was at our house. I could see it was a nice profession." Former players don't stop by Smith's home, but they phone him at the office or come by. Some, like Michael Jordan, take him on in golf, his sole form of exercise. Smith helps many of his ex-players by using his considerable pull within basketball or corporate circles to hasten their advancement. Others turn to Smith and his privately held corporation for financial assistance to complete their education or pay for a parent's funeral.

This week's meetings with current team members have been devoted to basketball matters, mainly understanding and embracing proper offensive roles. By now there's a sense of wanting to get on with things, to prove this won't be a repeat of last season, which included a 3–5 ACC road record and a four-game league losing streak, the first at UNC since 1965.

Carolina fans simply are anxious to see more wins, the more decisive and non–anxiety producing, the better. So there will be few boos when N.C. State takes the court shortly before 2:00 P.M. today—in the worst insult of all, the Wolfpack's presence is tacitly welcomed.

"Dean probably assigned the bus driver," Robinson says as he boards for the trip, laughing ruefully.

Forty minutes of driving in the sixtyish sunshine brings the Wolfpack entourage to the side of Carolina's campus nearest Raleigh and Durham, where the Smith Center looms like an otherworldly presence in a natural bowl. The arena is prodigious and modern and surrounded by grounds carefully sculpted to complement it. Approaching, you feel as though you've come upon an architect's rendering brought to life.

Inside, the playing area is awash in light blue, the color an enclosing theme from the trim on the banners hanging from the rafters to the outline of the state of North Carolina at midcourt. No clock except the game clock, no sense of immediate connection with a world beyond. No advertising logos, no overhead scoreboard. Just blue, that light blue.

"If God's Not A Tar Heel, Then Why Is The Sky Blue?" That tendentious question used to adorn bumper stickers throughout the Triangle. The stickers are rarely seen these days, though. It's Duke stickers that predominate. Most everybody loves a winner.

Unless, of course, the winner is Carolina. Where UNC's concerned, as Wake's Dave Odom says rather diplomatically, the state of North Carolina and parts beyond are divided into two camps: devoted Tar Heel fans and self-proclaimed "ABC" fans, rooters for Anybody-But-Carolina.

Fans of both persuasions nearly got the ultimate confrontation in 1991, when the Tar Heels and Blue Devils reached the Final Four and threatened to meet for the national championship. But UNC lost in the opener against a Kansas squad coached by Dean Smith's former ten-year assistant, Roy Williams, after which Duke upset undefeated Nevada–Las Vegas and marched to its first title.

That April in Indianapolis, Kansas fans were pleased but surprised to find their ranks swelled by Duke fans rooting not so much for the Jayhawks as against the Tar Heels, much to the lasting resentment of many UNC adherents.

Dislike of North Carolina is often based on vaguely populist sentiment, especially among N.C. State loyalists. Certainly Duke is the most elitist of the Triangle's major universities. Only 14 percent of the private school's students are from in-state, compared to 84 percent at N.C. State and 82 percent at North Carolina. (The stereotypical Dukie is wealthy, white, and from the Northeast, ironic considering Durham once was thought too bawdy a boomtown for proper society.) Yet State fans are more offended by what they perceive as an air of superiority emanating from their sister school in Chapel Hill, site of what Dean Smith is quick to call "the state's flagship university" and a liberal community Jesse Helms once said he'd like to wall in.

Pack backers often bristle at the widely held notion that it's much tougher to get into Carolina than it is to be accepted at N.C. State. In fact, among 1992 freshmen the mean SAT score at UNC was 1,111, compared to 1,053 at Raleigh. Not much difference.

The topic is in the news because a report released yesterday reveals there's not a single graduate among the basketball players who've entered N.C. State since 1985. Through the 1980s, only nine of forty-three eligible players received degrees. By way of comparison, using NCAA figures for 1983 and 1984 freshmen, Duke graduated 100 percent, UNC 83 percent, and N.C. State 13 percent.

It isn't only academics that's a sore point between N.C. State and UNC. The state's spending priorities are another. The legislature meets in Raleigh, but many of its members attended UNC's law school and prefer to roost not at Reynolds Coliseum but in the cushiest courtside seats at the Smith Center.

Many State folks also believe the media deck is stacked against them because of UNC, which has the state's only journalism school. Thus, when criticisms and unflattering stories arise regarding academic shortcomings or athletes' minor crimes, as happened repeatedly during Valvano's tenure, Pack backers tend to talk heatedly and defensively of a double standard rather than address the issues raised.

But no downtrodden wearers of red feel too feisty today as the Pack takes on the Heels, except perhaps the band of eight that pauses in a runway at the Smith Center, touches hands, whispers in private council, shouts "Pack!" and takes the court.

There they confront thirteen Tar Heel players (Brian Reese is sidelined with a pulled muscle in his upper back), more than twenty-one thousand Tar Heel fans, and athletic doom. It's like watching Grenada attempt to invade the United States, the results as predictable and sanguinary.

If there's any consolation in today's result, it is that disaster unfolds more slowly than it did at Duke sixteen days ago.

Robinson hopes the Pack can hang close by daring certain UNC players to shoot at one end, while running a highly selective delay offense at the other. Coach and team are buoyed by memory of perhaps State's best half of the year, achieved at home against Wake two days ago. Helped by the Deacons' charitable use of a zone, the Pack led by eleven points before losing 65–54.

But the Heels' superior size, strength, quickness, depth, experience, confidence and defense soon choke the visitors. Smith orders increased use of the traps that failed to catch the clever and gifted ball handlers at Wake and Duke. State has eleven turnovers in the first eleven minutes, and finishes the game with an astounding thirty.

During one first-half timeout, Robinson doesn't say anything for the first twenty or thirty seconds. "I didn't know what to say," he confesses. He reverts to the basics of the team's offense and defense, just as he'd outlined them on the first day of practice. "They were on the ropes like a boxer in a daze," Robinson says.

And that's not the worst of it.

Seconds after committing the last in a series of five straight Wolfpack turnovers, Marshall falls in a scramble for a loose ball. While he is lying face down, his head is inadvertently driven into the hardwood by a kick from teammate Todd Fuller's size-twenty athletic shoe.

Marshall, N.C. State's only semblance of a playmaker, doesn't return for the game's final twenty-nine minutes. Afflicted with a mild concussion and headache, for the rest of the afternoon he sticks his fingers in his ears when the band strikes up, or when Tar Heel fans amuse themselves by cheering and doing The Wave. Often the sophomore sits with head in hands, not unlike Robinson, who does so in response to the pain of watching his team in action.

Completing the day's physical casualties, Mark Davis reinjures his right wrist late in the game.

Still, State's little band plays on.

"The thing that I admire about that team is, they play hard," UNC guard Dante Calabria says. "With all the things that have happened to them, they play hard all the time. That's something you just have to admire about them. But if you're put in that same circumstance, I've thought about what would I do if I was put in that circumstance, and I don't know if I'd react the way they do. They come out and play hard every minute of the game."

Robinson coaches as hard as he can, but has fewer strings to pull than a freelance writer living outside New York. After waiting half a lifetime to get his dream job, in Robinson's third season it's come to this: being buried alive on a grand stage.

"We're not as bad as we were today," he says, "but we're fragile, very fragile."

By game's end Robinson has pulled a muscle in the right side of his face and expended his great reserve of enthusiasm. He sits rather quietly like a man watching an athletic version of the doomed charge at Balaklava in Tennyson's "Charge of the Light Brigade." The Smith Center ushers have much the same look, shaking their heads almost sorrowfully as Carolina's fresh, eager benchwarmers seize a chance to play and beat the hell out of State's battered little legion.

The 104–58 margin of defeat is the seventh-largest in ACC history.

"Our effort was there," Robinson says in the press room. "We played hard, but we didn't play smart. I credit Carolina with a great effort . . . it hurts to lose to anyone, it hurts to lose by one point or by fifty. It especially hurts to lose to Carolina. There is no question . . . wounds will heal and we'll come back again. We've had to do it all year and we'll just have to do it again . . . at least today our injuries were during the course of the game . . . I'm proud of these guys, they give their best every day and things are bound to start bouncing back."

Bound to.

"Personally, we're trying to stay positive," insists Kevin Thompson. "Right now, I don't know if we can get much lower. There's got to be brighter days ahead."

The game proves therapeutic and safe for North Carolina. "I realize N.C. State may not be an NCAA team, isn't an NCAA team," Smith says. "But they did a lot for us on execution. We graded out very well."

Also under discussion today are Smith's ideas about winning, touched off when he's asked how it feels to win again. "It feels wonderful," he says. "You know, I said as I grew older I would be able to feel better after a loss when we played well. Like Duke, we didn't shoot well but we played well. Then, after a win, say like down at Clemson . . . I've tried that. It just doesn't work for me. I feel better when it says North Carolina has more points." He pauses briefly, then takes his ever-racing train of thought onto a slightly different track.

"But I am concerned how we play. That's always been our top [concern] for the team, how are we going to play? We compare it to our potential and not to another team we're playing against. We play the golf course, we don't play the opponent." Today's opponent could use a day at the golf course, or anywhere else away from basketball.

Within fifteen minutes of Smith's remarks, after dropping their twelfth game against five wins, settling deeper into the ACC cellar, the largely silent N.C. State traveling party reboards the bus. The sun is at their backs as they head home to lick their latest wounds.

MONDAY, FEBRUARY 8

INDIANA, which Duke defeated in the '92 Final Four, has ascended to number one this week, the fifth team to hold the top ranking. Duke held it for every week of the 1991–92 season, becoming the first start-to-finish number one to win the NCAA title since North Carolina in 1982.

This week the Devils are ranked third, as most every South Carolina newspaper mentions in the headline for its Clemson game story. In fact, the ACC has four teams ranked in the top ten—Duke, UNC, Florida State, and Wake—for the first time since the '81 season.

Duke, highest-rated of the bunch, suffers from familiar problems in winning its eighteenth game: Bobby Hurley tends to look too much to the same people and to drift out of control on offense, Grant Hill's jumper is around the basket but usually won't go in, Cherokee Parks's first-half play is as flat and off-key as a bad singer's voice. Krzyzewski blisters the squad at halftime, with Hurley and Parks coming in for special attention.

Adding to Duke's problems, erstwhile starter Marty Clark plays just seven minutes. "My knees are killing me," he says later, ice pack on each knee, legs stretched before him. Clark says it's tendinitis. When the team returns home, he's placed on medication. But there are numerous good signs for the Blue Devils at Clemson, not the least of which is winning the game.

For whatever reason, the same Clemson squads that play fecklessly on the road display remarkable fire at home at Littlejohn Coliseum, especially against Georgia Tech and Duke. The Tigers have beaten Tech at Clemson six straight times, and over a the same span have beaten Duke three times and lost by two points and one point.

"If you can't get up to play Duke, you can't get up," says Lou Richie, a diminutive guard whose quickness bothers Hurley. "They're like the Chicago Bulls. Everywhere they go, people are up for them." Clemson led the '92 Blue Devils by nineteen points in the second half, the defending champs' largest deficit of the season. Angered by his team's lackadaisical manner—something he hasn't faced this year—Krzyzewski yanked his starters. The bench brigade, led by Erik Meek, smothered the flames and awoke its teammates, who returned and rallied for a 98–97 victory.

The Tigers are determined to win this time, or at least to atone for their execrable showing at Durham. "We're going to beat Duke," guard Andre Bovain tells a writer from Greenville, S.C. "You can write it down. We're going to beat them."

As happened last season, without television injecting artificial breaks, the pace is fast and furious, a delicious remembrance of how basketball is best played. Clemson uses the circumstances to test Duke's endurance and bench, and leads for the first fifteen minutes of the game. Not until Hurley hits his fourth bomb of the second half with 2:25 left does Duke's lead exceed six points, an advantage it stretches into a 93–84 victory.

"I tell you what—when are they going to start putting these games on TV?" a relieved Krzyzewski asks afterward. "The last two games down here have been some of the best in the conference. Tonight was a great basketball game. It's unbelievable how quick everyone was, how determined. We played well. They played great." Hurley has one assist in the second half as Duke reverts a bit to its NBA-style one-on-one offense. But the senior's sixteen second-half points come at crucial moments. He and Grant Hill, who controls the ball late, combine for nineteen of Duke's last twenty-five points.

The square-shouldered Hill, drawstring dangling from blue shorts and socks hidden inside black sneakers, leads all scorers with twenty-five points. Thirteen come at the foul line. Hill struggled with his free throw shooting early in the year; now, among all ACC players, he's second to Clark in accuracy in league competition.

"That's something I've worked on," Hill says. "I'm kind of like Bobby with threes. I want to shoot free throws." Hill has scored in double figures in all but one game this year.

He leads Duke in scoring and steals, is second in rebounds and blocks, is third in free throw and field-goal accuracy. And, as a pro scout at courtside in Littlejohn notes appreciatively, "He's just scratched the surface."

Yet, deep in his junior year Hill remains poised between confidence and genuine self-deprecation, a student of the game eternally finding flaws in the performer's execution. Thus what most strikes him upon reviewing his own effort are six turnovers, matching his performance in a lackluster win at Notre Dame two days earlier.

Thomas Hill likes what he sees on the stat sheet. His midseason funk ended, he shoots efficiently, earning fifteen points, and plays tough defense. A major Duke goal is shutting down Clemson's three-point attack; Hill's work helps hold the Tigers to five of nineteen accuracy from beyond the golden arc. Braggart Bovain is an especially ineffective shooter, though he does manage five steals.

Thanks to Duke's defensive emphasis and Clemson's hustle, Parks and Tony Lang get abused by the inside duo of Wright and Devin Gray, who combine for forty-three points, fourteen rebounds and six blocked shots. "They were ready to attack us," Krzyzewski says admiringly. Clemson hits 49.3 percent of its shots, among the best showings against Duke this season.

Parks's performance is especially irksome to his coaches, coming as it does so soon after Krzyzewski pronounced him dependable. "I think with him, he can be easily satisfied right now. The big question with him is, what are his goals as a player?" says assistant Mike Brey. "He should be seeing he can be a lottery pick. He can say it, but I don't know if he means it." To help convey the importance of that realization, the Duke coaches decide to start Meek when the team returns to Durham. Meanwhile Lang, the other player who's had his starter's status yanked and returned, seems to have responded well to the tactic.

"The last couple of games he's rebounding; he's being athletic. He's the player we know he can be," Grant Hill says. "He's kind of discovered his niche."

Helping improve Lang's frame of mind is the play of his bench buddies, Collins and Blakeney. "I think that Chris and Kenny came in and played real well. They kept the tempo up. I was like, if Chris and Kenny . . ." Lang's sentence peters out. "It sort of spread." Lang hates to say it, since he so recently accepted the rationale for being bumped to the bench, but it feels good to be starting again, too.

The evening's happiest development for Duke, though, is the play of Blakeney and Collins. The perimeter subs see twenty-seven minutes of action between them, much of it in the first half with Duke struggling.

They combine for eighteen points, make four of five three-pointers, and provide timely shooting, good ball handling and acceptable defense.

"For Chris and Kenny, this game was huge," Krzyzewski says. "To do that in this environment when you're down—hitting big shots, making big passes and playing good defense . . ." Recalling Lang's play as well, he adds, "This is a big game for us because those three kids have to feel much more confident after their contribution tonight in this win."

SATURDAY, FEBRUARY 13

MIKE Krzyzewski is forty-six years old today. Times are good. He and his family are healthy. His job is as secure as any can be in college athletics, which this week saw the University of California summarily dismiss basketball coach Lou Campanelli and last week saw the U.S. Military Academy, where Krzyzewski and Pete Gaudet once coached, dump Tom Miller.

This is perhaps Krzyzewski's busiest time of year. He's cut outside commitments to a minimum. With his team now facing its fourth game in eight days, fifth in ten, there's little time for distractions.

Krzyzewski finds his pleasures where he can, as from the bright presence of pansies blooming in his yard in the suburban outskirts of Durham. It's the first time he's planted pansies, and he's impressed not only with their beauty but with the hardiness that so directly contradicts the putdown that's common usage for "pansy." Gardening is one of Krzyzewski's few interests away from basketball and family, though of course he can't plant much just yet. He likes to garden "just to get away, so no one can ask for my autograph and ask me about repeating and three-peating," he says. "Not so much even to think as to be devoid of thinking. You know? Give yourself a rest. Running sometimes used to do that for me. I don't run as much as I used to. Maybe to think about what you shouldn't be thinking about. Why am I thinking about all these things? Here's what I should be thinking about."

Now that winter's facade is cracking, the Midwestern transplant finds there's a lot more to look at, too. Migrating robins have touched down, and thunderstorms. Dandelions, jonquils, and hyacinths join the pansies in subdued but colorful celebration of spring's approach. Maple buds are reddening. Everywhere bulbs upthrust greenly, daffodils topped by minarets of promise.

Professionally, early spring has especially happy connotations for Krzyzewski. It's the time of year he's become accustomed to taking teams to college basketball's brightest stage, the Final Four.

This season's team, third-ranked and seemingly rounding into shape, appears poised to duplicate the journey. The Blue Devils are on the verge of their tenth consecutive twenty-win season, have lost only three games by a total of ten points, and have given a determined, generally intelligent effort every time they've taken the court.

Statistics eloquently tell the story. The Devils are the ACC's most accurate shooters from the floor and the foul line. Conversely, their opponents are shooting poorly (.421), scoring sparingly (an average of 68.9 points), and committing three more turnovers per game than Duke.

Perhaps most significant in Krzyzewski's basketball calibrations, his team has made one hundred and nine more free throws than its opponents have attempted. This single stat reveals the successful achievement of numerous goals in Duke's system.

Defensively, Duke pressures the ball, contests passes on the wings, and stresses good positioning, double-teams, toughness, and hustle. Reach-ins, and the fouls that come from covering for teammates' mistakes, are kept to a minimum. A point of emphasis every half is to avoid the seventh team foul that puts an opponent on the free throw line with bonus shots. Woe to the Dukie who commits a foolish foul to put a rival into the bonus.

Duke prides itself on playing smart offensively too, dictating terms rather than simply taking what the defense gives. That means adjusting the motion offense to get the ball into what Krzyzewski and staff consider the proper hands. Reflecting that emphasis, almost half of this year's free throws have been attempted by leading scorers Grant Hill and Bobby Hurley, perimeter players who between them have made an excellent 78.3 percent at the line. Hurley and Hill, in fact most Duke players, are adept at attacking a defense off the dribble, which tends to attract fouls.

Given this thrust, it pleases Krzyzewski that Duke leads the ACC in the percentage of its total points achieved at the foul line. If that little-noted ranking holds true, it will be the tenth time in the last eleven seasons a Krzyzewski squad has been first or second in the league at cashing in via free throw. The sole exception was 1987, the last time Duke failed to reach the Final Four.

So the skies look bright for Duke as it prepares to host ninth-ranked

Wake Forest, fresh from a resounding loss at Florida State. To make Duke's prospects brighter yet on this windy afternoon, the Demon Deacons are without starting point guard Charlie Harrison, who's sprained his knee.

A win will bump Duke up to second in the national polls—though, oddly, only up to third in the ACC behind FSU and North Carolina.

"Once we get finished with Wake, we're on the road a little bit but we get more preparation time, we're over a big hump," Pete Gaudet confides. "It's turning out terrific. If we can beat Wake and watch the league manhandle each other a little bit, we're in great shape . . . nobody realizes what a good job we've done."

Wake and Duke players casually shoot together at the same basket an hour before the game. Wake's Randolph Childress shares shooting tips with Grant Hill, an acquaintance from high school days in the D.C. area. Hill is particularly good friends with Wake's Rodney Rogers, though not phone buddies like he is with Michigan's Chris Webber and Georgia Tech's James Forrest. (Actually the Dukies maintain friendly relations with players on most every ACC team except North Carolina.)

About three minutes prior to tipoff, the players are engaged in pregame warmups with their respective teams when the singing of "Happy Birthday" begins in the stands. This close to game time, Krzyzewski is, of course, all business. He recognizes the fans' serenade by standing before the bench and grinning modestly, then waves off the note of appreciation and resumes his seat.

Krzyzewski doesn't smile again once the game begins, though. Duke is off from the outset. Like Clemson on Monday, Wake thinks it can beat the Blue Devils to the basket, which it does on its first two possessions. Cherokee Parks, bumped as a starter against Georgia Tech by Erik Meek, is again slow to get going. So is Tony Lang, who picks up three fouls and no points in the first half attempting to guard Rogers and generate some offense.

Duke nevertheless builds an early nine-point advantage as the Hills and Bobby Hurley account for eighteen of the team's first twenty points. Grant Hill hits his first four shots, three of them jumpers. The junior has been fretting about his persistent failure to put together a personally satisfying game, but today he feels great. "I felt like I was in high school," he says. "I thought it would be a career night."

But after Wake rallies to pull within two, Hill falls injured during a scramble under Duke's basket. He tries to play on, but limps badly and takes himself out. Even when he returns for a few minutes, he isn't the same player.

"It was a jumble once Grant got hurt and Tony Lang got into foul trouble," Krzyzewski concedes. "We were horrible. We didn't rally around the flag. Grant gets hurt. We were in the lead. There were so many times when people could have stepped up and we didn't." Lang, Marty Clark, Meek, Parks, and Thomas Hill are thrown into the breach to slow Rogers, a collegiate version of Utah Jazz forward Karl Malone. Nothing works against the six-foot-seven Rogers. Put a big man on him and he blows past. Against a smaller man it's all power. Rogers does what he wants against the suddenly pliable Duke defense, crashing the offensive boards, driving the baseline, driving the lane, putting up feathery-soft jumpers that don't even touch the rim. After a while, few Dukies even try to get in his way.

The junior, who grew up across town from Duke in a public housing project as mean as any in a larger city, has twenty-four points in the first half alone. "I couldn't believe how easy it was to get him the ball," says Childress, marveling that Duke rarely fronts Rogers or double-teams him.

"They thoroughly outplayed us," a crestfallen Krzyzewski says after the game. "You name a phase of the game and if you were to judge us by today's game then you would say I don't coach very good defense, I don't coach very good shooting, I don't coach very good offense. You could go down the line and you'd be right. For today's game."

Duke leads 42–41 at halftime as Rogers gets the ball on the wing on Wake's first possession of the second half, drives around Parks and glides unmolested to the basket like a luxury car maneuvering among traffic cones. The Deacons, enjoying their best season in a decade, never trail again and go on to win 98–86.

Grant Hill meanwhile limps noticeably, favoring his left foot and in obvious pain. He can hardly keep up with the action and is a liability defensively. He sits down for the day with 16:36 to go. As if bracing for what's to come, the pair of pigeons that frequent Cameron fly high amongst the rafters behind and out of sight of Duke's bench.

Wake's total is the most scored by a Duke opponent at Cameron since 1983, Krzyzewski's last losing season. The Demon Deacons make 67.7 percent of their shots in the second half, 61 percent in the game. Rogers has thirty-five points, a career high, despite taking only sixteen shots.

"Rodney was sensational," Krzyzewski says. "That may be not giving him enough credit by saying it was sensational. I don't know. I have a limited vocabulary. He was better than that. And he did simple things that were great, absolutely great. It was one of the great performances, as good a performance as I've seen at Cameron in my thirteen years. If someone was going to perform that way, I'm glad it was Rodney because I really love him and how he plays and what kind of kid he is."

Coupled with the Virginia loss almost a month ago, the Wake defeat marks the first time since 1988 the Blue Devils have dropped two games at Cameron in the same season. The loss also ends a six-game Duke winning streak that began after leaving Tallahassee.

More important than the record is how Duke played and how badly Grant Hill is injured.

Krzyzewski says Hill's big toe is sprained. The player isn't convinced. "I think it's broken," Hill says before leaving the locker room with a bag of ice taped to his left foot. He broke the same toe as a junior in high school and says this injury feels identical.

The early diagnosis is indeed a sprain. Hill is expected to be out for one to three weeks. The timing is curious—Hill suffered an ankle injury almost exactly a year ago and missed three games. (The injury never heals; following the season, Hill undergoes an operation to repair torn connective tissue where his big toe attaches to his foot.)

As for Duke's performance against Wake, Krzyzewski acknowledges he's most disappointed with his team's defensive effort because, he says, "I think that's how everything starts. We were not an enthusiastic bunch today. That's my responsibility." He pauses, fumbling for words. "We deserved to lose." He laughs, though not happily. "Definitely. I mean, it wasn't even close. The team that deserved to win, won. And I think the team that put the most into the game won. And I admire that. Believe me when I say it about Rodney, like I really admire what he did today. I love that I saw that. I'm sorry that he was on the other team."

Proving once again that, even on our birthdays, we can't choose the presents we receive.

A few hours after Duke loses its fourth game, N.C. State wins its sixth. Typically, the game comes down to a final shot. Typically, it's the other team that has the ball in good position to score.

"I was shocked they got the ball all the way down there," Kevin Thompson says of Tennessee's baseline-to-baseline pass with three seconds remaining. "What can I say? I was holding on to the edge of my seat, just like against Clemson. And it was at the same basket too." The game is close throughout, with neither team strong enough to put the other away. Tennessee, 10–11 entering the contest, leads by a basket at halftime and by three points with 2:51 remaining. The Pack then reels off seven straight points, taking the lead for good when Lakista McCuller makes a steal near midcourt and goes in for a layup with 1:26 to go.

McCuller nearly made a similar play in N.C. State's previous game, a 75–66 loss at Virginia in which the Pack actually led through much of the first half and pulled within four in the late going. After losing its first four road games by an average margin of four touchdowns, the effort against a ranked team was encouraging. It wasn't enough because of a State defense that created only four turnovers and because Virginia guard Cory Alexander scored twenty-five points.

McCuller nearly forced a fifth turnover by the Cavs, but he overran the ball after knocking it loose. "Make that play," Robinson counsels the sophomore. "That's fine. But get the ball before you go." Against Tennessee, McCuller follows that simplistic advice, makes the steal and layup and, following a Volunteer timeout, makes a free throw too.

The crowd of about eight thousand senses victory and screams so loudly the lights on the operator-manipulated applause meter climb to the top and flash red. In the student section behind the team benches someone waves a sign that reads "Keep On Believing Pack." Tennessee inexplicably fails to get the ball to Allan Houston, a certain first-round NBA draft choice who was among the eight collegians enlisted as practice fodder last summer for the Dream Team. The Vols miss a three-pointer, miss a tap, and Mark Davis gets the rebound. Curtis Marshall is immediately fouled and makes the first of two free throws.

Now Houston's dad, Wade, the Tennessee coach, has his son bring the ball upcourt. The senior guard penetrates, is fouled by Marshall, and makes both free throws to cut State's lead to two points with forty-four seconds left. McCuller is fouled and makes both free throws. Houston responds by hitting a three-pointer. Timeout Tennessee, trailing by a point with 28.2 seconds to go.

When play resumes, Marshall is again fouled. Again he makes one of two. Timeout Tennessee.

This time the six-foot-six Houston backs six-three McCuller into the lane, turns, and hits a jumper. The game is tied with 14.3 seconds remaining.

During the preceding timeout, Robinson told his team what to do.

Now, remarkably, he gets what he asked for. State quickly inbounds the ball, McCuller races it upcourt and attacks the basket, only to throw up an off-balance shot against two defenders. The ball caroms off the glass and onto the weak side, where Thompson has positioned himself for just such an eventuality. He catches the ball and lays it back in.

State leads by two. Tennessee calls timeout with three seconds remaining.

"We executed with poise in a must situation, and that I was very, very proud of," says Robinson. "Because we could have choked right there, and we did not."

Instead the Pack almost chokes on the next play. Using Houston as a decoy, the Vols throw long to guard Chris Brand. Marshall leaps to intercept and misses. "I gambled," he admits sheepishly. "I'm sure we'll see it on the film tomorrow."

With Marshall out of position, Bland has a clear path to the basket. "I just turned and looked at it and said, 'Oh, no!'" recalls Marshall. But Bland rushes a jumper, missing everything. The ball goes directly to a teammate. But he too musters only a wild heave as the buzzer sounds, the crowd cheers and the applause meter spikes again.

Afterward there's the unaccustomed sound of laughter in the Wolfpack locker room. An awed flock of elementary-aged boys roams from player to player soliciting autographs. Their high spirits are contagious.

"We've been looking forward to this two-game stretch right here," admits Marshall, referring also to a game two days hence against a weak, sister school, UNC-Greensboro. "Really three games, because we thought we had a chance to beat Virginia." Mark Davis shares in the good feeling, but only to a point. He regrets he was on the bench, not the floor, for the final twenty-eight seconds. And he's still smarting after yet another miserable shooting performance—two of eight, keeping his glaring field-goal conversion rate around 28 percent.

"I don't know. I don't have anything else to say about it," he offers. "It's getting to the point where my confidence is coming back a little bit. I think I'm going to be one of the best shooters in the league."

He notes, as he has since the game at Durham nearly a month ago, that his shots are on line, just short or long. He insists, as he has since returning from his wrist injury nearly two months ago, that he'll continue to shoot with confidence. Never mind that he still looks anxious and unsteady with the ball in his hands, like a batter in a slump who grips the bat too tight.

Davis never before has experienced such failure and frustration, in basketball or any part of life. Asked how he copes, he says: "I call my mom. I guess she's the best remedy for me. I guess she gives me the pep talks of, like, a coach."

Davis's mother reminds him how he attacked things in high school, how he stayed in the gym on Friday and Saturday nights to work on his shooting. It's not so simple now, though.

"College is different," Davis says. "The schedule is so demanding. You have studies; you have tests." The aspiring civil engineer looks at the boys flitting about the locker room. "All these kids see in here are basketball players. They don't realize how tough it is to balance your schedule athletically and academically." Nor can the youngsters, or anyone else outside the N.C. State program, fully appreciate what this year has been like for the team, quite apart from wins and losses. Just today, Davis watched the Florida State–Maryland game on television and saw a commercial that included a clip of Tony Robinson in action.

"There's so many low points," Davis says of the season, "but the thing that really sticks out in my mind as the most disappointing thing for this team was Tony's death. Tony was always cheerful and kept everybody up. When he died I think he took a part of everybody with him."

TUESDAY, FEBRUARY 16

GRANT Hill is not shooting, stretching, and running with his teammates today. Instead, at trainer Dave Engelhardt's order, he's seated with his injured left foot propped on the scorer's table, naked toes peeping above a nylon casing, the nail black and blue on his severely sprained big toe.

Another departure from custom is the flock of elementary school kids in attendance. This is Duke's monthly autograph day, a fit time for the children to gather signatures from the Blue Devils, who each must sign several dozen balls in the Hall of Fame Room as well as an array of team posters lining almost the entire seventy-seat press row. (Fan favorite Bobby Hurley has an additional group of personalized photos to autograph.)

The heroes in blue quickly display their mortality, and in alarming variety.

First and most seriously, Moore dislocates his right shoulder contesting a shot. Just yesterday Krzyzewski told Moore he'd get a chance to play at meaningful times during games.

Now Moore clutches his arm and lists sharply to the right. Quickly, the trainer and a student manager escort him from the building, holding up his damaged limb as they go.

Not long afterward Marty Clark reinjures a jammed finger and comes to the sideline in obvious pain. The team takes a quick water break while Engelhardt rearranges Clark's finger and buddy-tapes it to a neighbor.

Even later Chris Collins, the smallest player on the team, takes a blow to the head and goes sprawling. He's up and about in a moment, shaking his head to clear his vision.

The ranks are so suddenly thin; with only incapacitated Grant Hill on the sideline, it's almost like N.C. State.

Hill has arrived at Cameron on crutches, and complains they hurt his armpits even through an Adidas leather jacket. It's the third straight year Hill has been sidelined by injuries. As a freshman he broke his nose and missed two games. For a time after his return he was plagued by headaches and wore a protective mask Krzyzewski said made him look like "the man from 'Star Trek.'" Later that season Hill also suffered a hip pointer and missed a game and a half. As a sophomore he sprained his ankle and missed three late-season games. Now this.

Hill had eschewed following in his father's football steps because he saw first-hand Calvin Hill's succession of painful injuries. But the son has apparently inherited a propensity for a hardwood version of "turf toe," the injury he suffered against Wake.

The prognosis is unpleasant and uncertain: Hill is sidelined indefinitely, a situation Krzyzewski calls "week-to-week, not day-to-day." The coach further announces "there's no way" Hill will play this week at Virginia and N.C. State.

Virginia's Jeff Jones prepares for Hill's participation anyway. He's been through this before with Duke, just last season in fact. It was against Virginia, after all, that Hurley returned from an injury—well ahead of schedule and on the very day Hill was to miss his first game of the year—and led the Blue Devils to a key late-February win.

Jones need not worry this time. There's a chance, not shared publicly, that Hill will be out as long as three weeks, or until the conclusion of the regular season. The length of the recovery may be dictated to a large degree by the team's ability to coalesce in his absence, an effort that would require increased consistency from Parks and Lang, and a step up by Clark, Blakeney, and/or Collins.

Lang, it seems, simply needs to believe his own positive words, uttered after most every game, and put together two good halves.

Prior to last week's game against Georgia Tech, Lang said "Coach Krzyzewski" (most players say "Coach K") told him to "just go out there and play freely." In fact, says one assistant coach, Lang is "begged" to shoot.

The result was more of the same, vintage Lang '93. In the first half against Tech, he played good defense on James Forrest but was otherwise a quiet cog, grabbing three rebounds, disdaining open baseline jumpers, taking just two shots and scoring a single point. Then in the second half he used his quickness and leaping ability to score nine points, get five rebounds, and block two shots.

Lang works hard and attempts to banish the lingering fixation on finding his niche, a distraction that he, his coaches, and his teammates believe has affected his consistency.

The junior admits, however, that he's also simply tired, his slender frame worn by the demands of school, life, and very serious play. He enjoys the benefits of basketball: the travel, meeting new people, and seeing new things. But there are hidden costs.

A player is handicapped socially, forbidden under NCAA rules to hold a job while attending school. Therefore Lang's modest spending money comes from his middle-class parents or from savings from summer-camp speaking engagements. That makes it tough to fit in at a school like Duke, where many students have the financial wherewithal to match their families' abilities to shell out more than eighty thousand dollars for a college education.

"The school that I went to had kids who came from projects. My father was from the projects," says Lang, whose high school in Mobile was all black. "The kids up here, a lot of them are well off. It's hard to fit in at the beginning, but you can after a while because you realize it's not a true representation of the world." Then, too, being black tends to ensure a certain social insularity at Duke, encouraging team members to band together. It's a widespread problem among African-American athletes at predominantly white schools, one that attracts a crew from CBS's "Sixty Minutes" to Duke's campus. Lang and Grant Hill are among the interview subjects for the story.

Meanwhile, with all the travel, practices, meetings, shoot-arounds, film study, and weight lifting, not to mention the interviews and community outreach, there's the matter of scholarship to be pursued.

"We're supposed to keep up with all of our class work when our schedule's not like regular students," Lang observes without rancor. "It's tough. Out here on the court, you're definitely competing with the highest level of competition. At Duke University, you're also competing with students at the highest level. It's double." So you "learn what it takes," says the history and economics major, and you juggle your commitments, striving all the while for excellence.

Lang's oncourt difficulties cost him a starting position for two games, but only that. Clark had a chance to seize Lang's spot, but regressed. With both juniors sputtering Duke's coaches eye what one calls "the big picture," which includes not only this year but next.

Four new players, two of them forwards, already have signed. The flock may add another wing if Baltimorean Keith Booth likes what he sees on a visit the last day of February, and if he can make seven hundred on the SATs.

Perhaps the toughest of next season's signees is big man Greg Newton, who's apt to push Cherokee Parks mightily, a prospect that quite pleases Duke's coaches.

Parks remains a bit enigmatic. Since the Carolina game, when Krzyzewski pronounced the sophomore's arrival as a solid starter, Parks has faded fast.

"That's frustrating," Thomas Hill says of Parks's play. "Maybe that's because he is young, maybe because he is only a sophomore. I don't think that's an excuse for him. It shouldn't be an excuse for anyone, to be honest."

Against Tech, Parks responds to demotion with a good effort in thirty minutes compared with Meek's ten. "It definitely pissed me off," Parks says of not starting. "I would not say I wasn't trying or putting forth, doing my best. That's just the way things went. But who's going to argue with Coach K's methods? They've been very successful. I'm not going to hold a grudge." Yet when Parks resumes his starter's role against Wake he again stumbles.

The way Parks's coaches see his performance is aptly summed up in a four-panel commentary that runs in the Duke *Chronicle*.

The student newspaper runs only three syndicated daily cartoons— "The Far Side" by Gary Larson, "Doonesbury" by Garry Trudeau, and "Calvin and Hobbes" by Bill Watterson. This week Watterson has bad-boy Calvin rolling a ball of snow nearly his own size while Hobbes, his stuffed-tiger friend, looks on.

"I'm making a monumental, heroic snow sculpture," Calvin announces, head thrown back and arm raised. "It will be called 'The Triumph Of Perseverance.'"

Hobbes, paws on hips, scarf nattily thrown about his neck, comments: "Very inspiring. What will it look like?" Calvin gestures with a mittened hand toward the near-formless ball beside him. "This."

"You're through?" Hobbes asks.

"I'm bored," Calvin says, walking away.

Parks isn't bored, but seems mentally unavailable at times. And he's still a bit formless, lacking a certain will to achieve. Perseverance has not yet triumphed.

Mike Brey says Parks has had a good year, considering he's been relied upon as a significant contributor for the first time, and came to Duke a bit naive about what he was getting into.

Parks says it's all a matter of perception. Asked why others feel it's difficult to motivate him, he replies: "I don't even know how to answer that. I guess it's just my personality. I am extremely laid-back. I guess my approach is different than everyone else's on the team."

Brey notes, "The big question with him is, what are his goals as a player?"

Brey says recruits are told there are two primary reasons for enrolling at Duke. The first is to get a good education. The second is "to play basketball at the highest level. And if you want to come here, you have to have an aspiration to play at the highest level." Parks has that aspiration. "I think it'd be real interesting," he says of an NBA career. "It would be a lot of fun. Occasionally I think that far down the road, but not much."

More often he appears content simply to be a student who plays basketball. "Right now, I think Cherokee is satisfied to be a Duke starter," Brey observes. "The basketball is secondary. What do you say to a kid? You can't get all over him. He should be seeing he can be a lottery pick. He can say it, but I don't know if he means it." What coaches and teammates see is an easygoing guy who hangs out with non-basketball friends and likes to do the sorts of things other students do. They don't begrudge him the experience, but they simmer over this failure to elevate the common enterprise, their common interdependent enterprise, to paramount importance.

"The reality with Cherokee Parks, as coaches and his mother all agree, it's as important for him to chase his basketball goals as his academic goals," Brey insists. "This is a kid, one of the few, he should make a living playing basketball. There's nothing wrong with that."

True. But herein lies the crux of what plagues intercollegiate athletics, even at a school as principled as Duke.

"There's incredible validity to the statement we're athlete-students, not student-athletes," Marty Clark says. "Basketball takes the best hours of your day. It takes priority over everything else. It takes more time. Easily, without any question. So to say we're student-athletes is incorrect."

So, for all the talk to the contrary, Cherokee Parks is supposed to accept that he's a preprofessional basketball player. He's not supposed to let his focus wander. He's not supposed to get too caught up in campus life, in unstructured fun, in questioning and challenging basic assumptions, in exploring realms that weaken discipline, undermine authority, or limit resolve.

Here he is, halfway through his college years, and he's not devoted first and foremost to honing professional skills. He's not thinking ahead to his career, to real life and the everyday responsibilities that await. He's acting like, well, a normal college student, or rather a non-eighties college student, enjoying the interlude of freedom between living under parental control and having to work to support himself.

"People may say he doesn't get motivated for games, but I know for a fact that he does," says Ryan Scannell, a premed student who rooms with Parks. "I think it's cool, because I don't think Cherokee approaches Duke basketball as much as a lifestyle as other players do. He also realizes that it's just a game. So you don't do well against Georgia Tech. What's the big deal? So you listen to your coaches and do better next time."

Parks's supposedly divided attention may be affecting his consistency. Certainly his lack of consistency is affecting the team. Older teammates, who sit around and talk about what it takes to win, wonder how to get him and the other less experienced players to step up their performance and commitment.

"Once you get everyone thinking about the same thing all the time, it's kind of like a passion," Thomas Hill says, recalling how it was during the two championship seasons. "What are your goals? What do you want out of life? That's definitely a question with a lot of guys on our team. Well, with a couple of guys on our team who are important."

Hill includes Parks, Blakeney, and Clark in that group.

"You wonder, what are you thinking about? What are your goals as a person and as a player? Are you more concerned about hanging out with your friends? Not to say being a regular student is bad or anything, but you're definitely here to play basketball. You're a basketball player. That doesn't mean you couldn't be anything else, but you wonder because we have such a great opportunity to do some good things. . . .

"It's hard to explain unless you're in that situation. I mean, you can definitely be both a player and a student, there's no question. But, like, I think in my case I know what's important. I know that basketball's not the only thing, the most important thing. I know school is important, and getting an education. But I can be both. I know that I have a future in basketball. That's how I can make money. That's how I can be a success or whatever. Not to say that that's the only thing I can do, but if that opportunity's there, why not go on that opportunity?"

NORTH Carolina defeats Clemson in Chapel Hill, 80–67. North Carolina always defeats Clemson in Chapel Hill. Has since 1926. The Tigers not only lose in Chapel Hill, they've now lost every game in the Triangle for six straight seasons.

The third-ranked Tar Heels improve their record to 21–3. Tonight at least it's a contest, Carolina's final margin of victory its smallest at home against the Tigers since 1983.

Donald Williams again faces a box-and-one alignment—still learning to move without the ball and stay focused despite special attentions, he takes four shots in the game, missing both three-point tries.

Yet when Dean Smith orders a spread offense to run time off the clock in the final four minutes, he turns to Williams. Last year's apprenticeship at point guard, widely second-guessed at the time, now serves Williams well. Carolina's most dangerous one-on-one player operates with aplomb, earning six trips to the foul line and two assists as the Heels pull away.

"I want our players to be very proud to beat a very good Clemson team having an excellent game," Smith says. "These are the kinds of games that many teams can lose, particularly when they start saying they haven't won in Chapel Hill—oh-for-history."

Perhaps the single most notable development tonight, and a major factor in holding Clemson at bay, is the play of Brian Reese.

Reese scores twelve of Carolina's first twenty points. He dunks after cutting to the basket and receiving a pass from Eric Montross, the fifth pass of the possession as the team works the ball purposefully. Reese scores a fast-break layup, changing speeds en route to elude a defender.

Clemson goes to a zone and concentrates on stopping Williams, so Reese spots up, takes a pass from Phelps, and hits a three from the right corner. Three possessions later Reese hits another bomb, this from the left side. Thirty seconds after that, the high-jumping forward gets behind the zone on the baseline, and even as the Clemson bench yells "Lob!" Reese slams the ball home on a pass from Henrik Rodl.

Reese finishes with eighteen points, his best scoring total since the opening game of the season. He passes with authority, displays an eye for getting the ball to Montross in the low post. Suddenly the Heels again possess the intermediate threat, the second reliable outside shooter, the explosive offensive force that glimmered tantalizingly late last season and intermittently in December.

"He just came out tonight to show that he was back," Montross says. "I've been waiting for that. He's an excellent player. He's been kind of hindered with a lot of injuries. He hasn't quite been up to full strength. I think that tonight was a time that he was able to come out and go as hard as he could and not worry about hurting himself."

Reese has been a devoted defender all year and one of the team's better passers. His willingness to work has never wavered. But he's been a lost basketball soul—confused, seeking, frustrated. Lately, the dissatisfaction has seethed just beneath the surface. "I have a year and a half left, that's all," he mutters. "I have a year and a half left here."

There's always a tension in Dean Smith's system between the creative and the structured, the "freelance" flexibility to read a defense and adapt as you choose versus the responsibility to stay within one's role, within the carefully meshed whole. "No matter how good a player you are, or whatever, if you don't listen to what he's teaching, you're not going to play," Reese says. "It's a team offense; it's a team defense. One person messes up; we're all just a shambles." Reese is quick to mention these truths. More than most players, he has spoken since arrival in Chapel Hill of his desire to fit, to blend, to balance selflessness and assertion in pursuit of victory. But it's a struggle.

"It was a big change for me, mentally, physically," Reese says of becoming a Tar Heel. "I'm from New York. I never ran a day in my life. Running track? Get in shape? I didn't know what that was. I rode buses, trains, cabs everywhere. Running? I didn't know what that was."

He found out.

"I thought I was on the track team," Reese says. "I was here the whole summer before my freshman year working out with George [Lynch] and them. I thought I was working out. I was like: 'Yeah, I ran this morning. I'll be all right for practice.'"

He found out different.

"I was throwing up, falling out," Reese confesses. "I'd never experienced anything like that."

Reese hadn't experienced anything like the intricacies of Smith's playing philosophy, either, particularly at the offensive end.

"You can see the moves I make; they come from the playground," Reese says. "Somebody is always wanting to try something new on you. Then, becoming an All-American in high school, you have to take shots. It's you, you, you. That is the way they put it to you. You have to be 'the man' every game."

Reese is a Fab-Five-type talent. He could have gone elsewhere and remained 'the man,' scoring twenty points per game. He chose instead to come to Chapel Hill, to play for the coach whose team impressed him on TV more than a decade ago while it was winning the '82 NCAA title. "You have to think about the future aspect of it," Reese said earlier this season. "Am I going to drop twenty points a game every year without playing with other good players?"

Reese said in picking a school he thought of Mark Macon, and how Macon struggled against double-teams for much of his career at Temple. In contrast, Reese feels "secure" at Carolina because "I'm always going to be playing with other good players, and they're going to help me . . . here, you're winning. Regardless of what everybody says, you know, 'You're not playing as much, you're not scoring as much,' and this, this. 'You don't be dunking.' It's just two points. I want to win."

But you can't join in pulling the wagon unless you're in the traces. At Carolina that means accepting a mental yoke designed by Smith. "He tries to build you up mentally," Reese says, "because, you know, he always says basketball is a mental game. That's all he's trying to do, prepare you and make you mentally strong." In pursuit of that strength, Carolina players endure repeated verbal testing, especially early in their careers. They're tested in team meetings, on the floor at practice, sometimes even in what Smith says about them to the media.

This fall, following the first week of practice, Smith announced Montross was performing below capabilities, probably because hype and expectation had made him nervous. Montross disagreed strongly.

Phelps laughed at the exchange, calling it one of Smith's typical "mind games." Montross preferred another term, but confirmed Phelps's assessment. "There's a message behind what he tells you anytime," the center says of Smith.

Sometimes the message simply is that there's no message other than to believe in yourself.

"It's like he'll show you something, and he knows the answer, and you probably know the answer, but he says something that makes you think different," Phelps explains. "Like, he'll show something on a film and you know you did it right and he knows you did it right, but the way he says something, he'll say something and then he'll say, 'Do you think that's right?' And you sit there and think about it like, 'I know that's right,' but the way he's talking he's making you change your mind and everything. You sit there like, 'Hmmm.' Then you probably change the story, like, 'No, that ain't right.'

"It's just a mind game like that, even though it was right. He just made you change it, just to make you think with yourself . . . he wants you to just really think for yourself and don't be scared. Just come out with it. You just won't have a problem, instead of changing your story because he says something."

Reese has been less sure than most, particularly about his role. That's made him a prime target for Smith's mental drills. "I'm the champion of that," Reese says without pleasure.

Reese's troubles this year also have a physical basis. He has suffered injuries to his hamstring, ankle, upper back, lower back, and finger. For the longest time he didn't believe he was holding back, but Smith kept telling him he was. Finally, Smith benched Reese entirely when N.C. State came to Chapel Hill so the forward's nagging aches could heal.

The tug of war over conditioning has been career-long for Reese, whose stamina has been a problem, supposedly due to asthma.

"The coach, he always gets on him on the asthma thing," Phelps notes. "Sometimes he'll run up and down the court, and he gets tired. Coach says, well, it's asthma, you know, and Brian don't want to be known as he got tired because he got asthma. Maybe he's tired because he's running up and down the court hard and everything. I think Coach Smith says things like that just to make him angry or play harder because he's saying things like that.

"I think that's the result, what's happening now. He needs to run, and he needs to get his stamina up. And all the things Coach used to say to him. I think right now he's really developed into a player. He's a junior now. I think he's just put it behind him, and he's just telling himself, 'I'm going out there and just play hard and do what I have to do out there on the floor.'"

Whatever the alchemy of his transformation, Reese has emerged from his funk, shedding his hesitancy virtually before everyone's eyes.

"All year I've played with an injury except these two games," he says of the last two outings, wins over Georgia Tech and Clemson. "It's uncomfortable to be out there playing with injuries. You're worried about it. When my butt bone was hurting, I didn't want to really box out hard enough. My ankle, I didn't want to really jump hard for fear of coming down on it. Or with my finger, when I would catch the ball I would be hesitant."

Whether Reese is in fact healthy again or merely has been given leeway to think he's healthy doesn't really matter. He's playing healthy. With that comes confidence and a sense of peace that until three games ago remained elusive.

"I think after the Duke game, we had a talk and he made up his mind that he has a lot of improving to do, and he started doing it," Smith says. "But he's always had a good attitude. He's very honest, not a con guy. Very nice. I like to visit with him."

N.C. State comes closer than Clemson to pulling off an upset tonight.

Ninth-ranked Florida State visits Raleigh without its two leading scorers, Bob Sura and Doug Edwards, both suspended for a game for cutting class. The Wolfpack is buoyed by its only two-game winning streak of the season. It leads by a point at halftime, makes eleven three-pointers, and stays within striking range until the bitter end.

The end does proves bitter, though, as FSU wins 72–71. Playing its third game in five days, the eight-man Pack runs out of gas down the stretch and falls to 7–14, 1–10 in the ACC.

Curtis Marshall finishes with a game-high twenty-two points. Mark Davis hits half his ten shots and rebounds well. Marc Lewis has ten rebounds.

But the Pack misses 60 percent of its free throws, including five of seven in the second half. "It's the sort of thing that keeps killing us," says Kevin Thompson, who misses five of seven foul shots in the game. "It just seems like it's always something."

THE mountains surrounding Charlottesville are little more than glorified hills, really, worn Appalachian outcroppings with flanks draped in velvet shadows and brows adorned by bare brown trees. Snow huddles where the sunlight can't reach, or lies in ragged hunks where it's been pushed to the roadside.

Grant Hill hasn't made the trip, staying behind to get treatment and rest. Mike Krzyzewski calls the Virginia game "a moment of need" in which other Blue Devils must step forward. He singles out Tony Lang to provide heightened leadership. And he says someone needs to contribute a double-figure rebounding performance. (Hint: Cherokee Parks.)

Krzyzewski also stresses a focus on "the big picture"—this team has won nineteen games in twenty-three tries and remains in good shape for a run at a national title. It can't win the ACC regular season race or concern itself with NCAA seedings, already a hot topic of press room conversation. Now is a time for improvement and exploration, for finding new strengths.

The Cavaliers are 15–5 and tied with Duke for fourth in the conference, primarily because they play tough defense, holding opponents to the lowest accuracy in the league (.409).

Duke, on the other hand, ranks seventh in the country and tops in the ACC in field-goal accuracy (.518). Only once in the past decade has a Krzyzewski team made less than 49 percent of its shots. The '93 Blue Devils also pace the ACC with .732 free throw accuracy; only twice in the past decade has Duke made less than a handsome 70 percent of its foul shots.

Tonight, the action suits Virginia: Defense dominates. The pace is slow.

Most offensive possessions are executed in half court. "I've never been in a more intense game defensively," Cav assistant Tom Perrin says. "Every point, every shot, I was drained on the bench."

The Cavaliers make 36.8 percent of their field goals, rotten accuracy that's not their worst this year. Duke's 35.9 percent shooting is, however, the worst at the school since a 1983 ACC Tournament loss to Virginia.

Throughout the first half, the Devil offense is as awkward as someone trying to order from a menu written in an unfamiliar language. Once again Bobby Hurley and Thomas Hill can't hit—the seniors make nine of twenty-eight shots, three of nine on three-pointers. "They try—it seems like Tommy and Bob try to lead by example," Marty Clark says. "When they don't play well, shoot well, there's less leadership on the floor. That's something we've talked about at team meetings."

And the team that thrives at the line misses nine of thirteen free throws.

Lang starts off hot, scoring on two of Duke's first three possessions. But he also fumbles a low, catchable pass from Hurley on an early fast break and doesn't see the ball much after that. Lang eventually fouls out after thirty-two minutes in which he attempts just five shots. Of those he does try, several are wide-open jumpers that he misses at key junctures late in the game.

Clark replaces Grant Hill in the starting lineup but takes little advantage of the opportunity. Rather, as happened when he took Lang's starting spot several weeks earlier against North Carolina, he's a virtual nonentity and barely leaves the bench in the second half.

"I think, for me, it's really important to hit my first or second shot, and when I don't my whole offensive game suffers," Clark admits. "And the first thing that goes is my three-point shot." Once among Duke's ace bombers, Clark tries a single three-pointer against Virginia and misses.

Clark has missed ten of eleven three-pointers since becoming a more prominent player in the Carolina game. The coaches keep encouraging him to shoot, but the more Clark misses, the less he feels like trying. "Me and Tony, we're kind of going through the same thing," he says.

The player who steps forward is Chris Collins. Kenny Blakeney tries, playing as much as Collins. He's OK defensively and has four offensive rebounds, but he squanders several golden scoring opportunities by hurrying shots.

Collins, on the other hand, plays with some poise and great enthusiasm. He draws a crucial charge and contributes his eight points in the final ten minutes. Included are a pair of three-pointers with the lead fluctuating, his second bomb launched about twenty-five feet from the basket as he comes to a running halt on the right wing, catches a Hurley pass, and bounces immediately into his shotput-jumper.

When it's clear the game will go down to the wire, Collins, not Blakeney or Clark, is on the court. Though he contributes an ill-advised three in the final minute, the freshman continues to clap, pat his older teammates on the back, and generally display the sort of positive attitude that impresses coaches and almost lifts Duke into overtime and potential victory.

"To me, hustle and positive play is very important," Krzyzewski says. "In fact, it's beautiful."

Parks has the best all-around outing among the starters. He has a game-high eleven rebounds, though none on offense. He also shoots efficiently, and is team-high with sixteen points. "When he shows up, he can have a tremendous influence on a game, without a doubt," Clark says.

Thomas Hill has fourteen points, but needs seventeen shots to get there. Teammates still consider the senior overly concerned with his NBA prospects, but tonight they appreciate his leadership.

Hill takes four of Duke's final eight shots and misses each—a baseline jumper after which Virginia takes the lead for good, a jumper in the lane on the very next possession, a pull-up three-pointer when two would do, and a hurried three-pointer after intercepting a Virginia inbounds pass. Hill's miss is the last shot of the game.

"Thomas had three or four open shots, it just didn't happen," Krzyzewski says.

This is an emotional game for Virginia and its eager fans, adding to Duke's difficulties. "Everybody before the game even started was out of their mind," center Ted Jeffries says of the Cav locker room.

Near the end, with victory in sight, that fever pitch works against the home team. "We were too emotional, beyond the point where it's a productive thing," Jones says afterward.

First, Parks makes a layup with eight seconds to go, pulling Duke within 58–55. Now all Virginia has to do is let the clock run down, then throw the ball long. That way, even if the pass is intercepted, there won't be enough time for the Blue Devils to score. But in the heat of the moment Jeffries gets nervous and hurries his inbounds pass, which is caught near midcourt by Thomas Hill.

Thinking his team leads by a safe four points rather than three, Cornel Parker leaves Hill free to drive as fast as he can toward the Virginia basket. Hill pulls up near the three-point line and lets fly in time to beat the final buzzer.

"I really couldn't grab the ball," Hill says. "I didn't know what time it was. And I was kind of off-balance. I just shot it. It really didn't feel like it was a good shot, but I was hoping it would go in." Jones laughs when asked what went through his mind. "Miss it! There's nothing real technical. Don't foul." Hill's shot falls short, the game ends, and Virginia students stampede the court.

"To be able to beat them is really a great feeling," Jones says in the wake of Virginia's first sweep of a regular season series with Duke since 1983. "We're thrilled. I think the reaction from our fans and our players after winning this game can be looked at as a tribute to Duke." Krzyzewski is similarly upbeat despite the loss and Duke's worst scoring output in eleven seasons. He lauds both teams' defensive performances and laments his team's inability to hit makeable shots, perhaps because players tried too hard.

"I'm not one to be down about losing when we have effort and preparation. Hey, let's go on to the next thing," Krzyzewski says. "You don't win championships by feeling sorry for yourself."

Duke's players aren't quite so quick to accept the result. "We were really looking to this game to come out as a team," Collins says as the Blue Devils make their way toward the bus and the bitter cold outside through corridors swarmed by autograph seekers. "It was a rough game to lose because of that. Some of the other losses we know we didn't give it our all. This game, maybe we didn't play as well as we can, but we played as hard as we can."

Tony Lang says much the same thing, and notes "it feels kind of weird" to lose consecutive games for the first time in his career. And Hurley, again the sole object of the crowd's hostility, says: "I'm not used to losing like I have, especially in the ACC. It's tough to deal with."

TODAY it's basketball second, emotion and mortality first. Reynolds Coliseum is packed more than an hour prior to game time. The occasion is a tenth anniversary celebration of the Wolfpack's 1983 national championship, a nine-game run that culminated with one of basketball's great upsets, a defeat of a heavily favored Houston team led by Akeem Olajuwon and Clyde Drexler. But even as the '83 Wolfpack's team doctor, trainers, student managers, assistant coaches, and many of its players are introduced, it's clear that the red-clad horde has come primarily to see Jim Valvano, the mastermind of that improbable victory.

This day is less a celebration of a distant achievement than it is a combination pep rally, testimonial and, frankly, elegy for the dying Valvano, making his first return to Reynolds since his ouster in 1990.

Valvano long ago received the assignment to serve as color analyst on this afternoon's ABC telecast of the Duke–N.C. State game. Anticipating the moment, Valvano insists he holds no grudges, pointing out he still wears his '83 championship ring, still holds season tickets to Wolfpack football and basketball games.

"I'm trying to dwell on the positive, I'm not a vindictive person," he said in January. "When I look back on State, sure, I think there were a couple of people there that treated me wrong. But when you look at the ten years I had there, who had a better run than I had? Who had more fun than I had?"

Yet there's little sense of fun in the air today.

Members of the school pep band wear T-shirts that say "Jimmy V" on the front and "Don't Give Up" on the back, a slogan Valvano has adopted in spearheading a drive to raise funds to fight cancer.

Appropriate to the occasion, the group of young men who get things rolling with an a cappella rendition of "The Star Spangled Banner" call themselves "The Grains of Time." The lights go down and the crowd listens to radio play-by-play of the final seconds against Houston, culminating with a buzzer-beating dunk by Lorenzo Charles to secure a 54–52 victory. The crowd cheers the moment yet again. As it does a spotlight catches the 1983 championship banner hanging at the arena's south end, the lights come up, and members of the magical squad troop onto the court.

Most of the ex-players here today were benchwarmers a decade ago. Three of the five starters can't make it. Point guard Sidney Lowe is busy at an NBA coaches' meeting; he's head man at Minnesota, where he must deal with iconoclastic rookie Christian Laettner. Charles and center Cozell McQueen—forever famous for saying he left South Carolina for N.C. State so he could attend school up north—are playing overseas.

Starter Thurl Bailey, a ten-year NBA veteran now with Minnesota, arrives late due to a snowstorm, but is there at the end of the bench as Valvano's appearance is announced by his broadcast partner, Brent Musburger.

Valvano enters to a great ovation, cut short by the band blaring the school fight song, an artillery version of "When The Caissons Go Rolling Along." Valvano, at forty-six, the same age as Mike Krzyzewski, moves stiffly down the line of well-dressed young men, exchanging hugs and quick greetings. He bows in front of Dereck Whittenburg, the voluble guard whose errant shot Charles stuffed home. For the six-foot-eleven Bailey he mounts a chair to achieve eye level.

"People don't realize what the guy did for us, not just as basketball players," Bailey says afterward. "He had such a big effect on our lives. I know he had a big effect on me, how I live. I've always wanted to write him and tell him, but how do you put that in words?"

Other former Valvano players are on hand, standing by the visitors' bench, including Washington Bullets rookie Tom Gugliotta.

Greetings concluded, Valvano moves toward midcourt with a gait slow and stooped, like that of a man thirty years his senior. He's pale, thin. But the hair remains black and full, the large eyes lustrous and fired yet with enthusiasm for life, for ideas, for laughter.

Football coach Dick Sheridan makes an extended address praising the '83 team and especially Valvano, the man who, as athletic director, kept Sheridan in Raleigh by paying him extremely well. One of Sheridan's most popular lines is an oblique reference to the swirl of allegations regarding academic irregularities and point-shaving that led to Valvano's ouster— "times when fantasy and myth prevailed." Valvano stands behind Sheridan, dressed in a blue ABC blazer and gray pants. Wife Pam is at his side, as she has been throughout an ordeal that began late last spring. Les Robinson is there too, his introduction greeted with solid applause. In contrast, the introduction of athletic director Todd Turner, hired after Valvano left but a UNC grad, meets with some boos.

Finally it's Valvano's turn.

Valvano, a delightful raconteur and highly sought motivational speaker, pulls the microphone from its stand with a pro's familiarity. For the next thirteen minutes he talks and paces gently to and fro upon the school logo, looking this way and that to include everyone.

Arrayed in a crescent toward the scorer's table Valvano sees dozens of cameras, still and TV, their attendant photographers standing or sitting in a double row. Valvano always has been a walking event, even when he hasn't tried to be. The attention always energizes him.

Behind Valvano, press row is nearly full, with many reporters standing to get a better look. Arrayed in another, larger crescent between speaker and scribes are paired male and female cheerleaders, at attention in red and white uniforms, hands on hips at matching angles.

Today's game officials stand under the south basket, dressed for action. Most members of the current Wolfpack squad cluster inconspicuously behind a nearby student grandstand, wearing game warmups.

The overhead scoreboard runs no commercials, only Valvano's electronic likeness with the legend "Coach 'V.'" At a distance, but no less present, are about twelve thousand fans and an unseen audience that counts posterity among its number.

Valvano's words are consistently hopeful and upbeat. There's no hint of sadness, no bitterness. There's only a glancing acknowledgment that this is probably farewell.

He opens with a salute to the '83 banner and a quip at his own expense. "I'm at a loss for words," he says, evoking laughter. "You knew that was too good to be true."

He tells a well-worn story from his early days at N.C. State about mistakenly going to Greenville in the wrong state (South Carolina) to address a Wolfpack Club his first week on the job.

He hums the school fight song, encouraging the crowd to fill in "Go State!" at the proper moment. "That's power! That's power!" Valvano sighs. "I miss that." He's speaking not of command so much as the heat of passion shared by thousands, the scent of competition, the sometimes-fierce pride raised when athletic city-states clash in combat. He had all that once, stood at the pinnacle of his profession right here, his touch golden and supreme. And now, a decade after achieving his dream, his body is killing him.

"I miss that," Valvano repeats about the fight song. "Now when I'm in airports and I go"—he hums a few bars—"they take me away and put me in a room." He pauses. "I miss that." No one enjoyed more than Valvano the matching of wits with other men and other teams. No one was better at reading a game's flow, improvising to seize or change it.

Jim Valvano also loves the immortal hunt of victory. Whether at basketball, commerce, darts, institutional politics, or electronic chess, his latest challenge, he loves most of all to learn new games and strategies, to fight a clever fight and to come out on top.

"Nobody had more fun that I did in the ten years that I was fortunate enough to be able to stand right there in that corner," Valvano tells the crowd, "right before every game, and thank God for the opportunity to coach at North Carolina State University." He speaks of the '83 team and the lessons it taught, particularly about "dreaming and the importance of dreams, because nothing can happen if not first a dream." The team also taught him, he says, "the persistence, the idea of never, ever quitting. Don't ever give up! Don't ever stop fighting!"

The lesson from that year that Valvano never did understand was why people felt discomfited by his eagerness to cash in on the title.

Fed by what became a crusade for Raleigh's *News and Observer* and its editor, Claude Sitton, resentment bubbled as Valvano conjured a wide range of endorsement and entrepreneurial opportunities. The extracurricular activity was nothing new for the restless, multifaceted coach, but it exceeded his previous efforts. Busier than ever, he didn't pay as close attention to his program as required. Mistakes mounted, repeated.

First went Bruce Poulton, the lightweight chancellor who promoted Valvano to be his own boss and readily countenanced a basketball program found by university-system officials to violate "the spirit, not the letter of the law." Eight months later it was Valvano's turn, the blow cushioned by a cash settlement in excess of six hundred thousand dollars, immediate acclaim as a TV commentator, and several coaching offers.

And now Valvano's back at Reynolds, the star attraction, wanting neither pity nor confrontation, but only to feel the good feelings again.

"Today I fight a different battle," he tells the Wolfpack faithful. "You see I have trouble walking, and I do. And I have trouble standing for a long period of time, and I do. Cancer has taken away a lot of my physical abilities. I can't run over and yell at John Moreau, the referee, like I'd like to do right now. I can't do the back flips I like to do with our world-class cheerleaders. I can't do those things anymore.

"But what cancer can't touch is my mind, my heart, and my soul. It can't touch those things."

Almost until his arrival, it's uncertain Valvano will make this speech. His bone cancer has worsened. He's missed his last two weeks of broadcast assignments. Yet not only is he standing and speaking now, but it seems to his friends he draws strength as he speaks.

"You look out there and you see the V you've always known," says Terry Gannon, a player from the title team who lately has subbed for Valvano on national telecasts. "He's not going to give up. Those aren't just words he used. Those are things he believes in." Valvano takes a moment to speak well of his successor. "I want you all to know from one coach to another that Les Robinson is going to hang his own banners up here in a couple of years. And Coach Sheridan is going to hang his ACC and national championship banners in a few years."

When the applause fades, Valvano adds: "I promise you, I will never give up my fight, and I'm going to be here to see those things happen to my friends." More applause. "And if by chance the Lord wants me," he says, clearly winding up, "he's going to get the best damn broadcaster and ex-basketball coach that they've ever had up there, I'll tell you that."

The last words are drowned by a great cheer. Valvano leads the crowd in a final verse of the fight song. Then he's presented a glass slipper representative of his team's Cinderella championship, and afterward moves to a seat beside Musburger to broadcast the game.

Fortunately for N.C. State, Grant Hill will not play. For today's game, the last of four straight home contests for the Wolfpack, Hill sits on Duke's bench wearing a brown suit and natty matching wing tips. He walks without crutches but limps noticeably. He hopes to return to action against UCLA next Sunday; it's an open secret that Bobby Hurley's jersey will be retired that day.

Another open secret revealed this afternoon is that N.C. State has jelled into a competitive basketball squad. "I don't think it's a coincidence that as we got rid of all the outside obstacles the second time, we started playing better," Robinson notes. "I think since Clemson we've played pretty well with the exception of Chapel Hill. We've been pretty consistent."

The game between the neighborhood rivals is hotly contested, with offense accented. Krzyzewski gives Chris Collins his first career start, bumping Marty Clark back to the bench. Collins winds up with a career-best fourteen points. Clark plays well too, hitting both three-pointers he attempts and playing good defense.

"That was kind of an eye-opener to me," Clark says of Krzyzewski's decision to start Collins. "You have to value your time when you're here. I'm not going to let anybody take anything away. I've paid my dues."

N.C. State doesn't change its lineup, but adds a new player—senior Tommy Kane, a manager who worked for Valvano his freshman year and is good friends with Gugliotta. "I thought it would have special meaning for him, so if I was going to do it for the tournament, why not do it now?" Robinson explains.

The coach is motivated, too, by what he learned prior to yesterday's practice. Kevin Thompson was taken to the hospital on Friday night with a badly swollen neck, an apparent allergic reaction to shrimp he'd eaten. The senior recovers quickly, but the incident confirms Robinson's decision to bolster his bench.

Certainly, against Duke Thompson shows no ill effects of his culinary mishap. Often subdued in public, even Thompson can't help but catch the fever of Valvano's last Reynolds afternoon, scoring a career-high thirty points accompanied by nine rebounds.

In fact, the same Wolfpack that trailed Duke 55–20 at halftime on January 21 leads the Blue Devils by five points, 43–38, at halftime on February 21. "That told me a lot, in a month's time how far this team has come," Robinson says. "Home court is big, but not a forty-point difference."

Rallying quickly after intermission, Duke takes a 51–49 lead with 16:40 left on a Cherokee Parks follow shot. Parks finishes with nineteen points, his fourth straight double-figure scoring effort, and ten rebounds. Duke builds its advantage to four points after a Parks fast-break dunk at the 13:02 mark, one of fifteen assists on the day for Hurley. That ties a school single-game record the senior set earlier this season against Oklahoma, and is counterbalanced by a single turnover.

What's more, Hurley goes over one thousand assists for his career, putting him in second place in modern NCAA history. The leader, State's Chris Corchiani, likewise recorded his one-thousandth assist at Reynolds.

Duke's tenuous advantage vanishes in barely a minute against a Wolf-pack playing its best game of the year. N.C. State will finish with season-high 55.7 percent field-goal accuracy, a draw on the boards, and just eleven turnovers against a demanding defense.

Mark Davis attributes some of that to Valvano. "The whole team was pumped up just hearing him speak," Davis says. "We thought this game was ours."

State takes a 61–60 lead with 11:51 to go behind Thompson's scoring. The advantage changes hands five times in the next five minutes. The score is tied at 71–71 with about six minutes remaining after Lakista McCuller hits a jumper. The guard who started the year with what his coaches call sixth-grade dribbling skills and no left hand finishes with two turnovers versus thirteen points, his fifth consecutive double-figure scor-ing effort.

But here Duke's toughness and experience take over. Hurley, as he's done so often in his career (though not lately), hits a three-pointer that tilts the balance in Duke's favor. Parks blocks a Todd Fuller shot, then dunks a Collins miss at the other end.

Fuller misses, Thompson misses. Clark drives the lane and scores on a feed from Hurley, who works off a screen on the next possession to hit another three. Suddenly it's 81–73 in Duke's favor with under two min-utes remaining.

"It's fun to play in an environment like this," Hurley says later. At least once during the game he takes time to stand, hands on hips, surveying the crowd. "It tests you in a big way. I enjoy the way we came together down the stretch."

For its part N.C. State responds to the pressure by coming a bit unglued, according to Thompson. "I think we kind of panicked a little bit at about the four-minute mark."

Interestingly, Thompson is among the few Pack members who doesn't go upstairs to hear Valvano. He stays in the locker room, readying for the game in his own way. Yet it was Valvano who recruited him.

Of course Valvano hasn't phoned Thompson, either, not since leaving State (but not the Triangle) three Aprils ago.

Thompson is a bit like an ancient mariner in these parts. Duke's seniors have enjoyed arguably the greatest sustained success in ACC history. North Carolina's seniors have remained in the highlands near the pinnacle, with a trip to the Final Four and an ACC title to their credit. Both teams have played under Hall of Fame–caliber coaches in stable programs considered national models of athletic rectitude.

Then there's the trouble Thompson has seen. Thompson is a guy with a positive attitude and a level head. He'll finish four years of school within a summer semester of graduating.

Thompson's freshman year was Valvano's last, with media from everywhere and an air of embattlement engulfing the program. Corchiani, the team's emotional leader, threatened to quit if Valvano was shown the door. Thompson was a reserve, playing about ten minutes a game on a team with four eventual NBA players.

His sophomore year Thompson and high school buddy Bryant Feggins started every game side by side. The Pack reached the second round of the NCAAs.

His third year only he and Gugliotta remained from the iron five of '91. Feggins was out with a torn knee. The team won twelve and lost eighteen.

And now, in Thompson's senior year, visitations from the Book of Job.

"I definitely think I've seen all ends of the spectrum," Thompson says in a quiet moment one day after practice. "Coming in, recruited by Coach Valvano. Then he resigned. Having Coach Robinson come in and his style of play. Then this year. I've pretty much spent the whole time trying to get better and working towards my degree and trying to improve on the court.

"I've pretty much had a full college career. Unfortunately there was the thing with Tony. A couple of guys having to sit out. Bryant hurting his knee and getting shot. I've seen it all, I'd say. I think it's made me a stronger person. When it comes time in life to deal with adversity, I'll be well prepared having to deal with so much over these four years."

Today, Thompson brings State within three points of the Blue Devils with a minute to go. A student frantically waves a sign that reads: "Jimmy V We Still Believe In Miracles." But Thompson's bucket is State's last gasp. Duke wins 91–82. State falls to 7–15, 1–11 in the ACC. Four more chances to avoid a twenty-loss season, with an excellent opportunity coming up at Maryland.

"We played our guts out," Robinson says. "The setting was there for us to pull a major upset. It disappoints me that we didn't win the game, but it disappoints me more that today couldn't be climaxed with a major upset-type victory." All is not lost. Robinson has repeatedly called upon tradition as a reserve of pride and inspiration. Now his team has seen tradition come to life.

TUESDAY, FEBRUARY 23

MIKE Krzyzewski is primed for an explosion as he arrives at practice this afternoon, though he doesn't realize it.

Things don't feel right. There's that persistent lack of inclusive leadership. Confidence remains elusive for several key players. Try as he might, Krzyzewski can't connect emotionally with his players, still a group of disparate elements rather than the fused whole he covets.

The coach has been concerned since preseason about the level of expectations created by the consecutive titles, and the effect on this new mix of veterans and unproven players, a group with a far smaller margin of error than its recent predecessors. His troubles now, as he attempts to conjure the accustomed late-season juggernaut, merely confirm Krzyzewski's worst fears.

"They started in an environment that was the same as far as expectations and all that, but that's not the environment that this team needed," he explains. "It needed to be able to fail, and find out about each other. Accomplish. It needed to live. It needed to do things that you hope your children would do in school.

"There were constraints put on them. I've spent the major part of this year trying to change some of that so that they could feel failure and success in the proper way. Failure as much as success." Even the losses in mid-January didn't alleviate the demands Krzyzewski considers unreasonable. "I think the losses just exacerbated the whole thing," he says. "It made it even worse. And, now, what was wrong? Instead of, 'Oh, yeah, these kids are just kids.' It almost made that worse instead of better." That pervasive attitude has had a dampening effect on the squad, as Krzyzewski tried to explain to his players on the bus returning from its impressive effort at Raleigh the other day.

"You see, up until the last couple of weeks, our guys never really got the confidence that success brings, or accomplishment brings," he says. "I'm not sure a lot of people would be twenty and five with the schedule that we've played, and not just games but how the games came about. And then, also, when you lose Grant. Although I think the loss of Grant has been one of the major good things for us, because I needed some help from my friends to knock this whole thing down and finally let these kids know, this is us."

Krzyzewski tells his team: "Forget about what anyone else says, what you did last year, who you were. This is us, and let's enjoy it. Let's make us better, and forget about everyone else."

The team had yesterday off. Today they come to Cameron at the usual time in late afternoon, and prior to practice Krzyzewski talks to the squad about going after loose balls and taking charges. He even dives on the floor after a ball to illustrate the hustle required. "We have to really go after this now," he says, "because something good is happening." The team watches film of Florida State, tomorrow's opponent, and goes over the scouting report. Then it takes the court.

There, Krzyzewski is aghast at what he encounters. "We were back to being either satisfied, into our own things, or still back on Sunday," he says. "Practice was horrible. Everybody. Every one of them was bad."

Suddenly, the frustrations of nearly four months come to the surface. Krzyzewski halts the workout and dispatches the team to the locker room. He's been known to launch blistering tirades in such circumstances, but this time he remains cool.

"It's a damn shame that we have something now that I know needs to be nurtured, developed and whatever, and we're going to let it go down the drain," Krzyzewski tells his team. "You guys are being selfish and holding on to whatever your individual things are right now. You saw in the last eight to ten minutes of that State game, giving everything to each other, what it will do, and you felt good about it. And for you not to do it now shows unbelievable immaturity." Krzyzewski storms out, storms back. This time he shouts, so angry he can't recall later what he said. He hasn't been this enraged in years.

The coach dismisses his team, ordering the players to return at 9:00 P.M. taped and ready to go. An apologetic Bobby Hurley approaches Krzyzewski and is rebuffed. "Get the hell out of here," Krzyzewski says. "I don't want to talk to you."

Krzyzewski appreciates the gesture, and asks an assistant to express that to Hurley. But he also wants to create a mood, wants his players to stew. "We need to destroy some stuff," he confesses. "While you build, you put up a new building, sometimes you have to knock down an old building. Sometimes you have to clear the trees." The problem is, while Krzyzewski knows how he feels, he doesn't know how to communicate it. He spends the next two hours on the Stairmaster, in the sauna. He does situps. Anything to clear his mind by purging the anger that consumes him.

Krzyzewski considers a classic punishment practice—forcing players to dive for loose balls and take charges. Instead he goes into the locker room and clears everything off the walls and the tops of players' cubicles except for fan mail.

"I wanted them to see the bare necessities," he says. "I wanted them to graphically get the picture that we needed to play poor, and in order to get anything we needed one another." When the players return, Krzyzewski lets go. He doesn't raise his voice. Rather he talks and he cries, "at an emotional end," he says.

"I'm going to tell you some things," he begins, "and when I get through, like, if you want to go and meet Mr. Butters [the athletic director], and you tell him you want a new coach, I'm gone. I'm telling you that, and I mean it. Because, I coach not to win or lose, I coach to have everybody on the same page with heart, mind, and soul. And if it can't happen, then I don't want to coach."

Krzyzewski asks the players when they last thanked the janitor, D.C., for cleaning up after them. He tells them he tries to speak with D.C. every day. "Maybe I do that because when I was going to West Point, my mom did exactly what D.C. did. At the Chicago Athletic Club from midnight until six o'clock in the morning, she scrubbed floors and cleaned offices, and she's the best person I've ever known." Speaking of his mother, Krzyzewski cries.

He goes on to tell the players about his father, an elevator operator he hardly knew "because he was always working," a man who changed his last name to Kross and died when Krzyzewski was a senior in college. "I always listened to my parents," says Krzyzewski, who attended West Point to please his folks. By comparison, he calls the players "dumb fucks" because they won't listen to him, one of the few people in life who, like his parents, will give them the truth. "That's what I promised you when I recruited you, that I'm going to tell you the truth. Now be men, and accept what I have to say." Individual critiques follow. No one is spared, not even the injured Grant Hill. Krzyzewski tells Hill, whom he considers one of the nation's top five players, to go hardship, just as he'd goaded Christian Laettner in previous seasons.

"Look, I only want to coach you if you want to let go," Krzyzewski tells Hill. "You still hold on to your humility and all that, but I think that's a crutch to really asserting yourself and I don't want ninety percent of you. You should go pro. You should go pro. Like, I don't want to coach you for ninety percent. When you get healthy, if you can't let go of that and assert, forget it." The coach later rues his remarks as the ranting of a "dumb Polack," but Hill takes it in stride. "To be honest, I thought it could have been worse," the player says.

Krzyzewski talks for about fifty minutes, coming back repeatedly to the importance of being honest with one another and of working in unison. "We don't want you to beat Florida State; we want you to do this, and then you'll beat Florida State," he explains. "In other words, let's internalize what we're doing." Words exhausted, Krzyzewski leads the team onto the court and has the players run the offense five against zero. He's after precision, elan.

Then Tony Lang, uncertain as ever, takes a shot. It's short. "Let's run motion again," the coach barks. Lang misses, short again.

"OK, let's run it again." Krzyzewski adds: "Tony, if you're short, I'm going to kill you. You either shoot an air ball, deep, or hit the shot. You have to be long. You have to be long." Lang misses, long.

"Let's do it again."

Lang misses. On the fifth try, he hits.

"OK," Krzyzewski says, "everybody sit down." Emotionally spent, the coach gives his players the schedule for tomorrow, and at about 10:15 sends them on their way.

"It was just a combination of all the frustration he had all year, coming out," Grant Hill says. "Unless you were there you just can't imagine how emotional it was, and how much it affected all of us . . . I don't think anybody took it the wrong way. Coach's job is to motivate you. Doing it by pampering you or yelling at you, that's something he's done well."

Krzyzewski notes later: "I'd like to say you plan everything. You don't know. It's like running motion offense—let's come down the court and see what happens. Because it's a day to day proposition in the development of your team."

The Tar Heels keep rolling along.

Two days ago they were in Charlottesville and beat Virginia by twenty points, leaving Cav players and coaches raving about UNC's defense, especially its traps. "You just have the sense there's no room," Virginia assistant Tom Perrin says. It's like you're playing on a racquetball court."

Dean Smith prefers to talk offense. He's liked his team's defense all season. "We're really, I think, a more confident offensive team right now, which is important," he says.

"I said we're a good offensive team, not a good shooting team." This season, as always, the Heels are making better than half their shots from the floor. But they've hit less than 70 percent of their free throws, an inferior effort by Smith's standards, and their three-point accuracy is dropping steadily.

Even with the flaws, something has changed for the Tar Heels since their consecutive losses at Wake and Duke. The offense with its plodding focus on the low post has been enlivened. Passes again reflect purpose rather than indecision. Opposing zones don't freeze all movement. Clogs and stutters no longer mark the start of every game. Donald Williams is again a confident, if not particularly accurate, shooter. Brian Reese has resurfaced as a creative penetrator, and both he and Pat Sullivan are less concerned with making mistakes and more intent on attacking the basket.

In short, with remarkably little fuss or bother the Heels have regrouped, functioning again as a model of efficiency and consistency.

Only three teams in the country have fewer losses than North Carolina as the regular season enters its final fortnight. The Heels are third-ranked, their highest standing since mid-January. They're tied with Florida State atop the ACC, and in excellent position to garner the top seed in next month's NCAA East Regional.

For all that, since its recalibration, Carolina has yet to face a daunting opponent. Three of the six teams it's beaten since the defeat at Duke possess losing records, and only Virginia is a first-division ACC team. The Tar Heels need to understand the fatal distance between confidence and real-

ity, need to know viscerally what it takes to beat a top team in difficult circumstances. Their biggest tests thus far—against Michigan in Hawaii, at
Wake Forest, at Duke—have resulted in defeat.

So the last sort of opponent needed tonight at the Dean Dome is a
shadow of glory like Notre Dame, which would be no match for N.C.
State.

Ever the good host, Smith finds nice things to say about his 9–15 visitors, both before his team destroys them and after. He covers all the bases
by also saying nice things about his 23–3 squad, and about his next opponent. "We're playing well together. We'll just have to go down to Florida
State. They may be the best team in the country. We don't know."

No one else knows either. Five teams have been number one this season. And that's before Indiana loses in overtime tonight at Ohio State,
where the Tar Heels won in December. That leaves one team ahead of
UNC in the national polls—Kentucky, the school chasing Carolina in all-
time victories.

If there is anything obvious this evening in college basketball, it's the
boredom gripping the Smith Center faithful.

The Fighting Irish are so bad that, during the first twelve minutes of the
second half, they record almost twice as many turnovers as points. The
teams are on even terms only in the final 10:29, when North Carolina
plays without its starters.

As for Notre Dame's John MacLeod, the ex–New York Knicks coach says
what there is to say after his team loses 85–56, then departs before
reporters can ask questions.

Fittingly, MacLeod's most interesting comment is not about his team.
"North Carolina is as good as any of those teams we've played this year,"
he says of a schedule that includes losses to erstwhile top dogs Indiana,
Michigan, Kentucky and Duke. "They're right there, in that group of six or
seven teams that have a chance to win."

Notre Dame is the second opponent against which Smith starts his
quickest lineup—Montross, Lynch, Reese, Phelps, Williams. It's Williams's
second consecutive start after coming off the bench most of the year
behind Henrik Rodl.

Perhaps a starter's role also will bolster Williams's confidence and
restore his flagging offense.

Williams averaged 16.8 points and was UNC's leading scorer through
thirteen games. Back then, people chuckled at Smith's insistence that the

sophomore is a streak shooter in need of work on his shot selection and form. Since then, something's gone awry and Williams's slump is worsening despite a pivotal seventeen-point second-half outburst in a win at Georgia Tech.

In his last thirteen games Williams has averaged a measly 9.2 points. His accuracy has plummeted: Over the first fifteen games he made better than half his three-pointers (52.9 percent); in eleven games since he's made 20.8 percent. Somehow the extent of Williams's slump has eluded notice, and the threat of his shot still distorts opposing defenses and opens things inside.

Williams's rise signals a corresponding decline for Rodl, the starting off-guard through the first two dozen games. "The event itself wasn't as frustrating as knowing that I didn't play better to play more," Rodl acknowledges. The senior says he can't resent Williams because "I've really, really enjoyed the friendship and the smile he always brings me. It's really helped me handle the situation." And he says whenever he feels sorry for himself, he compares the prominence of his role to that of classmates Scott Cherry and Matt Wenstrom, who mostly sit and watch.

Still, the demotion hurts.

"I think it's hard on every player to see that the coach has more trust in another player at his position," says Rodl. "I struggled with that, with not being better or whatever. I can't help it."

FLORIDA State is buried in an avalanche of fire. "They were possessed," Pat Kennedy says of the homestanding Blue Devils, who win by twenty-three points over his sixth-ranked squad.

Duke comes out smoking, fearsome desire restored, and leads for all but the opening two minutes and nineteen seconds. The Blue Devils score ninety-eight points, more than in any ACC game this season except the romp over Clemson in early January.

Tony Lang bursts forth with thirteen points in the first half alone. That's more in a half than he's scored in all but one game this year. "I was very hungry tonight," says Lang, who with Eric Meek came by Cameron for extra shooting practice earlier in the day. "I just had a lot of confidence in my shot."

Bobby Hurley breaks the school record for assists in a game, with sixteen. He pushes the ball upcourt with remorseless determination, yet has only two turnovers against an uptempo team whose strength is athleticism and trapping defense.

Duke hits 57.6 percent of its shots and has five players in double-figures. Thomas Hill and Cherokee Parks lead with nineteen points each. Parks has eleven rebounds, his third straight double-double.

Lang and Parks scorch FSU's Rodney Dobard and Doug Edwards at both ends. Dobard gets in early foul trouble and never scores a point. The quick-tempered Edwards misses most of his shots, becomes frustrated, and gets caught flagrantly fouling Lang.

Florida State finishes with its lowest field-goal percentage (40.0) since the third game of the season. "I'm a little shell-shocked," Kennedy says.

"We haven't had anybody be able to do that to us this year, including Indiana, to that extent." Kennedy isn't the only one shocked by ninth-ranked Duke's 98–75 win. Since Charlie Ward finished football and returned as starting point guard, freewheeling FSU has won thirteen of fourteen games, its sole loss at Chapel Hill after blowing a twenty-one-point lead.

So what if Ward is sidelined tonight with a recurrent shoulder problem? Duke is without Grant Hill, its best player. The Blue Devils didn't look all that great with Hill either. Even the Duke contingent among the reporters along press row doesn't hold out much hope.

But the ACC's appeal is built in part on its occasional unpredictability, as tonight's result attests. The fiery Blue Devils blow away Florida State, utilizing defense to create repeated fast-break opportunities. They lead 45–33 at halftime, then pull away, scoring on twenty-one of their last twenty-three possessions.

"Credit this one to Duke's defense," Kennedy says. "As usual, they were very physical from the beginning. Right from the start, they took us out of everything we wanted to do. We just didn't get many good scoring opportunities. When you face pressure like that—on the ball, in the passing lanes, inside—it will rattle you." Duke's players regard that aggressiveness as a direct result of yesterday's doings.

"It was an emotional game for us," Parks says. "Coach really opened our eyes."

Hurley calls the effort against FSU "the first time we've played a solid forty minutes," and says he's glad the team responded so well to Krzyzewski's concerns. "It was good to give something back to him, because he really gave us an awful lot yesterday," Hurley says. "It was good to have a performance like this for him tonight." Other than the fact the players were "thrown out of practice," details of yesterday's events are shared but sparingly. "I don't want to talk about it," Thomas Hill protests. "It was too emotional. All I can say is, it worked."

In fact, the motivational efforts have continued today. Krzyzewski tells his assistants to check with some of the players—Hurley, Lang, the Hills—to ascertain the team's mood. Then, just before the team goes out for pregame warmups, Grant Hill comes back to Krzyzewski's locker room area to talk.

The way Krzyzewski recalls the conversation, the player starts by telling him: "I was very concerned about you yesterday. I've never seen you like that."

"I've never been that way with you," Krzyzewski says. "So, how did you feel?"

"I thought what you said was true," Hill replies.

"Grant, I was just being honest with you guys."

"We appreciate that," Hill says. "I can do more, and I want to do more."

"You know," Krzyzewski says, "one of the things that I miss is, this has got to be a two-way street. This year's been more of a one-way street with me giving everything. I need something back, and you're one of the guys who can do it. I need some affection back, I need some feeling back, whether it be someone yelling back at me, holding my arm tight in a huddle or whatever."

"You know, Coach," Hill offers, "you've accomplished so much that I think in some respects it's intimidating to some of the guys."

"I understand that," Krzyzewski says. "That's one of the reasons I'm trying to show you that I'm a real person. And I am. That's what I tried to tell you last night. I'm still very hungry. I want, it's not to have the most wins, it's to have that feeling." Coach and player vow friendship, and Hill leaves. Departing from custom, Krzyzewski decides not to address the team until just prior to the game. He asks his assistants to take care of the last-minute strategic preparations.

When he finally faces the squad, Krzyzewski says: "There's a couple of things I want you to know before you go out for this game. One is that I love coaching you guys. There's not a team, or a group in the country that I would rather coach than you kids. I love you, and I'm in support of you. Just play together and do your best. That's all I want."

Krzyzewski displays little visible reaction during the game. He doesn't even say much to the officials, and not because he's given up cursing (and ice cream) for Lent, which begins today. Rather, Krzyzewski is numb, emotionally drained, so spent he has little energy even to rise from his seat. But he is pleased. "That's about as hard and as well as we can play together at this point," he says. "The defense was the key factor. We didn't allow any easy baskets. And we held our turnovers down. On the defensive end, it was tough to score against us."

Krzyzewski cares almost nothing about the opponent. Far more important are the win and the events yesterday that produced it. He thinks this may prove the turning point in Duke's season.

"Really, it was the first ballgame where there was no fear, no anything, and coupled with that a great sense of accomplishment," he confides.

"And they didn't have to have anybody say that it was. They didn't need to know, have anyone say, 'Well, it was great without Grant.'"

Given what he calls that "inward" focus, that long-sought self-satisfaction, Krzyzewski believes his team now has the wherewithal to mount another title run. "That doesn't mean we might not lose during the regular season or in the ACC Tournament," he hastens to add, "but by the time March comes, we now have a chance at this thing. Because, if it's developed, we've shown that we can do something that I don't think very many teams can do. Maybe nobody can do, in internalizing all this stuff."

SATURDAY, FEBRUARY 27

BOTH teams that started the week ahead of North Carolina in the polls have lost. Suddenly the Tar Heels, ranked no higher than third all season, are poised to ascend to number one. UNC hasn't achieved that lofty perch since the first week of the 1987–88 season, further confirmation this is Dean Smith's best squad in years.

The ranking would put Smith in a bit of a bind, though. He loves the role of underdog, sometimes contorting the facts to appear as one. Better to be the hunter than the hunted. Then again, he's been chasing Duke long enough, seen teams measured for too long against Krzyzewski's program, when once they strove most keenly to match his. Maybe it's time to let others try to catch North Carolina for a change.

But Smith is nothing if not consistent. Like most coaches he discounts the polls. Always has, at least during the regular season.

"I hope, I don't think our players pay any attention to polls," says Smith, who counsels them repeatedly not to.

In fact, Smith says a confluence of circumstances makes it "improbable" North Carolina will defeat Florida State. "We take it as a challenge. Three seniors, their last home game. They've won all their home games." Actually it's the last dance for five FSU seniors, and while the '93 team hasn't lost an ACC game at Tallahassee–Leon County Civic Center it has lost there to Florida.

Pat Kennedy's squad has beaten every team in the league this year except Carolina. His players readily recall blowing a three-touchdown lead in the Dean Dome. Now they're confident they'll finish the job they started in Chapel Hill.

Florida State also seems particularly inspired when playing the Tar Heels, perhaps because Kennedy, like many of the league's younger coaches, isn't overly fond of Smith. That spills over to the players, recalling the sort of bitter rivalry once common in the ACC.

Starting in the late sixties and extending well into the eighties, the hostility was directed from N.C. State's Norman Sloan and Maryland's Lefty Driesell toward Dean Smith. During the early eighties Jim Valvano says he was amazed when Smith left the room at an ACC coaches' meeting and Driesell immediately said, "We've got to get that guy."

Now it seems Kennedy's crew aches to upend North Carolina. But Florida State isn't up to snuff without Charlie Ward, still nursing a shoulder injury. That enabled Duke to expose several FSU flaws, most notably that, despite Kennedy's preseason talk about improving in halfcourt, his team doesn't care for hard-nosed, body-to-body defense.

"Florida State doesn't want to play defense," Smith says flatly. "They want to make you shoot."

By this time in their careers, the veteran-dominated Heels know better than to force a shot. Proper shot selection, including understanding the context in which each attempt is made, is eternally stressed by Smith. Careful measurement and evaluation, including detailed recordkeeping at practices, defines a good shot for each player. Then it's up to the individual to incorporate that information into the North Carolina basketball catechism and react accordingly.

Earlier in the year the Heels were susceptible to hoisting a few shots before the proper moment, creating repeated first-half difficulties. That tendency has receded since Smith recalibrated at midseason. Now when Florida State traps in hopes of precipitating a turnover or an ill-considered offensive foray, the Heels react as conditioned.

As Brian Reese summarizes Smith's thought on the subject: "On the first pass, I'll be wide open and I won't take the shot because that's too quick. We're not letting them spend much time on defense. Things like that, that's the way he teaches us. A lot of people go, 'You could shoot the three.' That's not our goal." Reese shows against Florida State how well he's learned his lessons, scoring a career-high twenty-five points and grabbing six rebounds in an 86–76 victory. "Maybe this was his coming-out party on offense," Smith says. Reese repeatedly slashes to the basket through FSU's zone, or simply beats the defense to the basket. "I still don't understand why they played box-and-one on Donald [Williams] when Donald didn't have a good shooting night, and Brian was going in for basket after basket," Henrik Rodl marvels.

Reese's postgame comments, like his oncourt performance, aptly reflect Smith's thinking. It's not a coming-out unless he does more than score, Reese points out. Being number one isn't as important as playing well, he says. And playing at Tallahassee, considering the circumstances, including a record crowd, "We shouldn't have had a chance."

Eric Montross and George Lynch help determine otherwise, pounding away inside for thirty-one points and fifteen rebounds as UNC dominates the boards.

Confounded by shifting Tar Heel alignments, prodded into quick shots by traps, then forced to let fly in a late attempt to catch up, FSU commits eighteen turnovers and converts three of twenty-one attempts from three-point range. "They're a team that has a lot of flash, but sometimes they're not very smart," Montross observes. "Obviously we're not best buddies. They talk a lot of trash, but we're sitting here with a 'W' under our belt. It's a good feeling to beat teams that talk trash."

Still, until the game's latter stages the action is intense and the issue unsettled, with numerous ties and lead changes. Florida State further spices the afternoon by talking plenty of trash, a team trademark.

The emotional highlight, though, comes when Kennedy screams in vain for a technical after Montross leaves the bench to see to Phelps, who's injured. (To his great credit, Smith interposes his body to block TV's ever-prying lens from zooming in on Phelps's anguished countenance. The coach says he's thinking of Linda Phelps, the player's mother. "I could see her watching television there at home and her son's grimacing. That was almost gruesome.")

Phelps, who reaches double figures in assists (ten) for just the second time this year, is leveled by a hard but legitimate foul delivered by FSU's Rodney Dobard on a breakaway layup. Both players leave the game with the game clock stopped at 4:39—Dobard with five fouls, Phelps with a possibly broken right forearm or elbow after crashing to the floor. Dobard departs first, heading to the FSU bench without any show of concern for the prostrate Phelps's welfare.

By then the game itself is largely settled, anyway, thanks to a Tar Heel explosion ignited by Williams.

As noted by Rodl, Williams remains in his shooting slump, missing nine of twelve shots including his first five three-point attempts. But with 7:44

remaining and the score tied at 56, Williams finally hits a bomb from the left side. Reese follows with six straight points, and the Heels are off on a decisive 13–2 run.

The victory raises North Carolina's record to 24–3. UNC's 12–2 ACC mark assures a finish atop the regular season standings for the sixteenth time under Smith but the first since 1988.

The Heels are unusually emotional throughout the game and do little to hide their satisfaction with the result. Several stand by the bench mimicking the tomahawk chop favored by FSU fans, who boo in response. Then the Heels take up the "Seminole War Chant" as they hit the showers.

"It's a great thing to sweep FSU," Kevin Salvadori says, calling the rivalry UNC's most heated after Duke. "FSU has sort of stepped in there because North Carolina State has struggled so much lately." In this season of paybacks, silencing cocky Florida State has been an unspoken goal. The Heels remember well being swept by the ACC newcomers last year, and how Cassell derided the Smith Center crowd. They recall how FSU strutted mockingly a month earlier at Chapel Hill. "They are confident, if not overconfident," Rodl observes.

But the injury to Phelps tarnishes the sweetness of victory, especially for Smith and others of the faithful who recall how a similar incident derailed one of UNC's greatest teams.

The '84 Heels, led by Michael Jordan and Sam Perkins, had won their first sixteen games when freshman playmaker Kenny Smith was fouled from behind on a breakaway layup against LSU. Smith broke his wrist when he fell, and though he came back late in the year the team never regained its previous overwhelming form.

Happily, on this occasion X-rays ultimately confirm trainer Marc Davis's evaluation at Tallahassee—the injury sustained by the left-handed Phelps is only a badly bruised right elbow.

No one in the ACC, perhaps in college basketball, has paid a heavier price for playing this year than Phelps. The guard injured his calf and knee in North Carolina's first 1992–93 preseason exhibition, wounds that prevented him from participating in the opener against Old Dominion. That's the only game he's missed in fifty-nine chances over two years. Yet since the regular season began Phelps also has sustained a concussion (at N.C. State), a hip pointer (at Wake), bruised ribs (at Duke), and several stunning blows to the head (at Georgia Tech). Now this.

SUNDAY, FEBRUARY 28

THE fight to escape the record books is over. N.C. State defeats Georgia Tech, thereby dodging the looming ignominy of twenty losses, more than any squad in school history. Les Robinson has been hoping to avoid that blemish since reading a newspaper article that discussed the possibility. "I'm not dwelling on it," he insists. Nor does he mention the prospect to his players. But Robinson, whose '92 squad set a school record for consecutive losses, has quietly calculated the probabilities of incurring this statistical black eye, and knows time is running out.

The victory on this icy, sunny Sunday afternoon is the Pack's second in ACC competition and third in its last six tries.

"Looking at the guys, I'd never believe we're eight and sixteen," Buzz Peterson says. "They're not carrying on like they want to get it over with. They're playing hard. I think a lot of that has to do with Les, the way he keeps guys going, keeps guys motivated." To give his squad something to aim for, Robinson portrays the last three regular season games as a sort of tournament. Today's final game is the first round, and mysteriously listless Georgia Tech, coached by Robinson's friend, Bobby Cremins, is the 68–60 victim. "I'm happy for Les. His team hasn't quit on him," Cremins says, perhaps a bit enviously.

The Yellow Jackets should be abuzz for this game, since the program's string of eight consecutive NCAA appearances remains in serious jeopardy. They seem to be on a roll, having won three straight. But, as Robinson points out, it's difficult for a team that routed the eight-player Pack a month ago to take it seriously now. "I don't think Bobby could convince them that this team could beat them. I really don't."

And that's a mistake.

"We're not the same team," Robinson says. "We've got our own personality now, our own rotation. Each game we're feeling better."

An hour later Duke plays UCLA at Cameron Indoor Stadium. Commenting on the game for ABC from a perch near the Cameron rafters is Jim Valvano, the man offered the Bruin job before it went to Jim Harrick.

How different things would have been for everyone had Valvano moved to Los Angeles, as seemed imminent during the early spring of 1988. But N.C. State invoked a five-hundred-thousand-dollar buyout clause in Valvano's contract, and he stayed in Raleigh. Two years later, when it became expedient for State to dump Valvano, it had to pay him that, and more.

Valvano also indirectly has a hand in today's pregame ceremony. When he signed point guard Chris Corchiani for the 1988 season, Valvano beat out Duke, among others. Thus the Blue Devils were still in search of a replacement for Quin Snyder when Hurley was a high-school senior in 1988–89.

Now, four years later, Hurley's Duke jersey is being retired. By way of preliminaries, about twelve minutes prior to the game, Mike Krzyzewski presents a ball to Hurley commemorating the guard's one-thousandth assist last Sunday at N.C. State. The two pat each other on the back. Hurley goes to his mother, Chris Hurley, standing by her seat behind the scorer's table, and gives her a hug and the basketball. Then outgoing Duke president H. Keith H. Brodie, a self-professed basketball fan, presents Hurley with a framed number eleven jersey with his name affixed. Hurley holds the framed jersey aloft and shows it to the cheering crowd at every side. His face remains impassive. Disdaining the waiting microphone at the foul line nearest Duke's bench—"I'm not really into all the individual attention," Hurley says afterward—he takes the jersey and presents it to his parents. His mother cries.

"I was a little nervous about everything that was happening today, because we had a game to play," Hurley says. "I didn't know what to do out there. I knew I'd feel really good, really proud. I'm glad my parents were there."

Hurley's is the seventh jersey number retired by Duke, and the fourth worn by a Krzyzewski-era player. (In contrast, UCLA has retired four jersey numbers, two belonging to women.) The first six numerals hoisted to the Cameron rafters were number 24, Johnny Dawkins (1983–86), 35, Danny Ferry (1986–89), 43, Mike Gminski (1977-80), 10, Dick Groat (1951, 1952), 25, Art Heyman (1961–63), and 32, Christian Laettner (1989–92).

Four were national players of the year—Groat in '51, Heyman in '63, Ferry in '89, Laettner in '92. Five made all-conference in at least three different seasons. (Groat played prior to the ACC's founding.) Hurley is the only honoree who belongs to neither of those exclusive groups. But he's also the only one who'll end his career holding a major NCAA record, that for assists.

And it's an achievement he cherishes.

"I think that's a great record to have because it's an unselfish one, it's one where you're looking for somebody else," Hurley says. "It will say I had a lot of chances. I've played a lot of games, I've played a lot of minutes and had a lot of opportunities and played with great players."

Judging by the pace at which Hurley has acquired assists lately, he'll surpass Corchiani's career total of 1,038 in Duke's final home game on Wednesday against Maryland. (Hurley already has received a telegram from Corchiani, which says in part: "Not bad for two boys from Jersey who learned the game from their fathers.") Hurley has fifteen assists against UCLA as the Blue Devils win 78–67. He had sixteen, a Duke single-game record, in the team's last outing, and fifteen in the game before that. Over the last three games, then, he's had forty-six assists and just six turnovers.

"You've got to be kidding me," Krzyzewski says in admiration. "I'm not sure you'll find anybody who's done it better than he does in this conference."

The prolific outburst is fueled by Krzyzewski's encouragement, Hurley's thirst for a record he's been eyeing since his freshman year, and several subtle alterations in Duke's motion offense. "I think you have to change during the season a couple of times in the ACC," Pete Gaudet says. "We've changed a lot of times at this point in the season."

Previously, Hurley was apt to penetrate and dish, and Duke kept two players posted inside. Now the Blue Devils set up screening pairs on different sides of the court and let Hurley read the moves of his cutting teammates. Also, when Hurley gave up the ball earlier in the year he rotated toward a corner to become a shooting threat. With Grant Hill out and Chris Collins starting, Hurley leaves those defense-stretching jumpers to Collins and rotates back to the key area, from which he can better survey the court.

Most of the starters prosper under the new arrangement. Cherokee Parks blocks four shots against UCLA, a school near his Huntington Beach home that courted him assiduously, and enjoys his seventh straight double-figure scoring performance. Tony Lang hits for fourteen points, matches Parks with seven rebounds, and plays with confidence and fire. Thomas Hill scores twenty-two.

That's not to say Duke's twenty-second win comes easily. UCLA is quick and determined. Once in each half the Blue Devils build eleven-point leads, but, as happened at Florida State in late January, they fritter each away. The second time UCLA pulls within 71–67 with just under three minutes remaining.

Lang misses the front end of a one-and-one with 2:17 left. Parks taps the rebound to Hurley and Duke resets its delay offense. But Thomas Hill commits a turnover as the shot clock winds down.

UCLA calls timeout with 1:31 to go. Challenged, Duke's defense stiffens. On their final three possessions the Bruins commit two turnovers, one on a steal by Lang, and have a shot blocked by Parks. The Duke cause is helped greatly by Kenny Blakeney's defensive work on UCLA scoring leader Shon Tarver. Meanwhile the Blue Devils score four straight times, their last points coming as Thomas Hill makes two of four free throws that result from a pair of technicals on UCLA coach Jim Harrick.

"Start the surfboard!" shout the Crazies as Duke seals its eightieth consecutive nonconference win at Cameron. "Start the surfboard!"

Dean Smith takes the day off, remaining in Florida while his team returns to Chapel Hill. It's his sixty-second birthday. He and his wife, Linnea, spend a quiet day near Panama City on the Gulf Coast, departing in late afternoon. It's the only time until season's end that Smith spends the entire day following a game without analyzing videotape of his team's performance.

WEDNESDAY, MARCH 3

THE rumblings of two multitudes presage the thunderstorm that passes through the Triangle tonight.

In Chapel Hill, as the Tar Heels finish throttling Wake Forest, some in the less-than-full Smith Center begin chanting "We want Duke!" But the cheer dies almost as quickly as it's born.

Perhaps the fans recognize the absurdity of calling for the head of an also-ran when their team is 25–3, top-ranked in the country, and already the ACC regular season champ at 13–2. They just can't help it, can't get that Duke burr out from under their saddles.

"I think since I've been here, the rivalry with Duke has been the best, has gotten the most attention of everybody," senior Henrik Rodl says. "Even yet, even Tuesday before the game, I had people come up and say, 'Beat Duke on Sunday.' We're playing Wake Forest, number fourteen in the nation on the next day, and they tell me to beat Duke on Sunday.

"I may have told you this before, but I think the whole Duke thing is just a little overblown. It's not our main purpose over the year to beat Duke. It's enjoyable to do that, but it's not our main focus of the season. We don't have a goal up on the blackboard that says, 'This year we beat Duke. Everybody else doesn't matter that much.' I think to a lot of people in this area it does. I guess at their workplace and stuff, it's either Duke or North Carolina that's important to them. But I think to the team it's not, even though we take part in the rivalry too."

Eleven miles down U.S. 15–501, Duke dismantles Maryland, with Bobby Hurley becoming the modern NCAA assist leader. Deep in the second half, perhaps looking toward Sunday but also simply rekindling an anthem heard at every game through every Duke season, the Cameron crowd chants: "Go to hell, Carolina, go to hell!" The sound fills the old building, every bit as much a war cry as the whoops at Florida State.

"Playing Carolina, it doesn't matter what else is going on," senior Thomas Hill says. "Playing them is the biggest game for me, at least. It's a big rivalry."

First, though, there's the matter of dispatching tonight's opponents, which proves rather a simple matter for both principals in Sunday's heavyweight match.

Carolina finishes its preliminary first. An awakened Brian Reese scores a layup off the opening tap. Two possessions later Eric Montross scores on a tap follow of a driving shot by Derrick Phelps. Wake returns fire, taking a 5–4 lead behind Rodney Rogers and Randolph Childress, the ACC's first- and third-leading scorers, respectively.

The game is barely two minutes old. Wake, winner of eighteen games and a certain NCAA entrant, will not lead again.

Donald Williams, long inaccurate, hits a three-pointer on Carolina's subsequent possession. Next time downcourt, Reese hits a three-pointer. Less than two minutes after that Williams hits another three. Bad news for Wake's plans to stay in a zone. Carolina leads 13–7.

That's just the beginning. Wake is within 19–15 when the explosion comes—a 19–1 run that lasts more than five minutes and settles the outcome. The Deacs never pull closer than ten points the rest of the night as they lose 83–65.

The Tar Heel defensive emphasis for the game is to limit Wake to one shot per possession. Carolina is so overwhelmingly successful, Wake fails to record an offensive rebound in the first half, a period in which the Deacs score on consecutive possessions just once. By game's end Carolina has more defensive rebounds than Wake has total rebounds, and both Childress and Rogers have fouled out, Rogers scoring nine points below his average.

Meanwhile the UNC offense is so efficient, the Heels make better than 55 percent of their shots and commit only nine turnovers, fewest against an ACC opponent this season. Injured Derrick Phelps has seven assists and a single turnover in thirty-one minutes. He was questionable for today's game due to a bruised right arm and a numb hand suffered in his fall at Florida State.

Reese and Williams punish Wake from outside, combining to make five of six three-point attempts. They finish with twenty-nine points between them. Williams's outburst puts opponents on notice that he remains a force to be reckoned with. Reese's emergence makes opponents' lives even tougher. "The last two weeks, his play has mirrored that of his team, or his team has mirrored that of him," Wake coach Dave Odom says of Reese. "He looks very good defensively. He's versatile. He's confident."

Two-pronged perimeter prowess makes things easier inside for Montross and George Lynch, who combine for thirty-five points and thirteen rebounds.

"We're learning the rules of the game according to Coach Smith," Montross says. Not a bad idea—this is the nineteenth season in which a Smith team has won at least twenty-five games. The next-closest coaches all-time are UNLV's Jerry Tarkanian with fourteen twenty-five-win seasons and UCLA's John Wooden with eleven. In fact, Smith's basic formula has produced three of this week's top ten teams—UNC, number-seven Vanderbilt, and number-eight Kansas.

Certainly Odom is impressed. He's impressed with any team that has as potent a pair of outside players as Williams and Reese, and as tough an inside duo as Montross and Lynch. "They've got all the pieces, they do," Odom says. "I think their defense is more consistent now. It looks like they have their system. I don't know how you put it. They look confident with their system."

The skies have opened up, and it's pouring by the time Duke seniors Thomas Hill and Bobby Hurley take the court for their last game at Cameron.

"Everything that I went through tonight I was thinking was for the last time, whether it was getting dressed for the game, stretching, everything went through my mind," Hurley says. "It was sad because I loved putting on the uniform and playing out here. There's nothing like it anywhere else. No matter what I do after this won't be the same as playing at Duke and all we've gone through." Sad as Hurley is, Thomas Hill feels happy as he prepares to extend a 55–3 career record at Cameron.

"I'm not happy that it's over, that it's the last game. But I've just seen other seniors and their experiences, and it makes me happy that I can experience it," says Duke's tough guy.

How he'll react when his name is called and he goes to stand at center court remains a mystery to Hill. At N.C. State and UNC, seniors are introduced for the last time with their close relatives. At Duke they stand alone, a symmetry Krzyzewski finds in keeping with the individual sacrifice that each player makes from the moment he appears in a Blue-White game until his final home bow.

"I'm not real emotional," Hill says. "I can have a stern look on my face but inside I'm real happy or whatever. We'll see. I don't know. I don't want to say how I might be without just ruining it. I just want to let it, how it is, just want to let it build up. I really don't want to think about it."

Keeping his mind a judgmental blank has become force of habit for Hill, whose fate it is to be overshadowed even now. On Sunday the school retired Hurley's jersey. Tonight Hurley figures to get the six assists he needs to establish a modern NCAA career record. Hurley is the talk of the media, both in North Carolina and nationally.

Hurley's even the talk of the locker room. "I think everybody wanted to be that guy on that trivia question: Who got the score on Bobby's assist to break the record?" Tony Lang says later. "I was hoping and praying that I was the one to get it so I could be on 'SportsCenter' smiling and stuff and saying, 'Hi, Mom!'"

Hill hasn't always been at peace with his semi-visible status.

"He gets pissed when he doesn't get recognition," cautions Duke radio voice Jay Bilas, perennially overshadowed by teammates on the 1986 Final Four squad, "and he's going to always be second fiddle on this team."

But Hill keeps his discontent to himself these days and expresses only pleasure as he recalls his final introduction to the Cameron crowd. "When I heard the clapping and all that, I thought about the two NCAA championships, the great players I've had a chance to play with here," Hill says. "That made me smile. I get a great kick out of thinking about stuff like that."

During the game itself, which Duke wins far more handily than the 95–79 final margin indicates, Hill finds his mind wandering years ahead.

"It was weird: What I'm doing after I graduate from Duke and stuff like that," he confesses. "I was thinking about how one day I might have to get a job or something. I was thinking about our tenth reunion anniversary, stuff like that."

Duke's coaches don't want players thinking so far ahead. More than a game ahead is too far, of course. Especially just now, when Mike

Krzyzewski is keen on bolstering the concentration, confidence and resolve of a group struggling to make do without Grant Hill. Duke's best player has been sidelined since February 13, so long a reporter approaches Hill and teasingly asks, "Grant who?" A ripple of recognition runs through tonight's assemblage when Hill appears for warmups in playing regalia, but he never leaves the bench during the game.

"We've got something good. Let's make it better, let's not lose it," Krzyzewski told the team at yesterday's practice. "People are talking to you about North Carolina. This game is more important than North Carolina. I'm telling you. Don't think North Carolina won't be important. But I'm telling you, nobody gives a shit about this game but the people right here."

Maryland, 11–13, comes to Cameron hoping to salvage a disappointing season. There's still an outside shot at a winning record, perhaps even an NIT bid. But such pretensions are short-lived. Duke leads 53–29 at halftime. The Terps never threaten during a second half marked by sloppy play and a floor slickened by condensation dribbling from the roof. Every healthy scholarship player sees at least fifteen minutes of action for Duke.

Hurley's long-awaited assist, number 1,039, comes with 11:02 left in the first half. Marty Clark and T. Hill fan wide in readiness to launch wing jumpers, but Hurley spots Erik Meek inside and gets him the ball. Meek powers for a layup and the crowd shrieks "Hurley! Hurley!"

The playmaker finishes with nineteen points, twelve assists, three steals, and five turnovers. (Hurley also is the ACC's career leader in turnovers.) "He's the perfect all-around point guard," Cherokee Parks says. "When you think of Duke, you think of Bobby Hurley."

Parks has sixteen points, twelve rebounds, and five blocked shots. It's his seventh straight game scoring in double figures since his disappearance at Clemson, his fourth double-figure rebounding total in the past five contests. Surely there's no question now that the sophomore center has arrived.

Lang ties season highs in scoring and rebounds. "I feel real good about myself and the team," says the long-faced junior. "I'm playing as well as I can play and the coaches want me to play." As it turns out, Lang's seventeen points tonight are more than he'll score over the remainder of the season.

Hurley is proud of his record, and pleased he didn't have to wait to break it in Chapel Hill. "I wouldn't want to even give Carolina the satisfaction of stopping the game there," he says. "These are the people I want to share it with. I don't want to share it with the people at Carolina."

"It's hard to imagine Duke without Bobby and Thomas," Krzyzewski says. "One of the really neat things that I'll always remember, when they first came off the floor, both of them, the very first thing they said to me, they said, 'Thanks, Coach.' For a parent or a teacher—the two are synonymous, really, parents and teachers—to hear that from your kid or your player or your student, 'Thanks' is probably the biggest compliment you can get."

The seniors traditionally get a last word, coming out to address the students who linger on the floor awaiting their return from the locker room. But the P.A. announcer speaks first. With a presumption bred by those two championship banners hanging at the east end of Cameron, he intones: "Before the seniors come out, thank you for a great season, have a safe trip home, and we'll see you in New Orleans."

SATURDAY, MARCH 6

NC. STATE is a brief candle trying to illuminate a long night, going strong for a while but ultimately and inevitably falling short. "Losing again today, it's like same book, same chapter, just different pages," Al Daniel says following an 80–68 defeat at Wake Forest. "But we played our ass off."

N.C. State is competitive for at least a half, maybe longer, then fades. It has led at intermission in eight of fifteen ACC games, and in seven straight prior to today. Here at Joel Memorial Coliseum the Pack trails by a point at halftime.

The problems are predictable, considering State's lack of size and depth. "As the body gets tired, the mind gets tired," Les Robinson explains. "As the mind gets tired, you start giving way." Mental fatigue is revealed in wavering concentration. The Pack, especially its guards, still make youthful mistakes and there's no great, poised athlete—as on most ACC rosters—who can compensate with a superior individual effort.

By now, too, once the team stumbles Daniel says it almost expects to fail, conditioned by months of watching leads dissipate and losses accumulate. "I think a lot of that is attitude: 'Well, here we go again.' I don't think it's a conscious thing." This afternoon the N.C. State candle flickers out when, after twelve lead changes and six ties, Wake Forest intensifies its defensive pressure and reels off fourteen unanswered points. Over the game's final twelve minutes N.C. State never draws closer than nine points.

Ex-manager Tommy Kane gets to play the final seventy-one seconds, recorded as one minute on the stat sheet. (Shortly after Kane enters the game, Wake's Rodney Rogers departs. The home fans chant "One More Year," aware their star will almost certainly turn pro following the season. He does.)

Word that Kane is eligible came at six P.M. yesterday as the Wolfpack boarded a bus for Winston-Salem. Someday Kane would like to be a TV commentator or a coach; for now the six-foot-two guard from Michael Jordan's hometown of Wilmington, N.C., is content to live what he calls "a dream come true."

Teammates even work the ball to set up two good shots for Kane from three-point range. The senior rushes the first, squares and shoots nicely the second time. Neither connects.

But the lingering image from this game is of Les Robinson. He's standing on the sideline. It's early in the second half. State is trailing by a basket. Mark Davis fires a pass to Lakista McCuller, who isn't there. Robinson is. Combining helplessness and self-defense, he catches the ball at his midsection and holds it a moment before surrendering control to an official and the remorseless advance of the clock.

SUNDAY, MARCH 7

DONNA Keane has a bad feeling about this game. Mike Krzyzewski's administrative aide, a devoted Duke fan, decided weeks ago not to venture to Chapel Hill to see the Blue Devils face North Carolina. The "hatred" directed at the Duke contingent in the Dean Dome is just too much to bear, she says. Now Duke also is without its best player, Grant Hill, while UNC is on a roll.

Rather than watch the game or even listen on the radio, Keane spends this Sunday afternoon in the office working on a backlog of correspondence.

Keane is onto something here. Even before the game begins, the mood in Chapel Hill is celebratory. Not because the Heels are top-ranked. Not because they're featured on the blown-up *Sports Illustrated* covers waved by fans. Not because a top seed in the East Regional may be on the line. Not because a win today would give North Carolina its first undefeated season at home since 1987.

This is "Senior Day," a moment for ritual salutation and final bows for those eldest sons wearing Carolina blue. Scott Cherry, George Lynch, Henrik Rodl, Travis Stephenson, and Matt Wenstrom are introduced with their parents or, in Rodl's case, his wife, Susan Rodl. The P.A. announcer calls the seniors "The Fabulous Five," an appellation that draws titters along press row and among the small group of Duke fans just behind the visiting bench, where Calvin Hill fights off a drunken fan.

Yet even the glories of Senior Day pale in comparison with the afternoon's underlying theme of redemption, an end to a pestilence that's seen Duke win three straight meetings and five of the last seven. UNC is marching to glory, weakened Blue Devils be damned. Demand for tickets is greater than at any time in the eight-season existence of the Tar Heel basketball temple.

"You could see in the building: We're number one, we won the league, we've had a great year, but we have to have this one," Duke's Mike Brey marvels. "I think we felt that way when they came [to Cameron]. We make each other better to the ultimate. Always one held out in front of the other."

As UNC's traditional last-game rival, Duke has been on the butt-kicking end of more than one emotional Senior Day. Perhaps that's why the second line of Duke's press notes today states: "Duke has spoiled the last two UNC Senior Days in 1989 and in 1991 when the ACC regular season title was on the line."

There's no spoilage today. North Carolina confirms its fans' fondest wishes and Keane's worst fears by winning resoundingly, 83–69. The victory raises the Heels' record to 26–3. They've won nine straight since their loss a month ago at Duke.

The Blue Devils fall to 23–6. They're 4–2 without Grant Hill, so sore after practicing briefly two days ago he doesn't even suit up to face the Tar Heels.

Without Hill, his ball handling and size, and perhaps even with him, it's quickly evident that Duke is no match for UNC today. The Devils are taken aback by the Heels' intensity, especially their suffocating defense. He who hesitates is trapped; he who shoots inside is apt to have the attempt rejected. Duke commits turnovers on five of its first ten possessions, finishes with season-low 35.5 percent accuracy, and has nine shots blocked. "I think defensively they played a great game," Tony Lang says of UNC. "First half, they got us out of sync a little bit."

While the Dukies stutter, the Heels, especially Donald Williams, sing. Ahead only 8–6, UNC runs off eleven unanswered points in barely two minutes as Williams hits a trio of three-pointers sandwiched around an Eric Montross dunk. Duke never again pulls within five points.

"Once we start hitting from outside, it's hard to guard us," says Derrick Phelps, who finishes with nine rebounds, eight points, seven assists and five turnovers.

Williams finishes with twenty-seven points, a career high. That Williams is so hot against Duke is no surprise to teammates. "Last night, he said, 'I'm ready to play now,'" Brian Reese reports. "He said, 'Watch me.' He thinks he had a poor game at Duke." That game, in which Williams was three for fifteen from the floor and missed seven of eight three-pointers, had a more profound effect on the sophomore than most people realize.

"He felt that it was his fault" we lost, Phelps says of his buddy. "He wasn't hitting those open shots, and he was so wide open he should have been hitting them. But I think he got down, and after that he shot badly in other games. And sometimes he didn't even shoot some games. He shot like three times, and I used to get on him about it, too. We used to always look and say, 'You only shot three times?' I used to, like, 'What's going on?'

"He used to be down, and he didn't know what was going on. He was just down on himself because he had like one bad game and we lost it, and he felt it was his fault. And we used to always tell him, 'Don't worry about it; it's just a small thing. It's just one game. Nothing to get down about.' I felt he was just waiting for this game to happen again, just to show that it ain't going to be his fault this game or whatever."

Williams's ten of fifteen shooting opens the inside. Lynch has twelve points and eleven rebounds. Eric Montross has eighteen points, seven boards, and a sobering effect on Duke's inside players. "He takes up so much space," Lang says. "You can't, there's no way in the world you can simulate him in practice. He's so strong and such a big target."

Lang plays aggressively, hanging around the rim all afternoon, his nine rebounds more than double the total compiled by any teammate. Less impressive is the work of Cherokee Parks, who disappears. "He hid," Brey says. "I think he's smart enough to know they were going to try to break him in half."

Collins, starting for the fifth time, plays a gutty game, taking and making a three-pointer on Duke's first possession. He finishes with a team-high fifteen points, ten in the first half, and five assists. Clark has a dozen points, hitting all three knock-kneed three-pointers he attempts. Meek has more rebounds than Parks in half the playing time.

As usual when Duke loses, Hill and Bobby Hurley shoot poorly and often—six of twenty-five combined from the field, two of twelve on three-pointers. Krzyzewski complains privately that he has no leadership on the court against the Heels. Certainly he doesn't get it from the two inward-directed seniors.

Hill had his coming-out here as a freshman, impressive with his poise and determination in a Duke loss. Today he commits four turnovers in the first dozen minutes, and though he plays tough defense on Reese is a modest factor in the game.

Hurley historically has had bad outings at the Smith Center. His freshman year he had a single assist and ten turnovers, tying a school mark for ball-handling errors. (Like most schools and leagues, Duke prefers to ignore turnover records.) Last year, as a junior, Hurley broke a bone in his foot at Chapel Hill when Duke incurred one of its two losses.

This afternoon Hurley is simply outplayed by Phelps, who shuts him down while enjoying one of his best all-around games. Several times Phelps simply drives for a layup past his All-America counterpart, who's cheating to help guard Williams. "Bobby Hurley's a great player; it's been said all along," Smith notes. "I think you'll be saying Derrick Phelps is a great player before long." Shortly after Duke mounts a second-half rally, both sides of the Hurley coin show brightly.

UNC pushes the lead back to fifteen behind a follow shot by Lynch and another three by Williams. Hurley responds by making his signature shot, a three-pointer, his only success in seven tries.

Montross replies with a layup and is clobbered from behind by Lang. The foul appears intentional, and is called such by referee Lenny Wirtz. Krzyzewski disagrees loudly.

Meanwhile Hurley moves toward the bench and says a few words of encouragement to teammates. Hurley walks back to Wirtz and, taking an emotional cue from his coach, mockingly claps in the ref's face. Wirtz gets the message and assesses a technical foul. "He felt that I showed him up," Hurley explains later. "I think maybe I did."

Krzyzewski strolls to the end of the bench, something he rarely does, and stares into the screaming blue vastness. With 6:13 remaining the game is essentially over.

"They really punished us for not playing well," Krzyzewski says before the short drive home along traffic-choked U.S. 15–501.

Krzyzewski isn't thrilled when the first questioner at his postgame press conference wants him to "rate this North Carolina team defensively" based on his years of observing the Tar Heels. Last year at this time, Smith was asked to evaluate Duke and called it the best Blue Devil squad he'd ever seen. And, Smith added to a round of laughter, "I think I've seen most of them, haven't I?" Krzyzewski is almost invariably gracious in defeat, but he isn't about to give so lighthearted an answer about the Tar Heels.

"You know, I don't really think that much about North Carolina," he says. "I think about Duke."

The questioner, Eddie Landreth of Durham's *Herald-Sun*, persists.

"I mean, they're good," Krzyzewski replies. "I'd have to think about that for a while. I mean, they're an excellent defensive team. It's like, when I was in my garden yesterday, I wasn't out there thinking, 'Let me see. The '93 Carolina team is . . .' I'm not making fun of you. Do you understand?"

Though it might seem otherwise, shying from discussion of Carolina is not mere pique on Krzyzewski's part. Rather it reflects a conscious effort to avoid the endless comparisons that envelop the less-than-friendly neighbors.

"It's a continuous battle," Krzyzewski confesses. "Because of the success of the two programs, people want to put you in that . . . I don't want to be a part of that . . . us beating North Carolina, that can never be, never be, the reason why you coach at Duke. Never. It kind of throws water on an oil fire—it looks like it's doing something, but it ain't."

Krzyzewski also perceives competitive dangers in defining oneself in terms of the rivalry. That became especially evident to him during the 1991 Final Four, when UNC lost in the first game before Duke went out to play supposedly unbeatable UNLV. "It can't be a theme for us," he says. "What if Carolina, they lose in the elite eight? Is our goal accomplished? That's what we fought in the Vegas game, that Carolina had already lost. That was a psychological hurdle that now it was OK to lose."

As for this afternoon's victorious coach, Dean Smith praises both his squad (especially the seniors) and "an excellent Duke basketball team" handicapped by the absence of Grant Hill. Smith's spirits surely are buoyed by the realization of the decisive win and unusually lively Dean Dome atmosphere.

Yet, Smith also shares Krzyzewski's attunement to the inordinate attention paid the rivalry with Duke, and is quick to dismiss the importance of today's result. "Usually this is for a seeding in the ACC or something, other than just for a Carolina guy to say 'Ha, ha,' or a Duke guy to say 'Ha, ha' at him," Smith observes. "Here we have problems in Yugoslavia, there are a lot more important things than this game."

MONDAY, MARCH 8

DUKE's best offensive player, best overall defender, and second-best ball handler has rejoined the team. He's immediately told to wear his practice jersey white-side out, signifying a starter. Chris Collins is bumped back to blue. "And if I need to do psychotherapy with Chris, we'll schedule that," Mike Krzyzewski tells an assistant.

The actual basketball part of this afternoon's practice lasts only an hour. Krzyzewski believes in reducing the length of workouts as the season wears on, lest players tire before the games are done. There's no complicated cascade of drills leading to a specific lesson today either. The goal is to reintroduce the Blue Devils to Grant Hill, and Grant Hill to the Blue Devils he's watched from the bench for six and a half games.

There's more chatter than usual among the players, more exhortation. Collins, hair unkempt and pushed up in front, remains hand-slap happy despite his demotion. "I think because Grant was back, everybody was a little fresher mentally," Mike Brey says later.

Everyone also recognizes the team's fortunes are sure to rise, which makes for good spirits. Everyone also knows "G" is limited—he can't go to his right, doesn't feel as explosive as before. "I don't think that we'll even see the healthy Grant this year," Brey admits. But a partial Grant Hill makes Duke a whole lot better, the third-best team in Brey's six years in Durham, he decides. Every one of the previous five reached the Final Four; Brey says only the two championship teams were better. Hill has used the enforced stillness to study tapes of himself and the team, to watch more closely what does and doesn't happen on the court. "I've learned a lot sitting out," he says. "I just learned more about myself, what I can do out there. I learned more about my team, individual players, what they can do. For me, maybe doing a better job of including them than I did before." Hill also has learned anew how much he "loves" basketball, even practice. "It just feels good to be back," he says. Missing the game this much after three weeks, Hill imagines how difficult it will be to "put the basketball down" when his playing career ends.

In fact, once the brief scrimmage commences Hill doesn't want to come out, even if the plan is to bring him along slowly, with frequent rests. "Every time he took me out I was pissed," he says of Krzyzewski.

Hill plays with apparent ease, as always. He makes lightning cuts and doesn't seem to hold back on his leaps and bounds. He dissects the defense off the dribble, alternately hesitating and rushing forward, first past Marty Clark then Erik Meek, keeping the ball in motion until he creates an open shot with a head fake. The next time downcourt Hill penetrates from the wing, and, when the threat of his shot draws the defense, deftly dumps the ball low to Lang, who dunks it.

Hill's purpose in passing to Lang is similar to his aim in talking trash to Clark. Leadership is among the qualities Hill has contemplated recently.

"I was like, 'Marty, you're letting me dog you with a bad toe,'" Hill says. From then on, Clark tries to blow past Hill each time he gets the ball. "He did a good job, I think he played well," Hill allows with an authoritative air.

For a while Hill frets that, though the team needs better leadership, he can't do much to provide it until he's a senior, until it's "his" team. But as his enforced timeout lengthens, Hill's perspective shifts. "That's the one thing I've gotten from being on the bench, is how much more of a leader I can be. That's what I was trying to do at practice."

Whatever conscious leadership Hill ultimately provides, to see him in action again is to realize how much he was missed. In fact, just today it's announced that he and Hurley made first-team all-ACC, the first pair of Dukies to do so since Mark Alarie and Johnny Dawkins in 1986.

Hill's mere presence injects a transforming element into what's at best a high-mediocre playing mixture. He makes it more difficult for opponents to match up with Duke defensively. He dribbles deftly against pressure, sees openings, hits jumpers, makes clever passes, battles for rebounds. He smothers his man defensively and helps bother other shooters. He's unpredictable, explosive, creative, fun to watch.

And he's got a sense of humor.

During the intrasquad scrimmage, Brey makes a call to which Hill objects. "Hey," Brey replies, "you haven't been around long enough to bitch about a call."

Hill smiles and points a finger to his chest. "First-team all-league," he replies eloquently if irrelevantly.

THURSDAY, MARCH 11

THEY don their red and white uniforms and await Les Robinson's instruction. By now the black badges of mourning affixed to jersey straps are so familiar a part of N.C. State's garb, they go virtually unnoticed. Yet they remain the signature of this season of disappointment and sorrow that began with Tony Robinson's suicide and could end here in the first round of the ACC Tournament.

But a tournament is a celebration of the possible. Put all nine ACC teams on the same court for a weekend, let them slug it out and see what happens. Thanks to the league's much-touted inner balance, this is not like a presidential convention, result preordained. The regular season champ has emerged victorious in the ACC Tournament less than half the time since 1954. That unpredictability has been even more pronounced recently. Since Georgia Tech joined the league in 1980, just four of thirteen first-place finishers survived to capture the conference title.

Commentators often gripe about the meaninglessness of it all. Fans know better. There's fun in not knowing, in the chance of an upset, the last-gasp opportunity for a bottom-dweller to redeem its season. There's appeal in watching the league's powers fight for supremacy at the end of a long season of refinement and testing, on the very eve of the NCAAs. There's intrigue in wondering whether fatigue, a hot streak, or a simple stroke of fate will intervene to confound expectation. All of which explains why the region's activities still come to a halt when the ACC Tournament is played, with observers at home, school, and work gathering 'round radios and TVs the way the entire nation once did for the World Series.

The ACC Tournament is regarded with comparable reverence by ACC athletic programs, though not due to its entertainment value. The event has been a sellout for nearly three decades, and as such boasts a rare capacity for producing funds, with boosters contributing four- and five-figure sums for the privilege of purchasing tickets.

The tournament is a premier social and cultural event for those in attendance. That goes, too, for the players, coaches, newspaper writers, magazine stylists, photographers, sports information staffers, radio voices, athletic department officials, TV talking heads, and ancillary media types (coach's show, booster tabloid, etc.) drawn by this gathering of the clan.

N.C. State had a distinct advantage during the ACC Tournament's early years. Back then, as the region's largest and most modern basketball facility, Reynolds Coliseum was the event's permanent home. Not until 1967, the ACC's fourteenth season and two years after the tournament became a sellout, did the league finally move its championship event off campus, to the Greensboro Coliseum.

Lo and behold, that year Dean Smith won his first ACC title. The following season the tournament moved to the new Charlotte Coliseum, which had a larger capacity (11,666) than Greensboro's arena and thus could accommodate more of those moneyed boosters. Not to be outdone, Greensboro expanded its seating to fifteen thousand and in 1971 got the tournament back.

The ACC Tournament remained in Greensboro for a decade with a single exception, until league policy dictated moving it to cities outside North Carolina. Twice during the eighties the tourney went to Landover, Md. Three times it went to Atlanta.

Then in 1990 the ACC returned to Charlotte, lured by a prodigious new coliseum (capacity 23,500). Georgia Tech and Virginia met in the title game that year, the first in league history lacking a team from the state of North Carolina. The arena was full anyway.

The ACC Tournament has remained since at the Charlotte Coliseum, but is about to move again. Greensboro expanded its arena to match the one in Charlotte, and will host the tournament from 1995 through 1997. After that greed could take the league to Atlanta's forty-thousand-seat Georgia Dome.

The locale may shift frequently, but the tournament's format has changed only twice. After South Carolina's 1971 withdrawal made it a seven-team league, the ACC awarded a first-round bye to its first-place regular season finisher. That practice ceased when Georgia Tech joined the fold.

The second change occurred last season, when Florida State became the ACC's ninth member. Restoration of the first-round bye for the regular season leader was considered, but ultimately the ACC stole a page from the Big East and adopted a Thursday "play-in" game between the eighth and ninth seeds.

Last year those teams were Maryland and Clemson. This year they're Maryland and N.C. State.

The Wolfpack has lost twice already to Maryland, but each time came away feeling it should have won. This past month the Pack also has played its best ball of the year, remaining competitive in every contest since its hapless showing at Chapel Hill. So the players regard tonight's play-in as more than an opportunity to prolong their season.

"We have been talking about coming out and showing people we're a better team than they think," Mark Davis says. "We want to prove that we're a better team than we showed everybody in the season. With all that adversity we went through, we're better than people thought."

The feeling in the locker room is calm as Les Robinson runs through the strategic keys to defeating Maryland. The most important thing, Robinson cautions his modestly gifted squad: "Do what you can do, and don't try to do anything you can't do." Just before he sends the players to the court to warm up, before the lights go off in the room and the words of The Lord's Prayer are raised, the coach adds, "The most important thing is, we want to be playing tomorrow."

There are ten players in uniform tonight, counting erstwhile manager Tommy Kane and Migjen Bakalli, who remains unsure his foot is up to the stress of playing. Marc Lewis is listed on the greenboard among the starters, and goes out to shoot with his teammates, but may not be able to play. He's suffering from a bad case of diarrhea. "I would feel much better if he was healthy," Robinson says. "It sounds crazy, but we've been lucky for about a month." The team returns. Lewis heads directly to the head, then rejoins the others in their plastic, teal-colored chairs.

Al Daniel reviews the scouting report once more. When he's through, Robinson adds a few admonitions about keeping the zone compact and contending with a press.

"Let's just play it one timeout at a time, one half at a time," Robinson tells the Pack. "Let's come in here at halftime in good shape. In good shape. Then we'll talk about winning the game." Robinson wonders how much time is left. A manager with a stopwatch tells him. Every player's eyes are on the coach.

"Let's everybody try to play the best game you've played this year, because this is the time to do it," he says. "Let them know right away. Let's see a Georgia Tech–type game where you play with intelligence and confidence."

That said, all that's left is the waiting. There's little talk. Todd Fuller passes the time on the floor, stretching. Bakalli stands nearby wearing his eternal grin. Lakista McCuller and Marcus Wilson pass around a can of spray that supposedly makes it easier to grip the ball. Curtis Marshall stands dribbling in place, the sound of the bouncing ball on the carpet like the beat of a mournful drum. McCuller starts dribbling too, twirling the ball. Last sips of Gatorade. The players huddle: "Let's go, men! Let's give it all up! Come on! Pack!"

The players depart. The sound of cheering drifts back to the locker room, where Robinson tells an assistant to apprise the game officials of Lewis's condition in case "he starts acting funny."

The first half is ugly. Neither team makes a third of its shots. N.C. State misses eight of nine three-pointers. During one stretch the Pack misses eleven straight field-goal attempts. Yet when Davis makes a shot inside to end the streak, and makes a free throw as well, it pulls his team within 17–15.

The deficit is 31–26 when the Pack returns to the locker room at halftime.

Before addressing the team, the coaches repair to an adjacent room to review the stats, particularly those compiled by team statistician John Griggs.

"We just shot too quickly," Robinson tells the players. "We've got our second wind now, we've got our second wind." Identify the hot three-point shooter and get him the ball, he tells them. Get the loose balls. Execute. Don't let Maryland make it a transition game. The zone is working, the Terps have hit 27 percent against the 2–3 alignment. "If we're ever going to be good, if we're ever going to be good, you're going to have to take a charge." A stadium official sticks his head into the room. "Five minutes," he says, and departs.

Robinson brings up the team's three-point shooting. "I could have handcuffed you and you would have gone one for nine. We're too good shooters for that," he announces. "I want to see twenty minutes of running the offense as well as we've run it all month, the last month. Run the offense!"

At first, it appears Robinson's words have had an effect. After falling further behind to open the half, the Pack mounts a 12–3 run, scoring on five straight possessions to forge a 38–38 tie with 15:12 to go. Thompson scores inside on a jumper off a pass from Davis. Lewis dunks a rebound of a Davis miss. Marshall hits a three. Davis hits a three. Thompson scores off a pass from Marshall. State is cooking. This is the team coaches and players want everyone to see. But that's the last time they see it.

Maryland—quicker, deeper, more athletic—replies with a 16–2 run of its own. The Wolfpack gives chase, edging within five points, only to fade down the stretch as the Terps win 76–55.

Maryland makes 59.1 percent of its shots in the second half, State 30.

Thompson misses a dunk, misses easy lay-ins, lets an inbounds pass go right through his legs. "If Kevin's having a bad night, we're in trouble," Robinson says. "We're in big trouble. And Kevin, who doesn't show a lot of emotion, you never know what's going through his head. He might have been too tight."

McCuller, who's averaged sixteen points over the past nine games, scores five, missing eleven of thirteen from the floor. As a team the Pack is four for twenty-one on three-pointers. Their 30.6 field-goal shooting is second-worst of the year.

The teams troop off the court as the crowd of nearly eighteen thousand flees the spectacle of ineptitude and hopes for a better tomorrow. Players from Maryland and N.C. State mingle in the hallway before heading to their respective locker rooms.

Maryland's Gary Williams has sold his team on the challenge and privilege of facing top-ranked North Carolina. Now they'll have to deal with the reality of that opportunity.

For the 8–19 Wolfpack there are no more opportunities. Mark Davis sits with head down, face buried in a white towel. A towel covers Curtis Marshall's head. Marcus Wilson shakes his head and slaps his thighs. The locker room is quiet other than a few coughs.

Robinson goes to Kevin Thompson and shakes his hand. "OK, men, this is a bad way to end the season, obviously," the coach says. "Losing's always tough. Losing the last game is always tough. This has been an extremely tough year, but I hope we've grown through the year. Most important, if we don't learn anything else, I hope we learned how to win. We've had excuses. We haven't talked about them."

There's more talk—of next season, of Maryland's superior play, of pride in Thompson. "We've got a lot to be thankful for," Robinson tells his team. Then one more muttered prayer and it's off to the showers. The coach and Thompson hug, Robinson gives Davis a consoling pat, and goes to meet the media.

"The ball wouldn't go in," laments Marshall, still slumped in his chair after a one for eight shooting performance. "It probably was our worst shooting night of the season. Wow, man. You're just amazed when you sit back and look at it. It's hard to explain." But he tries. "I think we wanted it a little bit too bad. We were a little overexcited out there. We wanted a chance to play North Carolina and show we could play with them. Because they destroyed us the first two times."

Mark Davis, who finishes the year with 34 percent shooting accuracy from the floor, 58.3 percent from the foul line, "hates" that the season's over. "My shot's back and everything's back," he declares. "I'm ready to play basketball."

These past few weeks Robinson has aimed his team at next year as much as this one. Everyone is expected to return in '94 except Thompson. Robinson would like to stay and watch the remainder of the tournament, but there's no time. While the ACC's other eight teams meet in the quarterfinals, he'll be off recruiting, seeking help.

"As far as the agony and all the attention that's been given this team—the trials, the tribulations, the excuses—I am tired of that; I'm not going to miss it," Robinson says. "All the scenario of this season has been unbelievable. I'm anxious to just get back to having a basketball team and not having so many outside distractions."

S HADES of 1987.

The day begins with Virginia edging Wake Forest, as it did in the opening round in '87. That earns the Cavs a spot in the semifinals against North Carolina, as in '87. The top-seeded Heels advance by routing eight-seed Maryland, as they did in '87. In the evening session, seventh-seed Clemson upsets number two, Florida State, as occurred with different teams in '87.

If form holds true, then, Duke will lose in the nightcap, as it did in 1987. That year, the Blue Devils played sixth-seeded N.C. State, which went on to win the tournament. Tonight Duke faces sixth-seeded Georgia Tech. Guess what? Tech wins 69–66.

During the afternoon Maryland stays with North Carolina for most of the first half before getting blown off the court like a bicycle caught in the wash of a passing tractor-trailer. The final damage is 102–66. Every available scholarship player scores for the Heels.

There are a few notable developments for UNC. Derrick Phelps gets in quick foul trouble, plays only fifteen minutes and is scarcely missed. Henrik Rodl has seven assists and a single turnover during a fifteen-minute stint, and Scott Cherry chips in five straight points to help UNC close out the first half with a 51–34 margin. Afterward Dean Smith is quick to praise Cherry.

Brian Reese continues to play with comfortable confidence, grabbing six rebounds and scoring sixteen points in twenty minutes. "Before, everyone came into the game thinking they had to stop Lynch and Montross," Maryland's Gary Williams says. "Now you have to worry about guys penetrating. They are just a better team." Still, it's Eric Montross and George Lynch who do the most damage, leading the Heels to a 57–33 edge on the boards. The well-muscled Lynch is especially overpowering, contributing twenty-two points, sixteen rebounds and three steals. Smith says of Lynch that he had to "hold him back by taking him out with eleven minutes to play. Otherwise he would have had a jillion" against the 12–16 Terps. As it is, the senior's point total against Maryland is his second-highest of the year.

Oh, yes. There's also the matter of a late wake-up call and a slow elevator, factors blamed by road roommates Reese and Montross for their eighty-second tardiness to the pregame meal.

Smith, a stickler for player promptitude, benches both starters for the first one minute and forty seconds of the game. Other than Senior Day, when Matt Wenstrom got the automatic nod, it's the only start Montross misses this year.

The victory raises Carolina's record to 27–3 and gives Smith career win number 767. That ties him for second all-time with Henry Iba, who recently died. The only Division I coach with more victories was Adolph Rupp with 875, a total Smith could match within four seasons.

Reluctance to stand out is quintessential Smith, a man in whom competitiveness and humility are in eternal conflict. Even to speak with Smith is to engage in verbal arm-wrestling; in conversation, as most every facet of life, Smith loves to win, to command, to hold the upper hand. Yet he's guided by strong religious beliefs that enforce a desire to deflect praise and credit, to shun ostentation and power. Some view Smith's seemingly contradictory actions, like professing modesty while allowing the Smith Center to bear his name, as signs of hypocrisy. More accurately, they reflect a very private man striving mightily to balance seemingly irreconcilable inner forces while engaging in a very public profession.

Despite the talk about Rupp's record, Smith insists he won't retire so long as coaching remains fun. Bill Guthridge, who knows Smith as well as anyone, insists he sees no signs of flagging interest on the part of his boss. Smith professes few interests outside basketball besides family and golf. Health never has been a problem, and both Smith's parents lived into their eighties.

Guthridge figured in one scenario Smith considered to finesse breaking Rupp's mark. Should he get close, Smith contemplated resigning in favor of Guthridge, but staying on as a volunteer assistant. Smith says that's no longer an option, but won't discuss what might happen instead.

As for tying Iba's mark, Smith says, "Oh, come on," when asked to comment. Pressed, he deflects discussion from himself to "Mr. Iba." "He was one of the great, special coaches of all time, friend to all of us," Smith says as he hustles from the Charlotte Coliseum, leaving it to Guthridge, as always, to shepherd the Tar Heels from locker room to bus to hotel.

Duke enters the ACC Tournament seeking to become the league's first repeat champion in more than a decade, just as last season it became the nation's first repeat champion in two decades. The plan for the weekend is to reintegrate Grant Hill into the lineup, slowly if possible, while maintaining the level of individual and group performance that's marked the team's play for the past several weeks.

Instead the Blue Devils get knocked out in the first round, which hasn't happened since 1987.

Worse, the loss to struggling Georgia Tech, coming on the heels of last weekend's defeat at Chapel Hill, leaves the Dukies' confidence shaken at the very moment they're about to embark on their annual NCAA run.

Afterward disappointment and anger swirl through the locker room. "We have to try to win six games to win the national championship," Bobby Hurley fumes. "I just don't see it happening. We're having too many inconsistencies."

Hurley knows what it takes to play for championships. His high school teams won four consecutive state titles, and he's been the ball handler for Duke teams that reached three straight NCAA title games. Tonight Hurley leads Duke with seventeen points and eight assists without a turnover. He feels he's done all he can, only to have that effort sabotaged by irresolute teammates, some of whom he calls "ghosts" of their recent selves.

It's obvious to whom Hurley refers—Marty Clark neither scores nor does much of anything else against Georgia Tech, and starter Tony Lang fouls out without scoring a point. Lang manages two rebounds and three shots, and fails to slow Tech's James Forrest, who scores twenty-seven points and misses only two of fifteen shots.

"I doubt our toughness, how much we want to win," Hurley snaps. "Before, it seems when I went into a tournament I was with a group of guys who were really tough. I think our team wants to win. But that toughness isn't there. It's definitely a bad feeling. I don't like where our team is at right now, where it's headed. We didn't give the kind of effort it takes to win a championship. If I was Coach, I don't know what I'd say to us right now. I have a lot of doubts."

As always following a loss, Grant Hill sits slumped, answering questions in a soft voice. "I just don't feel we played the best we could," he says. "It's very frustrating, that's all." Few realize it, but Hill is playing with two injuries. There's his sore sole, and also a bad ankle, the same ankle that bothered him at Maryland. That pain returned at yesterday's public workout, when Clark pushed Hill from behind to stop a layup attempt. Duke coaches joke they'll have to revoke Clark's scholarship. Hill remains angry, but focuses instead on what's wrong with the team.

"It really hurts to lose when you don't play well," he says. "Especially now, at this point in the season, you have to come out great, you've got to come out, like, bang!, and make the other team catch up."

At first, that's exactly what appears to be happening as the Devils jump to a 9–3 lead against the Yellow Jackets, who've lost more games than they've won since defeating Duke in mid-January.

Up and down all season, the Jackets enter the ACC Tournament uncertain that Bobby Cremins will remain as their coach. He's been wooed since January by South Carolina, his alma mater, and most Cremins intimates expect him to accept the job as Gamecock head coach.

This scenario leaves Duke's coaches nervous. They know Cremins's players, who regard him as something of a big brother, aren't about to let him go without a fight. They'll be "on a mission," as Mike Brey puts it. And Cremins isn't about to play Duke without marshaling his team's best effort. So it's no surprise when Tech responds to Duke's opening statement with a statement of its own, scoring seven unanswered points to take a 10–9 lead barely four minutes into the game.

That sets the tone for a half in which there are two ties and eleven lead changes as neither team can shake the other.

Hurley and Chris Collins each hit a pair of three-pointers for the Devils against Tech's zone during the half, while Cherokee Parks scores nine points inside. Duke twice leads by six, early on and with 2:36 left in the period after a running jumper by Thomas Hill. This is how it's supposed to be. Duke is expected to win, to strut its stuff. This is Duke's time of year. But any sense of control is short-lived. Duke finishes the half by missing its last four shots, Tech scores seven unanswered points, and takes a 36–35 lead at intermission.

Forrest does the most damage, hitting seven of seven shots in the period, including a dunk on a break that helps spark the comeback. Center Malcolm Mackey has six rebounds as the Jackets hold a decisive edge on the boards. The same Duke squad that's holding opponents to 43.5 percent shooting allows Tech 56.6 percent first-half accuracy.

Each team fails to score on its first three possessions of the second half, until Hurley hits a three to give Duke a 38–36 advantage with 18:56 remaining. It's the last time Duke leads.

Over the next three minutes the Devils fail to score on five straight possessions, allowing Tech to build a 43–38 edge. Trying to be aggressive, Lang charges on a fast break and misses a shot inside.

Duke seems uncertain in half court, and doesn't force many transition opportunities. Grant Hill misses jumpers, commits turnovers trying to create shots, and wears a pained expression. The Georgia Tech lead increases to 61–51 with 7:17 left.

Duke's not done, though. Proud and determined, it mounts a 13–3 run to tie the score at the 2:49 mark.

First Thomas Hill hits a three-pointer off an inbounds pass. Travis Best responds with a pair of free throws, Hurley waving in disgust at official Larry Rose as he's called for the foul. Grant Hill wants the ball now, gets it from Hurley and hits a three from the top of the key. This is Duke's thirtieth game of the season, and Hill's first successful shot from the bonusphere.

Next, with the shot clock running down, Hurley takes a charge from Best, the Tech guard's fourth foul. Grant Hill receives the ball on the right wing, backs freshman Martice Moore toward the basket, loses and recovers his dribble, goes low, spins, hits a six-foot bank shot and is fouled by Mackey. Hill makes the free throw, too, pulling Duke within 63–60.

Trying to steal the ensuing inbounds pass, Hill fouls Mackey. A lousy foul shooter, the Tech center makes one of two free throws. Immediately, Parks gets good position in the low post against Mackey, takes a pass from Thomas Hill, maneuvers to the basket, and hits a short jumper. (Parks has a good game, but pissed off teammates just as they were about to take the court. Last night ESPN had a feature on Hurley that included an anecdote about his resolve in finishing a ten-kilometer race as a child even after he'd fallen. As the players huddled, a fellow Dukie recalls Parks saying: "'Yeah, we can do it. We have to be like Bob was when he was little and he fell down and had that determination.' And he started laughing.")

Cremins calls timeout, lead down to two points with 4:36 left. It doesn't help. A nineteen-foot jumper by Grant Hill, his eighth point in barely three minutes, ties the score at 64–64.

Lang fouls out contesting a shot by Forrest, sending the forward to the line. "Great players make great plays, and he made great plays over and over," Lang says.

Forrest misses the front end of a one-and-one but Mackey rebounds and gets the ball to Drew Barry, who hits a running jumper. Next time downcourt Parks hits a turnaround shot in the lane, tying the score at 66–66 with 1:47 left.

Tech calls another timeout. When play resumes, Forrest, as happened down the stretch in Atlanta, is matched against Grant Hill and he delivers, his jumper giving the Jackets a 68–66 lead. Duke calls timeout. The Devils work the ball for a good shot, finally settling for a post-up jumper by Thomas Hill with the shot clock in single digits. His attempt is rejected by Mackey, who's immediately fouled.

Mackey misses both free throws, 23.4 seconds remaining. Moving the ball patiently, Duke gets an open three-point attempt by T. Hill. He misses. Mackey rebounds, is fouled again. Only 5.7 seconds remain. Mackey misses the first free throw, his fourth straight miss, but makes the second. Georgia Tech 69, Duke 66.

Duke decides to go without a timeout. Best faceguards Hurley, so Grant Hill quickly inbounds to Thomas Hill, who gets it to Hurley near midcourt. Drawing four defenders as he reaches the top of the key, Hurley kicks the ball to Chris Collins in front of the Duke bench. The freshman stops, pops. His jumper from the NBA three-point line goes in, out. Forrest rebounds. Game ends.

Long before the Blue Devils started recruiting him, Collins attended the ACC Tournament as a fan, sitting in the Duke section with his godfather. Back home in Illinois, Collins practiced what he'd do in an ACC Tournament, announcing the game as he played. And now he'd lived the moment he'd dreamt of, hoped for, and practiced, taken the shot he took "a million times" in his backyard.

"I thought the ball was in," he says. "It was right on line. It felt great. I was just thinking, 'Go in, go in.' It felt great. It was right in rhythm and then when it didn't [go in] my heart just kind of dropped. It's not a fun feeling."

Collins remembers Krzyzewski telling him afterward "to keep my head up and that it was a great shot; we couldn't have gotten a much better shot. That's a shot he wants me to take all the time, and to have the guts to take it was great." Thomas Hill and Tony Lang also make an impression, putting their arms around Collins and seconding the coach's message. "That made me feel a lot better," Collins says.

Lang, sporting a black left eye, is feeling rather bad himself. "Personally, I'm very frustrated because I feel I let myself down, and I let my team-mates down the way I performed today," Lang says. "It's also frustrating because this is the time of the year that we should play great together and we lose in the first round of the ACC Tournament. I mean, it's kind of hard to cope with, it's kind of hard to deal with. But you have to com-mend Georgia Tech, they played a great game. Some kind of way, we've got to put this game behind us."

Lang can't say why he "didn't come ready to play," why he was so unassertive, so quick to lose ground he'd gained while Grant Hill was absent. It's almost as if, with Hill back, he has an excuse to fade into the woodwork. In a way, he sees his effort as symptomatic of a team-wide malaise. "Sometimes you think that, well, with the success that we've had, that, hey, we're just going to win," Lang says. "But the years previous to this, we really went out there and made things happen."

That and other matters are discussed during a late-night players' meet-ing in a hotel room shared by Thomas Hill and Marty Clark. "It wasn't too productive because it was a lot of emotions," a participant says. If any-thing, the postdefeat conversation resurrects old conflicts that have divid-ed the squad throughout the season. "It's like a shipwreck. Everybody blames each other for the shipwreck. They blame the captain. They point the finger, instead of everybody accepting responsibility for themselves."

SATURDAY, MARCH 13

DERRICK Phelps gets his first view of The Blizzard of 1993 from a supine position, strapped to a stretcher at the rear of the Charlotte Coliseum. The huge outside doors remain open, and in the chill air Phelps's breath coalesces above him in puffs that match the color of the blanket covering his still torso and exposed limbs. Phelps's mother stands by his side wearing a yellow Mickey Mouse rain slicker and a concerned look. Across the player's body a uniformed paramedic speaks in a soothingly casual manner while awaiting the ambulance that navigates through the silencing snow amongst satellite dishes, parked cars, trucks, buses, and trailers.

"It was a lot of turmoil," Linda Phelps admits. "I just tried to stay calm because I didn't want to scare him." The preliminary courtside diagnosis is that there'll be no lasting damage from the savage spill Phelps takes near the end of North Carolina's 74–56 semifinal victory over Virginia.

The snowfall is part of what some weather forecasters and headline writers call the "storm of the century." (And people say sportswriters are prone to hyperbole.) More than one hundred deaths are attributed to the storm, which is six hundred miles wide and affects twenty-five states and Washington, D.C. Record snowfalls and low temperatures are recorded in many parts of the South. More than three million people are left without power, including for thirty minutes the 23,532 in the Charlotte Coliseum.

The teams stand by their benches at first while reserve lighting provides modest illumination. Tar Heel benchwarmers come out in the gloaming to get in extra shooting. Then the auxiliary lights fail and Jeff

Jones leads his team from the floor to the locker room. Seeing that (if dimly), Carolina too departs.

This is an odd moment for the Heels, because for the first time in their careers they confront a game situation they haven't practiced. Undaunted, when play resumes with 17:07 left in the game, they go on a 16–3 run that lasts a bit more than six minutes. Paced by six points from Eric Montross and four from Brian Reese, the outburst puts UNC in comfortable command. Virginia doesn't pull closer than a dozen points the rest of the way. "Maybe Coach will turn the lights off every day, we played so well after that," Henrik Rodl says, laughing.

Jones is not amused.

"When we had the delay and the lights went out, I think North Carolina showed great maturity and maybe showed their experience," he says. "They really seized that moment. I think it was more them. They had added intensity and really started pounding the offensive boards and were on the attack."

Dean Smith cites his team's performance subsequent to the stoppage as proof it's superior play, rather than depth and sheer numbers, that wears down Carolina opponents. Much to Jones's annoyance, Smith again complains about Virginia's defense despite an edge of more than two-to-one in fouls. "There was some contact inside, possibly, maybe," Smith says puckishly. "I wonder how far I can go and coach tomorrow. I could take a day off tomorrow and watch on TV." Not likely. For a while, though, it appears Phelps may have to watch the tournament finals from a hospital room.

North Carolina leads by twelve when Phelps gets behind the Virginia defense and drives for a layup. Racing desperately to overtake him, Virginia's Jason Williford tries to block the shot and instead fouls Phelps hard from behind. The UNC playmaker crashes to the floor, landing on his back.

"Anytime you go in the air and get knocked off balance, that's the worst thing," says a shaken Williford. "I don't want people thinking that I'm a dirty player or anything like that." Lying just beyond the baseline Phelps remains immobile, as players are taught to do should they sustain a serious injury. Phelps is accustomed to getting hurt. On this occasion he suspects the worst. His thighs are numb.

"At that time I was really panicking. I didn't know what was going on," he admits. "I was hurt. I was definitely crying. I didn't know what the injury was. I knew my legs were numb." His mother comes out of the stands to be by his side along with several doctors.

"I just asked him how did he feel," Linda Phelps says. "He said OK. He didn't look OK. I think he was scared. I was." Gradually the fear eases. A little. "My mother kept me calm, saying it's going to be all right," the player reports.

"That's an experience I don't want to go through again," Linda Phelps says afterward.

Eventually Phelps is placed on a stretcher and wheeled to the back of the building, from which he's taken to a local hospital for precautionary X-rays. He'll be released tonight. The diagnosis is that he's suffered a bruised sacrum (tailbone). Sore as he is, it's considered doubtful he'll play tomorrow against Georgia Tech, which outlasts Clemson in the second semifinal.

"Of course we can't replace Derrick," says Rodl, who'll doubtless be called upon to try. "He sets the tone of the defense and does all sorts of stuff for us."

Phelps takes it all in stride, the risks of the road, so to speak. "We just go hard each and every game we go out there. We just push and push and push to be better," he says. "I guess I've always been like that. That's in my nature."

Back in Durham, Mike Krzyzewski utilizes the unexpected day off to take his preteen daughter, Jamie, to the movies. They see "Groundhog Day," a comedy about a TV weatherman who wakes up repeatedly to find he must relive the same particularly bad day.

"I like Bill Murray, and Jamie explained it to me," Krzyzewski says several days later. "There were parts of it that I didn't understand. I was worried about certain things that I might have to relive, over and over, and I was hoping it wasn't going to be last Friday."

That, of course, was the day Duke lost to Georgia Tech.

SUNDAY, MARCH 14

TODAY's metaphorical exchange occurs as the final dozen seconds tick off the game clock, seemingly flowing faster because their passage is recorded in tenths of a second, the numerals flickering past like a sudden irreversible escape of gas from a balloon.

Down five, Donald Williams launches a three from the right side and misses. Eric Montross grabs the rebound, fires the ball back to Williams. He tries another three-pointer, another miss. Montross rebounds again and sends the ball back to Williams, whose shot goes down, the third time good but not the charm because the clock's run out on North Carolina's eleven-game winning streak, its number-one national ranking, and its gathering aura of inevitability.

"You know, I'm just kind of shocked," Bobby Cremins says after Georgia Tech wins 77–75. "Maybe I should consider another job every year."

Cremins, not generally respected for his coaching, now has three ACC titles, twice beating Carolina in the final, and has taken teams to four title games in nine years. He's the only coach at a school other than Duke, UNC or N.C. State to win more than two ACC championships.

Historically, members of the Triangle trio have held the ACC crown more than three-quarters of the time. Duke or Carolina has been in all but eight title games during the league's forty seasons.

Duke lately has been a fixture in the final, appearing in four of the five championship games preceding this one. The Devils have won three titles under Mike Krzyzewski, and nine overall. N.C. State has won ten, its last coming in 1987, hauntingly parallel 1987, when an inspired six-seed coached by Jim Valvano upset North Carolina.

"Up until '87, I'd never seen our mail complaining that we didn't win the ACC Tournament," Smith, winner of eleven ACC titles, recalls. "We played great the second half, maybe the best we had all year, and then all hell breaks loose." (Talk about fixtures: Smith has guided a team to the title game two of every three years since 1967, when Cremins and Krzyzewski were still underclassmen in college.)

Following the surprise loss to State in '87 by a team that had won sixteen straight ACC contests, Smith says he's "put a little more psychological, mental, emotional emphasis into" winning the tournament. It shows—his teams have been back to the final in all but one year since.

But here's a strange fact. Smith has taken eight previous teams to the Final Four, every one after it captured the ACC Tournament, none without doing so first.

This year's group intends to reach New Orleans, even if it has to beat Georgia Tech without Derrick Phelps, who enters the Charlotte Coliseum gingerly. He uses a metal railing to pull himself up a short flight of cement stairs near where he was wheeled out yesterday on a stretcher. The Jackets, a group of "shaky" ball handlers by Cremins's own estimate, have the ACC's worst turnover margin and are quite susceptible to defensive pressure tactics. They also tend toward mental torpor at crucial moments, and already have lost twice to UNC by an average margin of twelve points.

Yet it's the Heels who play catch-up for the majority of the contest. Their biggest second-half lead is five points, 50–45 with 13:59 left, an advantage that evaporates entirely within eighty seconds. The Jackets go ahead for keeps at the 8:54 mark on a follow shot by James Forrest. Forrest, a six-eight sophomore forward, is en route to the ACC Tournament's biggest scoring outburst—eighty points in three games on thirty-five of fifty-one shooting—since Albert King scored eighty-one for Maryland in 1980. He will become the unanimous tournament MVP.

Down the stretch, it figures the Heels, a thirteen-point favorite, will come to the fore. Instead, with a chance to become the first Smith squad since the national champs of 1982 to finish atop the regular season standings and win the ACC Tournament, it is Carolina, not Tech, that falters.

Williams misses jumper after jumper, fourteen misses in eighteen attempts. "The shots I would miss, they felt good, they were good shots," says Williams, who's forced to guard Travis Best in Phelps's absence, an assignment that costs the Heels' best outside shooter his legs.

Best is a quick, clever, relentless penetrator who, without Phelps to stop him, repeatedly insinuates himself into the gut of UNC's defense. Several times he and teammate Drew Barry drive coast to coast, something rarely seen against the Heels.

The Tech guard's disruptive effect highlights Phelps's value to Carolina. "He is the best defender in the league, Travis has a lot of trouble with him," Cremins says. Virginia players report Phelps is the only defender able to contain their playmaker, Cory Alexander.

In fact, Phelps turns out to be the single indispensable component in what's otherwise a squad of gifted, interchangeable parts. "Derrick has a kind of an air about him that says, 'On the court I'm the leader, and I'm going to tell you what to do and when you have to do it,'" Eric Montross says. "But it's not cocky, it's not, 'All right, do this because I'm the best,' or something like that." Phelps also sets the defensive tone. He's fun to play with. He clever and he's tough. Losing him, says George Lynch, is like being without Coach Smith.

With Phelps, this is perhaps the quintessential Smith squad, its members so well trained and integrated, so selfless, they operate the coach's system to near-perfection. They start with defense, holding opponents to the lowest field-goal accuracy of Smith's thirty-two-year tenure (41.4 percent). They force more turnovers compared to assists than any UNC squad since at least 1980. Offensively, they hit more than half their field goals and more than 70 percent of their free throws, outscore opponents by nearly eighteen points per game, and rank among the national leaders in rebounding margin. They're also the only first-place squad in the ACC's forty seasons that doesn't place a scorer in the league's top fifteen.

Without Phelps, who sits on the bench in tie and jacket beside Serge Zwikker, these Heels can't quite muster the acumen to play their customarily overwhelming brand of ball.

"We did everything to put ourselves in a position to win the ballgame," Rodl says. "We got good shots, played hard, but they played better. That's the end of it."

Reese is less forgiving. "I can't stand losing," he says, "regardless of who we played. There's no excuse. We did a good job. We could have done a better job."

Lynch is perhaps most realistic, or at least most calculating. "Let's see, we lost by two points without Derrick," he reckons aloud. "We would have won the game, no problem, if Derrick were in."

But now it's one misstep and the season's over, the easy camaraderie of common enterprise abruptly ended, and it's far from certain Phelps will play again or regain his previous level of efficiency.

Barely an hour after Georgia Tech wins the ACC title, the NCAA Tournament selection committee announces its pairings. For Duke athletic director Tom Butters, chairman of the committee, the announcement marks the culmination of perhaps the most difficult ordeal he's ever endured.

From Thursday night, when the eight committee members sequestered themselves in a Kansas City hotel, until the conclusion of this evening's press conference, revealing the tournament selections, Butters feels under tremendous pressure. He worries about saying or doing something that will "embarrass" the NCAA, the committee, or Duke. The weight of decision, of choosing a George Washington rather than a Providence, is especially heavy because he realizes acutely that "you're dealing with young kids' lives, what's important to them." Complicating the task are the weekend's "countless number of upsets." Tech's victory improves its seeding, but has no effect on North Carolina's fortunes. The Heels remain the top seed in the East, where they'll face East Carolina, the sixteen-seed, in the opening round at Winston-Salem. It's the twenty-third NCAA appearance by a Dean Smith squad, extending an NCAA record. Smith also has forty-nine tournament wins, most in NCAA history.

Six ACC squads make the field. The conference has placed a majority of its members in the NCAAs every season since 1984.

Speculation had Duke going either to the Southeast, where it might have a potential rematch with number-one-seed Kentucky on a sympathetic Charlotte floor, or to the West, abode of number-one-seed Michigan. Instead, the NCAA places the Blue Devils in the same bracket with teams they've beaten in the last two Final Fours, teams that at various times have been ranked tops in the country this year—Indiana, which finishes the regular season at number one, and Kansas.

"To be quite frank with you, I never thought we'd be in the Midwest," says Krzyzewski, fifth all-time in NCAA winning percentage at 33–7. "After looking at the entire bracket I wish I wasn't going to the Midwest. The bracket is unbelievably tough . . . the team that comes out of that region will certainly be deserving of being called a champion."

Duke is matched with Southern Illinois in the opening round, as the

Devils learn at a gathering in the Hall of Fame room that includes players, coaches and their families, and the sports information staff. The group snacks and watches TV as CBS announces the pairings.

Earlier in the day, preceding a team workout, the players held their own meeting, a bit more productive than the hotel-room session in Charlotte. A major theme is pulling together to defend their title. "This championship is ours," Grant Hill says. "Everybody's going to be coming at us and we've got to defend it. I know Coach doesn't want us to talk about defending, but it's ours."

The concept understandably is a bit remote to Collins, a freshman. Far more immediate is his enthusiasm about being part of an NCAA odyssey.

"To be there, to have your team be one of the teams waiting to see where you were going to go, it was a feeling of excitement," he says. "I remember, ever since I was able to write I would have my brackets out, sitting at home, writing where everybody was playing, predicting who I thought would go to the Final Four. To have my team be one of the teams playing, it's a memory. I'll never forget that first NCAA Tournament selection."

Participation and success in the NCAAs are nothing new, however, for the Triangle's ACC triumvirate. Pick a team category in the NCAA record book and you'll find the familiar names:

—Most Consecutive Tournament appearances: North Carolina first, now with nineteen, Duke tied for fourth with ten. (UNC's streak began the first season multiple entrants from the same conference were allowed. The next-longest run, fourteen by Georgetown under coach John Thompson, Dean Smith's longtime friend, ends this year.)

—Most Tournament appearances: North Carolina third with twenty-seven.

—Most Tournament wins: North Carolina third with fifty-six, Duke fourth with fifty.

—Highest Tournament winning percentage: Duke first, North Carolina seventh, North Carolina State ninth.

No other league has three teams among the top ten in NCAA winning percentage, let alone a threesome so intertwined they form a single, cozy basketball Triangle.

MONDAY, MARCH 15

THE public Mike Krzyzewski is cheerful and upbeat, excited about his program's latest NCAA bid. Unstated is the knowledge Duke can become the only program besides UCLA ever to win three consecutive championships.

Lurking in the background, though, is the realization this team isn't ready to win an NCAA title. And while he doesn't share that bit of knowledge with the world at large, Krzyzewski and staff let Duke's players know in a hurry.

The coaches approach this afternoon's practice with unusual intensity. Pete Gaudet's language is peppered with "Goddamns." Krzyzewski's is stronger still. Their words rise in a prodding chorus, murmurously merging like voices echoing in a hallway, as the players embark on the day's first drills.

"Rebound, Grant! Rebound, Grant!"

"Good job, Kenny!"

"Go, Erik! Go, Erik! Don't slow down."

"Grab the ball! Grab the ball!"

Krzyzewski, dressed in blue sweatpants and grey sweatshirt, tells the squad how to run a drill, then watches Erik Meek do it wrong. "So what the hell are you paying attention to?" he asks acerbically.

That's just the beginning.

A moment later Krzyzewski stops another drill. "You guys haven't contested a pass today," he says sourly. "It's sick watching you guys play defense."

He points out that the defenders are too intent on checking their own man rather than watching ball and man, and they aren't denying passes so much as they're guarding their man once he receives the ball. "There's nobody being alert on defense right now. Nobody," he says.

After a pass travels thirty feet to Cherokee Parks in the low post, Krzyzewski again stops play to lecture the group. On the next play Thomas Hill dives to the floor after a loose ball, scraping his left elbow. "You may as well get in your minds, it's the only way we're going to win," he says of a keener defensive awareness. "If you don't want to play badly enough then we'll play only one game, and we'll go to the beach."

A few moments later, Thomas Hill is matched with Chris Collins in ball denial. Thoroughly disgusted by the ease with which Hill receives passes, Krzyzewski intervenes. "If he gets the ball, you're not going to play in Thursday night's game," he tells Collins. Then for two possessions the head coach tries to get the ball to Hill, with Collins feverishly working to thwart the effort.

"You have to go back to playing defense like that, fellas," Krzyzewski says soon after. "It's like an old friend. We haven't seen that friend for a while."

Throughout, Grant Hill hobbles, stumbles, falls. There are no soaring moves from the injured junior. He's quiet, his expression pained, his brow furrowed, his demeanor quite at odds with the boldly determined statements he made at a lunchtime press conference.

"I've never really been pissed off like I was about the loss this weekend," Hill says of Duke's quick elimination in the ACC Tournament. He vows to maintain that angry attitude, and hopes his teammates too will display the cockiness, the confidence that Duke took onto the court in seasons past.

"Sometimes we can play so well, and we can play so bad. Sometimes you just don't know which Duke team is going to show up, which Duke players are going to show up," Hill complains. "I hope I know. I think you'll see us play our hardest, play our best. If you see us losing in the second round, the first round, whatever, you'll see us play our hardest."

But while Hill plays hard at today's practice, it's obvious his injured foot holds his attention. Krzyzewski quickly makes clear this isn't suitable, telling the team during a break that Hill won't be eased along as happened against Georgia Tech. "If Grant can't play, his ass is coming out of there," the coach declares.

Privately, Krzyzewski informs Hill: "You're not allowed to play and grimace, so forget it. You have to think about grimacing. You do. That means you're thinking about you. Basically, I'm just asking you to lead. I know you're not one hundred percent. But you need to be a leader."

Krzyzewski also tells the team to "forget brackets and defending championships and all that bullshit." The main issue, he says, is getting back to a winning attitude. "We haven't won because we've out-thought people," he reminds his players. "We've won because we've out-worked people and because we've initiated things. Let's attack and see how other people react."

The coach makes the remarks halfway through an unscheduled intrasquad scrimmage in chilly Cameron. Then he dispatches the team to the locker room to talk things over amongst themselves. Hill is told that if he concentrates on talking to teammates on the court, as he's supposed to, he'll shed his self-absorption and not notice the pain in his injured foot so much.

The advice seems to help. Hill's play is noticeably improved in the second half of the scrimmage. "We don't have time to be sick, we don't have time for anything except winning," Krzyzewski says.

He certainly doesn't have time for what he sees from Tony Lang, who contests a pass with a mere wave of his hand and no corresponding foot movement.

Krzyzewski immediately stops the scrimmage. "What the fuck?" he asks softly, moving close to Lang.

The volume of the coach's voice rises a level. "What the fuck are you doing?"

Now he's shouting. "Quit feeling sorry for yourself and play the fucking defense."

Lang paces down and back in the lane, clearly pained.

Several minutes later a trio of players earns a lecture for inadequate effort, while Bobby Hurley works feverishly on defense. Immediately the intensity level picks up. Bodies sprawl as players fight for position, contest passes. But within a few moments Krzyzewski complains the Devils aren't playing together. "That's why you haven't beaten a good team for two weeks!" he exclaims. "Duke beat Duke!"

Afterward, Krzyzewski tells the Dukies to always bring "talk and enthusiasm" to practice, factors absent when they arrived this afternoon for practice number seventy. "We came to practice today with a losing attitude," he says. "We need to play with emotion. We need to play with passion. How we get there is irrelevant."

TUESDAY, MARCH 16

THE thought for the day, which Pat Sullivan is asked to repeat at practice, comes from W. Somerset Maugham: "It is a funny thing about life; if you refuse to accept anything but the best, you very often get it."

Rather an apt starting point for the Tar Heels, licking their wounds after last weekend's venture to Charlotte. The return to Chapel Hill has been an especially painful one. Not only because the team lost, though that provides its demons too. This one's tough because of what happened to Derrick Phelps; in obvious discomfort, he stands much of the time as the bus heads north up I-85.

Now, after a day off and time to ponder, players and coaches are back in livery, hoping for Phelps's return and geared up to take on all comers, demonic and real.

Gone is that glorious number-one ranking, held for only two weeks. Absurdly, despite losing by two points in Phelps's absence the Tar Heels drop from first to fourth in the final AP poll.

Before the headlong rush to finality begins, the players have rituals to attend, like their final weekly autograph session, moving pen in hand from table to table on both sides of the carpeted Dean Dome hallway between locker room and press area, signing rows of *Sports Illustrated*s and game programs, T-shirts, basketballs, and other paraphernalia. And today there's a quick press conference, ten minutes with Lynch and Pat Sullivan, a bit more with Dean Smith. Later, Smith tells the team regarding this time of year: "We're starting press conference after press conference after press conference. It's good for you."

Sullivan enthusiastically violates sport's sacred one-game-at-a-time dictum, confessing excitement at the prospect to returning home to New Jersey's Meadowlands. That presumes North Carolina advances to the Sweet Sixteen, of course, but it's a safe bet, having happened every year since Sullivan was ten years old. "I don't think a great coach should be judged on how many national championships he has," says the junior, whose first basketball memory is the telecast of Smith's Tar Heels winning the '82 title. "I think it should be consistency, and he's the model."

Lynch, meanwhile, frets over the shooting touch that deserted him at Charlotte. Lynch knows his NBA prospects are uncertain without a reliable jumper. Not to mention, he's counted upon as the team's number two scorer as well as a "senior leader," a badge of honor and proud responsibility in the Tar Heel lexicon.

Lynch says: "I'm not going to put a lot of pressure on myself by saying, 'One game, we lose and we're out.' I want to go in and continue to play the kind of basketball Coach Smith has expected me to play all year."

After Smith finishes interviews with several local TV reporters he replaces Sullivan at the podium, and Lynch too departs. The writers at today's press conference don't ask Smith about Lynch's shooting. Few members of the media think Lynch can shoot, anyway.

But Smith is asked about the Tar Heels' misfires from the free throw line in the ACC Tournament final. Or, rather, the question is almost asked, with Smith interrupting to go off on a strange tangent that effectively stifles discussion.

Smith doesn't overtly bow to a superior intelligence prior to games, as Krzyzewski does by crossing himself, but he is superstitious. Not that he'll admit it. Smith is not worried himself, he insists rationally; he just knows it's best to avoid tempting fate. So he says: "The last time one of you asked about foul shooting, I said, 'Don't talk about it. We're fine. Talk about shank in golf! We're doing fine. We're doing fine. We're shooting fouls. We're a good shooting team. That's it.'"

Then, as if realizing the power he's just invested in the irrational, Smith partially contradicts his own remarks, denigrating those who believe rooting affects reality. "Somebody said, on television they just put under there: Montross had hit eighteen of eighteen [free throws]. Boy." Smith laughs. "The only time they put it was before he missed the two [late against Georgia Tech]. At least before he did it. Of course it had no effect on it whatsoever. But you'd be amazed how many people worried about that. Some guy did it on purpose. You know, put it down."

Everyone laughs.

"That's like, people wear different clothes for their team as if it had that kind of control over Eric's foul shooting. Human nature." Smith again laughs ruefully.

Smith also expresses concern with his team's performance down the stretch against the Yellow Jackets, a matter he'll review during a 7:00 P.M. team meeting prior to practice.

"We really haven't had that all year, where we're down, you know, with a minute and a half to play," he says of the catch-up situation. "Even though you practice it, it still isn't quite the same as years where you have a lot of those games." Without breaking stride, he proceeds to the flip side. "I guess I should be happy we got a lot of practice on a delay game this year. We had the lead late. But to come from behind late—we've come from behind, but not in the last five minutes."

Then there's the matter of facing East Carolina.

Just last week, Smith was asked about the possibility of an NCAA matchup with the Pirates, a team with a 13–16 record that earned an automatic bid as the winner of Colonial Athletic Association tournament. Typically, he congratulated the Pirates on being in the field and couldn't help adding, "I hope we are [too]." This despite his team's high ranking and incontrovertible prowess.

Now that he knows his team will face the number-sixteen seed, Smith insists that's his sole focus. "This is in all honesty: I couldn't tell you everybody who's made the East Regional, or even where we're seeded. I do know eight and nine are Purdue and Rhode Island. I know very clearly we're playing East Carolina, and that's all I want." But Smith knows something else too—he's never taken a team to the Final Four without first winning the ACC Tournament. He claims the stat is irrelevant; for him, the meaning of the ACC Tournament changed forever in 1976.

Prior to 1975, the NCAA field accommodated just one member per league. If you didn't win the ACC Tournament, and with it the league's automatic bid, you stayed home or maybe went to the NIT. The ACC's do-or-die finale was ridiculed for that reason, even as it intensified pressure on every coach and team, and fed a heady sense of competition that often devolved into envy, distrust and plain bad feeling.

Once Smith began dominating the league—winning five of nine titles from 1967 through 1975—he became a perennial target.

Carolina reached the 1976 title game, too, as well as four of the six after that. But in one of the great ACC Tournament shockers, forward Wally Walker and first-year coach Terry Holland led sixth-seed Virginia to the 1976 league title. What proved the Cavaliers' sole championship also was the first of three ever captured by six-seeds. The others also came against North Carolina.

While an official ACC title has lost its luster for Smith, the perennial pursuit of a national title has not. "All we talked about since November one was winning in New Orleans," he says of this season. "So that is a big change since '76." He can't resist stating the converse, though, punctuating it with a pained laugh. "But we've said that every year and we don't always do it."

Doing "it" is winning the NCAA title, or at least reaching the Final Four. The statement is barely out, though, before Smith's ever-active mind spins on, perpetually worrying each kernel of information like a hen poking at some resistant bit of food.

"It's nice that we're a contender every year. I think that's nice. If you're in the tournament, I guess you're a contender. If you're not in the tournament, I guess you can't be considered a contender. I know that isn't hard to figure out."

Watching tonight's practice, it also isn't hard to figure out that Derrick Phelps is hurting.

Phelps participates in an early "man-ball drill," throwing passes to teammates from a stationary position. Later he dribbles briefly beside the court and tries a few short jumpers on his own. But he spends most of practice seated beside the scorer's table along with the six-member battery of managers.

Practice ends about 10:15. Once the coaches leave, Sullivan and scrubs Travis Stephenson, Scott Cherry, and Ed Geth cavort near one basket, talking trash, laughing, shooting threes, taking turns hanging from the rim. Stephenson moves to the large white imprint of a tar heel at a corner of the playing floor and, as he does following most practices, heaves the ball toward the opposite basket. As usual he comes rather close.

Not so close, though, that he reaches the portable off-court basket where Lynch practices jump shots. With obliging student-manager Bobby Dawson feeding him ball after ball, Lynch works until eleven o'clock, long after everyone else leaves the silent Smith Center.

* * *

Today's Duke practice lacks the verbal lashes so evident yesterday.

There are, to be sure, a few acid remarks. "If you want to be singular, be singular," Mike Krzyzewski tells his team after one play. "We'll all go to our individual beaches on Friday." Mostly, though, it's a day for instruction, gentle critique and positive reinforcement. "Tony Lang, if you run the court like that, we're going to St. Louis," Krzyzewski says, implying two wins in Chicago.

The light workout concludes with a videotape review of Southern Illinois, Duke's upcoming opponent. Krzyzewski uses a TV set rolled onto the court on a metal stand, pointing out tendencies revealed during the second half of a Missouri Valley Conference tournament game. If the Blue Devils play their game, he says, SIU "can't even come close to us."

"Hey, let's not make it our last practice," Krzyzewski tells the team. "Let's make it the one that got us straight for our Chicago tournament. Let's make a statement to us—this is how we play."

THURSDAY, MARCH 18

DEAN Smith cringes at the moment of impact, feeling a sudden kinship with football coaches whose quarterbacks buck for the extra yard instead of sliding out of bounds or out of harm's way. Most Carolina players cringe inwardly. On the bench Brian Reese jumps up and yells "Oh, no!"

Henrik Rodl calls the act the most courageous he's ever seen on a basketball court.

Derrick Phelps, the object of all this attention, is merely being himself. So he makes sure his array of bulky padding is in place about hips and tailbone, gets up, and resumes playing. "I think he's a magnet for trouble," Eric Montross says evenly. "He does a lot of banging. He's a physical player in the sense he's always going after a loose ball; he's always going after a steal. He's a very aggressive player."

And a brave one.

Until tonight's tipoff, few outside the North Carolina basketball program know Phelps has been given medical clearance to play. Just yesterday the junior was so stiff and sore, Smith publicly doubted his readiness for the team's NCAA opener.

But Phelps wants to play, even if the soreness is still so bad he stands every time the team bus hits a bump along the snow-lined route to Winston-Salem's Joel Coliseum.

The decision on Phelps's participation is left to Smith, who knows better than anyone that Phelps is his squad's most indispensable member. "So much of our offense is from our defense," says Smith, who, earlier this week, is named ACC coach of the year for only the second time since 1979. "Of course I think Derrick is the best defensive player in the country."

Over the years Smith has seen several of his best teams meet premature ends due to late-season injuries to key players, either because the players couldn't return or because they did so as shells of their former selves, disrupting a team's inner harmonies just at the moment of truth. It happened in 1975 and again in 1977, in 1984 and again in 1985.

Smith decides to let Phelps play about five minutes in the first half. Then, assuming the guard looks comfortable and performs serviceably, he'll play as long as possible at the outset of the second half, coming out for good once he tires.

The coach also assumes Phelps will proceed with caution. "He really didn't say nothing about it," Phelps recalls following an 85–65 victory over East Carolina. "I guess he expected me to go out and play my game anyway. He thought I would be very ginger out there, make sure I didn't get injured again. I couldn't see myself doing that. I have to always be going all-out. I can't see myself backing off something." So once he enters the game, with Carolina up 21–12, Phelps plays as he usually does. Though admittedly "a little nervous," he steals the ball barely a minute after getting in the game, triggering a fast break that culminates with a three-point play by Rodl.

"He got us going," Reese says. "Then I started digging in a little deeper. He's the one that controls us. He's like Coach Smith out there."

The next time ECU tries to attack, the Heels spring a perimeter trap and the long-armed Phelps deflects the ball to Montross. Two possessions after that East Carolina's best player, guard Lester Lyons, steals the ball from Reese and races toward the UNC basket. And there, standing astride Lyons's path, body planted in perfect position to take the charge, is Derrick Phelps.

It's too late for Lyons to alter his path. Collision. Whistle. Offensive foul. UNC's ball. Cringes all around while Phelps almost visibly does inventory before regaining his feet.

"I think that's automatic. That's something I always do," Phelps says of taking a charge, with the contact that inevitably results. "I just wasn't out there not to play scared. I wanted to play my game, not to worry about my injury."

Reese understands "you can't be out there playing hesitant." Still, he too believes there's room for Phelps to go a bit easier. "Don't throw yourself farther than you have to go," he implores his friend. "When you fall, grab the ground." But Phelps ignores the advice. "He's a hard-nosed player," Reese says. "He's going to stick to his guns, no matter what. He has a lot of heart."

Phelps's fourteen-minute appearance, during which he's again fouled and sent sprawling while driving for a layup, is the emotional highlight of an otherwise workmanlike performance by the Heels. Truth be told, UNC is a bit flat. "It's hard, number-one seed against number-sixteen seed," Kevin Salvadori says. He also complains it's difficult retaining one's composure while getting fouled repeatedly.

"They were grabbing and holding and pushing," the seven-footer says of an East Carolina front line that goes six-four, six-eight, six-eight. "It's something we've seen all year. We're getting tired of it."

Imagine how the Pirates feel, though, as Montross towers over them like a skyscraper among purple-clad trees. ECU routinely practices shooting over players who hold broomsticks aloft, but that doesn't begin to simulate what it's like facing North Carolina. Montross, George Lynch, and top post sub Salvadori combine for forty points and twenty-one rebounds as UNC cruises to the finish.

Only Montross plays more than thirty minutes for the Tar Heels. Minutes played seems a bit of a sore point this weekend; the press release with UNC's stats somehow includes total minutes for each Tar Heel, a taboo number that's quickly blacked out by a Carolina functionary.

As for East Carolina's Lilliputian Pirates, they play with poise during their moment in the media sun, delighting friends and supporters by staving off a blowout until early in the second half. Lyons, the most athletic member of his team, darts through thickets of screens to launch a plenitude of jumpers worth twenty-seven points, the same output he had last year at Duke.

The respectable showing is especially gratifying for ECU coach Eddie Payne, who grew up in Winston-Salem and played for Wake Forest.

Payne attended summer basketball camps at Duke and wanted to play there, but never got a tumble from coach Vic Bubas. North Carolina assistant coach Larry Brown invited Payne to UNC's summer camp, but the Tar Heels weren't sufficiently impressed to offer a scholarship.

So Payne walked on at Wake Forest, where he played for Jack McCloskey, who later built the Detroit Pistons into NBA champs. By his senior year, 1973, Payne had a scholarship and was named Wake's most valuable player.

Payne's last season Wake had a losing record and the seven-seed in the do-or-die ACC Tournament, yet it upended North Carolina in the opening round. A key play was Payne's controversial court-length pass that produced a game-tying basket and overtime.

Given the encyclopedic nature of Dean Smith's memory and his penchant for holding on to arguments, it's no surprise that, two decades later, the mere mention of Payne's name at a pregame press conference sends him hurtling backward to that unsatisfying game.

All in the span of a paragraph, too, thoroughly perplexing those lacking a keen sense of ACC history.

"He was a very heady player," Smith says of Payne. "He's using that to be a very good coach. He was that far over the line when he threw that pass." Smith gestures widely.

Payne doesn't dispute Smith's version of the facts. But he adds that if he was inbounds, then the ball probably didn't nick the scoreboard two years later, either, when a long Wake pass was nullified at a crucial moment as Carolina rallied to a 101–100 tournament overtime victory.

Payne gathers coaching advice from ACC friends on how best to deal with the current Tar Heels. In the process, Frank McGuire and members of several coaching staffs tell Payne this is Smith's "best coaching job as well as his best team. Of recent memory." Nothing that transpires on the court causes Payne to think otherwise.

Duke blows away Southern Illinois, 105–70, in the snows of northern Illinois, hard by O'Hare Airport on the outskirts of Chicago. The Blue Devils lead 17–4, then 34–13, then 53–27 at halftime. Everyone plays except Kenney Brown. The margin of victory is Duke's largest in nearly two months, the sweetness of triumph a honeyed salve after consecutive defeats to conclude ACC competition.

The Blue Devils gain their thirteenth consecutive NCAA victory, second-longest streak in history behind UCLA's majestic thirty-eight. Mike Krzyzewski improves his NCAA winning percentage to 82.9 (34–7). Duke moves to 51–15 in NCAA competition, the best success rate among Division I schools.

Bobby Hurley and Thomas Hill now own a 17–1 NCAA record. Press accounts invariably relate the record to Hurley exclusively, since he's run the show for four years and is increasingly recognized as one of the great point guards of modern college history.

For all that, Hurley is not chosen ACC player of the year, losing a close media vote to Wake's Rodney Rogers. Achievement by Dukies has become so routine, not once this year has a Duke freshmen won ACC rookie of the week honors or any Blue Devil won league player of the week recognition. This rankles in Duke circles as another symptom of a disease they categorize under "Expectations." The malady by now has invaded the Duke entourage. Already there's talk of travel plans for St. Louis, next stop in the quest for a Midwest Regional title. Sports information director Mike Cragg, short on press guides, holds them back so he'll have enough for the Final Four.

Like the administrative meeting convened on campus prior to the NCAAs to plan this year's championship celebration, these are innocent acts born of habit and faith and five straight trips to the Final Four. But they're suppositions any self-respecting coach is loath to countenance, knowing well that predicting games is like forecasting the weather and that fate has a way of punishing pretension.

Still, the Southern Illinois game confirms the best about the Blue Devils. "We just came out with an incredible frame of mind as a team," Mike Brey says. The players ache to prove to others and especially themselves that they remain a force to be reckoned with, remain the Duke that's dominated March since most of them were in junior high.

"I thought we'd prove ourselves early in the season, and I guess we haven't," Grant Hill frets. "This is the last time this team can make its mark. We haven't done anything." In a way that's exactly the playing-poor attitude Duke's coaches covet. But it also reflects the chronic lack of satisfaction, the missing sense of achievement, that's plagued a squad triumphant in an impressive three-quarters of its games.

The blowout of Southern Illinois seems to banish the ghosts, though the Salukis are also defeated by their own fears and the mystique that surrounds Duke. "They were scared of us," Brey observes. "Then our shots started falling, and then it got contagious."

All Krzyzewski's talk at practice about making a statement has come to pass. "I knew they were a good team," says Saluki coach Rich Herrin, "but they're a better basketball team than I ever realized." The key, despite gaudy offense numbers, is defense. SIU hits barely 40 percent of its shots, commits nineteen turnovers compared to eight assists, and misses most of its three-pointers.

"We played great team defense," Gaudet says. "Yeah, we enjoyed it. We enjoyed it because we played well." There are other bright spots, too. Grant Hill shows signs of leadership, doesn't complain or wince despite his hurt foot, and flashes pre-injury form in soaring once for an unauthorized alley-oop pass from Hurley.

Cherokee Parks does a good defensive job on Ashraf Amaya, the Salukis' best player, who gets in quick foul trouble and is generally ineffective. When Parks isn't on Amaya, Erik Meek is. The inappositely named Meek leads the Blue Devils with seven rebounds, pounding whomever he's guarding with puppyish enthusiasm. "This is great, seeing you give a guy as much crap as you give our guys in practice," Gaudet tells Meek.

But the rout may have provided a misleading sense of potency, very much the way Krzyzewski says his starters achieve a false feeling of prowess by going against walk-ons every day in practice.

Generally overlooked in the postgame euphoria are continued subpar offensive showings by starters Thomas Hill and Tony Lang.

Neither is among the five Blue Devils who score in double figures though each plays at least twenty-five minutes. Hill continues to shoot poorly, making a third of his shots. During Duke's four games in March the senior has made a shade under 30 percent of his field-goal tries (thirteen out of forty-four).

Again, Tony Lang, left cheek still bearing a red mark from a Meek elbow that landed two weeks ago in practice, plays a modest subordinate role, contributing good defense, four points, three rebounds. This despite vows from teammates to get him more involved in the offense, and despite repeated requests from coaches for Lang to flash to an open spot for quick jumpers when Parks is double-teamed.

Hurley says he's learned "we can't win with three guys playing out there." And though he would "just love in the middle of a game for Tony to come up and yell at me and say I haven't touched the ball in five possessions," he knows that won't happen. It's not Lang's nature.

"He's a little fragile," Grant Hill explains. Understanding that, he and Hurley vow to take it upon themselves to get Lang going. "If he gets a few baskets early in the game, he gets his confidence," says Hurley, who greatly controls such opportunities with his passing. "And then he's going to play like one of our better players if he gets that confidence level."

Yet, for all that, against Southern Illinois Lang takes but two shots per half, scoring a layup once in each period.

SATURDAY, MARCH 20

BOBBY Hurley doesn't know where to look or what to do. Mike Krzyzewski stands by the Duke bench, applauding in salute and farewell.

As much as spring is the season of renewal, of youth and eternal return, it is also very much a time of parted ways, of buds nipped by frost and old champions fallen by the wayside, worn to death by winter. So, today, the vernal equinox arrives, and with it a stunning end to Krzyzewski's latest team, which until the last seems destined for glory as part of the natural order of things.

In fact, there is glory to be had tonight—captured by California and salvaged by Duke in a vain effort to stave off defeat far from the Gothic bastion where its championship banners hang in spotlighted glory like eternal flames in a temple of basketball worship.

After Cal wins 82–77, Krzyzewski traverses the long tunnel that connects the rundown Rosemont Horizon to the press area. There, at a podium with seniors Hurley and Thomas Hill by his side, the coach mourns and celebrates in a great gush of emotion.

"Bobby and Thomas have been like sons to me," says the man whom players joke loves Hurley more than his own three daughters. "They've taken me to places and to have experiences that no other college coach has had over the last twenty years. Every time"—Krzyzewski's voice grows emphatic—"that we went out on the court, I knew that they would give me their bodies, their minds and their hearts. I'm only sad that I can't do it any more with them."

Now the sadness wells up, filling his eyes and voice with tears. "All this stuff where people talk about college sports and things being bad, you have no—I want to whack everybody who says that." The whack is visible, delivered as a brisk back-and-forth gesture of Krzyzewski's right hand. "College sports are great. They're OK when you yell at each other, when you hug each other, and when you live.

"And, uh, I've been the luckiest guy over the last four years to have spent this time with these youngsters. It's been unbelievable." Again, sniffles and those burning, reddened eyes. "I wish you could feel what I feel. Losing a game, it doesn't mean a damn thing. It doesn't mean anything. Because I've won for so long with these guys, and I'll win for the rest of my life being associated with them."

It's the first time since 1985 that Duke hasn't reached the Sweet Sixteen. Other than a championship game loss in 1990 endured by Hill and Hurley, it's the first time any player on the squad has tasted defeat in the NCAAs.

For the longest time, tonight's defeat appears unavoidable. The University of California-Berkeley, with eight underclassmen in its top ten, plays inspired basketball and Duke does not. "They countered a lot of our stuff well. They were very good. Give them credit," Pete Gaudet says.

But the breakdown transcends coaching, or what Cal does and doesn't do. Rather, Duke is laid low by flaws hidden all season from public view, though acutely familiar to its players and coaches—the dangerous assumption of excellence, the individuality and self-doubt, the yearning for oncourt leadership and awkwardness in shouldering it. Under the pressure of Cal's assault, the weaknesses create fissures in Duke's facade, each setting another off like an ice floe cracking apart.

"What we needed wasn't Xs and Os, but the maturity level from the younger guys, the help from the old guys, that great sensitivity to meeting," Krzyzewski says. "We got it at different times, but we never got it for extended times. It was never the personality, whatever you want to call it, of our basketball team." Well into the second half, the Blue Devils have the futile look of a dog chasing a truck, with only Hurley's career-high scoring output and disgust for defeat enabling them to keep Cal's bumper in sight. "Holy shit!" Mike Brey thinks on the Duke bench. "We may get beat by thirty!"

The Cal lead reaches eighteen, sending Brey and cohorts searching for solace as well as answers. "You come up with different ways to keep yourself from going crazy," Brey says. "'Well, it's been a heck of a run.' Things like that come to mind. 'We didn't get the bounces all year we got the past two years. Maybe it was fate.'" The Golden Bears lead 70–53 with 13:26 remaining. Duke's deficit looms as more than an impediment to victory. It's a savage reminder of the burdens of achievement, of being aimed at game after game. A lopsided loss in an early round will be a bitter, unworthy dethroning, a betrayal of a tradition burnished by nearly a decade's worth of Dukies.

Not to worry. The Krzyzewski tradition includes a combative pride that predates Hurley. Now it fuels a fierce Duke rally. "We were terrific," Krzyzewski says. The Blue Devils take a 77–76 lead, with 2:21 remaining, on a Thomas Hill free throw. By this time Hurley has thirty-two points, most by a Duke player during the '93 season.

The game is within Duke's grasp as Hurley attempts the accustomed knockout punch with about a minute and a half left. "You couldn't ask for a better chance, Bobby taking a wide-open three to pretty much win the game," Brey says. "If he makes it, we go up four. Cal was starting to come apart a little bit."

But the shot won't fall, and neither will Cal.

"I thought we were going to win," Grant Hill says afterward, voice low and body hunched forward as always when discussing a defeat. "I thought the momentum had swung a little bit." Duke fails to score after Thomas Hill's go-ahead free throw, and in what seems an instant the undertow sweeps its season into oblivion. When the final buzzer sounds Cal players scream, "We shocked the world!" It's the school's first trip to the Sweet Sixteen since 1960.

Hurley stands with hands on hips looking upward uncertainly, this Horizon suddenly his last as a collegiate player. The final seconds tick away and the dazed senior trots off the court to find his way to the sanctuary of the Duke locker room, but not before taking a wrong turn in the unfamiliar arena. Once there, he and Krzyzewski hug tearfully, the embrace lasting perhaps a minute.

Hours later Hurley confides to a friend: "I can't believe it's over. I can't believe I'll never wear a Duke uniform again."

The Bears enter the game with ten victories in their last eleven games, a streak initiated when twenty-nine-year-old assistant Todd Bozeman replaced Lou Campanelli as head coach.

Some in the coaching profession think Bozeman maneuvered behind the scenes to speed his boss's midseason firing. One Pac-Ten coach refused to shake Bozeman's hand following a game. UNC's Dean Smith says during the NCAAs he's disappointed Bozeman didn't voluntarily walk the plank with Campanelli, the man who'd hired him. "I know if I ever got fired, Bill Guthridge or Phil Ford would never take the job. The big thing you want from assistants is loyalty." Whatever the case, Cal announces on the eve of the NCAAs that Bozeman, a popular choice with the players, has been awarded a three-year extension as head coach.

Disquieted Duke coaches see the hiring as a variation on the theme that carried Georgia Tech to the ACC title, with players rallying around their coach. Then they hear LSU's Brown tell the media about the Bears: "I don't think they have a prayer of beating Duke. They can use it as bulletin board material if they want. Duke is just way better than Cal."

Brown's remarks provide Bozeman with a golden motivational bullet. There's no greater challenge to gifted or determined athletes than the simple statement "No one thinks you can do it." Most coaches employ variations on that theme, from a Dean Smith jockeying for underdog's status and advocating "playing paranoid," to a Krzyzewski imploring his teams to "play poor." Now Brown's words create a symbolic bloody flag that Bozeman waves before his players as they depart the Horizon's cramped second-floor locker room to take the court against the two-time champs.

Duke's plan against California is to jump on top early, figuring to rattle the confidence of its young opponent. Instead, Cal sets the tone, scoring first on an alley-oop from guard Jason Kidd to Lamond Murray that results in a dunk. "I thought we had players in position," Gaudet says. "On a lob play, you send a message. You play the pass. You challenge for a charge. You pluck the ball away on the rim. You knock the ball away. Defensively, that's where you get to send a message too, not just offensively. We didn't do that."

Cal scores the game's second basket, too, on a layup fed by Kidd after stripping the ball from Thomas Hill.

Duke comes back to lead 6–4, and then 8–7 at the 17:17 mark; nearly thirty-five minutes elapse before the Blue Devils lead again.

In fact, it's Duke that appears rattled for much of the game, committing a dozen turnovers in the first half alone. Most stunning, perhaps, is the near-total lack of defensive intensity. Cal runs its offense with ease in the first half, recording fifteen assists on nineteen baskets. The Bears make 55.9 percent of their shots in the period, including an unexpected five of nine on three-pointers. They also get most of the loose balls, ricochets, and deflections.

The Blue Devils very much resemble the group that had Krzyzewski screaming at practice just five days ago. Defense is what fuels Duke's attack. Get Krzyzewski's teams in half court and they tend to struggle to score, which happens today as Duke hits 37 percent of its first-half shots.

"We weren't all on the same page for some reason," Krzyzewski says. "I really believed if we could get into the tournament, if we were on the same page, if we could get Grant just a little better, we had a shot" at the title.

Worse, as happens occasionally throughout the year, Cherokee Parks is taken aback when confronting a physical, mobile front line. Not even a quick first-half benching gets him going.

Nor is there a chance Parks can make amends in the second half. With the first half nearly over, he comes down on a Cal player's foot, badly twists his ankle, and falls to the floor in obvious pain. He's taken to the locker room for treatment, but his season is finished.

Krzyzewski is calm in the locker room at halftime. He doesn't raise his voice; in similar circumstances against Northeast Louisiana two years ago, he sent a chalkboard crashing to the floor in a Minneapolis locker room. Recalls Brey: "He said, 'We got knocked back on our heels. Go back and fight. We've got twenty minutes. We've got to scratch and claw, go after every loose ball, and we'll win.'" By his locker, Grant Hill seethes.

"It was frustrating because we talked about how we needed to start well against them, and we didn't. We talked about how we wanted to play defense, and if we played good defense we'd take care of business. And they scored forty-seven points in the first half. Forty-seven!"

He laments: "It seemed like that first half was how it was at times this year, when stuff was happening, we didn't attack it like we did last year as a team. We attacked individually. It was like the way it was all year—when the shit hits the fan it's like, 'I've got to get it back,' not, 'We've got to get it back.'"

With half the squad missing in action, Hill decides to be more assertive, to be the player his coaches have awaited. "I was like, 'I have to play my ass off because nobody else is. Bobby's by himself.'" Hill calls his change in mien being "more active." Call it what you will, the result is that Hill takes over the game.

But not until Cal opens the second half with eight unanswered points. Not until Hurley has scored all six of Duke's points to keep the game from getting out of reach. Not until Hurley yells "God damn it!" in teammates' faces after they fail to block out on a defensive rebound following a missed Cal free throw.

Grant Hill scores a dozen points in the second half. For the first time in his career he makes a pair of three-pointers in the same game. He has three assists, three rebounds, two blocked shots, and a single turnover in the period, along with six steals. His eight steals for the game are a Duke season high, and an indication of skills that ultimately earn him the Corinthian Award as the nation's top defender.

The Bear lead is 70–53 when Hill and Duke awaken. Suddenly the Dukies are running the break, flying around on defense, working patiently for good shots on offense. This despite using only six players for virtually the entire period—Hurley, the Hills, Lang, Meek and Kenny Blakeney.

The Blue Devils pull within 70–60 and Krzyzewski gets on hands and knees and pounds the floor, a traditional Duke signal that it's time to make a defensive stand. Cal turns the ball over, Thomas Hill scores at the other end, and the deficit is in single digits for the first time in an hour.

Duke closes within a basket with 8:32 left on a Grant Hill layup assisted by Hurley; that completes a run in which the Hills outscore Cal 16–2.

Duke pulls within a point at the 6:43 mark on a pair of Thomas Hill free throws; forges a tie at 3:56 as Hurley hits his last three; takes its sole lead of the half, 77–76, on Thomas Hill's free throw, after rebounding Hurley's missed three-pointer with 2:21 remaining. By now the Blue Devils are exhausted.

Cal misses a long, ill-conceived three-pointer, going dry on a night it still finishes ten of seventeen from long range. Duke calls "New York," a play designed to free Hurley for a jumper, and the little guard lets fly one of his thirteen second-half bombs.

"It's in. It's down in the bottom. It's out," Gaudet recalls. "They say golf's a game of inches. Basketball's a game of inches. We're up four, they have a tough time getting us. It didn't happen."

When the game ends Krzyzewski's mind links Hurley's miss with Thomas Hill's misses in the final seconds at Virginia, Duke's failures to put the game away at Florida State, Collins's errant three-pointer at the buzzer in the ACC Tournament. "I told my staff, it was like it's going in, but as it's going in, God says, 'Come on, it's someone else's turn,'" Krzyzewski says. "I can't tell you a time this whole year when something unpredictable happened where it came out for us. That's just the way the year was. What close game did we win this year?"

Following Hurley's miss, Kidd brings the ball into the forecourt, drives hard along the left wing. He collides with the ubiquitous Grant Hill, who appears to have established position to take the charge. The ball rolls out of bounds. No whistle. Cal ball. A pass inside is tipped by Hurley, but the ball eludes him. Kidd emerges from a mad scramble under the basket in time to throw up a prayer of a shot that goes in even as Grant Hill fouls him. The old-fashioned three-pointer puts California ahead to stay with 1:11 left.

Duke doesn't score again. Abruptly its reign ends. It's Jason and the Bears who don the mantle of destiny, who continue their pursuit of basketball's golden fleece. The stunned Blue Devils can only repair to a locker room where tears flow freely.

Soon, not soon enough, the Duke entourage is on a chartered jet headed back for North Carolina, a thousand miles distant. In flight Krzyzewski walks to the back of the aircraft and thanks the accompanying band members and cheerleaders for their support.

This afternoon in Winston-Salem, North Carolina performs a basketball version of vivisection on Rhode Island's Rams, winning 112–67. Early in the second half, his team trailing by thirty-seven, URI's Andre Samuel turns to TV commentators Billy Packer and James Brown and cries: "Help!"

The margin of victory against eight-seed Rhode Island is the largest ever in a second-round NCAA contest, and comes despite Dean Smith's decision to retire his starters for the game's final thirteen minutes. What's more, URI is a good team, good enough to win eighteen games entering the tournament and to top Purdue in the opening round.

But coach Al Skinner's squad can't match the Tar Heels' size, precision or physical play. The inevitable consequence is a "Rhode Kill," as newspaper headlines throughout the ACC region will put it tomorrow.

The Rams are still in the game about midway through the first half, trailing 22–16. By halftime the UNC lead is 50–21. The Atlantic Ten team scores on three of its final sixteen possessions of the period, while UNC scores on fourteen of sixteen. The Heels quash any notions of a Rhode Island rally by opening the second half with a 19–6 rush, completed when Derrick Phelps makes the seventh of his seven shots.

Rarely are stats more revealing. Rhode Island makes 22.9 percent of its shots in the first half, 31.9 percent for the game. The Tar Heels hit 56.8 percent. The Heels dominate the boards 50–34. Rhode Island's offensive breakdown is so complete, it records only one assist in the first half.

"They clearly have all the answers to the questions, especially if they shoot the ball as well as they did this afternoon," says Rhode Island coach Al Skinner, who spends the latter part of the contest in a veritable stupor, rarely calling plays or encouraging his team, neither looking at nor touching players as they foul out one by one. "I'm sure that they're going to be in the Final Four."

The margin is 75–31 when Smith starts clearing his bench. Scott Cherry and Matt Wenstrom each play thirteen minutes, their longest stints of the season. After demurring at first because of the flu, Ed Geth goes in with 5:21 remaining along with fellow bench jockey Travis Stephenson, whom the Tar Heel–dominated crowd exhorts to shoot every time he touches the ball. Stephenson declines until the game's final seconds, heaving the ball from near midcourt.

Smith concedes the URI rout is "about the best we've played" all year, though he sees "a lot of things we can improve." He also takes issue with comments by Rhode Island players that they've never encountered so physical an opponent. "It's nice that they think we're a physical team," Smith says. "I don't think we are. I wish we would be."

Smith's players are perplexed by this comment.

"I think when we play the type of defense we like to play, we definitely are physical," Henrik Rodl objects.

George Lynch agrees with Rodl. "I think we're a very physical team. I think we have to be that way in our conference, and I think Coach has prepared us for that."

MONDAY, MARCH 22

FOR the first time since 1985, Duke's basketball office is not humming with anticipation as the NCAA's third round heaves into view.

"It was weird waking up this morning and not still being involved," says Donna Keane, a championship ring hanging from her neck on a pendant. Outside her window, on a grassy embankment cut into a hillside, a squirrel checks out the meal options in bright sunlight. "It's definitely different. To see all this excitement going on, and all these teams still playing, and not to be a part of it, it's definitely different."

Not that activity has ceased. It rarely does at this level, where it takes several million dollars to fund the operation pf a basketball program. Let Southern University's Ben Jobe tell writers at the NCAA Tournament he takes naps on the bench, lets players run things, and does without extensive tape study and scouting reports. Let other coaches teach class or answer their own phone. This is the big time, the full time. (Except, of course, for Pete Gaudet, still facing the $16,000 annual income limit imposed by the NCAA on coaches who do everything except recruit.) There'll be a two-hour staff meeting this morning, and every morning for the next few days to map strategies for the immediate future. There'll be a team meeting late this afternoon at the usual practice time to touch bases, discuss ongoing training and academic concerns, and offer reassurances.

Then there's summer basketball camp to plan, a mammoth production involving hundreds of kids staying for a week at a time for four different weeks in June and July. And there's filling the holes in next year's schedule, and of course recruiting, always recruiting—touching bases here, looking under bushes there.

Krzyzewski wears jeans this morning, uncharacteristic for the office, making it feel more like a snow day. He appears quite relaxed, attending by phone to business deals, including a blockbuster shoe contract, and coaches' lobbying efforts in NCAA circles.

Later this week the coaching staff will meet with each player individually. "It's a way of showing them, don't feel you can't come into the office," Krzyzewski says.

Adds Gaudet, "Maybe it's a good time to do it while it hurts a little bit."

Keane, like her boss an avid Republican, decides there's a bright side to not repeating as champs—at least she won't have to go to the White House to meet President Clinton.

The coaches keep a stiff upper lip. There's no public show of turmoil. But they suffer to varying degrees, each according to his personality.

Gaudet, who will be fifty-one later this week, suffers more than most.

He reaches for positives: "Hey, we've got a week's head start on all those other teams," he says, knowing how silly he sounds. Then: Cal was very good; we don't begrudge anybody making the Sweet Sixteen; go ACC!; this is an ongoing process; wait till next year. And so on.

Gaudet defends Duke's players: "I read in the paper Duke hadn't reached its potential. They had a good year. They've gone through a lot of things the public doesn't understand. Maybe they had to deal with more things than other of our teams have gone through."

But Gaudet, whose special teaching responsibility is Duke's big men, also agonizes over the one-basket performance by Parks, Lang and Meek, in the loss to Cal. Why do guys like Parks and Lang, with all their talent, tune in and out from half to half, game to game? Gaudet wishes he knew. "I'm not a psychiatrist," he protests. "Quite frankly it isn't all part of our job description. Goddamn it! It's tough taking kids who are studying a good part of their day, take them for three hours a day . . . and in all aspects, including their heads, to make them thoroughbreds."

But why doesn't Thomas Hill dish the ball, or at least look for a possible assist, once he makes a move toward the basket? Why doesn't Grant Hill think of leadership as sharing the ball as well as being The Man? Why won't Tony Lang shoot? Doesn't Parks realize this is serious?

"You can carry it so far, and you do," Gaudet says. "But you go crazy if you try to think of all the answers." Which coaches do anyway, of course. "That's why we're in meetings all the time," Gaudet says.

Krzyzewski is more contained, perhaps because he's a bit drained. "I think for Mike it was a long year," Mike Brey observes. Recalling that Krzyzewski went straight from the 1991–92 college season to work on the '92 U.S. Olympic basketball coaching staff, and thence to the 1992–93 campaign, Brey adds, "He really never had a mental break. It's really been a tough year for him."

Krzyzewski agrees there's a physical relief in having the season end, but describes himself as the kind of guy who is always willing and able to run extra laps if necessary. "I'm going to do what it takes, and then think about being drained," he says. "Spiritually or mentally, it wasn't a relief. I wanted to keep going. I was sad in that case."

Brey turns thirty-four today, but his celebratory spirit is muted. He arrived at Duke when he was twenty-eight and hasn't experienced a birthday since that didn't include the excitement of a Final Four looming ahead. In fact, it's the first time in more than two years, since Duke won its initial national title, that the pressures of being top dog have subsided. "It was an unbelievable pace and expectation," Brey recalls, not altogether fondly.

Suddenly all that's changed.

Brey already has altered his activities. Yesterday, after the staff attended a funeral, instead of returning to the office he took time to play with his young children. Today he'll start pursuing a head coaching job that interests him. Later Brey will be among the finalists for the head coaching position at Vanderbilt, which goes to alum Jan van Breda Kolff, late of Cornell.

Four ACC teams remain in the NCAA field: Florida State, North Carolina, Virginia, Wake Forest.

No other league has so many entrants among the Sweet Sixteen. Not that this is anything new—it's the seventh time since 1980 that an ACC quartet has reached the Sweet Sixteen, a feat all the other conferences combined have managed just four times.

Now that Duke's eliminated, several folks in the basketball office confide they're rooting for Michigan because it's the team with the best chance to defeat North Carolina.

Grant Hill says he'll root for the Tar Heels, the ACC team, if they face Michigan, though he'd like to see his friend Chris Webber do well. He also predicts flatly that Webber will stay at Michigan and Anfernee Hardaway at Memphis State, and he bets writer John Feinstein one hundred dollars he's right. (A bet he loses when both underclassmen choose to enter the 1993 NBA draft.)

Both Hills and Hurley look forward to attending this year's Final Four, though only Thomas Hill will play, and that in an all-star game.

Others contemplate non-basketball matters. Erik Meek frets about an upcoming test in a class involving cadaver study of human lower extremities, a course popular among Duke players. Grant Hill tells him of another course at the hospital that's good for an A. Marty Clark happily considers which of two self-designed tattoos he'll have affixed to his ankle; both feature basketball-playing images of Calvin from the "Calvin and Hobbes" comic strip.

But, as Clark's tattoo attests, attention to basketball never really ceases at this level.

"I often say, you have to be a little, not neurotic, but different to be good at this level," comments UNC's Dean Smith. "You realize how many times you have to say no to other kids to go practice? That's true of golfers."

Already Tony Lang, stung by finger-pointing both within and beyond the Duke program, vows to add muscle in the weight-training room.

Basketball also is very much on Grant Hill's mind. Like many in the Duke program, the All-America seems unchanged on the surface but in fact seethes with disappointment, anger, frustration. He's disappointed in himself, his teammates, his coaches. He blames himself, his teammates, his coaches.

Here's Hill's year in a nutshell, with its contradictions and disappointments: He aches to lead, but is intent on being liked. He shies from confrontation, but knows that honesty demands directness. He takes prides in unselfish play, but has difficulty squaring that with a desire to control "the rock" at crunch time. He feels he played better in preseason, but led Duke in scoring (18.0) and steals (64), and finished second in rebounding (6.4 per game), blocks (36), and assists (72). He knows he can do virtually anything on a basketball court, but still can't quite believe it.

So what will become of Duke's Hamlet, who is capable of becoming the 1994 national player of the year yet wanders in perplexity upon the ramparts of greatness?

"My personality is that I want to be great," Hill offers freely, earnestly, almost innocently. "Part of me wants to be the best, but part of me doesn't. Part of me wants to be great in basketball, but I don't want to deal with all the stuff away from basketball . . . it's like right there. Do I really want to do it?"

Krzyzewski intends to coax forth that transcendent talent, and expects to throw Hill out of practice a few times next season to hasten the emergence. He also figures Lang's attention will be captured by the prospect of reduced playing time with freshman big men Joey Beard and Greg Newton on hand. "A lot of kids have to be kept on some edge," Krzyzewski says.

This season's squad is "as good a group of kids as I've coached," he insists, but also proved "very difficult" to harmonize. Already Krzyzewski looks forward to overcoming that failing, to transcending individual inadequacies through closer, keener identification with the whole. "I really think we had a hell of a year," he says. "It's not that the kids didn't try. There's just some things I wanted to do—my kids wanted a doll and a bike and I only had enough for the doll."

THEY shout "Heels!," break their pregame huddle, and take their places, in size order, in the corridor behind the end zone seats. Donald Williams, the shortest starter, and Scott Cherry, shortest senior, stand at the head of the line, each with ball in hands. "Let's go babe," Cherry says over his shoulder. "Let's go fellas!" And off they go, trotting onto the floor of New Jersey's Brendan Byrne Arena, alias the Meadowlands, their weekend test in basketball survival skills about to begin.

North Carolina's warmup drills are a businesslike calculus, no wasted motion, an apt reflection of their coach, Dean Smith, in his dark, conservative suit. Sober, in a word. Scrutinized, in another—among the seniors' privileges this season has been the choice to forgo having managers chart, and coaches monitor, layups missed in pregames.

Arkansas's Razorbacks show some flair, enjoy a little razzle-dazzle, strut their stuff now and again. Their coach, Nolan Richardson, wears cowboy boots and a suit of electric blue.

The fourth-seeded Razorbacks are young, quick, athletic and disciplined. They're good on the offensive boards and from three-point range. They're also pesky and unabashedly aggressive, and they love to trap, to force an opposing point guard to either give up the ball or wear down trying to protect it. "The brain of the team, that's what you have to go after," Richardson explains. "You cut off the head, the body ain't going anywhere."

Until recently Richardson had a chip on his shoulder nearly as formidable as the sequoia that weighs down Bob Huggins, the coach whose Cincinnati Bearcats defeat Virginia in tonight's first game. When Richardson had players like Todd Day, Lee Mayberry and Oliver Miller, he bragged about inflicting "forty minutes of hell" upon opponents, and he portrayed himself as an outsider with a style of play dismissed as "ratball, ghettoball" by the establishment. "My edge is to be bitter and angry, and to get where I need to go," Richardson said back then.

A year later his team has far exceeded expectations, and Richardson is pleased and proud. Only the media mentions forty minutes of hell, Richardson's angry rhetoric replaced these days by a professed kinship with a fictional detective played by Peter Falk. "I don't try to overcoach," Richardson says. "My favorite person when I watch TV is Columbo. He knows everything, but you don't think he knows anything. I love that. Crazy like a fox."

Richardson does an impressive imitation of Columbo when discussing North Carolina. Of Smith, he says: "He's probably the legend of basketball. He's invented so many things. I've never invented anything, but I can copy my ass off." And of these particular Tar Heels, he observes: "That's one of the biggest teams I've ever seen on the college level. I saw three seven-footers, and I saw one in a suit. I've never seen anything like that in my life and I've been to five cowboy shows, eight ropings, and two calf castrations." The Razorbacks are just the sort of team that figures to bother the more cumbrous Heels. They do, jumping to a 25–14 lead midway through the first half with swarming, quick-handed defense and a barrage of three-pointers. "Oooh, pig, sooey!" shout their fans in porcine pleasure.

Richardson insists prior to the game, "I don't like to watch any team play that passes the ball five times." But his Razorbacks do just that, and more, when confronted with UNC defensive alignments designed to minimize the difference in quickness. ("I never dreamed we'd play as much zone," Smith says.) Arkansas gets plenty of good shots, many from the perimeter, hitting eight three-pointers in the first half alone. The Razorbacks finish the game with eleven bonusphere hits, the most against Carolina all year.

What was billed originally as the easiest regional suddenly looks anything but.

Midway through the first half the Heels find they must rally simply to get even, and they duly mount a 14–3 run that ties the game at 28–28. The shift in tide starts with a Williams layup, assisted by Derrick Phelps after UNC beats a trap. The Razorbacks find Phelps the sort of cool head whom they can't frazzle; he plays thirty-five minutes and contributes seven assists, seven rebounds, two steals, and a single turnover. Phelps does this despite a new back injury incurred in practice earlier in the week. Combined with his lingering ACC Tournament bruising, the new hurt leaves Phelps in such pain he can hardly hide it. Concerned teammates approach the playmaker during stoppages of play to inquire after his health. "He's kind of nervous just making a layup," Brian Reese says.

Following the game, a tired Phelps confides the pain is so constant now he can't wait for season's end in order to take a long, luxurious vacation from athletics.

Arkansas rebuilds a 38–31 advantage with 3:50 left in the half, punishing Carolina's traps and beating the Heels for offensive rebounds. The Heels roar back with the loose-limbed Reese central to the action, and at halftime the teams are deadlocked at 45–45.

This scenario is all too familiar to Carolina fans, who've seen many of Smith's best teams stumble in similar circumstances. New York writers quickly strike upon this theme, noting that for all his great players and trips to the NCAAs, Smith has won a single national title. As one observer says of the Meadowlands trip: "I thought they would lose. It's a tradition, like a pumpkin for Halloween." If the '87 parallel holds true, the Heels will fall a round after Duke goes out. That would be today, amidst the concrete-choked swamplands of northern New Jersey, where mounds of dirty snow line roadways two weeks after the Blizzard of '93.

The Meadowlands, a 19,761-seat arena due west of Manhattan, has become the ACC's private portal to the Final Four. From 1986 through 1992 six East Regional championships were played here, and ACC teams won five—Duke over Navy in 1986, Temple in 1988, Georgetown in 1989, and Connecticut in 1990; and North Carolina in 1991 over Temple.

The sole exception to ACC rule occurred when Syracuse beat North Carolina in 1987. The Orangemen ultimately advanced to the national title game, losing to Indiana.

But this year's version of the Heels has a resiliency absent from many previous Smith squads that might well have been waylaid by quick, inspired Arkansas.

In part, it's a matter of team personality, as longtime observer Hugh Morton has noticed from his sideline photographer's perch. "Of course, different people make different teams," Morton says. "But I really think this crowd has the will to win more than any I've seen in recent years. The key here, I don't want to say killer instinct, but they have the same will to win Worthy and Jordan had." These Heels also have been adjusted and attuned by Smith, so they're ready for just such moments as this.

Since the Clemson game in mid-February, when Reese resurfaced and Henrik Rodl lost his starting spot to Williams, the Heels have become essentially a five-man unit. Smith may utilize eight to ten players regularly, but as the importance of the games increases so does the preponderance of playing time accorded the starters, who each average about thirty minutes per game. Conversely, veterans like Rodl, Pat Sullivan, and Kevin Salvadori have lost minutes, serving well defined, limited roles. Reserves like Dante Calabria, Scott Cherry, and Matt Wenstrom have all but vanished from sight.

Carolina's vaunted reserve capacity contributes two points and five rebounds against Arkansas. The only significant supporting roles are turned in by Rodl, with two assists and a steal, and Sullivan, who provides two rebounds and the reserves' scoring output.

But, with ball handling at a premium against the Razorbacks, and Phelps hurting, Cherry is pressed into service, to disastrous effect. Twice he comes in and twice he commits turnovers. The second occurs fourteen seconds after Cherry enters the game, as he foolishly goes to the sideline and picks up his dribble against a Razorback trap. Immediately yanked in favor of Rodl, Cherry comes to the sideline looking ready to cry. Bill Guthridge pats him on the back as Cherry takes a seat and hangs his head; by the next TV timeout the senior has sifted to the end of the bench, where he stays for the remainder of the weekend.

The most athletic five are left to carry the load, and all play key roles as the Heels steadily build the lead to 68–61 with 9:20 remaining. Richardson quickly calls timeout, the game threatening to slip away.

When play resumes, the Razorbacks start feeding freshman big man Corliss Williamson in the lane. Williamson scores consecutive baskets. Sullivan and Williams miss. Arkansas's Elmer Martin hits a jumper from the corner as the shot clock expires. Eric Montross makes a free throw, Williamson dunks, and with 6:26 to go the score is tied at 69–69.

Each team misses a shot before Reese, eyes seemingly glowing, weaves his way through traffic for a layup on a break. That puts the Heels ahead to stay. "I kind of like teams that're really athletic," Reese says. "I love that. I love that. I feel much more comfortable when people are on me."

The redclad Razorbacks run time off the shot clock against a UNC zone, but settle for a last-second, three-point try. The ball eventually winds up with Lynch, who finishes the game with ten rebounds. He starts upcourt, but doesn't get far before he's fouled from behind, falling to the floor near midcourt.

On the foul, Lynch cuts his left elbow on the NCAA emblem, and with blood trickling down his arm must be removed from the game under the NCAA's AIDS-inspired bloodletting guidelines. That enables Smith to reinsert Donald Williams, the team's best free throw shooter (81.8 percent). He converts both ends of a one-and-one, pushing the lead to 73–69 with 4:24 left.

Quickly Williamson responds with a basket inside. He's scored eight of his team's last ten points and finishes with sixteen to pace Arkansas.

Neither team gets off a good shot on its subsequent possession. With the game clock approaching two minutes, Phelps brings the ball upcourt against heavy pressure. The Heels try a thrust or two at the basket, then go to an isolation set with Williams handling the ball near the center circle. With about fifteen seconds left on the shot clock, he drives hard toward the right of the lane, is cut off, and has the ball tipped away momentarily by guard Clint McDaniel. Unfazed, Williams recovers possession, spins toward the baseline, leaps, fires, and hits a jumper.

Richardson had Williams at his home on a recruiting trip, and comes away from the game with vivid memories of one that got away.

"It looked like somebody threw him out of a cannon," the coach recalls of the pivotal shot. "He just jumped up over everyone and let one fly. He made some big shots under some tough defensive positioning. He had a great game. I knew he put it up nineteen times, I believe, and he came up with seven baskets. But a lot of times, in a game that we play, the teams that have great scorers, they kind of wear down. But I didn't think Donald was worn down. I think he was a little stronger than I thought he would be going toward the end." Down again by four, Arkansas throws up a quick three. Misses. Phelps rebounds, starts a break and gets the ball ahead to Lynch. But the pass is a little long, and by the time Lynch runs it down guard Corey Beck is there to draw a charge as the bigger man attempts to muscle to the basket.

Before the clock restarts Smith inserts his defensive platoon—Montross is replaced by Salvadori, the shotblocker, and Williams steps aside for Rodl, the large, solid wing. (Just the other day at practice, Williams's defensive efforts drew the ire of his coach. "What do you think we're doing out here?!" Smith yells.) The Hogs score anyway, a three-pointer from Darrell Hawkins over Rodl pulling them within 75–74 with 1:06 left.

Carolina calls timeout after getting the ball into the forecourt. Only 51.7 seconds remain.

The Heels noticed an opening earlier against Arkansas's overplaying defense, and now they decide to exploit it. Smith reinserts Montross and Williams and outlines a play one must always guard against when facing Carolina. "He just told us exactly where they were going to be playing us, what they were going to do when the ball is passed," Montross says. "It was like deja vu." Williams inbounds to Phelps. He gets the ball to Lynch, who dribbles from the right wing toward the top of the key. No big men post up near the lane. Williams, low on the right wing, runs away from the basket and beyond the three-point arc, as though to take a pass from Lynch, who spins his way. But, as Beck reacts and darts to intercept, Williams cuts the other direction, toward the basket, and lays in Lynch's perfect backdoor pass. "It's a play we use all the time," Smith explains, "but we drew it up specifically thinking they would probably think we were going to Montross." North Carolina leads by three with forty-two seconds remaining.

"Now you understand why we drill and go over it," Montross says of the backdoor play. "It paid off."

The evening's pivotal defensive stop comes on the very next play, courtesy of Lynch, whose vocal, emotional, exemplary leadership becomes more evident with each passing game.

Anxious to get off a shot, Arkansas's Robert Shepherd goes airborne near the top of the key, changes his mind when Lynch blocks his route and towers over him, and comes back to earth without ridding himself of the ball. That's a traveling violation and loss of possession with 23.4 seconds remaining. Lynch leaps high to celebrate, leaps again to slap hands with Williams, a quite un-UNC thing to do.

"I saw my whole career flash in front of me the last two minutes," Lynch says. "There was just a lot of things going through my head in the last couple of minutes. During timeouts, I was thinking anytime I have a chance to go to the basket, I'm going. Anytime I have a chance to box out, I'm going to. All the little things that Coach Dean Smith teaches during the year came back. If there is a chance, I'm going to put everything he taught me on the floor." The Hogs must foul to regain possession, so Carolina makes sure to get the ball in Williams's hands, and he makes three free throws that secure the final 80-74 margin.

Williams finishes with twenty-two points, one fewer than Lynch, and scores the Heels' final nine.

"All during the second half I was telling him to keep shooting," Reese says. "At least he's got enough guts to take the shot with the game on the line."

On the bus ride back to their Manhattan hotel the Tar Heels marvel among themselves, as dozens of Carolina players have marveled before them, at the backdoor play in the final minute, and what Williams calls "Coach Smith's genius."

"Coach Smith makes the game a lot easier for a player to have confidence in his teammates, because Coach Smith has something planned to make it easier," says Lynch. "A lot of people don't understand the things he teaches players to win the big games."

Adds Montross: "We believe in whatever he says is going to work for us."

SUNDAY, MARCH 28

BOB Huggins retains his hair. The Meadowlands keeps its nets. The NCAA dodges a potentially ugly controversy. Brian Reese avoids lasting ignominy as the guy who missed the dunk that would have taken North Carolina to the Final Four.

The Tar Heels survive Cincinnati in overtime, 75–68, winning the 1993 East Regional, but only by bringing to bear every resource of strategy, conditioning, talent, practice, personnel, and courage.

The Bearcats are the sort of team that makes you ache to beat them, the tone set by Huggins, their coach, and their senior guard, Nick Van Exel. Vanquishment by Cincinnati leaves such a bad taste in Virginia players' mouths, they depart from custom and root ardently for North Carolina.

On the court the Bearcats talk enough trash to cram a landfill. In a typical moment against Virginia, Van Exel yells at taunters in the U.Va. pep band: "Shut up, man! You're on spring break now!" Similarly classy conduct eventually earns Van Exel a technical foul.

Then, prior to playing North Carolina, Van Exel has the bad sense to strike upon a familiar theme sure to fire up the proud Tar Heels. "I think Dean Smith is a good coach with great players," he opines. "With all the talent he's had, who wouldn't have won all those games? To be honest, I think he should have won a few more championships. I don't really consider him a great coach." The Bearcats also greet the Heels in the hallway with a chant of "We hate Carolina! We hate Carolina!"

No wonder North Carolina's players seem drab by comparison. "It's funny how some of that is perceived," Bill Guthridge says. "They said dumb things. If that makes us dull, I'm glad we're dull. We should respect everybody."

After losing, Van Exel spurns repeated opportunities to compliment Derrick Phelps, the defender who shuts him down. He also comments: "The refs didn't give us a damn call. That's the way it's been all season, like playing five on eight." Such conduct only mirrors Huggins, a publicly dour and sometimes insolent man in his late thirties who perpetually pushes the limits of coaching decorum with officials and players. ("He's Dr. Jekyll and Mr. Huggins," says Terry Nelson, one of six seniors on the squad.) When Huggins isn't complaining about officiating, he's decrying the lack of respect for his program. "We're one of the elite programs in the country," Huggins says after his second-seeded squad falls a step short of a repeat trip to the Final Four. "If you don't believe that, you don't know basketball."

Cincinnati has built a 27–4 record, primarily on the strength of pressure defense that's every bit as relentless and perhaps less predictable than that employed by Arkansas. Opponents make but 40.6 percent of their shots and commit about seven more turnovers per game than the champs of the Great Midwest Conference. "We think speed can beat everything," forward Erik Martin says. "Size doesn't really matter." Other than six-foot-ten center Corie Blount, no Bearcat stands taller than six-seven.

For added incentive, Cincinnati's players have a promise exacted from Huggins in what he calls "a weak moment": If they reach the Final Four he'll shave off all the fine, wavy brown hair that's pushed back at the sides of his head and tufted high in the middle. "We're bringing the clippers right to the locker room," Nelson says.

So perhaps it shouldn't come as a surprise when Cincinnati immediately seizes command of the game, building a 29–14 edge thirteen minutes into the first half. Van Exel, UC's leading scorer, has been struggling with his shot in the NCAAs, but against the Heels he hits three-pointer after three-pointer. When he hits his fifth three-pointer of the opening period at the 7:09 mark, the score stands Van Exel seventeen, North Carolina fourteen.

While they fall farther and farther behind, the Heels commit eight turnovers and miss eight of thirteen shots. Brian Reese has especial difficulty, missing four shot attempts and committing two turnovers. Afterwards he describes Cincinnati's defense as "smack, smack, smack" every time he tried his cat-like slashes to the basket.

Soon after UNC falls behind by fifteen, TV mandates a pause. Many team huddles would be feverish at such a moment. Not Carolina's. Typically, inevitably, Smith has soothing words for his players. He tells them they're getting good shots, and to keep shooting. Smith hopes to halve the deficit by the end of the period, but says nothing. Many in the huddle also take solace from the rally against Florida State two months ago, when UNC was further behind and had much less time to play.

Little changes at first. Cincinnati has thirty-three points, and Van Exel one fewer than Carolina's twenty-two, when with 3:38 left in the half TV interrupts to do its bit to boost the nation's consumer spending.

"After he got to twenty-one points, he convinced me," Smith says of Van Exel, the Bearcats' left-handed bomber. Consequently, as the Tar Heels retake the court to resume play, Smith calls back Phelps, the guard whom he considers the nation's top defender, and directs him to deviate from standard operating procedure. "I whispered to Derrick, 'Don't leave him,'" Smith says. "I didn't want the others to hear it." The Heels thrive defensively on gambling and helping each other. Rarely does Smith countenance an undiluted head-to-head matchup. But this is an extraordinary circumstance, and the supposedly inflexible coach adapts accordingly. Over the remainder of the game, a shade under thirty minutes, Van Exel scores two points and misses nine of ten shots. Aches and all, Phelps winds up playing more minutes (43) than any Tar Heel.

Immediately following the timeout Eric Montross scores inside, his eighth point in three and a half minutes. But on the next possession an inadvertent elbow levels the junior giant, who's removed from the game and sits out the remainder of the period with an ice pack pressed to his face. Even without Montross, the Heels continue a 16–2 run spearheaded by George Lynch, who finishes the half with thirteen points, six rebounds, and four steals. His free throws, 37.6 seconds before halftime, give the Heels their first lead since the opening basket, but Nelson hits a jumper to give Cincinnati a 37–36 edge at intermission.

The teams stay within two baskets of each other for the remainder of regulation play.

Carolina forges the first of seven second-half ties at 44–44 on a pair of Montross free throws with 16:07 left in regulation. Reese scores his first basket of the game, swooping in from the left, to tie the score again at 46–46. Donald Williams achieves the next tie, 48–48, on a long jumper.

Cincinnati goes back ahead by four. Lynch scores on a follow shot of a follow shot for a 52–52 tie. "Cincinnata," as Smith calls it, builds its largest lead of the half, 57–52, at the 11:02 mark. Williams responds with his first three-pointer of the game, and after a blocked shot and a turnover Lynch dunks behind a zone on an alley-oop from Phelps to tie the score yet again.

UNC moves ahead by four, Cincinnati retakes the lead with 5:21 left. Carolina catches up on a Montross free throw after blowing a dunk, and builds its biggest lead during regulation play, 66–62, on a baseline jumper by Williams and a pair of foul shots by Reese with 1:44 remaining.

Smith replaces Montross and Williams with Salvadori and Rodl. Time to clamp down defensively. It doesn't happen.

Reese fouls Martin, who earns two of his sixteen points on free throws to cut the margin to 66–64. Now the Heels need to run time off the clock, to demonstrate their characteristic efficiency. Instead they allow the allotted forty-five seconds to expire without getting off a shot good enough to hit the rim. The buzzer sounds to indicate a violation, momentarily freezing the UNC players. But play doesn't stop, and the Bearcats quickly get the ball to Tarrance Gibson for a layup behind the defense.

Score tied at 66–66, thirty-five seconds remaining.

The Heels have the ball and hold for the final shot, letting time run down to single digits. Reese passes to Lynch posted to the left of the basket. Lynch—eventually chosen the regional's most outstanding player—misses a chip shot, the ball rolling around the rim and off with just over three seconds to go. The ball goes out of bounds off Nelson. Only eight tenths of a second remain, time for a quick scoring thrust but nothing more.

Each team calls timeout. As he did against Arkansas, Smith pulls a set play from his data bank of tricks. Expecting UC to focus on Montross, Smith runs Reese off a three-man stack along the right of the lane. The forward loops from the bottom of the stack to the middle of the lane and finds himself alone as he catches Phelps's inbounds pass near the apogee of a great, gulping leap.

Reese has been instructed to tap the ball toward the basket, "but I was so open that I had to try and shoot it," he says. He comes down with the ball. Half a second has expired. In one stride he's at the basket and airborne again. The red light going on to indicate the end of regulation play. Almost simultaneously, Reese launches a thunderous two-handed dunk.

Except he misses the dunk, which ultimately proves fortunate for all concerned. Fortunate because lead official Jody Silvester tells some reporters the shot would have counted, a sour way for Cincinnati to lose or for Carolina to win. And since UNC wins anyway, Reese escapes becoming almost as great a goat as boyhood acquaintance Fred Brown, who inadvertently threw a pass to James Worthy that sealed Georgetown's loss to the Heels in the 1982 title game.

Lynch is not pleased and tells Reese so, aware his teammate's greed squandered a golden opportunity.

Reaction is anguished on the Carolina bench, where the usual leaping demonstrations are even more emphatic. Serge Zwikker, the towering redshirt in street clothes, jumps backward holding his head. Ed Geth crumples to the court. Assistant Phil Ford does a full back-flip. "I've seen him do that before, but never in a suit and tie," Bill Guthridge says.

Smith has little outward reaction, other than a quick, almost furtive kick at the scorer's table. When Reese comes off the court, Smith tells him the shot wouldn't have counted.

"Generally when that happens, in overtime you let down," Smith says. "But we tried to regroup. We said, 'All right, we haven't had overtime. We need the practice.'" Actually the Heels practiced playing an overtime only recently. The day before departing for the Meadowlands—leaving the Smith Center to an invasion of Deadheads quite unlike Smith's obedient young gentlemen—North Carolina practiced a five-minute extra period.

Now, with the season on the line, Cincinnati scores first on a turn-around jumper by Blount over Montross. But that's it. The Bearcats fail to score again, missing their final eight shots.

"To be honest, we got tired. Maybe we wore down," Martin says. "I thought quickness beat everything, but I guess I found out today it doesn't beat size . . . they have, what, I don't know, eight seven-footers, it seems like. They just keep shuffling them on in. They kept it above our heads."

This, of course, is at odds with Smith's portrayal of his team, as he demonstrates yet again. "Our guards are six-two, six-three. Brian I hope is six-five, six-six. Everybody talks about tremendous size. I fail to see tremendous size . . . we're not short, don't get me wrong. I'm the shortest coach—five-foot-ten."

As usual when the game hangs in the balance it's Lynch and Williams who come through, whatever their size or "reaching height," Smith's preferred measure.

Lynch, now second all-time in rebounds at UNC, has four of his fourteen rebounds in the overtime. He also scores the last of his team-high twenty-one points to retie the score at 68–68 with 4:13 left in the extra period. "More than anybody else, he doesn't want the season to end," Rodl observes. "You can really tell in the way he approaches the game, the way he focuses and the way he talks to us." Huggins is impressed. "We were concerned about him all along," he says of Lynch. "All the tapes we watched the last couple of days, he is not as flashy as some guys. He just does the dirty work. He probably doesn't get enough credit."

Williams is less steady, but has developed a knack for exploding at the key moment. "I seem to concentrate when the game is more on the line than when the game is going on," he says. That's certainly true in the overtime—after the score is tied the Bearcats commit consecutive turnovers while Williams hits three-pointers on consecutive possessions. "As soon as the ball came to me, I could hear Coach Smith yell, 'Knock it down,'" Williams says. "Things like that give you a lot of confidence."

Suddenly UNC leads 74–68 with 1:53 left to play.

Despite repeated malfunctions trying to run out the clock, North Carolina emerges with a 75–68 victory, raising its record to 32–4. That ties the school standard for wins in a season, matched by the undefeated '57 national champs, the '82 champs, and the '87 squad that lost here in the regional final.

The '93 Heels don Final Four T-shirts and big grins immediately after beating Cincinnati, and the pep band breaks into "Born To Be Wild," hardly an appropriate theme song for this bunch. The celebration is actually quite brief. The players eschew cutting down the nets before winning a national title, and are hustled from the building to make an early flight back to Chapel Hill, where three thousand fans await at the Smith Center.

Among today's prime travel-party topics is Reese's missed dunk. "There will always be fun and games about the dunk he missed," says Phelps, who walks now with a hitched gait. "Brian Reese missing a dunk is shocking to me. If he says something about you, you can say, 'Yeah, but I didn't miss that dunk.'"

THURSDAY, APRIL 1

PRACTICE number eighty-six, last of the season in the Dean Dome. The rest of the Final Four entrants are in New Orleans. Michigan and Kentucky arrived yesterday evening. Kansas arrives today. "The Final Four is a lifelong dream, and I think we can more than make up for the time we're missing by bringing our tutors with us and having study halls on the road," Kentucky's Rick Pitino explains. He also took Providence to the Final Four in 1987. "This is a dream of a lifetime and I certainly won't let them [players] miss it."

The Tar Heels' contrasting approach is best expressed by Pat Sullivan in a statement as seemingly self-contradictory as it is revealing. "We're not going down to Louisiana to have fun and games, we're going down there to play a game," he says earnestly.

So, while others join the huge convention of basketball tourists eager to eat, drink, and most of all have ample cause to be merry, the Tar Heels practice one more time in the sober confines of the Smith Center, their personal dome, with only six onlookers seated in Section 225, from which Dean Smith's words gurgle like a voice heard through water.

There's no team meeting today. Assembly is at 1:45 P.M., far earlier than normal these past few weeks. The offensive emphasis is "Take pride in setting good screens, then turn and find ball!" The defensive emphasis is "Move when ball moves and be prepared to help on post!"

The thought for the day is from Epictetus, a Greek Stoic who philosophized that even apparent calamities are ordered for the best by a wise, divine providence: "Make the best of what is in your power: Take the rest as it happens!"

All fifteen players participate in the seventy-five-minute workout, including Donald Williams and Brian Reese, both sidelined yesterday by minor illness. As usual, the players are broken into predesignated groups of five. The starters are "White." Each is listed with the name of his primary substitute beside his own; "Rodl," listed for Phelps and Williams at both backcourt spots, comes complete with umlaut.

The atmosphere is overwhelmingly business as usual.

"I think that we're emotional people," Eric Montross says of the team, "but I think it takes a lot, one way or another, to really get us up or really get us down. I think that part of that is because of Coach Smith, and I'm talking about on the basketball court. I think another thing is because we have goals, and until we achieve a goal we don't get real excited."

Only in the basketball office does one find signs that these are extraordinary times.

The same balloons that arrived for the start of the NCAAs, names of each coach and player affixed, still float above the large table in the reception area. Nearby, further obscuring the corner where the 1991 Final Four trophy stands hidden by a plant, several montages from fans lean against cabinets.

Oddly, one montage includes a photograph of Clifford Rozier, the 1993 Metro Conference player of the year, who's been gone for two seasons.

SATURDAY, APRIL 3

THE Kansas–North Carolina game is played first, in late afternoon, at the dictate of television, and treated by most observers as a secondary event. "We think it'll be a good preliminary game," Dean Smith says facetiously.

Actually the game about fits its billing, with North Carolina leading virtually throughout, getting a good scare with about three minutes left but pulling away to a 78–68 victory. "Kansas may have been our best game of the year, [if] you count everything," Smith says.

The talk throughout a French Quarter and Superdome overrun by tourists adorned in shades of blue is primarily of the nightcap, of Michigan and most of all Kentucky, winner of four NCAA games by an average margin of thirty points. Popular wisdom favors the Wildcats, with Rick Pitino's pressing defense and three-point-oriented offense hailed as the style of the nineties.

Less confidence is expressed in Michigan's strutting, bald-shaven Wolverines, who arrive late for their own press conference. Participating in their second straight Final Four, they are nonetheless subject to incessant putdowns as underachievers, slackards who don't play fundamentally sound ball and don't always take seriously the task at hand.

The Carolina-Kansas matchup has an entirely different feel. It's a gathering of mirror images, a master-pupil face-off. "They know all our plays; we know all theirs," Kansas guard Rex Walters says. "It's going to be like a practice." In fact, Roy Williams enumerates plays as UNC does, closes practices, and has players memorize a thought and emphases for the day. Both teams also have seven-foot white guys who wear double-zero and austere haircuts, Eric Montross and Greg Ostertag.

Not a particularly gripping scenario, given that it echoes both of the past two Final Fours. Last season it was Duke and Indiana, Krzyzewski and Knight, the pupil victorious in a surprisingly unfriendly meeting. Two years ago it was Kansas against Carolina, Williams against Smith, with the pupil victorious.

Perhaps the game's familial nature contributes to Smith's remarkably buoyant spirits. He speaks freely of Final Fours past, including his half-minute playing appearance in 1952. He speaks of golf games with Williams, and allows himself to be drawn into a silly exchange about going one-on-one in basketball against Williams, sixteen years his junior. "In a one-minute game, I could beat him," Smith says.

Comment on Smith's easy manner, not only here in New Orleans but throughout the season, continues to amuse him. "I think people might have a preconceived idea of who, what I am, and then they get to know me a little," he says. "They think I've changed instead of, they never really knew me in the first place."

Smith's capture of a single national title, another topic repeatedly raised at press conferences, draws progressively less tolerant comments from Carolina players. Montross especially has grown impatient with such talk. "All year there was always somebody saying something about Coach Smith," he complains. "'When's he going to win another one? Is this going to be the year for him?' That kind of thing. He just deserves all the credit for the things he's done in the past. Very few coaches achieve a national championship, and those that do very rarely get a second time at it."

So George Lynch surely knows the emotional power of his words when, as the players huddle before taking the court to play Kansas, he exhorts them to help shut up Smith's critics.

That they come one step closer this evening is testament to their over-whelming inside game, Donald Williams's hot shooting, and Derrick Phelps's persistence.

Nineteen seconds into the game, the evening's tone is set on a power move by Montross after a pass from Brian Reese. "When I got the ball the first time, I wanted to make, not a statement but a strong move," the 270-pound center says. "Sometimes you can catch a team off guard with a quick move right away." The result is a 2–0 lead.

Kansas follows with a three-pointer at the 19:27 mark by handsomely named Adonis Jordan. That's the Jayhawks' sole lead of the game. They forge a pair of ties in the first nine minutes, but otherwise trail throughout.

The shape of Carolina's victory is so familiar it's almost formulaic. All but five of its first thirty points come inside or at the foul line. Montross and Lynch combine for thirty-seven points, a game-high twenty-three by Montross. He has eight at halftime, Lynch ten, as the Tar Heels lead 40–36. UNC opens the second half by ladling the ball repeatedly to Montross, who scores ten of Carolina's first dozen points.

"It's difficult guarding somebody that big, that strong, who takes up that kind of space," Kansas center Eric Pauley says of Montross. "His teammates did a tremendous job getting him the ball on the lob." Trying to slow Montross also lands several Kansas big men in foul trouble.

"We're proud of our banging," Montross says of the Heels. "If we were any more physical, we'd foul out in the first five minutes." Montross especially enjoys going up against the similarly sized Ostertag, a friend off the court, despite taking an elbow to the face and getting thrown once to the floor. "There were five hundred forty pounds of center out there, banging away and having fun," is how Montross describes it.

But while he's the dominant figure, Montross is hardly alone in his heroics. Lynch leads both teams with ten rebounds, five on offense, as the Heels outrebound the opposition for the eighteenth straight time. Kevin Salvadori adds six points and three rebounds, playing an unusually prominent role against a moderately athletic squad with only two players taller than six-foot-eight. Reese has six assists, demonstrating anew a flair for feeding the post. He has more assists during Carolina's 1993 NCAA run than in any previous period of his career, and he finishes the six games with one fewer assist than Phelps.

Carolina's leading scorer, though, is Williams, who's shaved his head for good luck and draws shouts of "Jordan! Jordan!" from adoring fans. Confidence high after his late-game heroics at the Meadowlands, Williams finishes with twenty-five points. When the Jayhawks collapse defensively around Montross and Lynch, the sharpshooter punishes them from the perimeter, hitting seven of eleven field-goal attempts, including five of seven from three-point range.

Williams's finest moment comes after Kansas fights back from several eight- and seven-point deficits to close within 68–65 with 2:48 to go. The Jayhawks trap a hobbling Phelps in the backcourt. He throws a long escape pass to Williams on the right wing. Without hesitation, the sophomore takes and sinks a three-pointer as Ostertag flies at him. "We encourage him to take it," Smith insists, contradicting the popular belief he'd countenance only inside shots at such a juncture. "Unless, of course, we go to our delay, and then shoot only layups."

Williams follows his three by forcing consecutive turnovers by Rex Walters. Then he makes a pair of free throws with 1:23 left, pushing the lead to a safe 73–65.

Williams's making a mark defensively especially pleases his coach. Between the Cincinnati game and this one, Williams was the only player called to the basketball office to view tape with Smith, who specifically critiqued his defense.

The Heels as a group are at the top of their game defensively, holding the Big Eight champs to 43.9 percent accuracy while hitting 53.8 percent themselves. Kansas scores but fifteen points in the game's final 12:47. "I don't think they were prepared for our kind of defense," Lynch observes.

The only Jayhawks to reach double figures are Jordan and Walters, who combine to hit ten shots from beyond the three-point arc. The nineteen points scored by each matches the total output of their starting front line.

Yet even there, the Heels force the KU backcourt into as many turnovers as assists (nine). And, after Walters scores thirteen points to lead all scorers in the first half, he's held to six in the second. Half of those come on a meaningless three-pointer that closes out Kansas's scoring.

Critical to that mastery is the play of Phelps, who struggles mightily to play thirty minutes after incurring yet another injury.

"I felt pretty good, like I used to early in the year," Phelps says of his condition prior to the game. "But it looks like no matter what I do, something happens."

This time it's a new hip bruise between the padding that protects his tailbone and a previous hip injury. The painful wound comes on a drive to the basket. Bumped slightly by Jordan, Phelps falls on his left hip, loses the ball out of bounds and is called for traveling with 13:07 remaining. He tries to play on, but limps and grimaces so noticeably he's brought to the bench after one possession.

"I think I just had to calm down a little on the bench," Phelps says following the game, seated by himself in a far corner of Carolina's huge locker room, blue towel draped over his bowed head. "I just sat down and let the pain go down a little, and when I was ready I told them."

Trainer Marc Davis, who tends to Phelps on the sideline, says the guard is the most courageous Tar Heel he can recall in more than a decade. Smith says he can think of plenty of players who competed with similar agonies, among them Phil Ford, who lost a tooth during one game in the late seventies, dribbled by the bench, threw the tooth over and kept playing. Phelps of course has heard the story too; Ford often is cited as a model, to the point that it's a source of good-natured amusement among the players.

Phelps is back within forty-one seconds. But, clearly hobbled by his injury, he's in and out of the lineup the rest of the way. "He was hurting pretty bad," Kansas's Jordan says. "I even asked him one time if he was all right. He said yeah. He's a tough kid." Kansas ends its season with a 29–7 record.

"People are going to ask about how it feels to lose to North Carolina, and it still feels crappy," Roy Williams says. "But, at the same time, I told the kids in the locker room that I loved them. And I feel the same way for those other coaches. I'll be pulling like heck for North Carolina Monday. If that upsets someone from Kentucky or Michigan, they don't understand what Roy Williams is all about."

The Kansas coach doesn't have to worry long about the feelings of Kentucky fans. In a nightcap considered the true heavyweight matchup, the Wolverines scratch the Wildcats in overtime, setting up a rematch with a North Carolina team they defeated by a point in December.

Back in Chapel Hill, where the weather turned notably cooler as soon as the Heels left town, an estimated ten thousand people throng the streets to celebrate a school-record thirty-third victory. With the national championship game two days away, a sign-toting fan cuts to the heart of the situation. "We're here," reads the placard. "Where's Dook?"

MONDAY, APRIL 5

THE sun has set only recently, signaling the start of Passover in this city beside the great river. While Jews around the world celebrate their deliverance from bondage thousands of years ago, the angel of defeat touches Michigan's Wolverines in the darkness. North Carolina's Tar Heels survive, 77–71, passing into basketball's promised land.

Tonight's championship game will be noted in popular shorthand for a fatal blunder by Michigan's Chris Webber, who, with eleven seconds remaining in a one-possession game, calls a timeout his team doesn't have, forfeiting possession of the ball and any remaining chance at victory. Now the Fab Five is unfulfilled in two title games, last year against Duke and now against the Blue Devils' next-door neighbor.

This is much more than a contest decided by a fluke. It's a game of runs, of timely three-point shooting, and crushing inside strength. The combatants are big, talented, determined people who have pointed all season toward this moment, and they play that way.

Prior to the game, outside a locker room several hundred yards from the Superdome court the Wolverines butt chests and heads like young rams. "Let's prove it again!" shouts Webber. "Let's show it again!"

Some North Carolina players observe uncharacteristic animation in Dean Smith's demeanor. "You just kind of sensed another little hop in his step," Eric Montross says. "He just seemed a little more vivacious, for lack of a better word. He just seemed a little bit more excited."

Before the Heels step into a real-life version of that doctored photo they received at the start of practice, George Lynch sounds a theme that worked against Kansas, that worked in 1982 when playmaker Jimmy Black told teammates much the same thing before facing Georgetown. "George just told the guys before we went out on the court, 'Let's not only do this for us, let's go out there and play hard and win this for Coach Smith,'" Donald Williams recalls. "So we kind of bonded together and also wanted to win it for him." Bill Guthridge, who's enjoyed his ritual pregame pop-corn-and-soda pit stop in the stands, says Smith is "calm and poised," as ever.

For his part, Smith insists he's "the same. I was more worried about what the players were thinking. Right before pregame, I wanted them, you know, relaxed and confident." Out on the court during player intro-ductions, Smith stands smiling, humming along as Michigan's pep band plays "Hail to the Victors," the school fight song. "I like that song," Smith tells NCAA officials seated at the scorer's table.

The game starts with each team missing its first two shots, and with Lynch leading with actions as well as words.

Webber misses a three, and Lynch rebounds. Lynch will finish with ten often-tough rebounds and a dozen points, his fourth consecutive double-double. He had sixteen rebounds in the teams' first meeting in Decem-ber, but also had perhaps his worst offensive showing, missing thirteen of eighteen shots as he struggled to accept his role. Now he gets to atone even as he leads his teammates to the summit.

At the other end Montross, whose normal offensive game is a model of straightforward simplicity, tries an unfamiliar turnaround jumper outside the lane and has it blocked by Webber. Brian Reese recovers the loose ball, one of his four offensive rebounds on the night. ("I want to win this so bad, it's ridiculous," Reese confides after the Kansas game.) But his fol-low shot is blocked by Ray Jackson and goes out of bounds off Carolina.

Jalen Rose drives baseline, something the Heels encourage, and misses a shot. Lynch rebounds, feeds Derrick Phelps, who leads the break, notices that no one's covering him, and takes the ball in for a layup at 18:57.

Lynch rejects a Juwan Howard shot, gets a pass at the other end and misses a layup. But Montross follows, gets fouled, and it's 5–0 Carolina. Lynch follows by taking a charge on Jackson, another Wolverine who swal-lows the bait and tries driving baseline.

Now Williams takes his first shot, a jumper near the right elbow, and misses. "At the beginning of the game I was a little nervous and I got tired," Williams admits. "But I came out and Coach Smith told me to start moving more without the ball." Michigan scores twice, including a dunk by Webber, after which he attempts to stare down Montross, who's dealt admirably with such bully-boy tactics all season. In fact, on the ensuing possession Montross gets an offensive rebound, is fouled, and hits two free throws. He'll finish with sixteen points.

Then Rose commits another ill-advised move against UNC's defense—he crosses midcourt along the sideline, is trapped, and picks up his dribble. Attempting an escape, his pass goes out of bounds. That eventually leads to a Lynch dunk on an alley-oop from Phelps, putting UNC up 9–4 at 15:59.

Phelps plays thirty-five minutes, more than any teammate, despite an array of aches and pains. The junior winds up with a game-high six assists and three steals, and he bothers Michigan's guards all night. Rose, the Wolverine playmaker, has six turnovers. But Phelps commits five, as many as he had in UNC's first four NCAA games combined.

Following a TV timeout and substitutions by both teams (they use twenty players between them), the Wolverines get hot, scoring eleven unanswered points. The catalyst is senior guard Rob Pelinka, who hits consecutive three-pointers against Pat Sullivan to give Michigan its first lead, 10–9. The Wolverines didn't make a three against Kentucky in four attempts; now Rose hits another, followed by a Webber drive through Sullivan. In the span of two minutes, Michigan has surged ahead 15–9.

The lead grows to 23–13 at the 11:32 mark on a fast-break layup by Howard.

North Carolina rotates most of its starters back into the game, mixes a 2–3 zone with its normal defense, and mounts a 12–2 run that knots the score at 25–25. The tying basket is a pull-up three by Williams from the right wing with just over eight minutes left in the half, his first points of the game.

The soft-spoken guard is playing with Jim Valvano in mind, having dedicated the game to him. The N.C. State coach was scheduled to be here for a testimonial dinner and an award recognizing his courage in battling cancer, but almost ten years to the day after he led N.C. State to a national title, Valvano is hospitalized, too ill to travel. He'll be dead by month's end.

"I dedicated this to him because he was the first Division I coach to recruit me," Williams says. "He started recruiting me in the ninth grade.

He's a great guy and a great man, and to see him struggle like this really hurts."

After Williams hits his three, the teams trade baskets for a few minutes before UNC closes the half with a 7–2 run. The final basket, giving the Heels their 42–36 halftime lead, is a long three-pointer by Williams off a screen by Phelps.

Like clockwork, the Heels open the second half by—what else?—getting the ball inside to Montross. The lead grows to 48–40. Michigan scores a couple of baskets. Williams responds with another three from the right side, then a driving jumper in the lane. Neither shot touches the rim as it goes through the net.

Michigan fights its way back to a 56–56 tie with 10:09 left on a fast-break dunk by Jimmy King, and takes its first lead of the half, 60–58, on a lob over Kevin Salvadori that Webber dunks with 8:35 remaining.

By now it's clear every possession is going to be precious, every play magnified.

Reese misses a three, rebound Webber. Rose misses a three, rebound Webber. In what proves his last college game, Webber finishes with eleven rebounds, along with twenty-three points. But he misses a follow shot now. Reese rebounds and passes to Williams. Unguarded, Williams dribbles alone up the right sideline, stops and lets fly from beyond the three-point arc before a lazing Rose moves out to contest the shot. As if drawn rather than thrown, the shot pierces the net with barely a ripple. UNC leads 61–60.

Howard hits a jumper to put Michigan ahead. The Heels race the ball into the frontcourt and call timeout with 6:50 to go. Many of UNC's players have been giving tired signals, asking to come out. So Smith inserts Montross, the sole starter resting on the bench, along with Sullivan, Salvadori, Henrik Rodl, and Scott Cherry. It's Cherry's first appearance of the game.

The wholesale substitution by a platoon of UNC's least-athletic reserves is met with incredulity by most observers. Had the game turned out differently, what happens with this lineup on the floor would have been almost as infamous as what befalls Webber in the final seconds.

"They moved the ball the way they're supposed to," Smith explains. "They're supposed to have gotten a shot, though. I told Scott Cherry, I said, 'Go!' He was right in front of me. But, you know, we moved them. Who knows? Maybe that tired them, because everybody really moved well without the ball." At the moment, though, putting the ball in the basket is of some importance too, and the collection of complementary players shies from shooting until the forty-five-second clock is about to expire. Finally Rodl forces up an off-balance heave that hits the side of the backboard and the Heels are called for a shot-clock violation.

In come Phelps and Williams, out go Cherry and Rodl. Rose provides a penalty by hitting a three from the top of the key, raising the Wolverines' advantage to 65–61.

Carolina spreads the floor and, with seven left on the shot clock, Sullivan finds Williams in the left corner. His penetrating jumper never touches the rim. Phelps pokes the ball away from Michigan at the other end. Sullivan gets it back to Phelps, but before the playmaker can push the ball past midcourt he loses it out of bounds, a wholly uncharacteristic unforced turnover. Chagrined, Phelps stands near midcourt holding his forehead with the long, elegant fingers of his right hand. Lynch, just returned to the lineup, comes by to offer encouragement.

King quickly makes UNC pay for the mistake, hitting a jumper to push Michigan's lead to 67–63. The game clock ticks under four minutes.

Now, at the turning point, all the elements of the penultimate Smith creation come into play: The patterned offense run with a sense of intelligent patience, resembling a predator picking a spot to pounce. The frustrating defense that's on you and above you and about you, holding NCAA opponents to 40.7 percent accuracy. The relentless focus on basketball's traditional inside-out construction method, resulting in 51.7 percent NCAA accuracy and forty more free throws made than NCAA opponents attempt. The sense of calm. The elevation of team above individual. The pointed finger to acknowledge an assist. The attention to fundamental detail. The benchsitters jumping in unison to cheer the slightest favorable turn in fortune. The lack of display. The sense of order, of system.

Phelps brings the ball to the right wing and tries to pass low to Montross, who's well covered by Webber. Thwarted, Phelps passes instead to Lynch, stationed beyond the top of the key. Lynch swings the ball to Williams, who swings it to Reese on the left wing. Montross has crossed to the left side of the lane and takes Reese's pass with Webber riding him away from the basket. Rather than force a shot, Montross passes to Phelps at the top of the key. Phelps rifles the ball—the sixth pass of the possession—to Williams, who's alone on the right wing.

Before the Michigan defense can adjust, Williams's three-point attempt is airborne. Swish. Again, it doesn't touch the rim. Carolina is back within one. Williams has scored eight straight points for the Tar Heels.

Less than a minute later, Phelps makes a fast-break layup that hangs tantalizingly on the rim, then falls in with 3:07 remaining. The Heels lead 68–67. They won't trail again.

Michigan misses a pair of jump shots. Lynch hits a turnaround, fallaway shot in heavy traffic, increasing the margin to 70–67 with 2:10 left. Rose turns the ball over in the lane, Williams picking off the loose ball and getting it to Phelps. Racing upcourt, Phelps is fouled by Rose, falling heavily to the court yet again.

Now Michigan fouls strategically to get the Tar Heels into a free-throw-shooting situation. But Lynch finds Montross alone for a dunk. UNC 72, Michigan 67, one minute remaining.

Ray Jackson quickly hits a jumper to cut the lead to three and Michigan takes its final timeout. Carolina immediately commits a turnover, Brian Reese receiving a pass and stepping on the sideline.

Smith goes to his defensive lineup. Rose misses a three over Rodl, but Webber follows with a layin over Salvadori. Thirty-seven seconds left, 72–71.

Sullivan is fouled with twenty seconds to go. A 78.9 percent free throw shooter, Sullivan makes the front end of a one-and-one. As he releases the shot, Rose steps into him. Carolina coaches scream for a foul, but none is called. An official warns Rose to cut it out.

On the UNC bench, players hold hands as Sullivan shoots again to secure a three-point cushion. The second free throw clangs off the back of the rim, into the hands of Webber.

Webber immediately starts to signal for a timeout, but thinks better of it. Then, with Lynch dogging him, he clearly travels with the ball as he starts upcourt. That's not called either. Nor does Webber get the ball to teammate Rose, signaling for the pass in front of the Carolina coaches, irate after the missed traveling violation.

Instead the forward races toward the end of Michigan's bench and into the jaws of infamy. Trapped by a Phelps-Lynch double-team, Webber hugs the ball to him and calls a timeout Michigan doesn't have.

That's an automatic technical foul, costing two free throws and possession of the ball. With eleven seconds left, the game is essentially over.

"When Webber called the timeout, I looked over at Coach Guthridge because I didn't know what was going on," Montross says. "Somebody just said they didn't have any timeouts. I didn't know who to believe because there was so much mayhem out there. Then I looked over at Coach Guthridge and he has this look on his face that's just like, 'They don't, and we're going to win.'"

Michigan, which lost to Duke in the '92 final because it didn't play tired, loses this time because it doesn't play smart. One can almost hear a collective sigh of relief from coaches everywhere—the team that seems to fight a coach's control loses because Webber either forgot or didn't listen to admonitions that his team had expended its timeouts.

"In the heat of the moment, strange things happen," Michigan coach Steve Fisher says. "Chris said he heard someone holler and call for a timeout. It's an awful way to have the season end when you've got a chance to get a shot to tie. No one feels worse than Chris, but we're not here if it's not for Chris."

The Heels have, of course, conserved their fouls. Assuming Webber escaped the trap, UNC could have fouled three times to prevent a last shot. Now it doesn't matter, as long as Williams makes the technical free throws. "I made believe I was back in the gym, practicing by myself," Williams says. He bounces the ball four times, lets fly. Nothing but net. Big breath. Bounces of the ball. Shot. Nothing but net.

Carolina inbounds. To Williams. He's fouled. He swishes both free throws. Williams finishes with twenty-five points, seventeen in the second half, and is voted the Final Four's most outstanding player. For the second straight game he hits five of seven three-pointers. That's two-game accuracy of 71.4 percent, a Final Four record. The same guy who was 14–47 from the bonusphere in the ACC Tournament is 22–44 from that range across the six games of the NCAAs.

"I thought he was going to make it every time it went up," Smith says. "What he's done here he did maybe one practice or two. I'm impressed."

Michigan gets a last, futile shot. Appropriately, Lynch rebounds, and Phelps gets to run out the last few seconds of the 77–71 victory.

Reflecting their coach to the end, and beyond, the Heels don't indulge in oncourt celebration until the final buzzer. Then they let go as bench players rush the court. For an instant Smith starts to run, caught in the spontaneous rush of emotion. But he quickly catches himself and walks to shake hands with Fisher.

Maybe Smith might have won more national championships if he didn't have to endure these scenes. Never the gladhander, the convention keynote speaker, the commercial shill, he escapes as quickly as possible after being called over for a TV interview.

Smith climbs the ladder last when it finally comes time to cut the nets. This is a family moment. He points to each of his players, then to the onlooking Tar Heel rooters—the assist signal, don't you know—before unleashing the final snip.

The players are less constrained. Unusually vocal, Williams yells repeatedly at the CBS camera about coming back to Chapel Hill to party. The festivities already have started without him—twenty-five thousand people stream onto Franklin Street to party in a cold rain.

Pat Sullivan, perhaps the team's premier cutup, threatens to upstage interviewer Jim Nantz by singing "One Shining Moment," the CBS theme song for this year's NCAAs. Sullivan's crackly crooning doesn't make CBS's postgame wrap, for some reason.

A few moments later, Sullivan, Williams and the gang move to midcourt for a ceremony delicious in irony. For the person presenting the national championship trophy—neighbor to neighbor, as though it's the bell kept by the victor in the annual Duke-Carolina football series—is Tom Butters, the Duke athletic director who chairs the NCAA Men's Basketball Selection Committee.

About that time, a solitary figure leaves the TV position and intermingles with the celebrating Carolina fans, waving a pom-pom, and posing for photos.

"I was just trying to bridge the gap," guest TV analyst Mike Krzyzewski says. "You don't have to hate them. Why do people have to hate each other? I try not to hate. Hate's not good. If you beat somebody, if hate's your motivation, how can you feel good?

"Was I somewhat envious of North Carolina? Yes. But I was envious of Michigan too, and Kansas, and Kentucky, because I wanted to be there. But I don't hate them." (Later, on the streets of the French Quarter, Carolina players are surprised when Duke players past and present stop to congratulate them.)

Back in the interview area, Smith, the original boy who cried wolf when it comes to complimenting seniors, makes sure to praise Cherry and Rodl. He corrects an interrogator's pronunciation of "Montross" and discounts talk of the blunders that ended both his national championship victories. "Neither one necessarily meant we wouldn't win," Smith says of

Webber's phantom timeout and the pass by Georgetown's Brown. "It's all part of the game. We've never said, I've often said, you have to be lucky and good. I thought Michigan and North Carolina were two of the best teams in the country. I'm not saying we're the best, but nobody said that's why we have this tournament. Otherwise we'd have four out of seven."

Still, it's as if Smith can't win even when he wins. Just yesterday he was being asked about monkeys on his back; now he's besieged by talk of winning on fluke plays, haunted by simile instead of simians. "I can't educate the world, and don't try," he says later. "And, you know, I'd rather talk about the plays Lynch made in the last two and a half minutes. He had the block, he forced the walk, it wasn't called."

Smith does allow himself a smidgen of public exultation.

"I'm pleased that we've been a national contender for a number of years," he says. "It is exciting to go out there and say, 'Hey, it's over. We won it.' We may not be the best team, but we're the NCAA champion."

But this is the best team, 34–4 with a single loss since the consecutive defeats at Wake and Duke two months ago. Even that loss, to Georgia Tech in the ACC Tournament final, occurred while Phelps was injured too badly to play. Now the Heels stand as masters of all they survey, including Durham. Their supremacy will endure at least until this time next year. And, with six of the top eight player returning, bolstered by the nation's top-rated recruiting class, there's already talk of repeating.

TUESDAY, APRIL 6

FIFTEEN thousand people show up at the Dean Dome, but not the man for whom the building is named. Crowd and celebration don't interest him; let his players enjoy that. Dean Smith leaves New Orleans before his team, and heads home for a little privacy. Tomorrow he'll fly to Philadelphia to sign center Rasheed Wallace, *USA Today*'s high-school player of the year.

The Smith Center's doors open long before the charter carrying the national champions returns to earth. By the time the plane lands at Raleigh-Durham airport and the Tar Heels' bus reaches Chapel Hill, the arena's spring-cushioned floor and lower deck are filled with people of all ages. Many sport newly purchased T-shirts, among the thirty thousand the university store sells today. It's a big day for Durham's *Herald-Sun* as well, as it prints a commemorative issue and peddles thirty-four thousand more newspapers than it's ever sold before.

The bus pulls to a guarded entrance at the building's rear and disgorges assistant coaches first, then players, all of whom wear white "NCAA Champion" hats. TV crews, photographers, police, reporters, and athletic department employees line the way. Donald Williams carries two NCAA emblems, each about four feet in diameter. The players disappear through the door marked "Varsity Hallway" and down the familiar corridor with the twenty-six tarred heels affixed to the blue carpet.

Out in the arena, the public address system carries the recorded radio play-by-play of last night's game, the crowd cheering again at key junctures. Electronic messageboards on the facade of the upper deck flash the scores of every UNC game this season in chronological order, then the names of the players, not alphabetically but by class.

At exactly 5:00 P.M.—the precision an accommodation to live telecasts on several Triangle stations—a huge roar goes up as the players appear from behind the blue curtain that's dropped for every practice. The pep band peps; the cheerleaders cheer. Matt Wenstrom, third in line, holds aloft the wood-mounted national championship trophy. Wenstrom's white ballcap is turned backwards. He and Montross advance with video cameras in hand. The players all wear ties and jackets, standard travel garb required by Smith.

Once the players are seated on a temporary stage, Woody Durham, whose game account only recently rang from the loudspeakers, takes the microphone as emcee. By now the crowd half fills the upper deck too.

Referring to a neatly printed note card, Durham's first comments are reckonings of past slights. "I understand Dick Vitale is in Ann Arbor, Michigan," he says to great applause. The TV commentator picked Michigan to win the national title. Then comes the inevitable: "I'll tell you what—this is some wine and cheese crowd." Glowing with barely subdued elation, Durham goes on to note proudly he's heard "Chapel Hill is still the beer-drinking capital of the world." Durham also points to a spot in the building's upper reaches where the '93 championship banner will hang in chronological order next to 1992, not set apart the way it's done at Reynolds Coliseum or Cameron Indoor Stadium. "And then '94 will go right next to it, and then '95," Durham says with a fan's dreamy greed.

Introductions begin with the team managers, their names read in rapid succession. The six stand in acknowledgment, and the players stand too, applauding their faithful gofers. Then Durham recognizes the assistant coaches, standing off to one side, and finally the players, freshmen first.

Dante Calabria, hat pushed back to reveal dark curls and a handsome face, elicits squeals that make it clear he has a future as a campus heartthrob. Ed Geth, most articulate of the first-year collegians, promises to bring back "four or five more national championships," quite a feat considering he has just three years of eligibility remaining.

Williams's introduction brings a great, sustained cheer. The sophomore walks down the first of two rows of players slapping hands with teammates. Lastly he hugs Brian Reese, Henrik Rodl, and George Lynch. Williams's hat looks way too big on his hairless head and sits just above the tops of his ears. After saluting his teammates and coaches, he observes, grinning broadly, "There ain't much more to be said but we're number one."

Later Williams says the title has special meaning for him and Travis

Stephenson, the only North Carolinians on the roster. "We probably remember the times, what happened in '82 and '83 when the local schools won it," Williams says, softly and rapidly as ever. "Even when Duke won it, the guys saw how they celebrated, the atmosphere around the area winning a national championship. I think it was one of the goals we were striving for at the beginning of the year. It really paid off, all the hard work we did in the preseason."

Pat Sullivan doffs his cap to the crowd and lauds the "family atmosphere" and unselfishness of the team. As Sullivan speaks, Montross loosens the stays of his eternal public reserve—first he plays an imaginary violin, then gets down on his knees, hands clasped angelically before him, all in silent mockery of his gushing teammate.

Next, Brian Reese, hat pulled low over his eyes, notes, "Coach Guthridge always said this team that we have is a special team. I think we went out and showed how special we was."

Durham introduces banged-up Derrick Phelps as a perfect spokesperson for Blue Cross–Blue Shield, and Phelps draws a laugh by carrying the theme. "First of all, I'd like to thank you fans for all the get-well cards," Phelps says. "I really appreciated them. That really cheered me up and made me want to come back and play for the team and help them win the national championship."

Montross, who started his own video following last night's game, steps to the podium and records a panoramic sweep of the adoring crowd. He expresses his pleasure at the turn of events, rebuts Cassell's putdown of the UNC crowd. "The next thing is, probably the most important, the fact that Dean Smith can no longer be challenged by critics about saying he never wins national titles."

Later, Montross admits he's glad it's all over: The practices and bus trips and jet flights, the bumps and bruises, the marshaling of mental resources, the donning of that unsmiling, unruffled game face. "It's kind of a relief, because it's been a long season. But at the same time these past three weeks have been the longest of any. It's hard to remember the ACC Tournament and losing to Georgia Tech and the end of the ACC season. It just seems like it was a long time ago. I think all the emotion and everything has come to a head, and now we're ready to relax and get our bodies back in shape."

The seniors of course address the crowd last. "I don't know who made it here, it was about five months and five days ago when this all started,"

Stephenson says. "We did a little thing on Halloween night called the Tar Heel Tipoff. It seems like yesterday."

Scott Cherry publicly thanks the coaching staff "for giving me a scholarship" and knocks "all the writers and doubters" who said he didn't belong. "When I walk around with that big fat ring on my finger, that'll speak for itself," he fairly spits.

Wenstrom, shirttail protruding beneath a blue sportjacket, begins, "As of last night I'm done as a collegiate athlete." Then he chokes up, steps back from the mike and tries to compose himself. But with teammates laughing and fans cheering supportively, Wenstrom can't stifle feelings that clamor for expression. He rubs his eyes, shakes his head, steps to the mike, steps back, snorts. Stepping forward again, he offers: "What I'm trying to get across is that I'll miss . . ." That's as far as he gets. The tears well up again and the seven-footer waves dismissively and retakes his seat.

George Lynch basks in the loudest cheers. He jokes about his leadership and teases Phil Ford, noting that while the coach's retired jersey hangs from the Smith Center rafters behind them, "There's one thing I have over him. I have a national championship banner." Lynch, an Afro-American studies major, abruptly concludes with a political comment, stating his support for the creation of the black cultural center that's engendered a raging campus debate, fueled by a fall visit by filmmaker Spike Lee and an upcoming one by Jesse Jackson.

But while Lynch speaks last, it's Henrik Rodl who again strikes the note that's lingered longest. Harkening like Stephenson to Halloween, when the '93 squad was unveiled, Rodl reminds listeners, "Like I said at the Tipoff classic, we could be so good it's scaaaary!"

Over in Durham, a Duke University transit bus flashes the eternal countervailing view on the electronic destination panel above its windshield: "Go to hell Carolina."

1992–93 DUKE BASKETBALL ROSTER

Name	Pos.	Yr.	Ht.	Wt.	Hometown
Kenny Blakeney	G	Jr.	6-4	190	Washington, DC
Kenney Brown	G	So.	6-2	180	Raleigh, NC
Stan Brunson	F	So.	6-6	195	Newark, DE
Marty Clark	G	Jr.	6-6	205	Western Springs, IL
Chris Collins	G	Fr.	6-3	175	Northbrook, IL
Grant Hill	F	Jr.	6-8	225	Reston, VA
Thomas Hill	G	Sr.	6-5	200	Lancaster, TX
Bobby Hurley	G	Sr.	6-0	165	Jersey City, NJ
Antonio Lang	F	Jr.	6-8	205	Mobile, AL
Erik Meek	C	So.	6-10	240	Escondido, CA
Tony Moore	F	Fr.	6-8	220	Kensington, MD
Cherokee Parks	C	So.	6-11	235	Huntington Beach, CA

1992–93 DUKE BASKETBALL SCHEDULE

Record: 24–8   ACC: 10–6

Opponent	Result	Score	Opponent	Result	Score
Canisius	W	110–62	San Francisco	W	117–73
Michigan	W	79–68	Maryland	W	78–62
Northeastern	W	103–72	North Carolina	W	81–67
Rutgers	W	88–79	Notre Dame	W	67–50
DePaul	W	89–73	Clemson	W	93–84
LSU	W	96–67	Georgia Tech	W	73–63
BYU	W	89–66	Wake Forest	L	98–86
Boston University	W	106–62	Virginia	L	58–55
Oklahoma	W	(ot) 88–84	NC State	W	91–82
Clemson	W	110–67	Florida State	W	98–75
Georgia Tech	L	80–79	UCLA	W	78–67
Wake Forest	W	86–59	Maryland	W	95–79
Iowa	W	65–56	North Carolina	L	83–69
Virginia	L	77–69	Georgia Tech	L	69–66
NC State	W	92–56	So. Illinois	W	105–70
Florida State	L	(ot) 89–88	California	L	82–77

1992–93 DUKE FINAL STATISTICS

Player	G	Field Goals		Free Throws		Reb	Avg	PF-D	A	TO	S	Pts	Avg
		M-A	Pct	M-A	Pct								
Grant Hill	26	185-320	57.8	94-126	74.6	166	6.4	61-1	72	63	64	468	18.0
Bobby Hurley	32	157-373	42.1	143-178	80.3	84	2.6	60-0	262	108	49	545	17.0
Thomas Hill	32	184-384	47.9	100-147	68.0	151	4.7	73-0	47	62	51	502	15.7
Cherokee Parks	32	161-247	65.2	72-100	72.0	220	6.9	68-0	14	56	25	394	12.3
Marty Clark	32	79-155	51.0	58-67	86.6	73	2.3	60-0	46	39	23	233	7.3
Antonio Lang	31	80-153	52.3	55-84	65.5	171	5.5	80-5	25	56	19	215	6.9
Chris Collins	29	56-139	40.3	20-32	62.5	33	1.1	26-0	34	23	15	169	5.8
Erik Meek	32	38-64	59.4	36-63	57.1	92	2.9	51-1	5	21	11	112	3.5
Tony Moore	12	16-27	59.3	3-3	100	24	2.0	12-0	4	7	2	35	2.9
Kenny Blakeney	30	32-77	4.16	19-29	65.5	45	1.5	32-0	20	33	11	87	2.9
Kenney Brown	15	0-5	00.0	4-9	44.4	5	0.3	3-0	0	1	0	4	0.3
Stan Brunson	8	1-6	16.7	0-0	—	1	0.1	2-0	0	0	0	2	0.3
Team													
Duke	32	989-1950	50.7	604-838	72.1	1153	36.0	528-7	529	469	270	2766	86.4
Opponents	32	911-2062	44.2	339-527	64.3	1156	36.1	680-13	458	572	209	2279	71.2

1992–93 NORTH CAROLINA BASKETBALL ROSTER

Name	Pos.	Yr.	Ht.	Wt.	Hometown
Dante Calabria	G	Fr.	6-4	186	Beaver Falls, PA
Scott Cherry	G	Sr.	6-5	180	Ballson Spa, NY
Larry Davis	G	Fr.	6-3	184	Denmark, SC
Ed Geth	F	Fr.	6-9	250	Norfolk, VA
George Lynch	F	Sr.	6-8	220	Roanoke, VA
Eric Montross	C	Jr.	7-0	270	Indianapolis, IN
Derrick Phelps	G	Jr.	6-3	181	East Elmhurst, NY
Brian Reese	F	Jr.	6-6	215	Bronx, NY
Henrik Rodl	G	Sr.	6-8	203	Heusenstamm, Germany
Kevin Salvadori	C	Jr.	7-0	224	Pittsburgh, PA
Travis Stephenson	F	Sr.	6-7	222	Angier, NC
Pat Sullivan	F	Jr.	6-8	216	Bogota, NJ
Matt Wenstrom	C	Sr.	7-1	260	Houston, TX
Donald Williams	G	So.	6-3	194	Garner, NC
Serge Zwikker	C	Fr.	7-3	248	Maassluis, Holland

1992–93 NORTH CAROLINA BASKETBALL SCHEDULE

Record: 34–4   ACC: 14–2

Opponent	Result	Score	Opponent	Result	Score
Old Dominion	W	119–82	Duke	L	81–67
South Carolina	W	108–68	NC State	W	104–58
Texas	W	104–68	Maryland	W	77–63
Virginia Tech	W	78–62	Georgia Tech	W	77–66
Houston	W	84–76	Clemson	W	80–67
Butler	W	103–56	Virginia	W	78–58
Ohio State	W	84–64	Notre Dame	W	85–56
SW Louisiana	W	80–59	Florida State	W	86–76
Michigan	L	79–78	Wake Forest	W	83–65
Hawaii	W	101–84	Duke	W	83–69
Cornell	W	98–60	Maryland	W	102–66
NC State	W	100–67	Virginia	W	74–56
Maryland	W	101–73	Georgia Tech	L	77–75
Georgia Tech	W	80–67	East Carolina	W	85–65
Clemson	W	82–72	Rhode Island	W	112–67
Virginia	W	80–58	Arkansas	W	80–74
Seton Hall	W	70–66	Cincinnati	W	(ot) 75–68
Florida State	W	82–72	Kansas	W	78–68
Wake Forest	L	88–62	Michigan	W	77–71

1992–93 NORTH CAROLINA FINAL STATISTICS

Player	G	Field Goals M-A	Pct	Free Throws M-A	Pct	Reb	Avg	PF-D	A	TO	S	Pts	Avg
Dante Calabria	35	24-52	46.2	7-9	77.8	29	0.8	26-1	21	29	64	64	1.8
Scott Cherry	33	20-33	60.6	25-35	71.4	23	0.7	15-030	21	9	69	69	2.1
Larry Davis	21	14-40	35.0	14-23	60.9	16	0.8	4-0	4	5	6	44	2.1
Ed Geth	21	16-25	64.0	12-17	70.6	28	1.3	14-0	0	7	4	44	2.1
Pearce Landry	1	0-1	00.0	0-0	00.0	1	1.0	1-0	1	0	1	0	0.0
George Lynch	38	235-469	50.1	88-132	66.7	365	9.6	85-3	72	89	89	560	14.7
Eric Montross	38	222-361	61.5	156-228	68.4	290	7.6	113-3	28	66	22	600	15.8
Derrick Phelps	36	111-243	45.7	56-83	67.5	157	4.4	68-1	196	110	82	293	8.1
Brian Reese	35	152-300	50.7	72-104	69.2	125	3.6	34-0	83	82	24	398	11.4
Henrik Rodl	38	58-117	49.6	25-38	65.8	57	1.5	50-0	136	60	39	163	4.3
Kevin Salvadori	38	66-144	45.8	38-54	70.4	138	3.6	79-2	12	24	7	170	4.5
Travis Stephenson	21	5-11	45.5	0-0	00.0	6	0.3	1-0	3	4	0	10	0.5
Pat Sullivan	38	88-170	51.8	60-76	78.9	92	2.4	43-0	51	35	26	245	6.4
Matt Wenstrom	33	34-61	55.7	16-27	59.3	47	1.4	17-0	7	1	31	84	2.5
Donald Williams	37	174-380	45.8	97-117	82.9	71	1.9	52-0	46	39	38	528	14.3
Team													
UNC	38	1219-2407	50.6	666-943	70.6	1561	41.1	602-10	698	581	357	3272	86.1
Opponents	38	978-2370	41.3	405-603	67.2	1222	32.2	750-20	536	686	273	2596	68.3

1992–93 NORTH CAROLINA STATE BASKETBALL ROSTER

Name	Pos.	Yr.	Ht.	Wt.	Hometown
Migjen Bakalli	G	Jr.	6-6	190	Belmont, NC
Mark Davis	G	So.	6-5	221	Utica, MS
Todd Fuller	C	Fr.	6-10	235	Charlotte, NC
Jamie Knox	F	Sr.	6-7	207	Vicksburg, MS
Chuck Kornegay	F	Fr.	6-9	215	Dudley, NC
Bill Kretzer	F	Fr.	6-9	225	Greensboro, NC
Marc Lewis	F	Jr.	6-8	218	Greensboro, NC
Curtis Marshall	G	So.	5-11	170	Omaha, NE
Lakista McCuller	G	So.	6-3	175	Andersonville, GA
Victor Newman	F	So.	6-7	195	Dothan, AL
Anthony Robinson	F	Jr.	6-9	230	Havelock, NC
Donnie Seale	G	Sr.	6-5	185	Eden, NC
Kevin Thompson	C	Sr.	6-10	250	Winston-Salem, NC
Marcus Wilson	F	Fr.	6-8	190	Monroe, NC

1992–93 NORTH CAROLINA STATE BASKETBALL SCHEDULE

Record: 8–19   ACC: 2–14

Opponent	Result	Score	Opponent	Result	Score
UNC–Wilmington	L	96–84	Clemson	W	72–70
UNC–Asheville	W	72–69	Wake Forest	L	65–54
Connecticut	L	81–74	North Carolina	L	104–58
Princeton	L	50–41	Virginia	L	75–66
Oregon State	W	69–68	Tennessee	W	74–72
Kansas	L	84–64	UNC–Greensboro	W	87–65
Iona	W	88–66	Florida State	L	72–71
North Carolina	L	100–67	Duke	L	91–82
Virginia	L	73–56	Maryland	L	88–71
Davidson	W	63–58	Georgia Tech	W	68–60
Florida State	L	70–54	Clemson	L	92–82
Duke	L	92–56	Wake Forest	L	80–68
Maryland	L	70–65	Maryland	L	76–55
Georgia Tech	L	85–74			

1992–93 NORTH CAROLINA STATE FINAL STATISTICS

Player	G	Field Goals M-A	Pct	Free Throws M-A	Pct	Reb	Avg	PF-D	A	TO	S	Pts	Avg
Kevin Thompson	27	176-324	54.3	66-114	57.9	246	9.1	64-1	54	62	24	419	15.5
Curtis Marshall	27	101-249	40.6	30-44	68.2	91	3.4	71-3	116	73	31	285	10.6
Lakista McCuller	27	102-259	39.4	30-46	65.2	70	2.6	46-0	58	56	26	278	10.3
Mark Davis	23	68-200	34.0	28-48	58.3	103	4.5	55-2	48	43	14	191	8.3
Marc Lewis	23	63-135	46.7	32-41	78.0	80	3.5	54-1	22	30	9	161	7.0
Todd Fuller	27	53-116	45.7	34-44	77.3	97	3.6	35-1	6	15	1	141	5.2
Marcus Wilson	27	40-112	35.7	16-29	55.2	52	1.9	53-1	27	43	12	110	4.1
Migjen Bakalli	11	34-78	43.6	11-21	52.4	25	2.3	22-2	17	17	8	101	9.2
Chuck Kornegay	7	24-43	55.8	14-20	70.0	34	4.9	11-0	10	6	5	62	8.9
Donnie Seale	7	21-53	39.6	4-15	26.7	25	3.6	14-0	16	23	6	49	7.0
Victor Newman	25	13-38	34.2	6-9	66.7	11	0.4	22-0	14	18	6	38	1.5
Jamie Knox	1	0-0	—	0-0	—	0	0.0	1-0	0	0	0	0	0.0
TommyKane	2	0-3	00.0	0-0	—	1	1.0	0-0	0	1	0	0	0.0
Team													
NC State	27	695-1610	43.2	271-431	62.9	914	33.9	448-11	388	389	142	1835	68.0
Opponents	27	768-1550	49.5	377-522	72.2	904	33.5	473-8	493	335	178	2072	76.7

INDEX